The Willard J. Graham Series in Accounting
Consulting Editor
Robert N. Anthony   *Harvard University*

Basic Auditing

Arthur W. Holmes, CPA
Professor of Accounting

Wayne S. Overmyer, CPA
Professor of Accounting

Both of the University of Cincinnati

Fifth Edition   1976

RICHARD D. IRWIN, INC.   Homewood, Illinois   60430
Irwin-Dorsey International   Arundel, Sussex   BN18 9AB
Irwin-Dorsey Limited   Georgetown, Ontario   L7G 4B3

© RICHARD D. IRWIN, INC., 1957, 1962, 1966, 1972, and 1976

Fifth Edition

First Printing, April 1976

Previous editions published under the title
Basic Auditing Principles

Portions of this publication are based upon *Statement on
Auditing Standards Nos. 1–5, The Code of Professional Ethics,*
and selected CPA examination questions and problems Copyright © 1973 through 1975 by the American Institute of Certified Public Accountants, Inc., and some passages are quoted
verbatim. Such passages have been reprinted by Richard D.
Irwin, Inc., with the permission of the American Institute of
CPAs.

ISBN 0-256-01778-6
Library of Congress Catalog Card No. 75–43165
Printed in the United States of America

Preface

This Fifth Edition of *Basic Auditing* is designed to fulfill the requirements of educational institutions offering a relatively short course in auditing. The concept that auditing is an independent intellectual discipline is established early. Because evidence is the basis for any audit conclusion, the importance of evidence is emphasized, together with the modern trend toward transactional auditing.

In the book we set forth the objectives of an audit and the reasons for the examination of each area of an audit. Our underlying plan for each chapter is to present audit objectives, properly applicable internal control features, and auditing standards and procedures applicable to materials under examination. We conclude each chapter with financial statement considerations for proper and adequate disclosure in reporting, in accordance with modern concepts of financial reporting.

In this edition, at the conclusion of each appropriate chapter, suggested additional optional reading material is presented; the suggestions are primarily from Statements on Auditing Standards issued by the American Institute of Certified Public Accountants.

In order to provide a rapid start into auditing, and to show the terminal visible audit product, we again present an audit report in the first chapter. The legal liabilities of public accountants and the requirements of the Securities and Exchange Commission are treated in the second chapter, and recent court cases and their implications are briefly discussed.

Our coverage of the use of the computer in auditing has been expanded in this edition, as have the materials on electronic data processing. The treatment of statistical sampling has been strengthened.

Realistically reproduced audit work papers appear throughout the book. If the audit report of Multi-Products, Incorporated, and all following work papers bearing the name of that company were removed from the book, they would constitute a complete audit file for that examination. Illustrative work papers bearing the name of the Blank Company provide additional material.

Once again there are more questions and problems in this edition than in the preceding edition. However, we have purposely limited the number of questions and problems in accordance with the plan for a short book; in addition, the work of an instructor in the selection of material for class preparation has been reduced. With regard to the questions and problems: Some are from or adapted from the uniform examinations offered by the American Institute of Certified Public Accountants, some are new, some are adaptations of questions and problems appearing in our *Auditing: Standards and Procedures*, 8th ed. (1975), and a few are the same as those appearing in that book.

Auxiliary materials that may be used with *Basic Auditing* include the Holmes and Kiefer *Audit Problem: Metalcraft, Inc.*, 6th ed. (1975), a 10- to 15-hour practice problem, and the Holmes and Moore *Audit Case: Colby Gears, Inc.*, 8th ed. (1975), requiring approximately 45 hours of preparation. (All of these are published by Richard D. Irwin, Inc., Homewood, Ill.)

March 1976   ARTHUR W. HOLMES
                                                WAYNE S. OVERMYER

Contents

Controls. Computers and Data Processing Developments. Distinctive Auditing Terminology.

Goods Sales. Rental Revenue. Profits on Long-Term Construction Contracts. Financial Statement Considerations.

Audit Objectives. Investment Classification. Internal Control of Investment Securities: *Reports to Management.* Audit of Investments in Stocks and Bonds: *Purchases and Sales of Securities. Revenues from Securities.* Audit of Investments in Life Insurance: *Cash Values and Cash Loan Values. Dividends and Interest. Policy Confirmation.* Audit of Investments in Funds. Financial Statement Considerations: *Temporary Marketable Securities. Long-Term Investments. Life Insurance. Investments in Funds.*

Audit Objectives. Necessity for Proper Inventory Valuation: *Responsibilities for Inventory Examinations and Valuation.* Internal Control of Inventories: *Pricing Inventories.* Audit of Inventories: *Observation and Quantity Testing. Original Count and Price Data, and Inventory Summaries. Work Papers. Cutoff of Purchases and Sales. Consigned Merchandise. Warehoused Merchandise. Purchase Commitments. Inventory Quality. Scrap Materials. Insurance Coverage. Miscellaneous Procedures. Inventory Certificates. Comments on Work in Process and Finished Goods.* Financial Statement Considerations: *Inventory Comments in the Audit Report.* Financial Statement Presentation.

Prepaid Expenses and Deferred Charges: Audit Objectives: *Preliminary Considerations.* Internal Control of Prepaid Items. Audit of Prepaid Items and Related Expenses: *Research and Development Costs.* Financial Statement Considerations.

Audit Objectives. General Comments. Internal Control of Fixed Assets. Audit of Fixed Assets: *Depreciation Considerations and Decisions. Management Reports. Land. Buildings. Machinery, Equipment, Tools, Office Equipment, Delivery Equipment. Related Expense Accounts. Insurance. Small Tools. Patterns, Dies, Electrotypes. Returnable Containers. Equalization Allowances. Extractive Industries Assets.* Financial Statement Considerations.

Classes of Intangible Assets. Audit Objectives. Internal Control of Intangible Assets. Audit of Intangible Assets: *Patents. Leaseholds. Copyrights. Franchises. Licenses. Organization Costs. Trademarks and Trade Names. Secret Processes and Formulas. Goodwill.* Financial Statement Considerations.

1

Professional Auditing and Audit Reports

Modern professional auditing is an intellectual discipline based on logic. Logic is devoted to the establishment of facts and the resultant conclusions as being valid or invalid.

Auditing may be briefly defined as the objective examination of the fairness of the presentation of the financial statements initially prepared by management. In the examination of the financial statements, an auditor relies upon:

1. The internal control procedures followed by a client.
2. The examination of accounting transactions and their underlying records.
3. The examination of evidence for the authority for and the validity of the transactions.
4. The examination of other financial and nonfinancial documents and records, and their underlying evidences for authority and validity.
5. Evidence obtained from outside sources—banks, customers, creditors, and others.

From the five preceding sources of information it is easily discernible that the basis of any audit decision must be *evidence* submitted by a client or obtained from others. *Statement on Auditing Standards (SAS) No. 1* and *No. 3*, issued by the American Institute of Certified Public Accountants (AICPA), recognizes the importance of evidential matters and internal control.

Statement on Auditing Standards No. 1 constitutes a codification of *Auditing Standards and Procedures No. 33* through *No. 54*. The student is advised to refer to SAS Nos. 1, 3, 4, 5, 6, 7, and to keep up to date on those to be issued in the future (including amendments). At the conclusion of many chapters of this book, references—not all-inclusive—are given for certain applicable sections and paragraphs of *Statement on Auditing Standards*.

While auditing is concerned with the evaluation of internal control, the examination of transactions, and the accumulation of evidence, it must be realized at this early stage that an auditor has tremendous ethical and legal responsibilities and still greater socioeconomic responsibilities. This is true because the results of auditing are judged by many organizations, agencies, publications, creditors, stockholders, courts, the news media, and others who may or may not have a direct interest in the results of auditing. In other words, the results of auditing are surveyed, or examined, and are judged by many of the adult population. In professions other than auditing—law, medicine, architecture, and so on—the results of professional operations *have been* limited to the professional practitioner, the client, and sometimes to the media. This is not true in auditing because, as indicated, the results of auditing affect and influence the entire socioeconomic environment. Consequently the dynamic social force and responsibility of auditing is so great that the intellectual imaginativeness of an auditor must never be diluted to a set of routine procedures and techniques.

In summary, auditing is a private profession rendering a totally public service. Professional auditing has a more commanding influence and voice than any other professional group.

Auditing is not a branch or subdivision of accounting because auditing measures and evaluates the results of accounting applications in business. Thus, it is independent of—or complementary to—accounting. Auditing does not measure and communicate business financial data (that is the function of accounting); it reviews and reports on the propriety or impropriety of management's measurements and communication of financial operations. Auditing is critical—not constructive—in the accounting sense.

The immediate objectives of an audit are to ascertain the reliability of the financial statements and to render an opinion of the fairness of presentation of those statements. Normally, the financial statements are the balance sheet, the income statement, the statement of retained earnings, and the statement of changes in financial position. It may be necessary to qualify the opinion, or it may be necessary to disclaim an opinion; in some cases an adverse opinion may be necessary, as will be pointed out later. These objectives—the review of past performance and the rendition of an opinion—are for information purposes.

The long-range objectives of an audit should be to serve as a guide to management's future decisions in financial matters, such as forecasting, controlling, analyzing, and reporting. These objectives have as their purposes the improvement of performances. An audit should not be viewed solely as an historical summing up but as the basis for future managerial guidance in the conduct of a business. Today there is an expanding concept of auditing in the area of financial reporting to include (in addition to the data necessary for management and owners) data required by governmental agencies, unions, the press, financial analysts, professional investment counselors, financial public relations personnel, and many others.

In auditing, the•scientific method must be used; this method consists of the following four parts: (1) defining the problem; (2) selecting, examining, and analyzing evidence; (3) drawing conclusions; and (4) verifying (or disproving) the conclusions by selecting and examining additional evidence—if necessary.

External Professional Auditing

An external audit is one conducted by an independent party of professional skill. The independent auditor is not an employee of the client, and has no relationship with management other than that of a professional person.

As already indicated, the immediate objectives of an independent external audit are (1) to judge management's representations, and (2) to report independently on financial condition and operating results. As one result of the audit work performed in order to obtain these objectives, there naturally evolves the detection of errors and fraud. Although the word "fraud" is frowned upon in connection with an audit objective, fraud exists. This is easily proved by an examination of recent court cases. Where fraud exists—with or without the acquiescence of management— the auditor would be remiss if an attempt was not made to discover it and disclose it. As another result of an audit, the auditor is in a position properly to advise and assist a client when the client requests management advisory services. Management advisory services constitute a separate engagement and are separately reported; additional material on this subject is presented below under "Independence."

Internal Auditing

An internal audit is one conducted by employees of management. Internal auditing is a staff functon. The internal auditor establishes and appraises financial and operating procedures, reviews financial records and accounting and operating procedures, evaluates the system of internal control, periodically summarizes the results of the continuous investigation, prepares recommendations for better procedures, and reports the results to top management—the president or the board of directors. The transmission of financial and operating information to management must emphasize the future effect of plans and decisions. An internal auditor is not independent of management, although the mental attitude should be one of independence.

Although the nature of the work of the internal auditor differs in many respects from that of the external auditor, in a broad financial sense the objectives of the internal auditor and the external auditor are similar—to appraise and report on financial statements and the reliability of their underlying data, and to determine the accuracy and integrity of the records.

Services of Certified Public Accountants

Professional certified public accountants offer the following principal types of services:

1. Auditing—the examination of financial statements and reporting thereon.
2. Management *advisory* services—the broad field of business managerial advisory services now increasingly demanded by clients. The areas covered are accounting, finance, personnel, product costs, distribution, general business policy, management information systems, data processing, EDP systems, operation research techniques, and so on.
3. Investigations—these are made for special purposes, such as the comparative cost of new versus the cost of retaining and maintaining present equpiment; an investigation of the system of internal control; preparation of budgets; a detailed examination of cash transactions in the event of suspected fraud; and many other purposes.
4. Representation—in tax matters, security registrations, contract termination, contract renegotiation, union negotiations, expert witness services, and many other matters.

Independence

Management relies upon the internal auditor for short-interval record examination, reporting, and recommendations. Management, owners, creditors, agencies, and others rely upon the independent auditor for critical examination of condition and operations, and reporting thereon. Therefore the independent auditor must be independent of management —not only in the relationship of client and professional person but also in thought and action. Stated differently, *independence* means freedom from influence or control of an *audit client*. The auditor must possess the independent judgment of any expert professional. The professional attitude of public accountancy is expressed in its independence, its competence, and its innate moral integrity. The auditor is not responsible for the financial statements of a client; but is responsible for an opinion

—unqualified, qualified, disclaimed, or adverse—of those financial statements.

Currently, there are two schools of thought regarding independence and the rendition of management advisory services (see the preceding section). One group follows the concept that an auditor—as an auditor—cannot maintain proper independence if management services are also rendered for the same client. The other group contends that independence can be retained for any client whose records are audited and for whom management services are rendered. Both groups should be able to attain total agreement if each would distinguish between management services and management *advisory* services. If management services are rendered, the auditor is taking over management's function and therefore is not totally independent. If management *advisory* services are rendered, the auditor is advising—not performing a function of management, and he is not performing operational work and is not acting in a management decision-making capacity. In the profession of accounting, management *advisory* services are not new—auditors have been advising clients for years. Within the past several years, advisory functions have increased in concept, scope, and emphasis. Much needless confusion has been interjected into the subject.

Obviously, in certain areas independence is not to be expected, as exemplified by assistance in establishing budgetary control systems, the installation of accounting systems, the preparation of tax returns, business consultations, and "write-up" work for small clients. In the preceding instances, the interests of a client should be placed above all other considerations, because independence is not required until an auditor evaluates and judges the results of a client's work.

EVIDENCE

In order to verify the validity of data and presentations in financial statements, adequate underlying evidence must be available. To determine the validity of an audit conclusion, an auditor must gather or obtain evidence, examine it, and evaluate it. Necessary audit evidence may be in existence at the time an audit is started; it may be created or obtained during the course of an audit; or it may be the result of logical deduction.

On the approximate basis of audit sequence—and at this point omitting the question of reliability and also omitting a full discussion of the types of evidence—audit evidence may be classified as follows:

A. Proper and adequate internal control procedures.
B. All accounting and financial records.
C. Documents: internally prepared and externally prepared, and readily available for substantiation; for example, bonds owned, copies of customers' invoices, creditors' invoices, and the like.

D. Information from independent outsiders: written or oral, and created during an audit.
E. Physical assets: cash on hand, inventories, supplies, fixed assets, etcetera.
F. Authoritative client representations: written and oral.
G. Auditor's examination of transactions, computations, and calculations, and comparisons with client-prepared data.

In judging the reliability of evidence, it must be remembered that classification is only a means to an end—a valid audit conclusion. As this book develops, various types of evidence will be discussed in greater depth.

PRINCIPLES, STANDARDS, AND PROCEDURES

A *principle* is a fundamental truth, or a primary law or doctrine. While auditing principles do not exist as primary truths or laws in the philosophical sense, they do exist in the sense of constituting rules which are derived from reasoning and experience and which guide the auditor. Therefore, auditing principles are the basic doctrines which indicate the objectives of auditing, and they suggest the manner in which the objectives are accomplished. For example: An auditor must determine that current-period revenues and expenses are properly matched in order to properly set forth periodic net income.

Stated slightly differently, accounting principles constitute the basis for the application of audit procedures in a logical manner which will fulfill the objectives of the examination. Auditing "principles" have never been codified and, perhaps, in the cause of nonregimentation, never will be. The American Institute of Certified Public Accountants is developing what is hoped to be an acceptable set of accounting principles that will be acceptable in the area of auditing. A principle may result from accepted practice—that is, a principle may develop as the result of general acceptance of a consistently applied procedure. To be very elementary, if a principle of accounting is to the effect that "for each debit (or debits) there must be an equal credit (or credits)"—that principle evolved from the practice of recognizing monetary equality in the recording of any financial transaction.

An auditing *standard* is a measurement of performance or a criterion established by professional authority and consent. Thus a principle is a primary law, while a standard is a performance-measuring device. An example of a standard: Through inspection, observation, and confirmation, sufficient competent evidence must be obtained to assure the proper matching of current-period revenues and expenses.

The American Institute of Certified Public Accountants has issued the following standards:

GENERAL STANDARDS:

1. The examination is to be performed by a person or persons having adequate technical training and proficiency as an auditor.
2. In all matters relating to the assignment, an independence in mental attitude is to be maintained by the auditor or auditors.
3. Due professional care is to be exercised in the performance of the examination and in the preparation of the report.

STANDARDS OF FIELD WORK:

1. The work is to be adequately planned; and assistants, if any, are to be properly supervised.
2. There is to be a proper study and evaluation of the existing internal control as a basis for reliance thereon and for the determination of the resultant extent of the tests to which auditing procedures are to be restricted.
3. Sufficient competent evidential matter is to be obtained through inspection, observation, inquiries, and confirmations to afford a reasonable basis for an opinion regarding the financial statements under examination.

STANDARDS OF REPORTING:

1. The report shall state whether the financial statements are presented in accordance with generally accepted accounting principles.
2. The report shall state whether such principles have been consistently observed in the current period in relation to the preceding period.
3. Informative disclosures in the financial statements are to be regarded as reasonably adequate unless otherwise stated in the report.
4. The report shall contain either an expression of opinion regarding the financial statements, taken as a whole, or an assertion to the effect that an opinion cannot be expressed. When an over-all opinion cannot be expressed, the reasons therefor should be stated. In all cases where an auditor's name is associated with financial statements, the report should contain a clear-cut indication of the character of the auditor's examination, if any, and the degree of responsibility he is taking.

These standards are more fully discussed in *Statement on Auditing Standards* (*SAS*) *No. 1.*

An audit *procedure* is an act to be performed. Audit procedures constitute the courses of action available to the auditor to judge the adherence to standards and the validity of the application of accounting principles. Examples of procedures necessary to adhere to Standard of Field Work No. 3, above, are (1) count the cash on hand, obtain a bank confirmation, and reconcile the bank statement balance wtih the cash ledger account balance; and (2) for inventories, compare vendors' invoice prices with prices used in the inventory calculation and compare with current market prices, observe the taking of the inventory, test the inventory count, and verify the accuracy of the client's extensions and footings of the inventories. Additional procedures will be developed as the book progresses.

Concepts are thoughts, ideas, or opinions based upon observations. While auditing concepts and methods are not as rigid as methods in the physical sciences, there is a similarity. For example, in auditing there is evidential support for every audit conclusion; otherwise there can be no audit opinion. In auditing, an "audit-scientific" method should be developed and followed, because any scientific method is concerned with searching for the truth based upon evidence. In any scientific method, unsupported ideas and prejudices must be excluded from consideration, due to lack of evidential support.

DISCLOSURE, CONSISTENCY, MATERIALITY, AND CONSERVATISM

In the performance of an audit and in the preparation of financial statements, the concepts of disclosure, consistency, materiality, and conservatism constantly must be borne in mind. These four concepts have been developed in earlier courses in accounting; consequently, only brief consideration and review are offered at this point.

Disclosure. Adequate disclosure is the keynote to proper financial reporting. Disclosure implies that all pertinent and adequate data and information be set forth in financial statements and accompanying notes. If full disclosure is not given to the results of managerial stewardship, pertinent data and information are withheld from persons interested in those financial statements. Disclosure would not be complete if long-term investments were classified as current assets in order to improve a current ratio; if fixed tangible assets were stated at other than acquisition cost figures, unaccompanied by an explanation; or if earnings per share of common stock were not shown as "primary" and "fully diluted." There are innumerable other examples.

Consistency. Consistency in the preparation of financial statements means that accounting principles have been applied in the same manner in both the current year and the prior year. For example, consistency would not prevail if inventories were priced at cost in one year and in the following year were priced under some other method. Consistency does not prohibit a change in the application of an accounting principle; but consistency does demand that a change in application be divulged in the financial statements or footnotes thereto, together with the effect of the change. If consistency does not exist for two consecutive years, that fact must be mentioned, together with an approval or disapproval of the change or changes in the application of the accounting principles involved.

Materiality. Materiality is a large or significant amount compared with a total or with a class of similar items. Materiality also is a practical concept involved in many problems of adequate disclosure. The following statement appears in the introduction to the Accounting Research Bulletins: "The committee contemplates that its opinions will have application only to items material and significant in the relative circumstances. It considers that items of little or no consequence may be dealt with as expediency may suggest. However, freedom to deal expediently with immaterial items should not extend to a group of items whose cumulative effect in any one financial statement may be material and significant."

The requirement of the Securities and Exchange Commission (SEC) is stated in Regulation S–X: "The term 'material,' when used to qualify a requirement for the furnishing of information as to any subject, limits the information required to those matters as to which an average prudent investor ought reasonably to be informed before purchasing the security registered." Inventories may be material in amount when compared with total current assets. Small, similar immaterial amounts may be material when totaled. Materiality also refers to nonrecurring expenses and revenues of a large amount in relationship to net income otherwise. The authors recommend that material nonrecurring items of revenue and expense be placed in the income statement—separately—following the normal figures of "Net income before federal income taxes." One point of materiality is that even if a nonrecurring item of expense or revenue of "material" amount does appear in one year, it still is expense or revenue of that year and should be set forth as such. Another point of materiality is: What is a "material" amount? This may be a matter of opinion; however, an item is material if it is of importance to the judgment of the statement reader.

Consequently, the accounting profession cannot quantify "materiality," because it is not quantifiable.

Conservatism. Conservatism means moderation or adherence to sound principles. Conservatism *does not* imply understatement, or pessimism as shown by writing fixed properties down to a nominal amount, or by always recording an unrealized loss but never recording an unrealized gain, or by charging capital expenditures to expense. Conservatism *does* mean that assets and revenues should not be understated to a point below their net realizable cash values, and that liabilities and expenses should not be overstated. The doctrine of conservatism is as follows: When two or more reasonable conclusions exist, the choice of the one that results in the least favorable *immediate* showing results in conservatism. Conservatism merely defers a favorable effect—because understatement in one period leads to overstatement in a subsequent period.

AUDIT REPORTS

The opinion of an auditor regarding the financial statements of a client is expressed in the form of a report. The report sets forth the scope of the audit and the auditor's opinion concerning the fair presentation of the statements.

Reports may be (1) short or (2) long. Ilustration 1–1 presents the commonly accepted standard short-form report recommended by the AICPA.

Short-form reports commonly are issued to nonadministrative stockholders and to creditors. Long-form reports (if requested by the client) are issued to management and may or may not be issued to stockholders, creditors, analysts, and others.

Illustration 1–1
SHORT-FORM AUDIT REPORT

BENNETT AND BENNETT

Certified Public Accountants

DATE March 1, 1977

TO THE BOARD OF DIRECTORS AND STOCKHOLDERS OF THE ABC COMPANY:

We have examined the balance sheet of the ABC Company as of December 31, 1976, and the related statements of income, retained earnings, and changes in financial position for the year then ended. Our examination was made in accordance with generally accepted auditing standards and, accordingly, included such tests of the accounting records and such other auditing procedures as we considered necessary in the circumstances.

In our opinion, the financial statements referred to above present fairly the financial position of the ABC Company at December 31, 1976, and the results of its operations and the changes in its financial position for the year then ended, in conformity with generally accepted accounting principles applied on a basis consistent with that of the preceding year.

Bennett and Bennett

In many companies, the probabilities are that the internal accounting staff is capable of preparing adequate financial statements, comparisons, analyses, statistical data displays, ratios, and comments which are necessary for management and control purposes. Consequently in such instances, the report of the auditor may be in short form, together with notes to the financial statements. In several large companies, members of the firm of auditors are on the premises daily.

In other companies, where the abilities of the internal accounting staff may be limited, management depends upon its auditor not only to render an opinion of the fairness of presentation of financial statements but also to render analyses, ratios, comparisons, and so on. In such cases a long-form report will be rendered, if requested.

The Robert Morris Associates and the New York Credit Men's Association both have stated that the long-form audit report is of greater value than the short-form report, because the long-form report is better for negotiations for credit and capital and because the short report does not spell out the scope of the examination for important items in the financial statements. The Securities and Exchange Commission is insisting upon better financial reporting, particularly in the area of adequate disclosure; the reader should watch these developments and their effect on published and unpublished audit reports.

Any audit report should be (1) dated, (2) addressed to the client, and (3) signed manually by the auditor (as in sole proprietor, or firm name, or corporate name). All audit reports must conform to the "Standards of Reporting" (page 7).

Modified Short-Form Audit Report. A "modified" short-form audit report sometimes is issued. The modified short-form report normally contains all of the elements of the recommended short form but opens with the opinion section illustrated below:

In our opinion, the accompanying balance sheet, statements of income, retained earnings, and changes in financial position present fairly the financial condition of the ABC Company as of December 31, 1976, and the results of its operations and its changes in financial position for the year then ended, in conformity with generally accepted accounting principles applied on a basis consistent with that of the preceding year. Our examination of these statements was made in accordance with generally accepted auditing standards, and accordingly included such tests of the accounting records and such other auditing procedures as we considered necessary in the circumstances.

A long-form report (Illustration 1–2) opens with the standard scope and opinion sections, followed by the financial statements, comments on operations, comments on financial condition, comments on certain audit procedures, and the presentation of various financial data.

In a long-form report, a description of audit procedures is not necessary. Occasionally there are included descriptions of unusual procedures, or procedures which might be of special interest to management, bankers, and others. If a recognized procedure is omitted, that fact should be mentioned in any report because, as will be shown later in this chapter, omission of recognized procedures may result in an opinion qualification or a disclaimer of opinion, or an adverse opinion.

Management's Review. Today, in the majority of annual reports issued by major companies, there will appear—preceding the audited financial statements and the accompanying footnotes—a management-prepared section titled "Financial Reviews," "Management's Discussion and Analysis of Financial and Other Activities," "Responsibilities for Finan-

Illustration 1–2

MULTI-PRODUCTS, INCORPORATED

TABLE OF CONTENTS

Illustration 1–2—Continued

BENNETT & BENNETT

Certified Public Accountants

Carew Tower

Cincinnati, Ohio 45202

March 3, 1977

The Board of Directors and Stockholders
Multi-Products, Incorporated

   We have examined the balance sheet of Multi-Products,
Incorporated, as of December 31, 1976, and the related
statements of income, retained earnings, and changes in
financial position for the year then ended. Our examination was made in accordance with generally accepted
auditing standards and accordingly included such tests
of the accounting records and such other auditing procedures as we considered necessary in the circumstances.

   In our opinion, the statements referred to above
present fairly the financial position of Multi-Products,
Incorporated as of December 31, 1976, and the results of
operations and the changes in financial position for
the year then ended, in conformity with generally accepted accounting principles applied on a basis consistent
with that of the preceding year.

Bennett and Bennett

Illustration 1–2—Continued

MULTI-PRODUCTS, INCORPORATED
BALANCE SHEET
DECEMBER 31, 1976, and 1975

ASSETS

	1976	1975
CURRENT ASSETS:		
Cash	$ 49,772	$ 79,602
Receivables, less allowance of $17,690 for 1976 and $17,448 for 1975	384,300	213,080
Inventories	562,582	548,708
Prepaid items	8,926	9,724
Total Current Assets	$1,005,580	$ 851,114
FIXED ASSETS:		
Land	$ 100,000	$ 90,000
Building	872,400	840,000
Machinery	579,560	558,560
Office equipment	54,020	49,300
Total	$1,605,980	$1,537,860
Less accumulated depreciation	428,480	354,830
Fixed Assets, Net	$1,177,500	$1,183,030
OTHER ASSETS:		
Cash value of life insurance	$ 11,150	$ 7,926
Sinking fund investments	116,500	113,050
Patents, at amortized cost	28,590	34,000
Total Other Assets	$ 156,240	$ 154,976
Total Assets	$2,339,320	$2,189,120

The accompanying Notes to the Financial Statements are an integral part of the statements.

3

LIABILITIES AND STOCKHOLDERS' EQUITIES

	1976	1975
CURRENT LIABILITIES:		
Accounts payable, trade.....................................$	74,752	$ 33,728
Notes payable, bank..	40,000	
Other current liabilities..................................	56,380	52,794
Debenture notes, current portion...........................	100,000	100,000
Federal income taxes.......................................	21,904	27,324
Total Current Liabilities.............................$	293,036	$ 213,846
LONG-TERM LIABILITIES:		
Debenture notes, 4%, maturing after one year..............$	300,000	$ 400,000
Total Liabilities....................................$	593,036	$ 613,846
STOCKHOLDERS' EQUITIES:		
Common stock:		
No par value; 50,000 shares authorized;		
40,000 shares are outstanding		
at a stated value of $20 per share ....$	800,000	$ 800,000
Additional paid-in capital on 40,000 shares of		
common stock at $5 per share..........................	200,000	200,000
Retained earnings..	746,284	575,274
Total Stockholders' Equities.........................$1,	746,284	$1,575,274
Total Liabilities and Stockholders' Equities........$2,339,320		$2,189,120

Illustration 1–2—Continued

MULTI-PRODUCTS, INCORPORATED
STATEMENT OF INCOME AND RETAINED EARNINGS
FOR THE YEARS ENDED DECEMBER 31, 1976 AND 1975

	1976	1975
NET SALES	$4,905,254	$4,167,186
Cost of sales	3,570,296	2,985,164
Gross profit on sales	$1,334,958	$1,182,022
Selling and administrative expenses	845,354	777,294
NET INCOME ON OPERATIONS	$ 489,604	$ 404,728
Interest and dividend income	5,450	4,134
	$ 495,054	$ 408,862
Interest expense	18,300	20,000
Net income before nonrecurring items	$ 476,754	$ 388,862
Gain (or loss) on sale of fixed assets (net of taxes)	(3,840)	1,400
Net income before federal income taxes	$ 472,914	$ 390,262
Federal income tax	201,904	187,324
NET INCOME FOR THE YEAR	$ 271,010	$ 202,938
Retained earnings January 1	575,274	452,336
	$ 846,284	$ 655,274
Dividends declared and paid	100,000	80,000
RETAINED EARNINGS December 31	$ 746,284	$ 575,274
Net income per share of common stock	$ 6.77	$ 5.07

The accompanying Notes to the Financial Statements are an integral part of the statements.

2

Illustration 1–2—Continued

```
                 MULTI-PRODUCTS, INCORPORATED
          STATEMENT OF CHANGES IN FINANCIAL POSITION
          FOR THE YEARS ENDED DECEMBER 31, 1976 and 1975
```

	1976	1975
Sources of Funds:		
Net Income	$271,010	$202,938
Charges to income not requiring use of working capital:		
Depreciation	73,650	68,254
Patent amortization	9,530	3,400
Machinery sold (loss included in net income)	15,000	1,400
	$369,190	$275,992

Uses

Application of Funds:		
Addition to land	$ 10,000	$ 20,000
Addition to building	32,400	-0-
Addition to machinery	36,000	77,000
Addition to office equipment	4,720	8,650
Increase in cash value of life insurance	3,224	2,964
Addition to sinking fund investments	3,450	2,800
Addition to patents	4,120	3,200
Dividends to stockholders	100,000	80,000
Reduction in long-term debt	100,000	100,000
	$293,914	$294,614
Increase (decrease) in net working capital	$ 75,276	$(18,622)

Components increasing (decreasing) working capital		
Cash	$(29,830)	$ 4,500
Accounts receivable, net	140,530	(61,222)
Notes receivable	30,000	(9,400)
Accrued receivables	690	410
Inventories	13,874	(5,211)
Prepaid items	(798)	2,818
Accounts payable	41,024	10,756
Notes payable	40,000	60,000
Social security and unemployment tax liability	1,306	1,321
Income taxes withheld	2,820	2,041
Accrued expenses	(540)	1,110
Current portion of debenture bonds	-0-	-0-
Federal income tax liability	(5,420)	(7,123)
Increase (decrease) in working capital	$ 75,276	$(18,622)

5

Illustration 1–2—Continued

MULTI-PRODUCTS, INCORPORATED

NOTES TO THE FINANCIAL STATEMENTS

ACCOUNTING POLICIES

The financial statements reflect the application of generally accepted
accounting principles, and are described and explained in the following notes to the financial statements.

RECEIVABLES

Receivables consist of the following:

```
Trade accounts receivable.....................................$327,300
        Less provision for doubtful accounts.....................  17,690
Trade accounts receivable, net..............................$309,610
Trade notes receivable......................................  74,000
Accrued interest receivable.................................     690

Net Receivables.............................................$384,300
```

As of December 31, 1976, trade accounts receivable were summarized
by invoice dates as follows:

```
        December, 1976..........................................$200,570
        November, 1976..........................................  96,532
        October, 1976...........................................  26,962
        Prior to October, 1976..................................   3,236
                Total...........................................$327,300
```

After adjusting for year-end sales and payments, no differences in account
receivable balances were reported based upon negative confirmations sent
to all customers. Based upon past experience, management is of the opinion
that the provision for doubtful items is adequate.

Credit terms are net cash in 30 days; in January and February,
1977, 95 percent of the open accounts receivable, and 70 percent of the
notes receivable were collected.

No differences were reported as a result of the positive confirmation of
the notes receivable; all are trade notes.

INVENTORIES

Inventories, determined by physical count, and priced at the lower of
cost (partly Lifo) or market, are compared below for two years:

| | December 31 | | Increase |
	1976	1975	(Decrease)
Raw materials.....................	$264,488	$258,294	$ 6,194
Work in process....................	120,604	111,212	9,392
Finished goods....................	170,880	166,706	4,174
Factory supplies..................	6,610	12,496	(5,886)
Total inventories.............	$562,582	$548,708	$13,874
Percentage of inventories to total net current assets...............	55.9%	69.4%	

6

Illustration 1–2—Continued

FIXED ASSETS

Land, building, machinery, and office equipment are originally recorded
at cost of acquisition. The company uses the straight-line method in all
instances. The depreciated cost of the building, machinery, and office
equipment represents that portion of original cost not yet allocated as a
charge against operations, and does not purport to be either a realizable
value or a replacement value. Net expenditures for fixed assets in 1976
totaled $83,120; gross book values of properties sold or retired totaled
$15,000.

	1976	1975
Building..	$ 872,400	$ 840,000
Machinery......................................	579,560	558,560
Office equipment...............................	54,020	49,300
	$1,505,980	$1,447,860
Less accumulated depreciation..................	428,480	354,830
Depreciated cost of building, machinery, and office equipment...........................	$1,077,500	$1,093,030
Land..	100,000	90,000
Total Fixed Assets, Net.......................	$1,177,500	$1,183,030

As of December 31, 1976, commitments for property additions and improvements
amounted to approximately $150,000.

An analysis of the fixed tangible assets and the related depreciation
provisions is presented below:

	Asset Balance 1-1-76	Net Additions 1976	Asset Balance 12-31-76	Accum. Depr. 1-1-76	Depreciation 1976 Rate	Depreciation 1976 Amount	Accum. Depr. 12-31-76	Book Value
Building.........$	840,000	$32,400	$ 872,400	$127,892	2%	$16,300	$144,192	$ 728,208
Machinery........	558,560	21,000	579,560	193,952	10%	52,020	245,972	333,588
Office Equipment.	49,300	4,720	54,020	32,986	10%	5,330	38,316	15,704
	$1,447,860	$58,120	$1,505,980	$354,830		$73,650	$428,480	$1,077,500

CASH VALUE OF LIFE INSURANCE

Included in the cash value of life insurance is the prepaid premium
portion of $2,706.

SINKING FUND INVESTMENTS

Under the terms of the debenture notes indenture the company is required
to maintain a sinking fund at least equal in amount to the note installment
next due for payment. The sinking fund assets are under company control.

Illustration 1–2—Continued

PATENTS

Patents represent purchased rights, and the remaining cost of all existing patents is to be totally amortized over the remaining four years ending December 31, 1980, because management is of the opinion that useful life will not extend beyond that date.

FEDERAL TAXES ON INCOME

In determining the amount of income subject to federal taxes, certain adjustments were made to the net income before taxes. The company is of the opinion that there are no contingencies for additional tax assessments or for tax refunds. During the year 1976, the company paid $180,000 on an installment basis, resulting in a remaining liability of $21,904 as of December 31, 1976.

DEBENTURE NOTES

Debenture notes in the amount of $1,000,000 were issued January 1, 1970, and are to be retired serially in the annual amount of $100,000 starting July 1, 1971.

As of December 31, 1976, $400,000 of notes are outstanding of which $100,000 is a short-term liability.

Under covenants in the indenture, the company is limited to $150,000 as aggregate annual payments which may be made for dividends on capital stock, or for redemption, purchase, or other acquisition of its capital stock.

MISCELLANEOUS LIABILITIES

Income taxes withheld	$19,248
F.I.C.A. tax liability	1,250
Federal unemployment tax	2,196
State unemployment tax	3,188
Accrued compensation insurance	1,548
Accrued interest payable	8,300
Accrued miscellaneous taxes	20,650
Total other liabilities	$56,380

STOCK OPTIONS

Under a stock option plan, as of December 31, 1976, there were outstanding options granted to certain employees to purchase 8,000 shares at the mean average market price at the date of grant, ranging from $131.00 to $162.50 per share. Options for 2,000 shares were granted during 1976. Options outstanding are not exercisable for two years, and expire five years after date of grant, with certain exceptions due to death or disability. During 1976, options for 4,600 shares were exercised at an average price of $143.00 per share, while options for 1,200 shares which have expired have reverted to unissued status.

Illustration 1–2—Continued

RESEARCH AND DEVELOPMENT COSTS

Research and development costs are charged to expense as they are incurred.

OTHER MATTERS

No litigation was pending as of December 31, 1976, and none is contemplated. It is the opinion of management that contingencies do not exist for assets or liabilities.

There were no foreign exchange adjustments for 1976 or 1975.

As of the date of this report, March 3, 1977, to the best of our knowledge, there have been no events subsequent to December 31, 1976, which would alter the financial statements as of that date.

COMMENTS ON OPERATIONS

Revenues, Expenses, and Net Income

The following summary sets forth the operations for 1976 compared with 1975:

	1976	Percent of Net Sales	1975	Percent of Net Sales	Increase (Decrease)
Net sales................	$4,905,254	100.0	$4,167,186	100.0	$738,068
Cost of sales............	3,570,296	72.8	2,985,164	71.6	585,132
Gross profit on sales....	$1,334,958	27.2	$1,182,022	28.4	$152,936
Selling expenses.........	335,126	6.8	317,620	7.7	17,506
Administrative expenses..	510,228	10.4	459,674	11.0	50,554
Net operating income.....	$ 489,604	10.0	$ 404,728	9.7	$ 84,876
Other expenses, net......	12,850	0.3	15,866	0.4	(3,016)
	$ 476,754	9.7	$ 388,862	9.3	$ 87,892
Nonrecurring items: Loss or gain on sale of fixed assets.........	(3,840)	0.1	+ 1,400	0.1	(5,240)
Net income before federal income taxes.........	$ 472,914	9.6	$ 390,262	9.4	$ 82,652
Federal income taxes.....	201,904	4.1	187,324	4.5	14,580
Net income...............	$ 271,010	5.5	$ 202,938	4.9	$ 68,072
Earned per share of common stock........	$ 6.77		$ 5.07		$ 1.70

The sales increase in 1976 of $738,068 was caused primarily by increased volume; price changes accounted for approximately $100,000 of the increase. The cost of sales increased at a slightly faster rate of increase than did sales. In terms of the cost of sales per dollar of sales, cost of sales increased from $0.716 in 1975 to $0.728 in 1976.

The rate of net income earned on net sales was 5.5 percent in 1976, and 4.9 percent in 1975.

Illustration 1–2—Concluded

SUPPLEMENTARY INFORMATION

MULTI-PRODUCTS, INCORPORATED
SELLING AND ADMINISTRATIVE EXPENSES
FOR THE YEARS ENDED DECEMBER 31, 1976 AND 1975

	1976	1975	Increase (Decrease)
Selling Expenses:			
Transportation-out	$ 26,004	$ 22,530	$ 3,474
Sales salaries	173,800	164,282	9,518
Travel expense	9,848	13,506	(3,658)
Advertising	92,832	80,460	12,372
General selling expense	32,642	36,842	(4,200)
Total Selling Expenses	$335,126	$317,620	$17,506
Administrative Expenses:			
Administrative salaries	$359,578	$337,500	$22,078
Depreciation of office equipment	5,330	4,850	480
Uncollectible accounts expense	13,092	8,436	4,656
Office supplies	4,648	5,350	(702)
Office operating expense	14,746	12,572	2,174
Insurance expense, general	9,292	9,160	132
Professional services	16,000	13,000	3,000
Miscellaneous taxes	35,654	22,614	13,040
F.I.C.A. tax expense	25,050	19,244	5,806
Federal unemployment tax	2,196	1,908	288
State unemployment tax	19,776	17,448	2,328
Workmen's compensation insurance	2,966	2,468	498
Life insurance expense	1,900	5,124	(3,224)
Total Administrative Expenses	$510,228	$459,674	$50,554

MULTI-PRODUCTS, INCORPORATED
STATEMENT OF COST OF SALES
FOR THE YEARS ENDED DECEMBER 31, 1976 AND 1975

	1976	1975
Inventories, January 1	$ 536,212	$ 509,220
Raw materials purchased	2,525,548	2,021,008
Transportation-inward	23,372	19,550
	$3,085,132	$2,549,778
Direct factory labor	674,102	645,722
Manufacturing overhead:		
Indirect factory labor	179,100	160,314
Depreciation of building	16,300	15,448
Depreciation of machinery	52,020	47,956
Building maintenance	14,470	13,040
Machinery maintenance	20,970	18,930
Research and development cost	25,500	21,600
Heat and Power	24,684	21,888
Factory supplies expense	24,460	23,300
Patent amortization	9,530	3,400
Total manufacturing overhead	$ 367,034	$ 325,876
	$4,126,268	$3,521,376
Inventories, December 31	555,972	536,212
Cost of sales	$3,570,296	$2,985,164

10

cial Statements," or another similar title. Purposely at this early stage such a section is not included here. If interested, the reader should examine the annual report of any major corporation.

THE AUDITOR'S OPINION

As stated, the opinion of an auditor may be unqualified, qualified, disclaimed, or adverse.

Unqualified Opinion. Illustrations 1–1 and 1–2 contain unqualified opinions. If as the result of an examination the auditor has no reservations concerning the fairness of the presentation of the financial statements, the application of accounting principles, or the consistency of their application compared with the prior year, the report will contain an unqualified opinion.

Qualified Opinion. If a client's application of accounting principles departs from generally accepted accounting principles, or if consistency in their application does not prevail resulting in a material (or significant) uncertainty of position, or if evidence is not sufficient, or if the client restricts the scope of the examination, the audit report should contain a qualified opinion—as the maximum.

A qualified opinion should always contain the phrase "subject to" or "except for" or "with the exception of" the item(s) or matter(s) to which the qualification is related. Three illustrations are presented below; there are, of course, many more. The reader should note that a "middle" paragraph is used to explain the reason for qualification.

The following report is qualified because of an unresolved matter.

To the Stockholders of the A Company:

We have examined the balance sheet . . . , etc.

As set forth in Note 1 to the financial statements, trade receivables at December 31, 1976, include $2,000,000, which the Company is seeking to collect through legal action. Pending the outcome of such action, it is not possible to form an opinion as to the adequacy of the provision of $100,000 for loss on this receivable.

In our opinion, subject to the effect of any losses that may be sustained in collection of the receivable referred to above, the accompanying financial statements present fairly the financial position of the Company as of December 31, 1976, the results of its operations, and the changes in financial position for the year then ended, in conformity with generally accepted accounting principles applied on a basis consistent with that of the preceding year.

Another type of qualification in an auditor's opinion is introduced by the words "except for."

Except for the possible effect on net income and net assets resulting from nonconfirmation of accounts receivable, as requested by management, in our opinion the accompanying balance sheet and statements of income and retained earnings, and changes in financial position, present fairly the financial position of the Blank Company at December 31, 1976, and the results of its operations for the year then ended, in conformity with generally accepted accounting principles applied on a basis consistent with that of the preceding year.

As an example of uncertainty of position, although there is no disagreement between an auditor and a client, an opinion might be phrased:

In our opinion, subject to the eventual determination of the amount to be realized for the company's investments in Saudi Arabia, the accompanying consolidated financial statements present fairly the consolidated financial position of The Global Company and its consolidated subsidiaries as of December 31, 1976 and 1975, and the results of their operations and the changes in financial position for the years then ended, in conformity with generally accepted accounting principles consistently applied.

Disclaimer of Opinion. If an auditor's exceptions to a client's failure to disclose material matters are of sufficient magnitude, or if the scope of an examination is so curtailed that exceptions would negate an opinion, the auditing firm should state that it is not in a position to render an opinion—and an opinion should be disclaimed, together with the reasons for disclaimer; the reasons for disclaiming an opinion should be set forth in a separate paragraph(s), as shown below:

(Scope Paragraph)

Except as set forth in the following paragraph, our examination was made in accordance with generally accepted auditing standards, and accordingly included such tests of the accounting records and such other auditing procedures as we considered necessary in the circumstances.

(Middle Paragraph)

We did not observe the taking of the physical inventories as of December 31, 1975 ($1,382,000), and December 31, 1976 ($1,456,000), since these dates were prior to our initial engagement as auditors for the company. The company's records do not permit adequate retroactive tests of inventory quantities.

(Disclaimer Paragraph)

Since we could not make adequate retroactive tests of the inventory quantities as of December 31, 1975 and 1976, and because of the significance of these amounts, we do not express an opinion on the accompanying financial statements.

As another illustration, the disclaimer paragraph might be as follows:

As indicated in the opening paragraph, the terms of our engagement excluded confirmation of receivables and the testing of inventory quantities. Because of the materiality of these items and the required omission of auditing procedures necessary to satisfy ourselves with respect to them, we disclaim an opinion of the fairness of the financial statements.

Adverse Opinion. An adverse opinion should be rendered when the financial statements do not fairly present financial position, results of operations, or changes in financial position prepared in conformity with generally accepted accounting principles. The reasons for the rendition of an adverse opinion should be set forth in a middle paragraph(s), together with the effect of the matter(s) on the financial statements; this would include reservations on the part of the auditor regarding the application of accepted accounting principles.

The opinion paragraph should include a reference to the paragraph(s) upon which the adverse opinion is based. Two examples are shown below:

(Separate Paragraph)

No provision has been made in the accounts for the company's warranty liability on products sold. This liability was estimated to be approximately $3,500,000 at December 31, 1976, and $2,400,000 at the end of 1975, after considering the related federal income taxes. Had such provisions been made, net income for 1976 and retained earnings as of December 31, 1976, would have been reduced by approximately $1,300,000 and $3,500,000, respectively.

Opinion

Because of the significance of the matter referred to in the preceding paragraph, in our opinion the financial statements do not present fairly the financial position of the ABC Company as of December 31, 1976, the results of its operations, and changes in financial position for the year then ended, in conformity with generally accepted accounting principles.

(Separate Paragraph)

Research and development costs deferred to the future are in the amount of $9,000,000. These costs were incurred in connection with the development of a new product, and the cost recovery depends upon the success of the new product at profitable sales prices; no research and development costs were charged to operations of the current year. See Note No. 3 to the financial statements. In addition, as stated in Note No. 4, the company is defendant in a court case involving $4,000,000 for patent infringement, and the company is suing for $2,000,000 in a counterclaim. At this time the outcome of this litigation cannot be ascertained.

Opinion

In our opinion, because of the matters set forth in the preceding paragraph, the financial statements referred to do not present fairly the financial position of the B Company as of December 31, 1976, or the results of its operations and changes in financial position for the year then ended.

Independent Audits

No two audits are identical. Each has its own peculiarities. There is only one audit—that which satisfies the requirements of an engagement and which adheres to recognized auditing standards, and procedures. As stated earlier, evidence and the examination of transactions are the bases for any audit conclusion. In order to arrive at a conclusion regarding financial condition and the results of operations for a period, it obviously would be impossible and ridiculous to examine each bit of evidence in existence. Therefore, tests of transactions and underlying data are made, and the results of these tests will form the basis for the overall audit conclusion. To summarize, in any normal audit, financial condition is examined and evidence data and transactions are tested and reviewed.

In outline form, an audit includes the following:

1. Examination of organization agreements—the corporate charter and amendments thereto, partnership contracts, and trust agreements.
2. Examination of minutes of the meetings of stockholders and the board of directors; examination of contracts; examination of the accounting system in operation.
3. Examination of the system of internal control; a good system of internal control reduces the amount of detailed audit work.
4. Proof that all assets owned are included in the balance sheet, and proof of the ownership of all assets included.
5. Proof that all liabilities are included in the balance sheet at proper amount.
6. Proof that owners' equities are properly set forth in proper amount, properly classified.
7. An analysis of charges and credits to Retained Earnings and other Nonstock equity accounts to assure their propriety.
8. Determination that financial statements are prepared in accordance with generally accepted principles of accounting, consistently applied.
9. Analyses of key items of material amount and/or significance.
10. Determination of proper periodic net income; this involves the analysis and test of revenue and expense transactions to the extent necessary to permit an expression of opinion.

Tests of transactions are made on theory that a proper sample will reveal errors. If errors revealed in the selected sample are judged to be too great, the *detail* of the examination is extended by selecting additional samples. The extensiveness of the testing in any examination is dependent on the following:

1. Adequacy of the system of internal control in operation.
2. Accuracy with which financial records are maintained.

3. Necessity of obtaining information in one audit which may not be important in another audit.

REQUIREMENTS FOR THE CPA EXAMINATION

Each of the 50 states, the District of Columbia, the Virgin Islands, Puerto Rico, and Guam has its own law setting forth the requirements for candidacy for the examination for the certificate of certified public accountant. These laws are not uniform; most jurisdictions require a college degree which includes recognized accounting courses. An additional requirement may be that the candidate shall have a minimum number of years' experience (one to five years, depending on the jurisdiction and on the education of the candidate) in public accounting under the employment of a certified public accountant or a public accountant. Depending upon the particular jurisdictional law, the required experience may precede or follow the taking of the examination; if it follows the taking of the examination, the certification is not conferred until the experience requirement is fulfilled. Most states have enacted legislation that a present noncollege graduate must obtain his certification prior to an established future date, after which date *all* candidates must possess a degree from a college or university offering recognized courses in accounting.

Under the jurisdiction of their boards of accountancy, all 54 jurisdictions offer the uniform CPA examination prepared by the Board of Examiners of the AICPA. The examination is offered in May and November. All jurisdictions employ the Advisory Grading Service of the Institute.

The CPA examination is divided into the following sections: (1) accounting theory; (2) accounting practice—problems; (3) auditing—questions and problems; and (4) commercial law. Several states also require that candidates be examined on the AICPA's *Code of Professional Ethics*. Properly, education—not practice—is the basic premise of the examination.

Each section must be satisfactorily passed; the commonly accepted passing grade is 75 out of 100 for each section. If all sections are not satisfactorily passed at the same time, the candidate may retake failed sections within a stipulated time without losing credit for sections already passed. The laws of some jurisdictions require a candidate who fails all sections taken at one time to wait a minimum period (usually one year) before being reexamined. After the passage of the elapsed time, all sections must be retaken.

STAFF ORGANIZATION OF PROFESSIONAL ACCOUNTING FIRMS

The organization of a firm (or corporation) of CPAs necessarily will vary, depending upon the personnel size of the firm, the occupational levels, and the types of services offered. The following personnel categories are prevalent in larger firms.

Partners. Partners are persons of top-level authority. Their judgment must be mature, and they must be resourceful. They select the staff, plan staff training, determine office operating policies, draft and/or review and approve audit reports, and determine that recognized auditing standards were adhered to in each engagement, in accordance with the objective of that examination.

Managers. Managers are responsible directly to partners. In small firms, partners may act as managers. In large firms a manager may perform many of the duties of a partner. A manager normally is in charge of many engagements at one time. Managers must possess the point of view of executives. Frequently they are in charge of personnel recruitment and staff training.

Supervisors. Supervisors are persons between the manager and the senior level. In small firms this category may not exist. Supervisors report to managers in large firms, and frequently are in direct field charge of many engagements. Supervisors do not extensively engage in SEC filings, management advisory services, or in liaison work.

Senior Accountants. A senior accountant should be a college graduate and a certified public accountant. The duties, responsibilities, and authority of a senior will vary with many factors, such as the personnel size of the firm, the type of engagement, the class of the firm's clientele, the ability of the senior, and his general training. Normally, a senior will be in immediate *field* charge of one or more engagements. He should be able to plan an audit and to supervise persons working with him; also, he should be able to complete an engagement, close all work papers, draft tax returns, and draft the audit report.

Semisenior Accountants. Semiseniors should be college graduates who have obtained or are obtaining CPA accreditation. They are in a class halfway between that of a senior accountant and a staff accountant. In small firms the classification of semisenior may not exist. In large firms, semiseniors may be placed in field charge of certain engagements, but in other engagements, they may serve as staff accountants.

Staff Accountants. Staff accountants are those persons beginning their professional public training. Under the supervision of a senior, a supervisor, or a manager, they perform routine detailed work on an engagement. Due to initial lack of training, their original responsibilities are limited; but their work is of importance to the senior, the supervisor, manager, the partners, the accounting firm, and the client. A few of the field duties of the staff accountant include verification of footing accuracies; verification of extensions and totals on invoices; proof of posting accuracy; tracing of transactional original evidence into the financial records; and preparation of reconciliations, confirmations, schedules, and analyses.

A staff accountant should be a college graduate. Many accounting firms now select college graduates on the basis of faculty recommendations, tests prepared by the AICPA, and selections made by personnel directors of accounting firms. While many of the duties of a staff accountant are detailed, he or she must remember that successful persons ranking higher, rose to their present positions because they were willing to do detailed and monotonous work; and at the same time, he or she must realize the importance of that work in terms of audit objectives.

In small CPA firms, the preceding personnel may be reduced—to partner, manager, senior, and staff accountant.

PROFESSIONAL ORGANIZATIONS

Each professional accounting society or organization is devoted to the fulfillment of its functions, and all are interested in the advancement of the profession of accounting.

The American Institute of Certified Public Accountants. This is the only national organization of CPAs. The Institute originally was established in 1887. The objectives of the Institute include the encouragement of cooperation among national organizations of accountants, coordination of state societies, improvement of professional personnel through advanced study (including continuing professional education), advancement of accounting collegiate education, and the creation of uniform national standards applicable to the requirements for issuance of the CPA certificate.

The Board of Examiners of the Institute prepares uniform CPA examinations. The AICPA formulates and follows a position on state and federal legislation affecting accounting practice; it cooperates with teachers of accounting in raising the standards of accounting education; and it establishes and enforces a code of professional ethics.

The Financial Accounting Standards Board. The FASB was established in 1973, and supersedes the former Accounting Principles Board of the AICPA. Its function is to establish standards of accounting and reporting. The board has seven full-time salaried members, and during their five-year period on the Board they may have no other business affiliation. When the FASB issues a *Standard* (after public hearing, comment, and change) it becomes binding on all members of the AICPA.

The Auditing Standards Executive Committee. This is the senior technical committee of the AICPA charged to issue pronouncements on auditing matters. It issues *Statements on Auditing Standards* (SAS) as interpretations of generally accepted auditing standards. Members of the AICPA must adhere to the *Statements*, or be able to justify their reasons for departure.

State Societies of CPAs. Certified public accountants have organized state societies within each state, and the state societies work in cooperation with the Institute. The objectives of the state societies, in general, are to elevate professional standards of public accounting, to promote the spirit of professional cooperation, to encourage proper education, and to direct and enforce continuing professional education.

The American Accounting Association. This is the leading national organization, with activities devoted primarily to accounting and related research, to the improvement of the teaching of accounting, and to the development of accounting principles. The original organization was founded in 1916. Its members include teachers of accounting and related subjects, and accountants who are privately and publicly employed.

Other Organizations. The *American Women's Society of Certified Public Accountants* was organized in 1933 in order to advance the professional interests of women certified public accountants. The *Institute of Internal Auditors* was formed in 1941. The *National Association of Accountants* is very important and active in the study and development of accounting practices and methods. It has an excellent educational program. The *Financial Executives Institute* is devoted to the further development of the functions of controllership. The *National Society of Public Accountants* was organized in 1945; its primary objective is education. *Beta Alpha Psi* is a national accounting fraternity with chapters in many universities.

The Association of Government Accountants. This (formerly the FGAA) is a national professional organization. Most of its members are primarily engaged in government accounting, auditing, budgeting, and related financial management areas. The members also include people from industry, education, and private personal service organizations interested in all government programs. The AGA has a code of professional ethics. The principal objectives of the association are (a) to unite professional managers in government service to perform more efficiently, (b), to provide an effective means for interchange of work-related and professional ideas, (c) to aid in improving financial management techniques, and (d) to improve financial management education in universities and in government.

The U.S. General Accounting Office. The GAO was created by Congress. It has a wide range of audit authority for government contracts with private companies, particularly those connected with national defense. The GAO has a code of audit standards, and it has the legal responsibility to approve all federal agency accounting systems—and there are approximately 325 systems. When a law is changed, an affected agency must change its system, after which the system change must be approved by the GAO.

The Cost Accounting Standards Board. The CASB is an agency in the legislative branch of the federal government and it came into existence in 1971. The function of the Board is to develop cost accounting standards for national defense contractors and subcontractors when the defense contract exceeds $500,000. The work of the CASB formerly was performed by the GAO. The Comptroller General of the United States is Chairman of the Board. He appoints four additional board members with background and experience in government, industry, professional accounting, and the community of academic accounting. The Board is responsible to Congress, it has an executive secretary who is a permanent employee, and it is served by a full-time staff of 20 to 25 experienced accountants and lawyers. Each professional staff member is assigned responsibility for a major research project, and the research projects are coordinated by a group of four project directors. At this time the CASB has issued several cost accounting standards.

PROFESSIONAL ETHICS

Professional ethics involves a system of moral principles and the observance of prescribed rules that govern the actions of a professional accountant in his operations and in his relations with clients, the public, and other accountants. Codified ethical rules of a profession are either mandatory or advisory, and they apply only to members of the organization establishing the code.

The AICPA has a mandatory code of professional ethics for its members. The Institute's code is divided into the following three major parts: (1) the *Concept of Professional Ethics*, (2) the *Rules of Conduct*, and (3) the *Interpretations of Rules of Conduct*. The first part is a philosophical essay; it does not establish enforceable standards, but suggests behavior. The second part consists of enforceable standards or rules. The third part consists of interpretations of the rules of conduct adopted by the Division of Professional Ethics of the Institute. The interested reader should become familiar with the entire code. Very briefly, the *Rules of Conduct* of the code (from which the statements are taken) may be summarized as follows:

A member or a firm of which he is a partner or shareholder shall not express an opinion on financial statements of an enterprise unless he and his firm are independent with respect to such enterprise. (Rule 101)

A member shall not knowingly misrepresent facts, and when engaged in the practice of public accounting, including the rendering of tax and management advisory services, shall not subordinate his judgment to others. (Rule 102)

A member shall not undertake any engagement which he or his firm cannot reasonably expect to complete with professional competence. (Rule 201)

A member shall not permit his name to be associated with financial statements in such a manner as to imply that he is acting as an independent public accountant unless he has complied with the applicable generally accepted auditing standards promulgated by the Institute. (Rule 202)

A member shall not express an opinion that financial statements are presented in conformity with generally accepted accounting principles if such statements contain any departure from an accounting principle promulgated by the body designated by Council. . . . (Rule 203)

A member shall not permit his name to be used in conjunction with any forecast of future transactions in a manner which may lead to the belief that the member vouches for the achievability of the forecast. (Rule 204)

A member shall not disclose any confidential information obtained in the course of a professional engagement except with the consent of the client. . . . (Rule 301)

Professional services shall not be offered or rendered under an arrangement whereby no fee will be charged unless a specified finding or result is attained, or where the fee is otherwise contingent upon the findings or results of such services. However, a member's fees may vary depending on the complexity of the service rendered. (Rule 302)

Fees are not regarded as being contingent if fixed by courts or other public authorities or, in tax matters, if determined based on the results of judicial proceedings or the findings of government agencies. (Rule 302)

A member shall not endeavor to provide a person or entity with a professional service which is currently provided by another public accountant. . . . (Rule 401) (Note: there are certain exceptions, indicated in Rule 401.)

A member in public practice shall not make a direct or indirect offer of employment to an employee of another public accountant on his own behalf or that of his client without first informing such accountant. . . . (Rule 402)

A member shall not commit an act discreditable to the profession. (Rule 501)

A member shall not seek to obtain clients by solicitation. Advertising is a form of solicitation and is prohibited. (Rule 502)

A member shall not pay a Commission to obtain a client . . . (Rule 503)

A member who is engaged in the practice of public accounting shall not concurrently engage in any business or occupation which impairs his objectivity in rendering professional services or service as a feeder to his practice. (Rule 504)

In accordance with the bylaws of the Institute, its Trial Board may try and punish a member charged with violation of its code of professional ethics. Punishment may run from reprimand to dismissal from the Institute. Following the decision of the Trial Board, the certificate of the charged certified public accountant may be suspended or permanently revoked by the jurisdictional authority which granted the certificate.

SUGGESTED ADDITIONAL READING

Statement on Auditing Standards No. 1, Section 110, paragraphs .01–.09; Section 150, paragraphs .01–.06; *Statement on Auditing Standards No. 2,* pages 1–18 (which replaces Sections 510–516 of *Statement No. 1*); *Code of Professional Ethics* of the AICPA.
Statement on Auditing Standards No. 5.

QUESTIONS

1. *a)*   What is auditing?
    b)   Who is interested in the results of an audit other than the auditors?

    c)   What are the functions of the auditing standards issued by the AICPA?

2. What are the differences between each of the following, considered independently of each other.
    a)   accounting
    b)   independent auditing
    c)   internal auditing, and
    d)   public accountancy?

3. Why are client internal controls important to an independent auditor?

4. *a)*   How much evidence should be examined to arrive at an opinion of the fairness of presentation of a client's financial statements?
    b)   In general, how may audit evidence be classified?
    c)   To a businessperson, what are the advantages of an audit?

5. In an examination of financial statements, an auditor is interested in the accumulation and examination of accounting and other financial evidence.
    a)   What is the objective of accumulating and examining accounting and other financial evidence during the course of an audit?
    b)   The source of evidence is of importance in the auditor's evaluation of its quality. Evidence may be classified according to its source; for example, one class (assume bank checks) originates with the client, passes through third parties, and is returned to the client where it may be examined by the auditor. List the classifications of accounting evidence according to source and briefly discuss the effect of the source on the reliability of the evidence.

6. What are the objectives of a short-form audit report?

7. *a)*   In general, what are the types of services rendered by professional certified public accountants?
    b)   Do all services rendered by certified public accountants require independence? Explain.

8. For nine consecutive years you have performed the audit for a client. Unqualified reports always have been issued. Early in 1976 you recommended that the company change from Fifo to Lifo for costing sales and pricing inventories. Your recommendation immediately was placed in operation. What effect, if any, would this change have upon the audit report for the year ended December 31, 1976?

9. *a)*   What is meant by a qualified audit opinion? Set forth your assumptions and prepare an illustration of a qualified report.
    b)   Under what circumstances should an auditor disclaim an opinion in his audit report? Prepare an illustration.

10. *a)*   Under which of the following circumstances should an adverse opinion be rendered?
       (1)   The scope of the examination was limited by the client.
       (2)   Sufficient auditing procedures were not performed to form an opinion of the financial statements as a whole.
       (3)   Exceptions to the fairness of the presentation of the financial statements are so great that a qualified opinion is not justified.
    b)   An unqualified short-form report implies or states which of the following statements?

> (1)   States that all material items have been disclosed in conformity with the application of generally accepted accounting principles.
>
> (2)   Implies that only items disclosed in the financial statements and accompanying footnotes are properly presented and assumes no position on the adequacy of disclosure.
>
> (3)   Implies that disclosure is adequate in the financial statements and accompanying footnotes.
>
> (AICPA, adapted)

11.   Is it possible to qualify an audit opinion without also invalidating the related financial statements? Explain.

12.   Based upon the following audit report, (a) prepare a list of criticisms and (b) draft a proper report:

> To the Pour Company:
>
> We have audited the accounts of the company as of October 31, 1976, and we have tested the records and accounts and the accounting methods and procedures employed by the company.
>
> We reviewed the report of Toron & Toran, CAs, Toronto, who audited the records of the subsidiary company located in that city.
>
> Accounts receivable were not confirmed. We verified inventory summaries for clerical accuracy, and the board of directors certified that the inventories are valued at not in excess of replacement cost. In accordance with the accounting records, all liabilities are in the balance sheet.
>
> In our opinion, the accompanying balance sheet and income statement correctly present financial condition and operating results as of October 31, 1976.

13.   a)   From your knowledge of financial reporting, why are footnotes to financial statements frequently desirable or necessary?

   b)   Prepare a list of several different examples of information which might be disclosed in footnotes to financial statements.

   c)   Prepare a list of several different examples of information that might be contained in an audit report which probably would not appear in the financial statements or footnotes thereto.

14.   You are auditing the financial statements of Robin, Inc., which opened its first branch in 1976. During the audit, the Robin president raises the question of the accounting treatment of the branch operating loss for its first year, which is material in amount.

   The president proposes to capitalize the operating loss as a "startup" expense to be amortized over a five-year period and states that branches of other companies engaged in the same business normally suffer a first-year loss which is invariably capitalized, and you are aware of this practice. The president argues that the loss should be capitalized so that the accounting will be "conservative"; further, it is argued that the accounting must be "consistent" with established industry practice.

   a)   Discuss the president's use of the words "conservative" and "consistent" from the standpoint of accounting terminology. Discuss the accounting treatment you would recommend.

   b)   What disclosure, if any, would be required in the financial statement

(1) if the loss is charged to expense, or (2) if the loss is capitalized?

(AICPA, adapted)

15. If the major portion of the income of an auditor is received from one client, can the auditor be considered to be independent?

16. Management advisory services constitute one of the major operating areas of the professional certified public accountant. How could the CPA be of service in determining the advisability of a proposed capital expenditure for the expansion of a client's operations?

17. An independent CPA should not express the opinion that the financial statements present fairly the position of the company and the results of its operations, in conformity with generally accepted accounting principles, (1) when exceptions are such as to disclaim an opinion, or (2) when the examination has been less in scope than considered necessary to express an opinion on the statements.

   a) Describe a situation in which an auditor cannot express an opinion because the exceptions are such as to disclaim the opinion. Present an explanation of the criteria applicable in making this decision.

   b) Describe a situation in which an auditor cannot express an opinion because the examination has been less in scope than considered necessary. Explain why you think no opinion should be expressed in the situation which you describe.

   c) Draft an appropriate short-form audit report which an auditor might submit in the situation given in your answer to (*b*).

(AICPA, adapted)

18. An auditor and a client agreed that the audit fee would be contingent upon the number of days necessary to complete the audit. Did the CPA violate the *Code of Professional Ethics* of the AICPA? Present reasons for your answer.

19. In rendering an unqualified standard short-form audit report, set forth four circumstances in which an auditor may be considered as having acted in a professionally discreditable manner.

20. The *Code of Professional Ethics* of the AICPA states that a member shall not endeavor to obtain clients by solicitation. Because advertising is a form of solicitation, it is prohibited.

   a) Discuss the reasons for the rule prohibiting advertising.

   b) When a CPA starts his own practice, how can he ethically obtain new clients?

21. A member of the AICPA performed the following services for a corporate client: Write-up work, adjusting entries, and financial statement preparation. The financial statements are acceptable to all agencies of the state of incorporation. Is the auditor independent? What are the reasons for your answer?

PROBLEMS

1. For each of the following examples, indicate the type of opinion expressed by the accountant as: qualified, unqualified, adverse, or disclaimer.

a)   In our opinion, subject to the effects, if any, on the financial statements of the ultimate resolution of the matter discussed in the preceding paragraph, the financial statements referred to above present fairly. . . .

b)   In our opinion, because of the effects of the matters discussed in the preceding paragraph, the financial statements referred to above do not present fairly, in conformity with generally accepted accounting principles, the financial position of X Company as of December 31, 1976, or the results of its operations and changes in its financial position for the year then ended.

c)   Since the Company did not take physical inventories and we were unable to apply adequate alternative procedures regarding inventories and the cost of property and equipment, as noted in the preceding paragraph, the scope of our work was not sufficient to enable us to express, and we do not express, an opinion on the financial statements referred to above.

d)   In our opinion, the aforementioned financial statements present fairly the financial position of X Company at December 31, 1976, and the results of its operations and the changes in its financial position for the year then ended, in conformity with generally accepted accounting principles applied on a basis consistent with that of the preceding year.

e)   In our opinion, subject to the effects of such adjustments, if any, as might have been required had the outcome of the uncertainty referred to in the preceding paragraph been known, the financial statements referred to above present fairly. . . .

f)   In our opinion, except for the effects of such adjustments, if any, as might have been determined to be necessary had we been able to observe the physical inventories. . . .

g)   Since the Company did not permit the written confirmation of accounts receivable and we were unable to apply adequate alternative procedure regarding the existence and amounts of accounts receivable, as noted in the preceding paragraph, the scope of our work was not sufficient to enable us to express and we do not express, an opinion on the financial statements referred to above.

h)   The accompanying balance sheet of X Company as of December 31, 1976, and the related statements of income and retained earnings and changes in financial position for the year then ended were not audited by us and accordingly we do not express an opinion on them.

i)   In our opinion, the accompanying balance sheet presents fairly the financial position of X Company at September 30, 1976, in conformity with generally accepted accounting principles applied on a basis consistent with that of the preceding year.

j)   In our opinion, because of the material exceptions expressed in the middle paragraph, the financial statements presented do not present fairly, in conformity with generally accepted accounting principles, the financial position of W Company as of December 31, 1976, or the results of operations and changes in financial position for the year then ended.

2. Using the facts stated below, write the middle paragraph for the auditor's opinion:

   a) Lease obligations (with a life in excess of three years) in the amount of $500,000 have not been capitalized. In addition to the affect on long-term debt and fixed assets, retained earnings, net income, and earnings per share have been affected.

   b) Client X, whose sales are made on the installment basis, records the sales in full at time of sale. However, for income tax purposes, income is reported on the installment basis.

   c) A client has not taken a physical inventory in several years. In addition, fixed asset records have not been maintained and alternative methods do not permit the determination of the value of the inventory or the fixed assets.

   d) The engagement letter stipulates that the auditor will not examine records supporting the client's investment in a foreign company.

   e) The engagement of the auditor was not made until after the closing date of the client's records, thus making it impossible to observe the taking of the physical inventory.

   f) Part of the examination relating to inventories is made by another independent auditor, which is an associated firm and whose work is acceptable to you based on your knowledge of the professional standards and competence of the firm.

   g) Your client has just completed a pooling-of-interest transaction and has requested you to prepare financial statements for two prior years. In addition, other auditors have examined two of the other entities which are to be included in these statements.

3. From the following information prepare a statement of changes in financial position for the year ended December 31, 1976:

Purchase of land	$ 20,000
Retirement of 10% bonds—1926–1976	100,000
Sale of X Company stock	31,500
Sold $20,000 of our par value common stock	21,200
Net income from operations	41,600
Depreciation of fixed assets	10,000
Purchased new machinery	25,000
Retired $10,000 of our par value preferred stock	10,700
Sold land	9,000
Issued $80,000 of authorized 6% bonds, maturity 2000	82,000
Paid cash dividends as follows:	
Preferred 3,000	
Common 6,000	
Contributed cash to 9% bond sinking fund	4,000
Purchased new delivery trucks	4,000
Paid 1976's installment on long-term unsecured notes	10,000
Paid for extraordinary building repairs	7,400
Sale of retired machinery	2,000

4.   The following year-end financial statement was prepared for you by the White Pine Company.

WHITE PINE COMPANY
Statement of Financial Condition
May 31, 1977

Assets

Current Assets:

Cash	$ 35,000
Marketable securities (Note 1)	36,000
Trade accounts receivable, net	72,000
Inventory	160,000
Office supplies	1,000
Total Current Assets	$304,000

Property, Plant, and Equipment (at Cost):

Furniture and fixtures, net of $2,300		
accumulated depreciation	$ 6,000	
Equipment (Note 2), net of $1,600		
accumulated depreciation	8,000	
Land	16,000	30,000
Total Assets		$334,000

Liabilities and Stockholders' Equity

Current Liabilities:

Trade notes payable	$ 80,000
Trade accounts receivable assigned	1,000
Trade accounts payable	109,000
Stock dividend payable	5,000
Total Current Liabilities	$195,000

Long-Term Liabilities:

Obligation on equipment lease (Note 2)	1
Total Liabilities	$195,001

Contributed Capital:

Common stock, $10 par (10,000 shares		
authorized, 5,000 shares issued		
and outstanding	$ 50,000	
Preferred stock, 5%, $100 par, cumulative and		
nonparticipating (1,000 shares autho-		
rized, 909 shares issued and outstanding . .	90,900	
Paid-in capital from sale of common stock		
in excess of par	2,069	
Total Contributed Capital	$142,969	
Retained earnings (Deficit)	(3,970)	
Total Stockholders' Equity		138,999
Total Liabilities and Stockholders'		
Equity		$334,000

Notes to the statement of financial condition:
1.   Marketable securities are net of the $25,000 Federal Income Tax liability.
2.   On January 5, 1976, the corporation entered into a six-year noncancelable lease of $67,500 of equipment with a useful life of 15 years. The lease provides for rentals of $13,750 annually during the first six years and of $750 annually for the duration of the life of the equipment when the lease is renewed for an additional nine years.

What are the weaknesses in presentation, disclosure, and classification in the preceding financial statement? Explain why you consider them to be weaknesses and what you consider to be the proper treatment of the items. Do *not* discuss terminology or prepare a revised statement. (Assume that the arithmetic is correct.) *Not sufficient footing to explain explicit detailed disclosure*

(AICPA, adapted)

5. Part A: The internal accountant for Kary, Inc. (which uses the calendar year as its fiscal year) made the following errors of omission or commission:

   a) A $2,000 collection from an account receivable, received December 28, 1976, was not recorded until it was deposited in the bank on January 2, 1977.

   b) A vendor's invoice for $3,200 for inventory received in December 1976 was not recorded as a purchase until January 1977. Based on physical count and pricing, inventories were properly stated as of December 31, 1976.

   c) Depreciation for 1976 was understated $1,800.

   d) In October 1976, an invoice for $400 for office supplies was charged to travel expense. The supplies were totally used in 1976.

   e) The December 31, 1976, sales on account—$6,000—were recorded in January 1977.

As the CPA for Kary, Inc., and assuming that no other errors were made, and ignoring all taxes, answer the following:

Net income for 1976 was: (1) understated $1,000, (2) understated $4,200, (3) overstated $5,000, (4) correct, or (5) none of the preceding.

Part B: Assume the same facts as in Part A, and answer the following:

Working capital as of December 31, 1976, was: (1) understated $6,000. (2) understated $1,000, (3) understated $2,800, (4) correct, or (5) none of the preceding.

6. In his opinion of a client's financial statements, a CPA must comply with the generally accepted standards of reporting. One of the reporting standards relates to consistency.

   a) Discuss the statement regarding consistency that a CPA is required to include in his opinion. What is the objective of requiring a CPA to write a statement about consistency?

   b) Discuss what statement, if any, regarding consistency, a CPA must make in his opinion relating to his first audit of the financial statements for: (1) a newly organized company ending its first fiscal year, and (2) a company established for several years.

   c) Discuss why the changes described in each of the following cases would or would not require recognition in a CPA's opinion regarding consistency, assuming that the amounts are material.

   (1) The company disposed of one of its three subsidiaries that had been included in its consolidated statements in prior years.

   (2) After two years of computing depreciation under the declining balance method for income tax purposes and under the

straight-line method for reporting purposes, the declining-balance method was adopted for reporting progress.

(3)   The estimated remaining useful life of plant property was reduced because of obsolescence.

(AICPA, adapted)

7.   Income statements for two consecutive years are presented for Debco, Inc. After examining the statements, answer the following questions:

   a)   Is full disclosure of all material data set forth in both statements?
   b)   Are the statements prepared on the basis of consistency?
   c)   Are the items marked with an asterisk material in amount?
   d)   Are the income statements prepared in accordance with modern practice? This is in addition to your answer to (*a*), (*b*), and (*c*).

In each case, set forth specifically the reasons for your answer.

DEBCO, INC.
Income Statement
For the Years Ended December 31

	1976	1975
Net sales	$3,600,000	$2,800,000
Cost of sales	1,980,000	1,500,000
Gross profit	$1,620,000	$1,300,000
Selling and administrative expenses, including 1976 loss of $100,000 on sale of obsolete inventory	$1,000,000	$ 740,000
Net operating income	$ 620,000	$ 560,000
Other expense, net	20,000	50,000
Net income before extraneous items	$ 600,000	$ 510,000
Organization costs written off	20,000	
	$ 580,000	
Profit on sale of fixed assets (net of taxes)		40,000
		$ 550,000
Refund (or assessment) of prior years' taxes	−50,000	10,000
Net income before federal income tax	$ 530,000	$ 560,000
Federal income tax	260,000	280,000
Net income for the year	$ 270,000	$ 280,000
Retained earnings, January 1	$1,080,000	$1,096,000
	$1,350,000	$1,376,000
Organization costs amortized		6,000
		$1,370,000
Add (or deduct): Profit or loss on sales of investment securities (net of taxes)	$ 140,000	−20,000
Retained Earnings, December 31	$1,490,000	$1,350,000

8.   Select the best answer for each of the following items relating to financial statements and the auditor's report.

   a)   An auditor's opinion exception arising from a limitation on the scope of his examination should be explained in:
   (1)   A footnote to the financial statements.
   (2)   The auditor's report.
   (3)   Both a footnote to the financial statements and the auditor's report.

      (4)   Both the financial statements (immediately after the caption of the item or items which could not be verified) and the auditor's report.

b)   An auditor need make no reference in his report to limitations on the scope of his audit if he:

      (1)   Finds it impracticable to confirm receivables but satisfied himself by other procedures.

      (2)   Does not audit the financial statements of an unaudited subsidiary that represents 75 percent of the parent's total assets.

      (3)   Omits confirmation of receivables at the client's request but satisfies himself by other procedures.

      (4)   Does not observe the opening inventory and is unable to satisfy himself by other procedures.

c)   Footnotes to financial statements should not be used to:

      (1)   Describe the nature and effect of a change in accounting principles.

      (2)   Identify substantial differences between book and tax income.

      (3)   Correct an improper financial statement presentation.

      (4)   Indicate bases for valuing assets.

d)   Assuming that none of the following have been disclosed in the financial statements, the most appropriate item for footnote disclosure is the:

      (1)   Collection of all receivables after the year-end.

      (2)   Revision of employees' pension plan.

      (3)   Retirement of president of company and election of new president.

      (4)   Material decrease in the advertising budget for the coming year and its anticipated effect upon income.

e)   An exception in the auditor's report because of the lack of consistent application of generally accepted accounting principles most likely would be required in the event of:

      (1)   A change in the rate of provision for uncollectible accounts based upon collection experience.

      (2)   The original adoption of a pension plan for employees.

      (3)   Inclusion of a previously unconsolidated subsidiary in consolidated financial statements.

      (4)   The revision of pension plan actuarial assumptions based upon experience.

f)   A CPA is completing his examination of the financial statements of the June Service Company for the year ended April 30, 1976. During the year June's employees were granted an additional week's vacation, and this had a material effect upon vacation pay expense for the year and the accrued liability for vacation pay at April 30, 1976. In the opinion of the CPA, this occurrence and its effects have been adequately disclosed in a footnote to the financial statements. In his audit report, the CPA normally will:

      (1)   Omit any mention of this occurrence and its effects.

(2)   Refer to the footnote in his opinion paragraph but express an unqualified opinion.

(3)   Refer to the footnote and express an opinion that is qualified as to consistency.

(4)   Insist that comparative income statements for prior years be restated or express an opinion that is qualified as to consistency.

g)   While assisting Phoenix Company in the preparation of unaudited financial statements, Jackson, CPA, noted that Phoenix had increased property, plant and equipment to reflect a recent property appraisal. In this circumstance, Jackson's reporting responsibility is met by:

(1)   Issuing the statements on plain paper without reference to the CPA.

(2)   Advising Phoenix's management of the deviation from generally accepted accounting principles.

(3)   Describing the deviation from generally accepted accounting principles in his disclaimer of opinion.

(4)   Stating in the disclaimer of opinion that Phoenix's financial statements are unaudited.

h)   The primary responsibility for the adequacy of disclosure in the financial statements and footnotes rests with the:

(1)   Partner assigned to the engagement.

(2)   Auditor in charge of field work.

(3)   Staffperson who drafts the statements and footnotes.

(4)   Client.

i)   The use of an adverse opinion generally indicates:

(1)   Uncertainty with respect to an item that is so material that the auditor cannot form an opinion on the fairness of presentation of the financial statements as a whole.

(2)   Uncertainty with respect to an item that is material but not so material that the auditor cannot form an opinion on the fairness of the financial statements as a whole.

(3)   A violation of generally accepted accounting principles that has a material effect upon the fairness of presentation of the financial statements, but is not so material that a qualified opinion is unjustified.

(4)   A violation of generally accepted accounting principles that is so material that a qualified opinion is not justified.

j)   The use of a disclaimer of opinion might indicate that the auditor:

(1)   Is so uncertain with respect to an item that he cannot form an opinion on the fairness of presentation of the financial statements as a whole.

(2)   Is uncertain with respect to an item that is material but not so material that he cannot form an opinion on the fairness of presentation of the financial statements as a whole.

(3)   Has observed a violation of generally accepted accounting principles that has a material effect upon the fairness of

presentation of financial statements, but is not so material that a qualified report is unjustified.

(4) Has observed a violation of generally accepted accounting principles that is so material that a qualified opinion is not justified.

(AICPA, adapted)

9. The following items apply to an examination by Johns, CPA, of the financial statements of Central Leasing Company for the year ended December 31, 1976.

A cash advance to AAA Credit Corporation is material to the presentation of Central's financial position. AAA's unaudited financial statements show negative working capital, negative stockholders' equity, and losses in each of the five preceding years. Johns has suggested an allowance for the uncollectibility of the advance to AAA Credit.

All of the capital stock of both Central and AAA Credit is owned by James Ray and his family. Ray refuses to consider an allowance for uncollectibility, and insists that AAA eventually will be profitable and be able to repay the advance. Ray proposes the following footnote to Central statements:

Footnote to Financial Statements

At December 31, 1976, the Company had advanced $500,000 to AAA Credit Corporation. We obtained written confirmation of this debt from AAA Credit Corporation and reviewed unaudited financial statements of AAA. AAA is not in a position to repay this advance at the time, but the Company has informed us that it is optimistic as to its future. AAA Credit Corporation's capital stock is wholly owned by Central Leasing Company's common shareholders.

Several of the following items set forth assumptions about this situation. Unless otherwise stated, each assumption is independent of the others and applies only to that particular item.

a) With respect to Central's advance to AAA Credit, Johns:

(1) Needs no disclosure in the audit report because the common ownership of the two companies has been adequately disclosed.

(2) Needs no disclosure in the audit report because the auditor is not expected to be an expert appraiser of property values.

(3) Should be concerned in formulating an audit opinion primarily with the issue of collectibility from Central's viewpoint.

(4) Should be concerned in formulating an audit opinion primarily with the consolidated financial position of the two companies.

b) A deficiency in the given footnote is that it:

(1) Does not identify the auditor.

(2) Is worded as a representation of the auditor.

(3) Does not state the auditor's conclusion or opinion.

       (4)   Includes the client's representation as to collectibility.

   c)   Assume that Johns concludes, based upon appropriate audit procedures, that the advance to AAA Credit will not be repaid. The audit report will include:

       (1)   A "subject to" qualification or disclaimer of opinion.

       (2)   An "except for" qualification or disclaimer of opinion.

       (3)   A "subject to" qualification or adverse opinion.

       (4)   An "except for" qualification or adverse opinion.

   d)   Assume that Johns concludes, based upon appropriate audit procedures, that Ray's optimism concerning AAA Credit can neither be substantiated nor disproved and that the matter is so uncertain that an opinion cannot be formed concerning the advance. The report will conclude:

       (1)   A "subject to" qualification or disclaimer of opinion.

       (2)   An "except for" qualification or disclaimer of opinion.

       (3)   A "subject to" qualification or adverse opinion.

       (4)   An "except for" qualification or adverse opinion.

   e)   Assume that Johns starts the opinion paragraph of his audit report as follows: "Because of the uncertainty with respect to the collectibility of the advance referred to in Footnote 1, we are unable to express an opinion . . ." This is:

       (1)   A disclaimer.

       (2)   Negative assurance.

       (3)   An adverse opinion.

       (4)   An improper type of reporting.

   f)   Assume that subsequent to the completion of field work (but prior to issuance of Johns' report) Ray and his family sell all of their stock in AAA Credit and the new owners repay the advance from Central. Johns opinion as to Central's 1976 financial statements will be:

       (1)   Unaffected because the sale of AAA Credit stock occurred subsequent to the audit date.

       (2)   Unaffected because the sale of AAA Credit stock occurred subsequent to the completion of field work.

       (3)   Qualified unless the repayment of the advance is recorded by Central's as a December 31 transaction.

       (4)   Unqualified because the issue of collectibility is now settled.

                               (AICPA, adapted)

10.   Select the best answer for each of the following items.

   a)   Flack, CPA, has a small public accounting practice. One of Flack's clients desires services which he cannot adequately provide. Flack has recommended a larger CPA firm, Gordon & Company, to his client, and, in return, Gordon has agreed to pay Flack 10 percent of the fee for services rendered by Gordon for Flack's client. Who, if anyone, is in violation of the AICPA's *Code of Professional Ethics?*

       (1)   Both Flack and Gordon.

       (2)   Neither Flack nor Gordon.

    (3)   Only Flack.

    (4)   Only Gordon.

b)   Jackson, CPA has a public accounting practice. He wishes to establish a separate partnership to offer data processing services to the public and other public accountants.

    (1)   Jackson cannot be a partner in any separate partnership which offers date processing services.

    (2)   Jackson may form a separate partnership, but it will be subject to the *Code of Professional Ethics.*

    (3)   Jackson may form a separate partnership as long as all partners are CPAs.

    (4)   Jackson may form a separate partnership, but he must give up his public accounting practice.

c)   Smith and Jones, CPAs, wish to incorporate their public accounting practice.

    (1)   An appropriate name for the new corporation would be the Financial Specialist Corporation.

    (2)   Smith and Jones need not be individually liable for the acts of the corporation if the corporation carries adequate professional liability insurance.

    (3)   Smith's ten-year-old son may own stock in the corporation.

    (4)   The corporation may provide services that are incompatible with the practice of public accounting as long as a non-CPA employee performs the services.

d)   Regina, CPA, has agreed to audit the financial statements of a church which she does not attend. She has agreed to perform the audit without compensation if the church will acknowledge her work in its bulletin and mention the name of her firm. This is a violation of the *Code of Professional Ethics* because:

    (1)   It is a form of solicting business.

    (2)   Regina is not independent.

    (3)   Regina is holding herself out in the bulletin as a church-accounting specialist.

    (4)   Regina would not do satisfactory audit work in order to cut costs of a non-fee engagement.

e)   The *Code of Professional Ethics* considers *Statements on Auditing Standards* (formerly *Statements on Auditing Procedure*) issued by the Institute's Auditing Standards Executive Committee (formerly the Committee on Auditing Procedure) to:

    (1)   Supersede generally accepted auditing standards.

    (2)   Be separate and independent of generally accepted auditing standards.

    (3)   Not be part of the *Code* since specific rules pertaining to technical standards are established by the *Code* itself.

    (4)   Be interpretations of generally accepted auditing standards.

f)   Beyer & Company, CPAs, has a computer which it uses only five hours per day. It wishes to rent computer time to others but will not provide any services to the user.

(1)   Beyer & Company can only offer time to its clients.

(2)   Beyer & Company can advertise the rental of the computer time as long as it does not disclose its name or the fact that it is a CPA firm.

(3)   Beyer & Company cannot offer the time to anyone.

(4)   Beyer & Company can only offer the time to other CPA firms.

g)   William, CPA, has sold his public-accounting practice to Janet, CPA.

(1)   William must obtain permission from his clients before making available work papers and other documents to Janet.

(2)   William must obtain permission from his clients for only audit-related work papers and other documents before making them available to Janet.

(3)   William must return the work papers and other documents to his clients, and Janet must solicit the clients for his use of the materials.

(4)   William must obtain permission from his clients for only tax-related work papers and other documents before making them available to Janet.

h)   West, CPA, has made arrangements with a bank, which is his client, to allow him to prepare, in the bank lobby, tax returns for the bank's customers for a fee. The bank mailed its customers a notice of the fact that West will provide this service and an estimate of the fee for various returns.

(1)   West is in violation of the *Code of Professional Ethics* if he approved the mailing.

(2)   West would not be in violation of the *Code of Professional Ethics* if the bank were not his client.

(3)   West would not have been in violation of the *Code of Professional Ethics* if the bank had not mentioned the fee in the mailing.

(4)   West would not have been in violation of the *Code of Professional Ethics* as long as the mailing did not give his business address nor mention that he was a tax expert.

i)   Grace, a practicing CPA, has written an article which is being published in a professional publication. The publication wishes to inform its readers about Grace's background. The information regarding Grace should not:

(1)   List the degrees held by Grace.

(2)   State with which firm Grace is associated.

(3)   State that Grace is a tax expert.

(4)   List other publications by Grace.

j)   Adams is the executive partner of Adams & Company, CPAs. One of its smaller clients is a large nonprofit charitable organization. The organization has asked Adams to be on its board of directors, which consists of a large number of the community's leaders. Membership on the board is honorary in nature. Adams & Company would be considered to be independent:

(1)   Under no circumstances.
(2)   As long as Adams's directorship was disclosed in the organization's financial statements.
(3)   As long as Adams was not directly in charge of the audit.
(4)   As long as Adams does not perform or give advice on management functions of the organization.

(AICPA, adapted)

2

Legal Responsibilities
of Professional Accountants;
SEC Requirements

PROFESSIONAL ETHICS AND LEGAL RESPONSIBILITIES

Professional ethics, including the *Rules of Conduct* set forth in Chapter 1, encompass the concepts of independence, competence and moral integrity—all of which, when reflected in an audit report, automatically result in certain legal responsibilities. The responsibilities may or may not result in liability. Because independent auditors are members of a skilled profession, they have certain legal rights and legal responsibilities. The liabilities of professional accountants are not fully defined in all areas of alleged error, negligence, fraud, or fraud with the intention to defraud in the conduct of an audit. Legal responsibilities are great, but that is not a reason for fear. Every person and organization in the world has certain legal responsibilities and certain legal rights or privileges, and every community has certain elements who will act illegally—knowingly or unknowingly.

Audit reports move outside the client-auditor circle, and even third parties—not parties to the contract—may allege injury. Consequently, in his report, the auditor must:

1. Clearly indicate omitted auditing procedures.
2. Set forth the reasons for omitting auditing procedures.
3. Limit the report to a statement of findings.
4. Qualify, disclaim, render an adverse opinion, or not permit his name to be associated with the financial statements.

Under existing rules of law the liabilities of a professional accountant may be classified as follows:

1. Liability for breach of contract.
2. Liability for negligence.
3. Liability for fraud.
4. Liability for fraud with the alleged intention (even though not intentional) to defraud—as interpreted by the courts today.
5. Liability under the various federal securities acts.

The lines of demarcation between the five divisions often are shadowy and indefinite; one division *often* merges into and overlaps another—as may be determined in any particular court case.

Several legal cases are cited later in this chapter.

Auditing has become of such great public interest in modern financial activities that individuals and groups other than owners must be satisfied with the accuracy, clarity, and unequivocality of audit reports. These other groups (many times without a reason other than to obtain money) rely upon opinions rendered by auditors of independence and high moral integrity—and today if the opinions are considered to be unreliable, *it is almost certain that a lawsuit will follow.*

In the past, the auditor was responsible *for his opinion of the financial statements;* he was not considered responsible *for* the statements. However, today the courts are holding the auditor responsible *for* the statements—as exemplified by such cases as *BarChris Construction, Texas Gulf Sulphur, Yale Express System, Continental Vending, Westec Corporation, National Student Marketing, 1136 Tenants Corporation,* and many others. Many of these cases have resulted from the broadened concept of Rule 10b–5 of the SEC. The financial statements are the representations of the client, but the opinion rendered is that of the auditor. The opinion must carry the weight of professional competence and integrity, and it must be expressed independently and without concession.

In a jury trial, CPAs often become the victims of their reputation for professional capability.

At this point, the differences in the roles of accountants and attorneys is to be noted. An attorney is expected to be an advocate of his client's interests, while an independent auditor is independent and objective. The rules of professional ethics of both groups requires both to be ethical and honest.

Liability for Breach of Contract

Under the general laws of contracts, a liability to a client exists if the auditor breaches the contract. If the subject matter of a client-auditor contract is illegal, a valid contract does not exist. An auditor must not withhold information from a client, and he must not disclose the affairs of a client to third persons.

Liability for Negligence

Negligence is failure to do that which a reasonable and careful person ordinarily would have done under similar circumstances; or negligence is the performance of an act which a reasonable and careful person would not have done under similar circumstances. The professional accountant is holding himself forth as an expert, skilled in accounting and auditing. Ignorance of his duties and obligations—even though remote—does not constitute a defense against action, as exemplified by many recent court cases. There must be no pretense to knowledge when knowledge does not exist. The skill of a competent professional person is expected.

Difficulty may arise because what amounts to lack of skill in one case may be of no consequence in another case. The auditor must determine whether or not the financial records of a client represent actual conditions, and not merely ascertain that they are mathematically correct. He is under legal obligation to show accuracy of condition commensurate with the exercise of reasonable professional skill. A legal obligation may or may not be incurred if true conditions are not disclosed after the exercise of reasonable skill. In a lawsuit the accountant must convince the court of the exercise of reasonable skill—and sometimes of a superhuman skill.

Formerly, the liability for negligence was restricted to the client with whom the auditor had a contract; however, under the Securities Acts, and in recent court cases, negligence may be extended to a third party— a stockholder, a nonofficer director, or a creditor. The purpose of the audit and the extension of auditing procedures may either limit or extend the contractual obligation between an auditor, and a client, and an outside party, and thereby assist in determining the degree of legal responsibility. To be liable for ordinary negligence under a contract, the auditor normally—

1. Must owe a duty to the client plaintiff.
2. Must have violated or breached that duty.
3. Must have caused injury to the plaintiff resulting directly from the negligence, or
4. Must have caused injury by ignoring contributory negligence on the part of the client.

Contributory negligence is not a defense if it has not contributed to the accountant's failure to perform his duty.

An auditor bases his opinion on the results of testing, in accordance with recognized auditing standards. Sampling and testing may or may not unearth defalcations. If an examination is conducted in accordance with recognized auditing standards and if irregularities exist, normally they should be discovered, unless a client hides information. Beyond this point the auditor should not be responsible for the discovery of dishonest acts of a client's personnel, unless a court rules otherwise (and this is not uncommon today).

Liability for Fraud

In the preceding sections, negligence has been construed as "ordinary" negligence. The auditor customarily is liable only to his client for ordinary negligence. However, if the negligence is "gross" negligence, it may be held to be *constructive or technical fraud*. In fraud, there is deceit; negligence does not include deceit. It must be remembered that the charges of negligence, fraud, and fraud with intent to deceive have existed in England since 1854, and since 1905 in the United States.

In the *Ultramares* case (*Ultramares Corporation v. Touche*, 74 A.L.R. 1139; 255 N.Y. 170; 174 N.E. 441) (1931), the late Justice Benjamin Cardozo created the concept that gross negligence resulted in constructive or technical fraud; and if fraud is present, a right of action for damages is open to *anyone* who suffered because he relied upon the accountant's report. In order to establish fraud, there need be no contract between the accountant and third parties whom the accountant has never seen and whom he does not know. If it is possible to demonstrate to the satisfaction of the court that there existed a misstatement of an essential fact, or if there is an omission of an essential fact, and, today, if a third person suffered because of such misstatement or omission, the auditor may become liable to those third persons regardless of his competency, carefulness, and caution. Thus an inexcusable error constitutes neglect toward the client, and it may be construed as fraud toward injured third persons. In the *Ultramares* case, the court held that test and sampling were proper but that failure to detect fictitious receivables, inflated inventories, and errors in accounts payable, and failure to discover that the same receivables were pledged at several banks, constituted negligence, and that the jury should decide whether the offense was ordinary negligence or gross negligence amounting to fraud.

The *Ultramares* case and the cases of *Lawrence v. Fox* (20 N.Y. 268); of *Rhode Island National Bank v. Schwartz and others* (U.S.C.A. *Fourth Circuit*, No. 71–1284 *Norfolk, Va., 1971*); of *1136 Tenants' Corporation v. Max Rothenberg & Company*, Index 10575/1965, New York County Trial Term, Part VII (1970), and other cases have narrowed the space between negligence and fraud, and have caused fraud to be easier to establish. If fraud is proved, privity of contract is no defense to the suit. The *Lawrence* case was the first decision in the United States which clearly eliminated the necessity of privity of contract in order to allow a third party to sue. The case did not mention deceit, fraud, or negligence; but it paved the way for another case (*Ultramares v. Touche*)—and third parties. Legal cases are on record where the purchaser of a commodity has sued and recovered directly from a manufacturer for damages caused by defective manufacture, when the purchaser obtained the product from a dealer. A slight extension of these cases to the field of public accounting would render an auditor more directly liable to third persons for what a court might consider to be ordinary negligence—and that is exactly what happened in the 1960s. In the *State Street Trust Company* case (278 N.Y. 104), one court placed the accountant under direct responsibility to third persons who relied upon the accountant's statements, even without proof of gross negligence amounting to fraud, as established in the *Ultramares* case. In the *State Street Trust Company* case the plaintiff had loaned money to the accountant's client prior to the receipt of the accountant's statements.

In order to establish fraud other than that arising from gross negligence, there must be fraudulent intent. The auditor may be liable for fraud (1) if he is guilty of making a statement known to be untrue or without reasonable grounds for believing it to be true or with total disregard for the truth, made with the intent that another person shall act thereon; (2) if that person acts thereon; and (3) if the act causes injury to the person acting thereon. In the past no legal obligation was incurred by the auditor if a client set up restrictions that had the effect of not enabling the auditor to disclose fraud and these restrictions were disclosed; suspicions of fraud must be disclosed to avoid liability. The auditor should not be responsible for premeditated fraudulent plans if reasonable skill would not reveal them. In his report the auditor must disclose all essential facts pertaining to the audit; he must set forth any restrictions placed upon him during the examination which might have prevented the securing of essential data. Departure from recognized professional practice must be reported.

Under common law in the United States, it was generally held that accountants are liable to third parties for the practice of fraud; liability for negligence was limited to the client based upon the privity of contract between the auditor and his client. The cases and court decisions set forth these general rules. In a text of this nature, these cases are purposely briefed.

In the case of *Landell* v. *Lybrand* (264 Pa. 406; 107 Atl. 783; 8 A.L.R. 461), the plaintiff purchased capital stock in a company audited by the defendants. The report of the auditor had been shown the plaintiff by an outside party, and the plaintiff had relied upon that report. In his suit the plaintiff charged the accountants with negligence and carelessness. The Supreme Court of Pennsylvania ruled that the accountants had no liability to the plaintiff because there was no contract between them.

In similar manner the United States Circuit Court of Appeals, in the case of *O'Connor* v. *Ludlam* (92 F. [2d] 50), ruled as follows: "Since there was no contractual relationship between the plaintiff and the defendant, liability (to a third party) could be imposed only for fraud;

a mistake in the balance sheet, even if it were the result of negligence, could not be the basis of a recovery."

In the case of *Ultramares* v. *Touche* (255 N.Y. 170; 174 N.E. 441), the plaintiff was a third party who had relied upon the report of the auditors. The case was based upon misrepresentation of accounts receivable, but the case would be no different had the alleged misrepresentations involved any other assets. There were two charges: (1) misrepresentations that were the result of negligence and (2) misrepresentations that were alleged to be fraudulent. The certified balance sheets in the case were used for credit purposes. From the following excerpt, quoted from the court decision, it is apparent that, for negligence, the liability of the accountant was limited to the client, but that the accountant may be held liable to third parties for fraud. The excerpt from the court decision is as follows:

. . . To creditors and investors to whom the employer (client) exhibited the certificate, the defendants owed a like duty to make it without fraud, since there was notice in the circumstances of its making that the employer did not intend to keep it to himself. A different question develops when we ask whether they (the defendants) owed a duty to the creditors and investors to make it without negligence. If liability for negligence exists, a thoughtless slip or blunder, the failure to detect a theft or forgery beneath the cover of deceptive entries, may expose accountants to a liability in an indeterminate amount for an indeterminate time to an indeterminate class.

The court went on to state that the opinion of an expert may be fraudulent if the basis of the opinion is such that there was no sound belief in support of the opinion; also, if there was a statement of fact in the certificate, whether believed to be true or untrue, the accountants are liable for deceit—that is, fraud—in the event that the statement of fact is false.

In the case of the *State Street Trust Company* v. *Ernst* (278 N.Y. 104, 704; 15 N.E. [2d] 416; 16 N.E. [2d] 851; 120 A.L.R. 1250), the same rules were followed. A quotation from the court follows:

. . . We have held that in the absence of contractual relationship or its equivalent, accountants cannot be held liable for ordinary negligence in preparing a certified balance sheet even though they are aware that the balance sheet will be used to obtain credit. Accountants, however, may be liable to third parties, even where there is lacking deliberate or active fraud. A representation certified as true to the knowledge of the accountants, when knowledge there is none, a reckless misstatement, or an opinion based on grounds so flimsy as to lead to the conclusion that there was no genuine belief in its truth, are all sufficient upon which to base liability. A refusal to see the obvious, a failure to investigate the doubtful, if sufficiently gross, may furnish evidence leading to an inference of fraud so as to impose liability for losses suffered by those who rely on the balance sheet.

Another case is that of *Commercial Investment Trust Financial Corporation* v. *P. W. R. Glover et al.,* in which C.I.T. lent money to Manufacturers Trading Corporation. C.I.T. relied on Manufacturers Trading Corporation's CPAs report of examination in making and continuing to make loans to Manufacturers Trading.

C.I.T. was not a client of the CPAs involved but was a creditor of the accountants' client. C.I.T. contended that Manufacturers Trading Corporation's receivables were worthless and uncollectible, or did not exist; that required collateral did not exist or was insufficient to cover the loans; and that the provision for bad debts was inadequate. The plaintiff, C.I.T., attempted to prove that the defendant accountants' audit report representations were materially false and misleading. The defendant accountants claimed a denial of opinion of the receivables and underlying collateral, which appeared in the audit report. Had the plaintiff won, the effect of the case could have been an extension of the concept of the *Ultramares case*—involving liability to third parties for fraud—to liability to third parties for mere negligence. The plaintiff did not prove ordinary negligence to the satisfaction of the courts. The decision of the lower court for the defendants was upheld by the United States Court of Appeals. The Court of Appeals stated that "we do not believe we should attempt to go beyond the standards of the market place, as reflected in current judicial decisions." Evidently, the references were to the *Ultramares* case and to that of *O'Connor* v. *Ludlam* (92F. [2d] 50).

Several months after the verdict in the *C.I.T.* case, arose the case of *The First National Bank and Trust Company of South Bend* v. *Small et al*. In this suit, the bank claimed it had relied upon the accountants' audit reports in renewing a $100,000 loan to Manufacturers Trading Corporation of Cleveland, Ohio. The jury, by a vote of 11 to 1, found for the plaintiff. The audit reports were the same as in the *C.I.T.* case. Thus, the concept of negligence is still confused.

Recent Cases

An in-depth study of recent cases will clearly indicate that the courts are changing the concept of "let the buyer beware" to "let the seller and/or director beware."

In the 1960s, a flood of new cases was brought into court, involving not only alleged fraud but fraud with the intent to defraud. Many of these cases were tried before a jury which had little knowledge of auditing, if any. Many were and are being settled out of court. A book of this nature and size does not permit a full description of these cases, because that would require an additional volume. In the news media, a suit against a firm of CPAs draws front page attention, but the final disposition is seldom mentioned. A *few* cases are briefed below.

In 1962 the BarChris Construction Company became bankrupt (*Escott* v. *BarChris Construction Corp.*, 283 F. Supp. 643.705 S.D. N.Y., 1968). A

U.S. District Court Judge ruled that the bond underwriters, outside directors, and the auditors had not made a *reasonable effort* to check the facts —even though the suit did not accuse the underwriters, the outside directors, or the auditors of *attempting to deceive anyone*. In fact, this case really involved SEC Rule 10b–5 which falls under the Securities and Exchange Act of 1934. This will be discussed later.

In 1964, Yale Express System, Inc., announced an unaudited profit of $904,000 for the first nine months of the year, but the 12-month audited *loss* was $3.3 million. Innumerable stockholders suits were filed against the CPA firm involved, on the basis that the CPA firm should have had sufficient information to realize that the unaudited statements for the first nine months were incorrect! The cases were settled out of court for an undisclosed few million dollars. This is the case of *Stephen Fischer et al.* v. *Michael Kletz et al.*, U.S.D.C. Southern District of New York, 65 Civ. 787.

In 1968 the Second Circuit Court (New York City) handed down its decision in the Texas Gulf Sulphur case involving stockholder suits of approximately $100 million—and the decision was against the corporation, its directors, and others. This case aroused the entire accounting profession and the law profession.

Also in 1968 the collapse of Westec Corporation (*Carpenter* v. *Hall*, Complaint C.A. No. 68–H–738, S. D. Texas, Houston, 1968) resulted in approximately $100 million in stockholder lawsuits. Also, the trustee for Westec decided to take action against the CPA firm. In addition to the lawsuits, the SEC took under consideration administrative proceedings against the CPA firm involved under Rule 2–E of the SEC's Rules of Practice; if these administrative proceedings were involved, the accounting firm involved could be subjected to anything from public rebuke up to an order denying the CPA firm, or some of its partners, or other personnel the right to certify reports to the SEC. This suit centered around the differences between pooling of interests and purchase of stock procedures.

In the case of the *Rhode Island Trust National Bank* v. *Schwartz, Bresenoff, Yavner, Jacobs and others*, U.S.C.A., *Fourth Circuit*, No. 71–1284, Norfolk, Va., 1971, the Court of Appeals ruled negligence in the audit of International Trading Corporation and related companies, resulting in a loss to the plaintiff bank in excess of $100,000. The lower court ruled for the defendants, but the Court of Appeals disagreed regarding negligence and reversed the decision. The audit report contained certain reservations regarding fairness, such as "our examination included a general review of the accounting procedures and such tests of the accounting records as we were permitted to make." The report also pointed out that detailed cost records were not kept of certain capital improvements made by company employees. A disclaimer of opinion was rendered, but the work papers allegedly showed that no material cost had been recorded for the improvements. The case demonstrates the necessity for an adverse opinion based upon client-imposed restrictions which cause doubt, or if a disclaimer was decided upon, it should be strongly worded—and in short form, or the client should not be audited.

The *Stephens Industries* case (*Stephens Industries, Inc.* v. *Haskins and Sells,* 438 F2nd 357), and the same case in the U.S. Court of Appeals (10th in.) January, 1971, Term No. 229–70, the Court was aware of certain limitations placed on the auditor, and held that an accountant may be liable to a client for either fraud or negligence, but liability may be found for third parties only if there is fraudulent conduct on the part of the auditor. Briefly, this case holds to the concept that when a CPA starts with an engagement letter which properly sets forth all terms of the engagement, and if the CPA works through to the preparation of a report which follows these terms, the report will stand the test of a sophisticated court examination.

One of the latest cases is the *Equity Funding Corp. of America,* which became bankrupt in April 1973. It involves the sale of over $2 billion in fictitious life insurance policies. At least three accounting firms have been mentioned as being connected with audits of the company and its subsidiaries. Three accountants were sentenced to three months in jail on July 22, 1975, and placed on probation for four years. Many former executives of the company have been indicted for criminal fraud and 25 have pleaded guilty; the heaviest sentence (eight years in jail) was given to the former chairman.

Unaudited financial statements and the responsibilities of the auditor were brought into sharp focus in the case of *1136 Tenants' Corporation* v. *Max Rothenberg & Company,* Index 10575/1965, New York County, Trial Term, Part VII (1970). The annual accounting fee was $600 and the judgment was for $237,278. The plaintiff was a company which owned a cooperative apartment building; the defendants were CPAs who—according to the Court—were engaged not only for write-up work, but also for audit purposes. One of the partners admitted to some audit work. The building was managed by Riker & Company, which collected maintenance charges from tenants, deposited collections in its own bank account, from which it paid bills. Each month Riker sent the plaintiff data supposedly setting forth all incomes and expenses—and the defendant entered these data on the records of the plaintiff. The CPA firm had no connection with Riker & Company, other than being hired by Riker personally. Allegedly, Riker & Company appropriated some collections and did not pay all bills. A strong disclaimer of opinion was in order.

If the reader is interested, additional suggested cases include: *Continental Vending; Gold* v. *D.C.L., Incorporated* (S.D.N.Y. para. 94,036); *MacNerland* v. *Barnes; National Student Marketing Corp.; Home–Stake Production Co.;* and many others.

ADDITIONAL OLDER CASES

For persons interested in additional material concerning legal responsibility and civil liability, the following cases are cited from chapter 6 of the *C.P.A. Handbook*, published by the AICPA.

Smith v. *London Assurance Corporation*, 109 Appellate Division 882; 96 N.Y. Supp. 820 (2d Dept. 1905).

Maryland Casualty Company v. *Jonathan Cook et al.*, 35 F. Supp. 160 (E.D. Mich. 1940).

O'Neill et al. v. *Atlas Automobile Finance Corporation*, 139 Pa. Super. 346; 11 A. 2d 782 (1940).

In re: London and General Bank. The Accountant Law Reports (Gee & Co., London, 1895), vol. 21, pp. 173–92; reprinted in *Dicksee's Auditing* (Gee & Co., London, 1951), pp. 584–98.

In re: Kingston Cotton Mill Company. The Accountant Law Reports (Gee & Co., London, 1896), vol. 22, p. 77; reprinted in *Dicksee's Auditing* (Gee & Co., London, 1951), pp. 598–601.

The Irish Woolen Company, Ltd. v. *Tyson.* The Accountant Law Reports (Gee & Co., London, 1900); reprinted in *Dicksee's Auditing* (Gee & Co., London, 1951), p. 615.

Craig v. *Anyon*, 212 App. Div. 55; 208 N.W. Supp. 259 (1st Dept. 1925). Affirmed 242 N.Y. 569; 152 N.E. 431 (1926).

Board of County Commissioners v. *Baker*, 152 Kan. 164; 102 P. 2d 1006 (1940).

National Surety Corp. v. *Lybrand*, 256 App. Div. 226; 9 N.Y.S. 2d 554 (1st Dept. 1939).

Dantzler Lumber and Export Company et al. v. *Columbia Casualty Company*, 115 Fla. 541; 156 So. 116 (1934).

Flagg v. *Seng*, 16 Cal. App. 2d 545; 60 P. 2d 1004 (1936).

Fidelity and Deposit Company of Maryland v. *Atherton*, 47 N.M. 443; 144 P. 2d 157 (1943).

Landell v. *Lybrand*, 264 Pa. St. 406; 107 Atl. 783 (1919).

Ultramares Corp. v. *Touche et al.*, 229 App. Div. 581; 243 N.Y. Supp. 179 (1st Dept. 1930). Reversed in 255 N.Y. 170; 174 N.E. 441 (1931).

Glanzer v. *Shepard*, 233 N.Y. 236; 135 N.E. 275 (1922).

State Street Trust Company v. *Ernst*, 251, App. Div. 717; 298 N.Y. Supp. 176 (1st Dept. 1937). Reversed in 278 N.Y. 104; 15 N.E. 2d 416 (1938).

O'Connor v. *Ludlam*, 92 F. 2d 50 (2d Cir. 1937). Cert. denied, 302 U.S. 758 (1937).

Doyle v. *Chatham & Phoenix National Bank*, 253 N.Y. 369; 171 N.E. 574 (1930).

Chandler v. *Crane, Christmas & Co.*, 2 K.B. 164 (1951); 1 The Times L.R. 371 (1951).

Shonts v. *Hirliman*, 28 F. Supp. 478 (S.D. Cal. 1939).

Ipswich Mills v. *Dillon et al.*, 260 Mass. 453; 157 N.E. 604 (1927).

Ex parte Frye, 155 Ohio St. 345; 98 N.E. 2d 798 (1951).

Himmelfarb v. *United States*, 175 F. 2d 924 (9th Cir. 1949). Cert. denied 338 U.S. 860 (1949).

Gariepy v. *United States,* 189 F. 2d 459 (6th Cir. 1951).
United States v. *Stoehr,* 100 F. Supp. 143 (M.D. Pa. 1951). Affirmed in 196
  F. 2d 276 (3d Cir. 1952).
Petition of Borden Co., 75 F. Supp. 857 (N.D. Ill. 1948).
Hopkins v. *The People,* 89 Colo. 296; 1 P. 2d 937 (1931).

SECURITIES AND EXCHANGE COMMISSION REQUIREMENTS

Liability under the Federal Securities Acts

In addition to liabilities as established by the courts, and in addition to adherence to professional codes of ethics, accountants who express opinions on financial statements of companies whose securities are registered with the SEC must meet all requirements of the Commission.

As administered by the Securities and Exchange Commission, the Securities Act of 1933, the Securities Exchange Act of 1934, the Public Utility Holding Company Act of 1935, the Trust Indenture Act of 1939, the Investment Advisers Act of 1940, and the Investment Company Act of 1940 have gone further in establishing liability for a public accountant than has the common law.

Essentially, the Securities Act of 1933 is a disclosure act. It provides for the disclosure of data and information pertinent to a registrant company's business and securities. The data and information must be available to potential investors deciding whether or not to acquire securities of that company. The Act also is designed to prevent misrepresentation, deceit, and fraud in the sale of securities. The SEC does not pass judgment on the merit of the securities, and the Commission neither approves nor disapproves a security offering; it simply insists that adequate information is available for determining the desirability of a security by a person wishing to purchase.

The Securities Exchange Act of 1934 provides for the control of securities exchanges, securities listed on the exchanges, and brokers dealing in securities. The general purposes of the Securities Exchange Act are to protect the investing public by preventing improper practices regarding prices and transactions, to curtail speculation, to prevent the manipulation of stock prices, and to review the annual and other periodic reports of companies subject to registration. The Securities Exchange Act has placed additional responsibilities on the accountant. The Commission does not view the accountant as the *originator* of the financial statements of a registrant but as an expert lending his opinion.

Over the past few years, the demands of the SEC have been increasing at an accelerating rate, thereby placing additional expensive burdens on both business and the professional accountant. Many persons have considered some of the demands of the Commission to be arbitrary and activist-oriented.

On August 20, 1964, the Exchange Act was amended in order to give investors in publicly held over-the-counter securities the same protection provided investors in securities listed on stock exchanges. The objective of this amendment is to obtain full disclosure of all material data and information for investors in over-the-counter securities. Under the Regulations, Rules, and Accounting Series Releases issued by the SEC, an accountant may be liable for negligence and/or fraud to owners and purchasers of securities.

Qualifications

The various laws that grant the SEC authority in the matter of issuing securities and in dealing in the securities of registered companies grant the Commission the privilege of requiring certification of financial statements filed with it. Rule 11 of the rules of practice of the Securities and Exchange Commission is as follows:

(e) The Commission may disqualify, and deny, temporarily or permanently, the privilege of appearing or practicing before it in any way to any person who is found by the Commission after hearing in the matter:

(1) Not to possess the requisite qualifications to represent others; or

(2) To be lacking in integrity or character or to have engaged in unethical or improper professional conduct.

Independence

Present-day concepts of the independence of professional accountants are critical. The standards by which independence is judged are rigorous. In addition to the *Code of Professional Ethics* of the AICPA, the concept of professional independence has been further intensified by the Securities and Exchange Commission. With respect to professional independence, the Commission has adopted the following rule:

REGULATION S–X, Rule 2–01: QUALIFICATIONS OF ACCOUNTANTS

(a) The Commission will not recognize any person as a certified public accountant who is not duly registered and in good standing as such under the laws of the place of his residence or principal office. The Commission will not recognize any person as a public accountant who is not in good standing and entitled to practice as such under the laws of the place of his residence or principal office.

(b) The Commission will not recognize any certified public accountant or public accountant as independent who is not in fact independent. For example, an accountant will be considered not independent with respect to any person or any of its parents or subsidiaries in whom he has, or had during the period of report, any direct financial interest or any material indirect financial interest; or with whom he is, or was during such period, connected as a promoter, underwriter, voting trustee, director, officer, or employee.

(c)   In determining whether an accountant may in fact be not independent with respect to a particular person, the Commission will give appropriate consideration to all relevant circumstances, including evidence bearing on all relationships between the accountant and that person or any affiliate thereof, and will not confine itself to the relationships existing in connection with the filing of reports with the Commission.

The *Rules of Practice* of the Commission place that body in a position to enable it to enforce its regulations with respect to the qualifications of accountants certifying to financial statements filed with the Commission.

Specific additional requirements of the SEC with respect to independence are detailed in releases of the Commission under its jurisdiction over the Securities Act of 1933, the Securities Exchange Act of 1934, the Public Utility Holding Company Act of 1935, and the Investment Company Act of 1940.

Thus, independence is not based solely upon honesty in the preparation of financial statements but upon any accountant-client relationship which in any manner detracts from the objective independence of the auditor. Independence may be held to be lacking in the following instances: if the auditor owns an interest in his client's business, if he serves as director and auditor, if he serves as a voting trustee, if disclosure is not full and proper, if he subordinates his opinion to that of his client, if he is associated with another accountant who owns an interest in the business of his client, if the client indemnifies the accountant against loss, if the accountant serves as promoter, if family relationships exist, and perhaps if he receives a substantial percentage of his total professional income from one client.

Independence and Tax Practice

In the majority of audit engagements, the CPA prepares tax returns for a client. Does the preparation of tax returns for an audit client impair independence? Independence is not impaired if the tax service is limited to assistance and advice and does not involve legal decision-making processes. This is true because an audit is one operation and the preparation of tax returns is separate from the attest function.

Registration Statements

The Securities Act of 1933 requires that a registration statement and a prospectus be filed with the Commission prior to the issuance of securities for sale in interstate commerce if the issue exceeds a defined amount.

Minute detail is required in the registration statement, including a complete economic history of the registrant company. In preparing registration statements, company personnel, legal counsel, underwriters for the securities, and the independent auditor combine their efforts and talents.

Registration statements may or may not include interim financial statements, which may or may not be certified. If they are certified, the auditor is informed of the affairs of his client up to a current date. If the financial statements are not certified, the auditor may be requested to furnish the registrant a letter setting forth the fact that an examination was not made for the interim period, but that limited procedures were applied, and that inquiries were made, and that the results of the application of the limited procedures and the inquiries led to the belief that the uncertified interim statements did not require amendment.

In the event that the securities registration does not include interim financial statements, the auditor may be requested to furnish the registrant a statement concerning material changes in the client's financial condition during the period between the last certified statements and the registration date. The statement of the auditor would be based upon the audit procedures and inquiries made subsequent to the date of the financial statements. The statement of the auditor also must satisfy the Commission.

Regarding periodic reports, companies covered by the Exchange Act must file: "(1) Such information and documents as the Commission shall require to keep reasonably current the information and documents required to be included in or filed with an application or registration statement, (2) Such annual reports . . . certified if required by the rules and regulations of the Commission by independent public accountants, and such quarterly reports as the Commission may prescribe."

Principles

Except for public-utility holding companies and registered investment companies, the SEC does not indicate a statement of accounting principles; it prefers that principles originate in the accounting profession. However, under the law, the Commission has the power to prescribe accounting terms, principles, practices, and reporting requirements for financial statements filed with it. Where the experience of the Commission has disclosed serious discrepancies in practice as between companies and accountants, and where the Commission has been of the opinion that uniformity in practice would benefit investors, the conclusions have been expressed by rule or regulation of the Commission or in an opinion of its chief accountant.

Accounting regulations and requirements of the Commission are published in Regulation S–X, relating to financial statements and to auditing regulations, in the Commission's *Accounting Series Releases;* and in formal findings and opinions of the Commission. The rules contained in Regulation S–X prescribe the method of presenting pertinent data in financial statements to be included in registration statements and reports to be filed. The original purpose of the *Accounting Series Releases* was to contribute to the development of uniform practices in major accounting questions. These releases are now a part of the regulations (Rule 1–01 [a]).

A short time ago the SEC issued *Accounting Series Release No. 115,* dealing with the certification of financial statements. It is as follows:

There have recently been filed with the Commission a number of registration statements under the Securities Act of 1933 which include accountants' opinions that are qualified as to matters of such significance to the registrant that there is serious question as to whether the certificate meets the requirements of Rule 2–02 of Regulation S–X.

Following is the important part of an audit report regarding this type of situation:

"Substantial losses have been experienced during the past four years and nine months and continuation of the business is dependent upon the Company's attaining sufficiently profitable operations and/or additional capital to satisfy all of its liabilities as they become due.

"In our opinion, subject to the Company's ability to attain profitable operations and/or to successfully obtain additional capital, the accompanying financial statements . . ." (From the *Journal of Accountancy,* May 1970).

The Commission, of course, does not expect an accountant to express any opinion as to the future earnings of the registrant. However, where, as here, the financial statements are prepared on a "going concern" basis while at the same time the accountant's opinion is so qualified as to indicate serious doubt as to whether or not the preparation of financial statements on that basis is warranted then a significant question arises whether the financial statements were certified as required by the Securities Act of 1933 and the rules and regulations thereunder.

Rule 2–02 (*a*) of Regulation S–X states that "The Accountant's certificate shall state clearly: (i) the opinion of the accountant in respect of the financial statements covered by the certificate and the accounting principles and practices reflected therein . . ." In *Accounting Series Release No. 90,* the Commission reached a conclusion as to certification requirements as follows:

"If, as a result of the examination and the conclusions reached, the accountant is not in a position to express an affirmative opinion as to the fairness of the presentation of earnings year by year, the registration statement is defective because the certificate does not meet the requirements of Rule 2–02 of Regulation S–X."

The problem is an important one. If the business will not continue and the proceeds of the present offering will simply be used to pay existing creditors, then the offering may be deceptive to the public. The Commission does not expect accountants to express opinions that are unwarranted in the circumstances. Indeed, if there is a question as to whether the business will continue, no amount of changing the accountant's certificate would appear to solve the underlying problem.

The Commission has concluded that a registration statement under the 1933 Act will be considered defective because the certification does not meet the requirements of Rule 2–02 of Regulation S–X when the accountant qualifies his opinion because of doubt as to whether the company will continue as a going concern. The Commission does not intend to preclude companies with pressing financial problems from raising funds by public offerings of securities. It does, however, believe it clear that an accountant's report cannot meet the certification requirements of the 1933 Act unless the registrant can arrange its financial affairs so that the immediate threat to continuation as a going business is removed. The independence of the accountant must be satisfied that it was appropriate to use conventional principles and practices for stating the accounts on a going concern basis before a registration statement under the 1933 Act can be declared effective.

Under the Investment Company Act of 1940, the prescription of the form of preparing financial statements of investment companies has the effect of providing a reasonable degree of uniformity in the accounting principles to be applied by the registered investment companies in maintaining their accounting records.

Audit Reports

The rules of the SEC applicable to the certifying accountant's rendition of a report, opinion, and changes in the application of accounting principles are as follows:

RULES 2–02: ACCOUNTANT'S CERTIFICATES

a)   Technical requirements
The accountant's certificate shall be dated, shall be signed manually, and shall identify without detailed enumeration the financial statements covered by the certificate.

b)   Representations as to the audit
The accountant's certificate (i) shall state whether the audit was made in accordance with generally accepted auditing standards; and (ii) shall designate any auditing procedures generally recognized as normal or deemed necessary by the accountant under the circumstances of a particular case, which have been omitted, and the reason for their omission.

Nothing in this rule shall be construed to imply authority for the omission of any procedure which independent accountants would ordinarily employ in the course of an audit made for the purpose of expressing the opinions required by paragraph (c) of this rule.

c)   Opinions to be expressed
The accountant's certificate shall state clearly:
        (i)   the opinion of the accountant in respect of the financial statements

covered by the certificate and the accounting principles and practices reflected therein;

(ii)   the opinion of the accountant as to any material changes in accounting principles or practices, or adjustments of the accounts, required to be set forth by Rule 3–07; and

(iii)   the nature of, and the opinion of the accountant as to, any material differences between the accounting principles and practices reflected in the financial statements and those reflected in the accounts after the entry of adjustments for the period under review.

d)   Exceptions

Any matters to which the accountant takes exception shall be clearly identified, and the exception thereto specifically and clearly stated, and, to the extent practicable, the effect of each such exception on the related financial statements given.

RULE 3–07: CHANGES IN ACCOUNTING PRINCIPLES AND PRACTICES

a)   Any change in accounting principle or practice, or in the method of applying any accounting principle or practice, made during any period for which financial statements are filed which affects comparability of such financial statements with those of prior or future periods, and the effect upon the net income for which financial statements are filed, shall be disclosed in a note to the appropriate financial statement.

The requirements of the Commission relieve the auditor of no responsibility, but they do recognize that the finding of liability under the act may be affected by the scope of the audit. Thus the representations of the accountant must be free *both* of negligence and of fraud. Therefore, if the accountant is innocently negligent and not guilty of fraud, the liabilities are as great as if a financial condition had been knowingly misrepresented. However, in order to defend a charge of misrepresentation, the accountant must not stop at proving that, after reasonable investigation, reasonable ground existed to believe that the registrant's financial statements were true—that the auditor was free from negligence; the accountant must also show that he believed his representations were true, the effect of which would be to establish that he was not conscious of misrepresentation at the time of making the report and therefore was not guilty of fraud. After the accountant proves that he was not negligent —that is, that he had reasonable ground to believe that his representations were true—it would generally be possible to show that he believed his representations were true and that he was therefore innocent of fraud.

Thus the SEC (1) distinguishes between auditing standards and their methods of application, (2) directs certain recommendations to assure observation of acceptable auditing standards, (3) thus far, leaves with the accounting profession the determination of the auditing standards, and (4) recognizes varying applications of auditing procedures in conformity with the circumstances of each case.

Disclosure

The SEC has adopted amendments to Rules 14a–3, 14c–3, and 14c–7 under the 1934 Act, which are intended to improve disclosure in annual reports to security holders and the dissemination of annual reports on Form 10–K or 12–K. The effective date is for fiscal years ending on or after December 20, 1974.

In Release No. 11079, issued October 31, 1974, the amendments require that annual reports to security holders include the following: (a) Audited financial statements for the last two years, (b) a summary of operations for the last five years, together with management's analysis thereof, (c) a brief description of the company's business, (d) lines-of-business information for the last five years, (e) identification of the company's directors and executive officers, including their principal occupations and employers, (f) the principal market in which securities entitled to vote are traded and a statement of market price ranges of, and dividends paid on such securities for each quarterly period during the last two years.

The amendments also require the company to furnish, on request and without charge, to its security holders on the record date a copy of its Form 10–K or 12–K for the most recent year and to provide copies of the exhibits of such reports upon payment of a reasonable fee.

The SEC emphasized that the annual report to security holders will retain its status as a nonfiled document and nonproxy soliciting material, so that it is not subject to the civil liability provisions of Section 18 of the Exchange Act.

Post-Statement Disclosures

The SEC has indicated its attitude with respect to the disclosure of events taking place after the date of the financial statements. Both the 1933 Act and the 1934 Act create certain possible liabilities for the accountant based upon the inclusion of an untrue statement of material fact or the failure to state a fact required to be stated or necessary to make the financial statements not misleading—not only at their effective date but also at their later date of issuance. The contention, in effect, is that if the responsibility of the accountant ceases at the date of the financial statements, the assumption would be that he is not required to possess knowledge of events occurring subsequent to that date.

Financial statements normally are representative *only* as of their date —not at their later date of issuance. This is not the situation with respect to financial statements incorporated in a registration statement filed with the SEC, under the Securities Act of 1933; under that act the statements supposedly represent conditions and operations as of the date of the registration statement. Therefore, the auditor *must* investigate nonroutine events occurring between the date of financial statements and the effective date of the registration statement. How to meet the provisions of the act has never been conclusively interpreted by the courts or by the Commission.

Financial Statements

The Securities Act of 1933 provides that financial statements required to be filed with the Commission shall be certified by an independent public accountant. The concepts of independence are rigid. The Commission holds that a public accountant who has performed some service such as journalizing and posting a client's transactions is not in fact independent. An opinion of the financial statements in these cases will not be accepted by the Commission.

If an accountant "prepared or certified" the financial statements of the registrant, the written consent of the accountant is necessary to use his name in connection with the statements. If statements submitted are not prepared in accordance with recognized principles of accounting, the Commission presumes that such statements are misleading or inaccurate, even though footnotes are appended to the statements. A qualified opinion is not acceptable.

Article 5 of Regulation S–X governs the certification, form, and content of the financial statements, including the basis for consolidation, for all companies except investment companies, insurance companies, banks, and companies in a developmental stage. Under Article 5 the balance sheet is in the order of "current to fixed"; the income statement shows sales, cost of sales, selling expense, general expense, administrative expense, other income, other deductions, special items, and net income before and after federal income tax provisions. An analysis of retained earnings is required; the income statement may be combined with the statement of retained earnings, if such combination is not misleading and does not obscure annual net income.

Rule 3–01 of Regulation S–X, as amended, provides that "financial statements may be filed in such form and order, and may use such accepted terminology, as will best indicate their significance and character in the light of the provisions applicable thereto." Thus, full and adequate disclosure in the financial statements reduces the necessity for reporting accounting methods in detail. In certain instances the Commission has held that the financial statements did not result in full disclosure when the accompanying report offered explanations; and in other instances it has held that the financial statements need not be recast when the report proper afforded disclosure. These varying decisions are caused by the circumstances in each case. "It is the philosophy of the various Securities Acts that financial statements shall be so prepared to make it possible for individuals to determine on their own account the investment of their funds to the management of a given corporation or to increase or decrease their present investments." This philosophy is disappearing.

Regulation S–X, Rule 3–11, requires a statement of the policy followed for the fiscal period for which income statements are filed with respect to the following: (1) the provisions for depreciation, depletion, and obsolescence of physical properties, including the methods and, if practicable, the rates used in computing the annual amounts; (2) the provision for amortization of intangibles, or allowances created in lieu thereof, including the methods, and, if practicable, the rates used in computing the annual amounts; (3) the accounting treatment for maintenance, repairs, renewals, and betterments; and (4) the adjustment of the accumulated depreciation, depletion, obsolescence, amortization, at the time the properties are retired or otherwise disposed of.

This policy statement must be incorporated in the income statement or must accompany it. In the preparation of balance sheets for all companies, Regulation S–X requires that accumulations for depreciation, depletion, amortization, or retirements be shown as deductions from the assets to which they are applicable. Further requirements of Regulation S–X are, in part, as follows: If a director, officer, or principal stockholder, other than an affiliated company, owed the corporation at any date during the fiscal period more than 1 percent of the total assets, or $20,000, whichever is the lesser, such information must be filed. A schedule of indebtedness owed the registrant by each affiliated company at the beginning and at the close of the fiscal period must be filed.

The balance sheet must disclose the preferences of senior stock issues in the event of involuntary liquidation, when the excess of the preference over par value or over stated value is significant; it also must disclose any restrictions, or the absence of restrictions, upon retained earnings, resulting from the fact that the preference of the senior shares, in involuntary liquidation, exceeds its par or stated value. Stockholders' equities other than capital stock must be properly subdivided. If significant in amount, discount on capital stock shall be shown separately and deducted from the capital stock or other proper item. All of the requirements of Regulation S–X are minimum requirements, to which shall be added all necessary additional information and material.

Certain accounting releases of the Securities and Exchange Commission deal with the description of "surplus" following a quasi-reorganization. These releases require "that a clear report be made to stockholders of the proposed restatements and that their formal consent thereto be obtained." The minimum disclosure considered necessary when an operating deficit has been charged off against Paid-In Capital (noncapital stock sources) by resolution of the board of directors, not accompanied by approval of the stockholders, is as follows:

. . . Until such time as the results of operations of the company on the new basis are available for an appropriate period of years (at least three) any statement or showing of earned surplus should, in order to provide additional disclosure of the occurrence and the significance of the quasi-reorganization, indicate the total amount of the deficit and any charges that were made to capital surplus in the course of the quasi-reorganization which would otherwise have been required to be made against income or earned surplus.

The Commission also requires that the new retained earnings be dated in the balance sheets subsequent to the quasi-reorganization; it also requires that full disclosure be granted the entire transaction and that an explanation be given of the possible effect on future dividends.

If, upon review by the Commission, financial statements are found to have been prepared contrary to generally accepted accounting principles, or if they otherwise fail to meet the requirements of the Commission, a deficiency letter is prepared and sent to the company allegedly at fault. The deficiency letters, followed by correspondence and/or conference with the registrants and their accountants, frequently constitute a method of resolving accounting questions which might otherwise have to be settled through formal hearings.

The Investment Company Act of 1940 and the Investment Advisers Act of 1940, which brought investment companies and their advisers under the supervision of the Commission, requires—in part—that the registered investment company file the following information:

1. A balance sheet, together with a statement of the aggregate value of investments at the date of the balance sheet.
2. A schedule setting forth the amounts and values of the securities on the balance-sheet date.
3. A statement of income for the period covered by the report, which must be itemized for each income and expense category which is in excess of 5 percent of the total income or expense.
4. A statement of retained earnings, itemized for each item which is in excess of 5 percent of the total charges or credits during the period.
5. A statement of the total remuneration paid to all directors and members of the advisory board, to all officers, and to each person to whom any officer or director of the company is an affiliated person.
6. A statement of the total dollar value of purchases and sales of investment securities, other than government securities.

In addition, the same information must be transmitted to shareholders at least semiannually. The Commission has ruled that for investment companies, the records of original entry, general ledgers, and any other important data must be retained forever.

The SEC has held that the primary responsiblity for the accuracy of financial information filed with it rests with management and not with the auditor; the client, therefore, must understand that the accountant is not assuming managerial responsibilities but that he is acting as a check against the accounting of the client.

Reliance on System of Internal Control

In addition to professional recognition of the reliance upon the system of internal control, the SEC has recognized the importance of the system of internal control in its relationship to the amount of testing in an audit. Regulation S–X, Rule 2–02 (b), requires the accountant, in the determination of the scope of the audit made for the purpose of reporting on financial statements filed with the Commission, "to consider the adequacy of the system of internal check and control" and "to consider the system of internal audit regularly maintained by means of auditors employed by the registrant's staff."

Reliance on Other Accountants

With regard to reliance upon the work of other accountants, Rule 2–05 of Regulation S–X of the SEC is as follows:

If, with respect to the certification of the financial statements of any person, the principal accountant relies on an examination made by another independent public accountant of certain of the accounts of such person or its subsidiaries, the certificate of such other accountant shall be filed (and the provisions of Rules 2–01 and 2–02 shall be applicable thereto); however, the certificate of such other accountant need not be filed (a) if no reference is made directly or indirectly to such other accountant's certificate, or (b) if, having referred to such other accountant's examination, the principal accountant states in his certificate that he assumes responsibility for such other accountant's examination in the same manner as if it had been made by him.

Rules 2–01 and 2–02, mentioned above, refer to the requirements as to accountants' qualifications and accountants' opinions, respectively.

Damages

The Securities Act has made the accountant liable to third-party investors not only for fraud but also for innocent, though negligent, misrepresentation, as stated early in this chapter.

After proper filing of the registration statement, 20 days elapse before the obligations and rights of the Act become effective. After the effective registration date, a security purchaser may decide to sue the certifying accountant for misrepresentation of a material fact or for the omission of a material fact in the registration statements. In order to recover, the plaintiff must prove loss; but he is not required to prove that the loss resulted from the misrepresentation. If the plaintiff purchased the securities later than one year following the registration date and after more recent financial statements were available to him, the plaintiff must prove that the loss resulted from misrepresentation in the statements submitted for registration.

The defenses of the accountant against such action are as follows: (1) proof that the financial statements filed with the Commission were not fair copies of the statements prepared by the accountant; (2) proof that, prior to the registration date, written notice was given the Commission by the accountant that he would not be responsible for the financial statements filed with the registration statement; (3) proof that the statements were true and proper and that they contained no omission or misstatement; (4) proof that the financial statements were used with the registration statements without the knowledge of the accountant and that the accountant, upon learning of the use of the statements, gave public notice to the situation and also notified the Commission to withdraw his authority for the propriety of the statements; (5) proof that the plaintiff investor possessed knowledge of incorrectness in the statements at the time the securities were purchased; (6) proof that the loss of the investor was caused by reasons other than the accountant's error; (7) proof that the accountant acted in good faith in conformity with a regulation of the Commission; (8) proof that the accountant relied upon a technical expert for some phase of the financial statements and that the accountant had no reason to question the accuracy of the figures of that technician; (9) proof that action by the plaintiff was brought subsequent to three years from the date on which the security was offered to the public, in accordance with the Act; and (10) proof that action by the plaintiff was brought subsequent to one year from the date the plaintiff learned of the accountant's misrepresentation.

In accordance with the Act, the recovery of the plaintiff is limited to the difference between the price paid for the security (not in excess of the public offering price) and (1) the value at the date the suit was instigated, or (2) the price at which the plaintiff sold the security before filing suit, or (3) the price at which the plaintiff sold the security after filing suit but before judgment.

The burden of proof is placed upon the accountant, and as many suits as are instituted against him must be defended. The liability of the accountant attaches to prospectuses issued in connection with a proposed security sale as well as to the registration statements.

Section 11 (*a*) of the Securities Act of 1933 provides possible liability for false or misleading registration statements, as follows:

In case any part of the registration statement, when such part became effective, contained an untrue statement of a material fact or omitted to state a material fact required to be stated therein or necessary to make the statements therein not misleading, any person acquiring such security (unless it is proved that at the time of such acquisition he knew of such untruth or omission) may, either at law or in equity, in any court of competent jurisdiction, sue. . . .

The possible liability may exist against—

Every accountant, engineer, or appraiser, or any person whose profession gives authority to a statement made by him, who has with his consent been named as having prepared or certified any report or valuation which is used in connection with the registration statement, with respect to the statement in such registration statement, report, or valuation, which purports to have been prepared or certified by him (Section 11[a] [4]).

The preceding possible liabilities may not exist when—

As regards any part of the registration statement purporting to be made upon his authority as an expert, (i) he had, after reasonable investigation, reasonable grounds to believe and did believe, at the time such part of the registration statement became effective, that the statement therein were true and that there was no omission to state a material fact required to be stated therein or necessary to make the statements therein not misleading (Section 11 [b] [3] [B]).

Under federal security legislation, therefore, the accountant may be charged with liability for failure to protect prospective investors and present stockholders. A liability may exist for carelessness and negligence, even though fraud did not exist.

As a result of federal security legislation, the accountant has been placed in the position where he must differentiate between the rights and privileges of the various groups interested in the financial statements— that is, the rights and privileges of the government and its agencies, preferred stockholders, common stockholders, bondholders, and so on. These obligations of the accountant spring from the legal requirements governing the relationships existing between the various classes of financial interests; the application of these legal requirements depends upon business data, properly prepared, classified, and presented in the financial statements.

The Securities Exchange Act, with respect to the recovery of damages, provides that if the accountant "proves that any portion of all of such damages represents other than the depreciation in value of such security resulting from such part of the registration statement, with respect to which his liability is asserted, not being true or omitting to state a material fact required to be stated therein or necessary to make the statements therein not misleading, such portion of or all such damages shall not be recoverable."

The Securities Exchange Act sets forth the liability for statements which may prove to be misleading, as follows:

Any person who shall make or cause to be made any statement in any application, report, or document filed pursuant to this title or any rule or regulation thereunder or any undertaking contained in a registration statement as provided in subsection (*d*) of section 15 of this title [Title I, Sec 18], which statement was at the time and in the light of the circumstances under which it was made false or misleading with respect to any material fact, shall be liable to any person (not knowing that such statement was false or misleading) who, in reliance upon such statement, shall have purchased or sold a security at a price which was affected by such statement, for damages caused by such reliance, unless the person sued shall prove that he acted in good faith and had no knowledge that such statement was false or misleading. A person seeking to enforce such liability may sue at law or in equity in any court of competent jurisdiction. In such suit the court may, in its discretion, require an undertaking for the costs of such suit and assess reasonable costs, including reasonable attorney's fees, against either party litigant.

Investment Company Securities

Of interest to accountants is a ruling of the SEC under the Investment Company Act. This rule pertains to securities of registered management investment companies which have been placed in the custody of a company that is a member of a national securities exchange, as defined by the Securities Exchange Act. The custodian company may accept such securities only upon a written contract with the investment company. The securities must be completely segregated from securities of the custodian or of any customer. The segregation must be both physical and separately identified in the accounts of the custodian. The custodian may not assign, hypothecate, or otherwise dispose of such securities, except upon the direction of and for the account of the registered management investment company. Such securities must be verified by physical examination by an independent public accountant retained by the management investment company at the end of each annual and semiannual fiscal period, and also must be examined by the accountant at least one other time during the fiscal period, which time shall be selected by the accountant. The accountant must render a certificate to the Commission, in which he must state that he made the examination, and in which he must describe the examination; the securities shall be subject to examination by the Commission at all times.

Long-Term Leases

The accounting profession recognizes the necessity for disclosing the existence of long-term leases, particularly the now widely used buy-build-sell-lease type of agreement. The requirements of Rule 3–18 (*b*) of the Securities and Exchange Commission are as follows: "Where the rentals or obligations under long-term leases are material there shall be shown the amounts of annual rentals under such leases with some indication of the periods for which they are payable, together with any important obligation assumed or guarantee made in connection therewith. If the rentals are conditional, state the minimum annual amounts." The SEC interprets Rule 3–18 to apply to leases which extend more than three years from the balance-sheet data.

Inventories

With regard to inventories in the financial statements of registrants, the requirements of Regulation S–X, Rule 5–02, 6 (*b*), are as follows:

The basis of determining the amounts shown in the balance sheet shall be stated. If a base such as "cost," "market," or "cost or market, whichever is lower," is given, there shall also be given, to the extent applicable, a general indication of the method of determining the "cost" or "market," e.g., "average cost" or "first-in, first-out."

SUGGESTED ADDITIONAL READING

Code of Professional Ethics of the AICPA, particularly the *Rules of Conduct*. New rules of the Securities and Exchange Commission. *Accounting Series Releases* of the SEC. The final disposition of such legal cases as *National Student Marketing Corp., Equity Funding*, and others.

QUESTIONS

1.   *a)*   A client, not in bankruptcy, has not paid its CPA's billed fees for the past two years. Is the CPA still independent?

     b)   A university faculty member, with tenure, who also is a CPA, is asked to audit the financial statements of the fund of the student senate. The university is connected with the fund in the following manners: (1) the basic administration-faculty-student relationship, (2) the university collects student fees and remits them to the senate, (3) the university requires that an administration officer approve student senate checks and sign them.

        Would the independence of the CPA be impaired under this situation? Would independence be impaired if the faculty member was in public practice and served as a part-time faculty member?

2.   *a)*   A client, in bankruptcy, had not paid its CPA firm for services rendered prior to the date of the declared bankruptcy. Would the independence of the CPA firm be impaired as a "debtor in possession" or as a trustee in bankruptcy because of existing claims against the bankrupt client?

     b)   A CPA in public practice was asked to serve a client both as general counsel and as auditor. Would the independence of the CPA's firm be impaired with respect to this client?

3.   For each following case, state whether you believe the proposed action would be considered proper or improper according to the *Code of Professional Ethics* of the AICPA. Justify your decisions.

a)   A firm of CPAs is considering the use of an outside mailing service to handle confirmations of the accounts receivable of clients upon whose financial statements the firm is to render an opinion. The mailing service would mail the requests, receive the replies, remove the replies from the envelopes, and return them to the auditors.

b)   A CPA, now on the staff of a firm of CPAs but contemplating public practice in his own name, plans to send announcements of his opening of practice to clients of the firm by which he is now employed, as well as to friends and acquaintances. Some such clients have indicated that they would like him to continue with them, but they are not yet aware of his decision to enter upon practice for himself.

e)   A CPA, in the sale of his entire practice to another CPA, proposes to turn over to the latter all of his work papers and business correspondence.

d)   A CPA plans to initiate discussions with an accountant who is at present employed on the staff of another CPA firm with a view to persuading the accountant to come to work for him.

(AICPA, adapted)

4.   What is the difference between negligence and fraud?

5.   What are the liabilities of the independent auditor under the federal Securities Acts?

6.   What are the rules of the SEC with regard to audit reports?

7.   How have the Securities Acts made the independent auditor liable to third-party investors?

8.   What are the legal responsibilities of the independent auditor for inventories?

9.   To what extent does the SEC require independence of the public accountant?

10.   Do you think the SEC will invoke its authority to prescribe accounting principles? Discuss.

11.   An auditor frequently requests that the client supply him with a certification of (*a*) inventory quantity, pricing, and condition; (*b*) receivables, particularly with respect to their collectibility; and (*c*) capital assets, particularly if appraised amounts are used in the accounts.

   To what extent may an auditor use these certifications as safeguards against charges of negligence and at the same time assume full responsibility for the engagement?

12.   You are the auditor for Rose, Inc. Foster, a member of the board of directors, owns all of the capital stock of Anders, Inc., which you also audit. Rose, Inc., buys all of its raw materials from Anders, Inc. Foster is the only member of the board of Rose who knows that you audit the records of Anders, Inc. In the report of your examination of Rose, Inc., what would you indicate with respect to this situation?

13.   What are the legal responsibilities of a public accountant with respect to the work done by him as a professional auditor? Discuss.

14. Without consulting its CPA, a client has changed its accounting so that it is not in accordance with generally accepted accounting principles. During the regular audit engagement, the CPA discovers that the statements are so grossly misleading that they might be considered fraudulent.

   a) Discuss the specific action to be taken by the CPA.

   b) In this situation, what obligation does the CPA have to outsiders if he is replaced? Discuss briefly.

   c) In this situation, what obligations does the CPA have to a new auditor if he is replaced? Discuss briefly.

   (AICPA)

15. Should an accountant report material events that took place after the effective date of the financial statements but prior to rendition of the audit report? Explain.

16. An auditor, you are requested by a client corporation to sign published statements of anticipated earnings. What position would you take with respect to this request? What are the reasons for your answer?

17. a) Why does an auditor review the system of internal control of a client, and to what major questions does he seek answers in undertaking the review?

   b) Compare the extent of an auditor's review of the system of internal control for the first examination of a new client with the review of the system of a client whose records he has examined regularly over a period of years.

3

Internal Control for Manual
and Electronic Systems;
An Audit Program

INTERNAL CONTROL

Internal control constitutes the methods followed to (1) protect assets, (2) protect against improper asset disbursements, (3) protect against the incurrence of improper liabilities, (4) assure the accuracy and dependability of all financial and operating information, (5) judge operating efficiency, and (6) measure adherence to company-established policies.

The evaluation of a system of internal control is the keynote to the determination of the extent of the examination of financial transactions. The influence on auditing of the operation of an adequate system of internal control is to the effect that auditing now assumes an application revolving around transaction review, analyses, and sampling and testing —culminating in mature evaluation and final judgment regarding fairness of presentation of financial data.

Internal control may be administrative or financial. Administrative internal control normally pertains to activities which are not directly financial in nature, as exemplified by a company policy that each of its traveling salesmen must prepare and send to the home office a daily report indicating calls made, orders received, and rejections and the reasons therefor. Financial internal control pertains to financial activities (2, 3, and 4, above) and may be exemplified by the separation of the duties of personnel in handling cash and recording related cash transactions. Financial internal control may also be described as a system wherein the monetary accountability and work of one person is verified by another person—without duplication of function or effort.

Both financial and administrative internal control are functions of management. In many cases financial and administrative internal control interweave—there are no mutually exclusive boundaries. Proper financial internal control is accomplished by management's verification of financial transactions and financial recording. In an audit, the auditor is more concerned with financial internal control than with administrative internal control. In a nonaudit engagement involving management advisory services, the auditor may be more interested in administrative internal control than in financial internal control. In this book attention will be focused on financial internal control.

Effective operation of a system of financial internal control is dependent upon (1) accounting and financial records which are properly designed and effectively operated and (2) the effective segregation of the duties of company personnel.

Principles of Financial Internal Control

Due to the fact that effective financial internal control is based upon the concept of charge and discharge of responsibility and duty, the basic principles of financial internal control are as follows:

1. Accounting and financial operations must be separated, and no one person should be in complete charge of a business transaction. One employee should not have access simultaneously to an accounting record and to the material or data underlying that record. To illustrate: One employee should not have authority to disburse cash and to record those disbursements.
2. Responsibility for the performance of each duty must be fixed in each person.
3. Accuracy proofs should be utilized in order to assure the correctness of the underlying operation and the subsequent accounting. To illustrate: The total of daily cash receipts should be proved against the totals of cash register tapes, or sequentially numbered sales invoices, or retail price tags removed from merchandise sold.
4. If possible, employees should be rotated on a job, and vacations for those in positions of trust should be enforced. In this way the opportunities for fraud are reduced.
5. Employees should be bonded—in order to protect the employer and to deter a tempted employee.
6. Instructions should be reduced to writing in the form of operations manuals.
7. The controlling account principle should be used in all possible instances. The use of controlling accounts serves as accuracy proof between account balances and between employees.
8. A double-entry system of accounting should be used. However, it is not a substitute for protective financial internal control.

9.   Mechanical or electronic equipment, with built-in proof features, should be used if possible. However, fraud still is possible.

Review of and Reliance upon the System of Internal Control

Preliminary to an audit, or during its course, the professional auditor will review the system of financial and administrative internal control in operation. The purposes of the review (particularly of the financial internal control) are:

1.   To arrive at a decision regarding the amount of detailed examination work to be performed during the audit.
2.   To ascertain the weakness or strength of the system.
3.   To judge the adequacy of the system as one of the bases of expressing an opinion concerning the fair presentation of the financial statements.

An auditor normally will initiate his review of internal control before entering into transaction verification. This is logical because conclusions regarding internal control affect the scope or detail of an examination. However, conclusions regarding all phases of internal control cannot be made until an auditor has almost totally completed all phases of his examination. Therefore, many auditors interweave their review and evaluation of internal control with the actual audit processes. For example, an auditor's review of internal control over cash receipts and a test of cash receipt transactions may convince him that cash receipts are properly controlled, accounted for, and recorded. However, a review of internal control over cash disbursements may convince him that cash disbursements are under proper control, but an examination of cash disbursement transactions may result in the conclusion that they are improperly controlled. Consequently the auditor would change his original evaluation of internal control over cash disbursements and extend his examination of disbursement transactions.

A system of financial internal control is easy to operate, and proper internal control methods may be placed in effect in any business organization. However, any system of financial internal control may be manipulated if collusion exists between two or more employees.

A proper system of financial internal control, effectively operated, saves an auditor much time, reduces examination cost to a client, and assures the auditor of the reliability of the financial transactions. Also, effective financial internal control reduces the work of the internal auditor. If a business transaction is carelessly handled at its origin, auditing becomes difficult and costly, and the reliability of the examination is limited. To illustrate: A bookkeeper opens incoming mail containing checks and cash received from customers, and, therefore is in a perfect position to steal remittances and then debit an expense account and credit accounts receivable or sales. An auditor would be forced to extend the examination of the offsetting debits when receivables or sales were credited.

One recognized auditing standard provides for reliance upon the effectiveness of the system of internal control as a guide to the auditor in determining the amount of detailed verification necessary during the course of an audit. In addition, both the Securities and Exchange Commission and the New York Stock Exchange have rules recognizing the importance of proper internal control in relationship to the amount of detailed transaction examination necessary in an audit.

The review of the system of financial internal control may take the form of oral questioning, or it may take the form of prepared questionnaires for each section of the audit. In an initial examination, it is advisable to approach the review of internal control from the point of view of financial transactions, so that the flow of work and the accountability of the personnel may be determined.

Each appropriate chapter of this book contains a discussion of the financial internal control features applicable to the item or items under examination, and also contains internal control questionnaires for each functional section of an audit. The questionnaires may be expanded or curtailed for each examination, as the circumstances demand.

Internal Audits, Independent Audits, and Internal Control

Coordination between internal auditors and professional CPAs is established by a mutuality of interest existing between the two groups. The growth in the size of business organizations, the volume of transactions, and the complexity of the transactions have made necessary internal auditing, internal control, and the examination of the internal control and the internal audit procedures by the independent certified public accountant. Financial statement accuracy is management's responsibility, and the independent auditor relies on data collected and proved by management. The internal auditor and the independent auditor cooperate for the production of reliable financial statements. To illustrate: If the internal auditor is able to produce an aging schedule of accounts receivable, the independent auditor will test it and draw his conclusions from it, and will not be forced to prepare one. If the internal auditor has confirmed accounts receivable, the independent auditor may restrict his confirmation requests to a smaller percentage of the total. If the internal auditor has prepared proper inventory schedules, properly priced, the independent auditor may curtail his testing of the schedules and the pricing to the point where he is satisfied with the results. There are many other examples of cooperation.

Financial internal control deals with the operation of the financial system. Internal auditing deals with the internal verification of recorded data. An adequate system of internal auditing in no sense implies that the work of the independent auditor is performed for him. The independent auditor does not accept the results of internal auditing as a substitute for his own examination. After examination, the independent auditor merely relies on the results of internal auditing in order to decide upon the reliability of the accounting and to decide upon the volume of transaction verification. Thus the effect of internal auditing is to give the independent auditor greater reliance upon the system of financial internal control than would be possible if internal auditing did not exist.

Systems of Financial Internal Control

When financial internal controls are placed in operation, personnel should be segregated by functions, as follows:

1. Those who initiate or authorize transactions.
2. Those who execute the transactions.
3. Those who have responsibility for the asset, liability, expense, or revenue resulting from the transaction.

After internal controls are installed, they must be observed and controlled, since they will not operate without supervision. Management must be alert to employee carelessness in carrying out assignments in the internal control area. Any system of internal control must adhere to the principles of financial internal control set forth on page 77.

Each proper chapter of this book will open with the internal controls necessary for the asset, liability, capital, expense, or revenue being discussed. In order to offer the reader an early concept of the operation of a satisfactory system of internal control in a small business organization, the following section is presented.

From the point of view of internal control, business transactions may be divided into the following classes: (1) purchases of assets and services, (2) sales of assets and services, (3) receipt of cash, (4) disbursement of cash, and (5) company internal transactions.

Financial Internal Control in a Small Organization

Internal control is of equal importance to both a small and a large company, and there are more small companies than large ones.

Assume a single proprietorship, consisting of the owner, one bookkeeper-office employee, and five salesclerks. The owner is without technical accounting knowledge. In order to effect satisfactory financial internal control, the duties of the owner may be outlined as follows:

1. *General*
   a) Be personally acquainted with the bookkeeper-office employee.
   b) Engage a CPA for an annual audit and for interim visits.
2. *Purchases of Merchandise for Resale*
   a) Maintain a sequentially prenumbered list of all purchase orders placed.
   b) As vendors' invoices and goods are received, note the receipt on the proper purchase order.
3. *Payrolls*
   a) Compare the payroll record with the employees' names, authorized gross pay, deductions, and net cash—and *add the total payroll.*
4. *Sales of Merchandise*
   a) If cash registers are used:
       (1) Assign each clerk to one register or one drawer (if possible).
       (2) Remove the cash register tapes—daily.
       (3) Compare the totals of the daily register tapes with the daily debit to Cash and with the amount deposited in the bank.
   b) If sales invoices are used:
       (1) Use and keep a record of sequentially numbered sales invoices.
       (2) Daily, account for all sales invoices used.
       (3) Daily, total the sales invoices and compare with the daily debit to Cash and to Accounts Receivable.
       (4) Daily, compare the Cash debit with the bank deposit.
5. *Cash Receipts*
   a) Follow items 4(*a*) (3) and 4(*b*) (3) and (4), above.
   b) Personally open *all* mail, list the remittances received from customers, and *retain* the list.
   c) Deposit all cash receipts daily.
   d) Compare the remittance list total with the Cash debit and with the bank deposit.
6. *Cash Disbursements*
   a) Disburse by prenumbered and controlled checks.
   b) Stamp vendors' invoices and the related purchase orders "Paid."
   c) Total the daily disbursements and compare with the credit to Cash entered by the bookkeeper.
   d) Maintain a petty cash fund and sign each petty cash voucher.
   e) Review (or prepare) the bank reconciliations.
7. *Accounts Receivable*
   a) Compare sales invoices with periodic statements sent to customers.
   b) Personally mail the statements.

8. *Inventories*

   a) If possible, use the retail system, preferably on a unit-control basis.

   b) Personally supervise the periodic inventory count.

ERRORS AND FRAUD

One of the purposes of a system of internal control and internal audit is to prevent errors and fraud. Accounting errors are either *unintentional* or *intentional*. If not detected and corrected, an error results in incorrect financial statements. An unintentional error is one in which accounting principles are incorrectly applied, or one with an arithmetical error, or one of omission—in which case there is failure to make an accounting entry.

An intentional error is the result of deliberate planning. It may be an error involving the proper application of accounting principles; or it may be one of omission of an entry; or it may be one of commission, in which case accounting records are deliberately misstated. Intentional errors usually are made by dishonest individuals who have fraudulent intentions.

Embezzlement constitutes the conversion of property of another to personal use—without permission or authorization. Trespass need not exist. *Fraud* is a deceitful and dishonest act and may be used to cover embezzlement. Fraud consists in (1) taking property from its owner without the owner's knowledge or permission or (2) misstating a situation—either knowingly or by gross negligence. *Larceny* is a form of fraud in which there must be unauthorized trespass. To illustrate: Burglary constitutes larceny. A cashier may embezzle money or other property.

Legal actions for any form of fraud may be originated by the state or its subdivisions, or by an injured person. Fraud may constitute a misdemeanor or a felony. Bonding of employees who are in a position of trust frequently serves as an effective prevention to a fraudulent act. As an interesting sidelight, a current FBI announcement (September 1975) estimated that employee frauds in the United States were over $40 billion annually. Losses from outside sources (robbery, larceny, burglary, and automobile theft) were approximately $1.5 billion per year!

Proper internal control assists in the prevention and detection of fraud. To prevent and detect fraud effectively, one must be familiar with the fraudulent methods used in the theft of assets. Several of these fraudulent methods are described below.

Thefts of Assets Other than Cash. If inventory control systems are inadequate, and even if individual thefts are small, merchandise thefts in total may be material. *Remedies:* Maintain adequate control of the physical items of inventory. Periodic physical inventories should be taken by persons other than clerks or other inventory custodians. Employees' packages should be checked in and out of the premises. Shopping services and detective agencies may be employed. If more than one clerk is present, an automatic deterrent exists against both employee and nonemployee.

In manufacturing concerns, there are many thefts of small tools and supplies. *Remedies:* Establish centralized control of the items. Proper inventory records should be maintained. Issuance should be only by properly authorized requisition.

Thefts of escurities may require forgery in order to cash them. *Remedies:* Double-key safe-deposit boxes should be used. Securities should be so registered that two signatures are required prior to cashing.

Thefts of Cash. The methods used to steal cash are legion. A few of the methods are illustrated below:

1. Cash sales money may be stolen at the time a sale is made. The stolen sales money is not recorded on a sales invoice or on a cash register. This type of theft may be difficult to detect because records do not exist. Only a portion of the sales price may be rung on a cash register and the difference stolen. *Remedies:* Use central cashiers and visible cash registers. Give the customer a copy of the sales invoice or a receipt ejected from the cash register. Use detective agencies and shopping services.

The following methods involve record manipulation. The internal controls are summarized in the internal control questionnaires in each applicable future chapter.

2. Cash may be stolen from sales money or accounts receivable collections. The correct amount of cash is debited to Cash and credited to Sales or Accounts Receivable. In the cash receipts record the totals of the cash debits and the sales or accounts receivable credits are underfooted. Therefore, after posting, the Cash account balance will agree with the reconciled bank statement balance. If checks are stolen, forgery is necessary in order to cash them. To illustrate: If $10,000 cash was received, and if $1,000 was stolen, and if an entry is made debiting Cash and crediting Sales for $10,000, the cash ledger account balance will be $1,000 over the reconciled bank statement balance. If the Cash debits and the Sales credits in the cash receipts record are each underadded by $1,000, the bank statement and the cash ledger account balance will agree, after reconciliation. *Remedies:* Separate the function of receiving cash and recording cash entries. Prove the accuracy of footings in the cash receipts records. Match cash record debits with bank statement deposits.

3. In the cash receipts records, sales discounts allowed customers may be overstated, followed by theft of the amount of the overstated discounts. *Remedies:* Separate the function of receiving cash and recording cash entries. Examine discount entries and compare the recorded discounts with allowed discounts. Match cash record entries with the detail of bank statement deposits.

4. When cash is received from a customer, an expense account may be debited; the cash is stolen, and the customer has received proper account credit. *Remedies:* Trace accounts receivable credit entries to the contra

debits. A variation of this method is to write off a collectible account and when the customer remits to steal the remittance.

5. When a charge sale is made, debit a fictitious customer. Collection from the actual customer will not be recorded because there is no account with him in the records. The remittance is stolen. Later the fictitious customer's balance is charged to bad debts. *Remedies:* Separate the function of receiving cash and recording cash entries. Confirm accounts receivable, and the request to the fictitious customer will be returned to the sender. Obtain executive approval of all accounts charged to bad debts. A variation of this method of fraud is to undercharge a customer *on the records;* when the customer remits, the difference between the billing and the receivable is stolen.

6. Lapping cash receipts involves withholding current cash receipts without making an entry. At the time of a subsequent cash receipt, the entry for the first cash receipt is made and the second receipt is not recorded. To illustrate: Customer A remits $100 on account. The cashier-bookkeeper retains the $100 and makes no entry. Later, Customer B remits $160 on account. Customer A is credited with $100, and Customer B with $60. The shortage remains at $100, but the shortage in A's account is covered. Later, Customer C remits $120 on account. Customer B is credited with $100, and C receives no credit. The total shortage is $120. These manipulations may continue indefinitely. *Remedies:* Separate the function of receiving cash and recording cash entries. Match individual cash receipts with credits to customers' accounts. Confirm accounts receivable balances. Compare bank deposits with the detailed listing of customer remittances.

7. Unclaimed dividend and payroll checks may be stolen and cashed. *Remedies:* Do not permit the cashier or the accountant to open returned mail. Do not return unclaimed checks to the accounting department. Have employees sign for their payroll checks. Independently mail Form W–2 to employees, either at the end of the calendar year or at the employment termination date.

8. Money may be stolen from petty (or other) cash funds. This form of theft usually is accompanied by forging approvals to petty (or other) cash vouchers, or altering the amount on an approved voucher, or altering dates on vouchers used in a prior reimbursement period. *Remedies:* Permanently stamp all used petty (and other) cash vouchers. Place the control of the unused cash vouchers in a person other than the fund custodian. Sequentially prenumber all vouchers. Demand proper approval of all disbursements from the fund.

9. Checks may be forged and cashed. These checks may be destroyed when they have cleared the bank. If they are destroyed and if cash disbursements entries have not been made, cash disbursement record totals must be raised; or unrecorded cash receipts must be deposited in the bank. *Remedies:* All check numbers must be accounted for. The person

preparing and/or signing checks must not have access to paid checks returned by the bank. Foot cash receipts and disbursements records, and trace postings.

10. The date on an already paid vendor's invoice and/or voucher may be changed. A check then is prepared, stolen, and cashed. If an accounting entry is made, a debit to an expense or an asset is duplicated. If an accounting entry is not made, the cash disbursements records must be overadded in order to provide agreement between the Cash account balance and the reconciled bank statement balance. A variation of this method is to prepare false invoices and/or accompanying vouchers, enter them in the records, prepare the checks, extract them, falsify endorsements, and cash them. *Remedies:* Persons signing checks should compare them with vendors' invoices and accompanying vouchers. The invoice— and, if used, the voucher—should be stamped "Paid." The payment date should be placed on invoices and accompanying papers—ineradicably. Officials signing checks should know the names of creditors. Unusual endorsements should be examined, such as a stamped endorsement followed by another endorsement, usually an individual's. Checks should be mailed by the last person who signs them, or mailed under his control.

11. Kiting of checks occurs when a check drawn on one bank is deposited in a second bank, but no entry is made reducing the cash balance in the first bank. This type of transaction occurs at the end of a month and is not fully recorded in order to cover a shortage in the second bank. If the check drawn on the first bank has not cleared at the end of the month, the effect is to overstate the amount of cash in bank. *Remedies:* Compare cash deposits per bank statements with cash debits—especially toward the end of a month. Directly from the banks, obtain bank statements and paid checks approximately one week after the end of the month if possible (or wait until the next bank statement mailing date) and compare the paid checks with cash record entries. Foot cash disbursements records and extract the ledger account balance of each cash account.

12. Purchase discounts may be understated, underfooted, or apparently not taken—and the discount extracted from cash receipts. *Remedies:* Compare purchase invoice terms with cash disbursements entries and the checks. Verify footings.

13. Payrolls may be manipulated by (*a*) padding the earnings of employees, (*b*) overfooting payroll records, (*c*) adding names of fictitious employees to the payroll records, (*d*) not removing names of terminated employees from the records, (*e*) stealing unclaimed wages, and (*f*) not recording deductions from employees' gross pay.

The independent auditor and the internal auditor must be on guard at all times in order to prevent and to stop criminal practices. However, no accounting system exists which cannot be manipulated by a person either working alone or working in collusion with another person. Both the auditor and the employer are more interested in preventing fraud than in tracing it after it has occurred.

AN AUDIT PROGRAM

In order to understand, report, and render an opinion, an auditor must *inquire, examine, and authenticate.* As an aid to inquiry, examination, and authentication, the auditor prepares a program of auditing procedures for each examination. An audit program is a logically planned procedure of examination. In addition to serving as a logical procedural guide during the course of an audit, the predetermined audit program serves as a checkoff list as the various sections of the audit progress and as successive phases of the audit work are completed.

For any one client, an audit program must be revised periodically, in conformity with changing conditions of the client's operations and in accordance with changes in auditing standards and procedures.

In each chapter of this book, there will be presented the audit procedures applicable to the particular asset, liability, proprietorship, revenue, and expense under discussion. An audit program must be developed in accordance with accepted auditing standards and procedures. In practice the entire audit program and the entire internal control questionnaire are filed as a unit for reference in future examinations.

A suggested audit program for petty cash is shown in Illustration 3–1. This audit program should be expanded or contracted in accordance with the requirements of each engagement.

Many CPA firms use a standard preprinted audit program and internal control questionnaire. When preprinted in standard form, applicable and nonapplicable items must be noted for each client.

In developing an audit program and a questionnaire for a specific client, care must be exercised to include all procedures and questions applicable to the operations of that client. In the development, common sense and good judgment must be exercised. Petty items should be excluded; major items concerning the program and the internal control questionnaire must be included in accordance with the circumstances of the engagement. For a new client the auditor must study all of the operations and existing conditions. In a repeat engagement the auditor reviews his program and questionnaire of the prior period, and changes the program and questionnaire in the light of alterations made by the client in his operations, personnel, products, and accounting procedures.

The Effect of Electronic Data Processing on Internal Control and an Audit Program

In order for an EDP system to function at its best, clear lines of authority and responsibility must be established. The functional responsi-

Illustration 3–1

Prepared by_____   AUDIT PROGRAM
Date_____   PETTY CASH FUND
Company _____
Period Covered_____

---

1. Simultaneously control all cash and negotiable securities.

---

2. Count and list all items in the fund.

---

3. Obtain the signature of the fund custodian, acknowledging return of the fund items.

---

4. Obtain responsible written approval for all expense vouchers, receivables, and employees' checks in the fund.

---

5. Reconcile the fund with the general ledger fund account at the proper date.

---

6. Trace all checks in the fund to subsequent deposit tickets and to the bank statement.

---

7. Examine original disbursement evidence and compare the cash fund vouchers with the covering reimbursement voucher; inspect distributions and approvals.

---

8. Verify footings and crossfootings of the reimbursement vouchers.

---

9. Trace reimbursement vouchers to the disbursements medium.

---

10. Obtain responsible written acceptance and approval of any shortage in the petty cash fund.

---

11. From company personnel obtain direct confirmation of the amount of fund cash held by them at the end of the period.

---

12. If the examination takes place after the end of the fiscal period, reconcile the account back to the end of the fiscal period-end date.

---

bilities should provide for the separation of initiation and authorization of a transaction and the recording of the transaction. Further separation is desired in establishing responsibility for the protection of the assets. If such separation is built into an EDP system, efficiencies from specialization will result and it will also be possible to make cross-checks that promote accuracy without duplication of effort. As a result of EDP systems, there has been made possible a great deal of centralization of processing of financial transactions.

Since the data processing is carried out in one department, importance of control cannot be overemphasized. Keeping in mind that there must be separation between people who authorize transactions, record transactions, and are responsible for the safeguarding of assets, satisfactory internal control can only be maintained if adequate procedures are provided. In an EDP system, just as in a manual system, we must keep in mind the requirements of such groups as the Securities and Exchange Commission, the AICPA, and the New York Stock Exchange. The auditor must be satisfied as to the adequacy of the system of internal control. For example, if a salesman sends in an order to be filled and, after inspecting it for description manually, the order is processed by a computer system, the auditor must be able to determine the integrity of the system by determining that the authorization of the transaction was properly executed, that the recording function was properly executed, and that the information storing function has been properly executed. To insure these major aspects of internal control, there must be physical as well as operational segregation of the disk packs and the scheduling of personnel from machine room operations.

How much control is possessed by the department originating the data to be processed is largely dependent upon the size of the company. Where large companies are involved, one will find many using departments, and this requires extensive internal control. Frequently the final checking or coordinating of the material is through someone outside the data processing department.

Even though great care may be taken in developing programmed controls, output controls must be provided. Comparisons of control totals of data processed with totals independently arrived at by departments responsible for original source data are mandatory if a satisfactory system of internal control is to be maintained. A definite sampling program of individual items processed will also provide another means of output controls. By breaking down the sampling procedures among the several interested groups or departments, the inaccuracies that frequently develop with routine sampling are eliminated.

In order for an EDP system to provide maximum internal control, administrative controls are absolutely necessary. Complete documentation of systems design and programming must be maintained so that the system can be evaluated and modified when necessary. Lack of documentation can and will create chaos in an EDP system. Data system survey, data systems study, and programming must be provided for if an EDP system is to operate with any degree of reliability.

Accurate computer programming cannot be overemphasized. The preparation of flow charts, program listings, and computer operating instructions must be complete in every detail. It cannot be assumed that the machine will do any more than it is instructed to do. Since more and more users of EDP equipment are using off-premises facilities, a tight control of all phases of the program must be maintained. At the very least a programming manual should be set up and currently maintained. This should consist of a written record of all policies, procedures, and techniques that are to be standard throughout the departments that are using the computers. This would insure well-formulated and well-documented procedure changes, and thus should prevent the manipulation of the system by unauthorized persons.

Summary of Internal Computer Controls

1. Whenever changes are made in memory records, such as the fixed asset control account, payroll, inventory, and other records, the changes should be initiated by persons other than those immediately involved with the changes. For example, the personnel department should initiate the information regarding a person joining or leaving the firm; a superintendent or division head should not initiate this information.

2. Serially prenumbered documents should be used authorizing changes to master records. A prenumbered document should be recorded at the point of issue and in the data processing department, where authorization for the change should be verified.

3. Computer operating personnel should never be permitted to check and record the receipt and distribution of input, output, and traffic between the program and the machine steps. In addition, computer programming personnel should *not be permitted* to use the computer.

4. Batch totals of the number of documents or total dollars, or hash totals, the adding of invoice numbers, and so forth, would assist in providing suitable controls for master records. In this manner, control information is maintained independently of the computer for each type of master data. For example, control accounts should be maintained for each type of deduction from a numerical or financial item.

5. Accurate records should be kept on all data file maintenance and its updating. The original notifications should be kept on file in the data processing department and it should also contain a copy of the notification of the updating that was sent to the point of issue.

6. To assume that source data is being verified, master file data should be printed out periodically.

7. The following records of movement of data should be accurately maintained by the data processing control group:

    (*a*) A receipt indicating the source of data.

    (*b*) A log indicating when the data were processed by the computer.

    (*c*) A log indicating when the data was returned from being processed, and a receipt indicating the return of the data to the source.

    (*d*) A log listing all output records and reports received from processing.

(*e*)   A log detailing the distribution of output records and reports.

8. Input controls are essential and the records control group in data processing should possess the following:

(*a*)   A document count.

(*b*)   Control totals for hours, rates, dollars, units, pounds, voucher numbers, and so forth.

(*c*)   Batch controls consisting of document count and control totals.

(*d*)   Batch summary totals run daily, weekly or on some other cycle which will provide the necessary check.

(*e*)   Finally, a system summary total which will control the tremendous variety of document batches involving the total system. For example, all the facets of accounting for a payroll.

9. Output controls are essential and the records control group in data processing should have the following:

(*a*)   All columnar totals.

(*b*)   Hash totals, like totals of voucher numbers in a batch, so that it can be determined that all data have been included.

(*c*)   Record counts which clearly relate to the number of specific records involved in a transaction or an account balance, or the total system balance.

(*d*)   Complete cross-footings to verify columnar total or totals.

(*e*)   Limit checks. These are instructions which cause the computer to reject listings of any data not within the programmed limits.

(*f*)   During processing, check points should be established which will provide a means of locating errors early and quickly, thereby making it unnecessary to rerun an entire program when an error is discovered.

(*g*)   The establishing of a zero balance is desirable to prove accuracy of computations within a known total.

10. A parity check, which assures that proper sequence of data is maintained, should be built into the computer program.

11. Preauthorization of *all* computer usage, especially overtime, should be required and a record maintained. Also contained in this preauthorization of usage would be the operating instructions, programs to be used, reference files to be drawn from the data processing library, and planned start and stop time of the run.

12. To complement the preauthorization of computer use, computer operators should maintain operating logs which would include estimate versus actual run time.

13. Whenever possible, no operator should be permitted to operate the computer alone. A second person should be present and both initial the operating log.

14. Whenever errors are made, a register of errors should be maintained

supported by a printout of the error, action taken, and record of the manual intervention. It is highly desirable to maintain a printout record of all manual interventions.

15. When control totals are programmed, they should be checked by someone other than the computer operator. An even more desirable procedure would be to have the program build up and check its own controls against the input data. No output should leave the data processing department without passing through the records control group for verification.

16. Magnetic media should be kept in a library and someone other than the programmers or computer operators should be responsible for their safekeeping. That person should:

   (*a*) Maintain a record of each tape or disk with the history of its use, including content, updating, run numbers, number of passes, reference label, and any other information needed to identify the reel or disk.

   (*b*) Definitely tie in media usage with the preauthorization procedure so that no tape or disk can be issued without proper preauthorization.

   (*c*) Use a follow up or trailer label with control totals of selected items updated during processing; the record control group should maintain similar but independent controls for comparison.

   (*d*) Not permit any reference or master tape or disk to be overwritten during an amending or updating process. A new tape or an updated disk should be written so that generation identification can be maintained.

   (*e*) Provide different locations for security for master tapes or disks of exceptional importance. It is also desirable to keep the supporting documents.

   (*f*) Provide a safe file for disks and tapes at point-of-use.

17. Data processing operations should include a register of all changes regardless of their nature and cross-references to other programs which might be affected by the change should be noted. Changes or new programs should not be allowed to operate until they have been tested and approved by the head of data processing.

18. If possible, only one person should be responsible for an operation at any one time. There must be a division between the employees who authorize a transaction and produce the input, as well as those who process the data and those who use the data.

19. Employees should be rotated within the data processing group. This should prevent an employee from so dominating an area of operations that losses from fraud or error are not detected.

20. In addition to rotating personnel, it is desirable to bond key personnel. This will impress the persons involved with their responsibilities

and should prompt a review of a firm's internal control of its computer operations by an insurance company.

Computers and Data Processing Developments

In the past 25 to 30 years, computer technology has developed at a rapid rate, starting with the vacuum tube, to the transistor, to integrated circuits using the basic logic known as the *flip-flop*. Thus, the monstrous vacuum tube computer has gradually been replaced by small equipment using a semiconductor chip with up to 1,000 flip-flops in one semiconductor, which is so small that it is barely visible and contains 4,000 bits per chip. According to one authoritative source, the cost per flip-flop has been reduced from approximately $30 to $0.01, while physical space has been reduced from approximately 250 cubic feet to .05 cubic feet for 32,000 memory bytes. The cost of a processing unit with 32,000 bytes has dropped from $650,000 in 1950 (approximately) to $500 in 1973—and if semiconductor technology continues to develop, in ten years the total cost of a computer and its operation will be negligible per operation.

DISTINCTIVE AUDITING TERMINOLOGY

Certain terms distinctive to auditing are introduced at this point. Accountants commonly employ these distinctive terms to designate a function related to auditing.

Analyze: To separate into elements or parts. To illustrate: A selling expense account may be analyzed by separating and classifying each entry in a systematic manner in order to obtain accuracy and proper classification.

Check: To control. In auditing, it should mean a tick-mark placed after an item, after the item has been verified.

Checking: To compare one number in two or more places. The terms "check" and "checking" are used too loosely in auditing; the use of both words should be avoided.

Compare: To note the similarity or dissimilarity of items. To illustrate: The net income of 1977 may be compared with that of 1976; the total of a sales invoice may be compared with the corresponding entry in the sales record.

Confirm: To obtain proof from a source other than the client or his records. To illustrate: A bank confirmation is obtained directly from the bank in order to confirm the client's bank balance according to its own cash ledger account.

Examine: To investigate, to inspect, or to test accuracy. To illustrate: An invoice may be examined in order to assure the accuracy of prices, extensions, and footings.

Foot: To determine the accuracy of vertical subtotals and totals.

"Crossfoot" means to determine the accuracy of horizontal subtotals and totals.

Inspect, Scan, Scrutinize: To review and investigate, *without* complete verification. Complete verification would result in an unwarranted amount of work. To illustrate: Petty cash vouchers may be inspected for reasonableness.

Reconcile: To bring into agreement two separate and independent sets of related figures. To illustrate: The cash balance according to the bank statement may be reconciled with the cash balance according to the cash ledger account.

Test: To verify the accuracy of a *portion* of a total of similar data. To illustrate: The accuracy of every tenth sales invoice may be proved; postings to general ledger accounts may be proved for two nonconsecutive months of the year. If the results of the tests are satisfactory, the assumption is that other similar data will contain the same percentage of reliability.

Trace: To determine that an item is properly disposed of in accordance with original authority.

Verify: To prove accuracy. To illustrate: The accuracy of footings and posting from journals may be verified; the ownership of assets may be verified by proof of ownership.

Voucher: Any documentary evidence in support of a transaction. A voucher commonly is thought of as an authorization to disburse money; this is not true.

Vouching: The examination of underlying evidence which is in support of a transaction; or the substantiation of an entry by proving authority, ownership, existence, and accuracy.

SUGGESTED ADDITIONAL READING

Statement on Auditing Standards No. 1, Section 320 except Appendix A and B; Sections 640 and 641.

Statement on Auditing Standards No. 3.

QUESTIONS

1. What does a company plan to accomplish through its system of internal control?

2. Define administrative and financial internal control.

3. Upon what does the effective operation of a system of internal financial control depend?

4. What steps are involved in a conceptually logical approach to the auditor's evaluation of a system of internal control whose purpose is to prevent or detect material errors and irregularities in financial statements?

5. *a*)   At the outset of an audit, you reviewed the client's internal audit procedures and found them to be excellent. Does this indicate that a portion of your work is completed?

    b)   How does internal auditing assist the independent auditor?

    c)   Name several distinctive features of internal auditing.

6. What are the principal characteristics of a satisfactory system of internal control?

7. With regard to any given system of financial internal control, list five sources of evidence which are available to an independent auditor. State briefly how the evidence from each source can be used in the evaluation of the system of internal control.

8. An internal control questionnaire includes the items listed below. For each item, explain what is accomplished by the existence of the controls involved.

    a)   Are costs and expenses under budgetary control?

    b)   Is a postage-meter machine used?

    c)   Are statements of account mailed to all customers once each month?

    d)   Has the depository bank been instructed not to cash checks made payable to the order of the company?

9. You are auditing the financial statements of a corporation that manufactures men's suits. Sales are made by five salesmen to approximately 1,500 retail shops. Because of his familiarity with the trade, the sales manager has been asked to approve each order before shipment is made. In the case of past-due accounts, it will also be his responsibility to determine whether additional credit can be extended. Also, he will recommend the write-off of uncollectible accounts. One bookkeeper and two billing clerks handle the accounting records. As an auditor, in what way is your audit program affected by the credit procedures of this client?

10. Three people constitute the accounting staff of a small wholesale company. In addition to the three persons mentioned, two men are in the warehouse and two more are drivers of the company's delivery trucks. The warehousemen handle all goods coming in as well as assist the drivers in loading their trucks to make daily deliveries. In some instances, the drivers make collections before deliveries are permitted to be made. Outline a satisfactory system of internal control for cash. The cash receipts and disbursements are approximately $500,000 per year.

11. What types of payroll manipulations should an auditor look for as part of his internal control review?

12. The following questions relate to internal computer control:

    a)   How should changes in memory records of a fixed asset control account be handled?

    b)   What feature should be present when authorizing changes to master records?

    c)   What should computer operating personnel *not* do?

    d)   What records of movement of data should be accurately maintained by the data processing control group?

e) Since input controls are essential to internal control, what should the records control group in data processing possess?

f) Since output controls are of equal importance to internal control, what should the records control group in data processing possess?

g) What is a parity check?

h) What is the procedure when errors are made?

i) What is the procedure when control totals are programmed?

j) What should a register of data operations include?

13. The audit of the financial statements of a client that utilizes the services of a computer for accounting functions compels the CPA to understand the operation of his client's EDP system.

a) The first requirement of an effective system of internal control is a satisfactory plan of organization. List the characteristics of a satisfactory plan of organization for an EDP department, including the relationship between the department and the rest of the organization.

b) An effective system of internal control also requires a sound system of records control of operations and transactions (source data and its flow) and of classification of data within the accounts. For an EDP system, these controls include input controls, processing controls, and output controls. (Confine your comments to a batch-controlled system employing punched cards and to the steps that occur prior to the processing of the input cards in the computer.)

(AICPA, adapted)

14. What should an auditor's review of a client's system of accounting control encompass?

PROBLEMS

1. Indicate by number and letter the best answer for each of the following items which relate to internal control. Choose only one answer for each item.

(1) The best statement of the CPA's primary objective in reviewing internal control is that the review is intended to provide

a) Reasonable protection against client fraud and defalcations by client employees.

b) A basis for reliance on the system and determining the scope of other auditing procedures.

c) A basis for constructive suggestions to the client for improving his accounting system.

d) A method for safeguarding assets, checking the accuracy and reliability of accounting data, promoting operational efficiency, and encouraging adherence to prescribed managerial policies.

(2) A Company holds bearer bonds as a short-term investment.

Custody of these bonds and submission of coupons for interest payments normally is the responsibility of the

a) Treasury department.
b) Legal counsel.
c) General-accounting department.
d) Internal-audit department.

(3) Operating control of the check-signing machine normally should be the responsibility of the

a) General-accounting department.
b) Treasury department.
c) Legal counsel.
d) Internal-audit department.

(4) Matching a supplier's invoice, the purchase order, and the receiving report normally should be the responsibility of the

a) Warehouse-receiving department.
b) Purchasing department.
c) General-accounting department.
d) Treasury department

(5) A CPA learns that his client has paid a vendor twice for the same shipment, once based upon the original invoice and once based upon the monthly statement. A control procedure that should have prevented this duplicate payment is

a) Attachment of the receiving report to the disbursement support.
b) Prenumbering of disbursement vouchers.
c) Use of a limit or reasonableness test.
d) Prenumbering of receiving reports.

(6) To minimize the opportunity for fraud, unclaimed salary checks should be

a) Deposited in a special bank account.
b) Kept in the payroll department.
c) Left with the employee's supervisor.
d) Held for the employee in the personnel department.

(7) A responsibility that should be assigned to a specific employee and not shared jointly is that of

a) Access to the company's safe deposit box.
b) Placing orders and maintaining relationships with a prime supplier.
c) Attempting to collect a delinquent account.
d) Custodianship of the cash working fund.

(8) For control purposes the quantities of materials ordered may be omitted from the copy of the purchase order which is

a) Forwarded to the accounting department.
b) Retained in the purchasing department's files.
c) Returned to the requisitioner.
d) Forwarded to the receiving department.

(9) XYZ Company has an inventory of raw materials and parts consisting of thousands of different items which are of small value

individually but material in total. A fundamental control requirement of XYZ Company's inventory system is that

a) Perpetual inventory records be maintained for all inventory items.

b) The taking of physical inventories be conducted on a cycle basis rather than at year-end.

c) The storekeeping function not be combined with the production and inventory record-keeping functions.

d) Requisitions be approved by an officer of the company.

(10) The sales department bookkeeper has been crediting house-
account sales to her brother-in-law, an outside salesman. Commissions are paid on outside sales but not on house-account sales.
This might have been prevented by requiring that

a) Sales order forms be prenumbered and accounted for by the sales department bookkeeper.

b) Sales commission statements be supported by sales order forms and approved by the sales manager.

c) Aggregate sales entries be prepared by the general-accounting department.

d) Disbursement vouchers for sales commissions be reviewed by the internal audit department and checked to sales commission statements.

(AICPA, adapted)

2. The following eight functions are to be performed by three clerical employees of a client:

a) Maintain the general ledger.

b) Maintain the accounts payable ledger.

c) Maintain the accounts receivable ledger.

d) Prepare checks for signature.

e) Maintain the cash disbursements records.

f) Issue credits for returns and allowances.

g) Reconcile the bank account.

h) Handle and deposit cash receipts.

There is no problem regarding the ability of the three employees. You
are requested to assign the listed functions to the three employees in a
manner to achieve the highest degree of internal control. The three employees will perform no accounting functions other than those listed;
accounting functions not listed will be performed by other client personnel.

a) Distribute the listed functions among the three employees. Assume
that with the exception of the preparation of bank reconciliations
and the issuance of credits for returns and allowances, all functions
require an equal amount of time.

b) What are four unsatisfactory combinations of the listed functions?

(AICPA, adapted)

3. The board of trustees of a local church requests you to review its accounting procedures. As a part of this review you have prepared the

following comments relating to the collections made at weekly services and to the record-keeping for members' pledges and contributions:

a)   The board of trustees has delegated responsibility for financial management and audit of the financial records to the finance committee. This group prepares the annual budget and approves major disbursements but is not involved in collections or record-keeping. No audit has been considered necessary in recent years because the same trusted employee has kept church records and served as financial secretary for 15 years.

b)   The collection at the weekly service is taken by a team of ushers. The head usher counts the collection in the church office following each service. He then places the collection and a notation of the amount counted in the church safe. Next morning the financial secretary opens the safe and recounts the collection. He withholds $100 to meet cash expenditures during the coming week and deposits the remainder of the collection intact. In order to facilitate the deposit, members who contribute by check are asked to draw their checks to "cash."

c)   At their request a few members are furnished prenumbered predated envelopes in which to insert their weekly contributions. The head usher removes the cash from the envelopes to be counted with the loose cash included in the collection and discards the envelopes. No record is maintained of issuance or return of the envelopes, and the envelope system is not encouraged.

d)   Each member is asked to annually prepare a contribution pledge card. The pledge is regarded as a moral commitment by the member to contribute a stated weekly amount. Based upon the amounts shown on the pledge cards, the financial secretary furnishes a letter to requesting members to support the tax deductibility of their contributions.

Describe the weaknesses and recommend improvements in procedures for

a)   Collections made at weekly services.

b)   Record-keeping for members' pledges and contributions.

(AICPA, adapted)

4.   Morgan, a CPA, is examining the financial statements of the Cincinnati Sales Corporation, which recently installed an off-line electronic computer. The following comments have been extracted from Morgan's notes on computer operations and the processing and control of shipping notices and customer invoices:

a)   To minimize inconvenience Cincinnati converted, without change, its existing data processing system, which utilized tabulating equipment. The computer company supervised the conversion and has provided training to all computer department employees (except key punch operator) in systems design, operations and programming.

b)   Each computer run is assigned to a specific employee, who is responsible for making program changes, running the program and answering questions. This procedure has the advantage of elimi-

nating the need for records of computer operations because each
employee is responsible for his own computer runs.

c) At least one computer department employee remains in the computer room during office hours, and only computer department
employees have keys to the computer room.

d) System documentation consists of those materials furnished by the
computer company—a set of record formats and program listings.
These and the tape library are kept in a corner of the computer
department.

e) The Company considered the desirability of programmed controls
but decided to retain the manual controls from its existing system.

f) Company products are shipped directly from public warehouses
which forward shipping notices to general accounting, where a
billing clerk enters the price of the item and accounts for the
numerical sequence of shipping notices from each warehouse.
The billing clerk also prepares daily adding machine tapes ("control tapes") of the units shipped and the unit prices.

g) Shipping notices and control tapes are forwarded to the computer
department for key punching and processing. Extensions are made
on the computer. Output consists of invoices (six copies) and a
daily sales register. The daily sales register shows the aggregate
totals of units shipped and unit prices which the computer operator compares to the control tapes.

h) All copies of the invoice are returned to the billing clerk. The
clerk mails three copies to the customer, forwards one copy to the
warehouse, maintains one copy in a numerical file, and retains one
copy in an open invoice file that serves as a detail accounts receivable record.

Describe weaknesses in internal control over information and
data flows and the procedures for processing shipping notices and
customer invoices and recommend improvements in these controls
and processing procedures. Organize your answer sheets as follows:

Weakness	Recommended Improvement

(AICPA, adapted)

5. An audit of the records of the Tabor Company disclosed that the treasurer
was short in the Company cash in the amount of $15,000. The shortage
was concealed by increasing inventories $12,500 and land $2,500.

The treasurer pointed out deficiencies in internal control and admitted
the shortage. In restitution he offered to surrender the 150 shares of
the common stock of the company owned by him; the treasurer's stock
is to be surrendered at book value, after adjusting for the shortage. The
board of directors accepted the offer, with the agreement that the
treasurer would pay any deficiency from his other resources, and that
the corporation would pay the treasurer the excess of book value over
the shortage, if an excess existed. The treasurer's 150 shares, after being

acquired by the company, were distributed pro rata to the remaining stockholders.

As of the date of the preceding agreement, there were issued and outstanding 1,000 shares of $100 par value common stock, retained earnings were $40,000, and reserve for contingencies was $35,000.

a) What amount of money should the treasurer pay the company, or the company pay the treasurer?

b) Prepare the entries necessary to record all transactions.

c) What is the amount of the stockholders' equities—in detail and in total—after distribution of the stock of the treasurer?

6. Robat, Inc., became your client in 1976 when its former CPA died. You have completed your initial examination of the Robat, Inc., financial statements for the year ended December 31, 1976, and have prepared a draft of your audit report containing your unqualified opinion which was addressed to the board of directors according to instructions. In addition, you have drafted a special report in letter form outlining deficiencies in the system of internal control noted in the course of your examination and your recommendations for the correction of these deficiencies.

When your reviewed the drafts of these reports with Robat's president, he instructed you not to render the internal control letter. The president stated that he was aware the deficiencies existed and would give them his personal attention. Because he felt the board of directors should be concerned with major policy decisions and not with day-to-day management problems, the president believed the board should not be burdened with such matters.

a) What factors would you consider before deciding whether or not you should render the internal control letter?

b) If you decide to render the internal control letter to Robat, Inc., should it be rendered to the board of directors or to the president?

(AICPA, adapted)

7. Three separate features of the operating methods of the Fielding Company are described below. You are to point out (a) any existing weaknesses in internal control, including an explanation of possible errors or manipulations that might occur because of each weakness; and (b) recommendations for changes in procedure for the correction of each weakness.

a) When materials are ordered, a duplicate purchase order is sent to the receiving department. Upon receipt of the materials, the receiving clerk records the receipt on the duplicate purchase order and sends it to the accounting department to support the accounting entry. The materials are then taken to the storeroom where the quanity is entered on bin tags.

b) Time cards of employees are sent to a data processing center which prepared punched cards for use in the preparation of payrolls, payroll checks, and labor cost distribution records. The payroll checks are compared with the payrolls and signed by an official of the company, who returns them to the supervisor of the data processing center for distribution to employees.

c) A sales branch of the Company has an office force consisting of the branch manager and one assistant. The branch has a local bank account from which branch expenses are paid. The account is in the name of "Fielding Company, Special Account." Checks drawn on the account require the signature of either the branch manager or the company treasurer. Bank statements and paid checks are returned by the bank to the branch manager who reconciles the account and retains all materials in his files. Disbursement reports are prepared by the branch manager and submitted to the home office on scheduled dates.

(AICPA, adapted)

8. Select the best answer for each of the following items:

a) An auditor should be concerned about internal control in a data processing system because
   (1) The auditor cannot follow the flow of information through the computer.
   (2) Fraud is more common in an EDP system than a manual system.
   (3) There is usually a high concentration of data processing activity and control in a small number of people in an EDP system.

b) Control totals are used as a basic method for detecting data errors. Which of the following is not a control figure used as a control total in EDP systems?
   (1) Ledger totals.
   (2) Check-digit totals.
   (3) Hash totals.
   (4) Document-count totals.

c) Bell's accounts-payable clerk has a brother who is one of Bell's vendors. The brother will often invoice Bell twice for the same delivery. The accounts-payable clerk removes the receiving report for the first invoice from the paid-voucher file and uses it for support of payment for the duplicate invoice. The most effective procedure for preventing this activity is to
   (1) Use prenumbered receiving reports.
   (2) Mail signed checks without allowing them to be returned to the accounts-payable clerk.
   (3) Cancel vouchers and supporting papers when payment is made.
   (4) Use dual signatures.

d) Casper Company received a substantial sales return on December 30, 1976, but the credit memorandum for the return was not prepared and recorded until March 4, 1977. The returned merchandise was included in the year-end physical inventory taken on December 31, 1976. The most effective procedure for preventing this type of error is to

    (1)   Prepare an aging schedule of accounts receivable monthly.

    (2)   Prenumber and account for all credit memorandums.

    (3)   Reconcile the subsidiary accounts-receivable ledger with the general-ledger control account monthly.

    (4)   Prepare and numerically control receiving reports for all materials received.

e)   Smith Company's accounts-receivable clerk has a friend who is also Smith's customer. The accounts-receivable clerk has issued fictitious credit memorandums to his friend for goods supposedly returned. The most effective procedure for preventing this activity is to

    (1)   Prenumber and account for all credit memorandums.

    (2)   Require receiving reports to support all credit memorandums before they are approved.

    (3)   Have the sales department independent of the accounts-receivable department.

    (4)   Mail monthly statements.

f)   Which of the following is a responsibility that should not be assigned to only one employee?

    (1)   Access to securities in the company's safe-deposit box.

    (2)   Custodianship of the cash working fund.

    (3)   Reconciliation of bank statements.

    (4)   Custodianship of tools and small equipment.

g)   Salesmen's commissions are based on sales. Sales continue to increase; but uncollectible accounts receivable are also increasing at an alarming rate. The most effective procedure for preventing the increase in uncollectible accounts receivable is to

    (1)   Have the sales manager review activity of individual salesmen.

    (2)   Age accounts receivable regularly.

    (3)   Have the write-off of accounts properly approved.

    (4)   Have the credit department approve credit extended to customers before shipment.

h)   When evaluating internal control, the auditor's primary concern is to determine

    (1)   The possibility of fraud occurring.

    (2)   Compliance with policies, plans, and procedures.

    (3)   The reliability of the accounting information system.

    (4)   The type of an opinion he will issue.

i)   A sales clerk at Sweet Company correctly prepared a sales invoice for $5,200, but the invoice was entered as $2,500 in the sales journal and similarly posted to the general and receivable ledgers. The customer remitted $2,500, the amount on his monthly statement. The most effective procedure for preventing this type of error is to

    (1)   Use predetermined totals to control posting routines.

    (2)   Have an independent check sales-invoice serial numbers, prices, discounts, extensions, and footings.

    (3)   Have the bookkeeper prepare monthly statements which are

verified and mailed by a responsible person other than the bookkeeper.

(4) Have a responsible person who is independent of the accounts-receivable department promptly investigate unauthorized remittance deductions made by customers.

j) In evaluating internal control, the first step is to prepare an internal-control questionnaire or a flow chart of the system. The second step should be to

(1) Determine the extent of audit work necessary to form an opinion.

(2) Gather enough evidence to determine if the internal-control system is functioning as described.

(3) Write a letter to management describing the weaknesses in the internal-control system.

(4) Form a final judgment on the effectiveness of the internal-control system.

(AICPA, adapted)

9. You are the in-charge accountant examining the financial statements of the Blue Company for the year ended December 31, 1976. During late October 1976, you, with the help of Blue's controller, completed an internal-control questionnaire and prepared the appropriate memorandums describing Blue's accounting procedures. Your comments relative to cash receipts are as follows:

All cash receipts are sent directly to the accounts-receivable clerk with no processing by the mail department. The accounts-receivable clerk keeps the cash-receipts journal, prepares the bank-deposit slip in duplicate, posts from the deposit slip to the subsidiary accounts-receivable ledger, and mails the deposit to the bank.

The controller receives the validated deposit slips directly (unopened) from the bank. He also receives the monthly bank statement directly (unopened) from the bank and promptly reconciles it.

At the end of each month, the accounts-receivable clerk notifies the general-ledger clerk by journal voucher of the monthly totals of the cash-receipts journal for posting to the general ledger.

Each month, with regard to the general-ledger cash account, the general-ledger clerk makes an entry to record the total debits to cash from the cash-receipts journal. In addition, the general-ledger clerk on occasion makes debit entries in the general-ledger cash account from sources other than the cash-receipts journal, e.g., funds borrowed from the bank.

Certain standard auditing procedures, which are listed below, have already been performed by you in the audit of cash receipts. The extent to which these procedures were performed is *not* relevant to the question.

a) Totaled and cross-totaled all columns in the cash-receipts journal.

b) Traced postings from the cash-receipts journal to the general ledger.

c) Examined remittance advices and related correspondence to support entries in the cash-receipts journal.

Considering Blue's internal control over cash receipts and standard auditing procedures already performed, list all other auditing procedures and reasons therefor which should be performed to obtain sufficient audit evidence regarding cash receipts. Do not discuss the procedures for cash disbursement and cash balances. Also do not discuss the extent to which any of the procedures are to be performed. Assume adequate controls exist to assure that all sales transactions are recorded.

(AICPA, adapted)

4

Starting an Audit;
Audit Work Papers

PRELIMINARY ARRANGEMENTS

Prior to beginning any audit, certain preliminary arrangements must be worked out between the client and the auditor. To some extent the preliminary arrangements with a client depend on whether the examination is an initial or a repeat engagement. Working together, the client and the auditor plan the work in advance of the actual examination. Today, surprise audits are used only in instances required by legislation and in cases involving suspected fraud.

If the audit is a first engagement, the auditor should—

1. Study the client's business, obtain organization charts and work-flow charts, study the chart of accounts, prepare a schedule of all books and records, and visit the operating premises of the client.
2. Examine the client's system of internal control.
3. Examine the client's system of internal audit.
4. Examine the general plan of the accounting system in operation.
5. Ascertain the purpose for which the audit is to be made.
6. Ascertain the period to be covered by the audit.
7. Clear with the client such points as—
   a)   The confirmation of receivables.
   b)   The time of starting the examination.
   c)   Fees to be charged.
   d)   The preparation of tax returns.
   e)   Whether or not the client's records are to be closed prior to the start of the examination.

If the audit is a repeat engagement, work papers and correspondence of prior years should be reviewed.

Illustration 4–1

LETTER OF ENGAGEMENT CONFIRMATION

BENNETT & BENNETT

CERTIFIED PUBLIC ACCOUNTANTS

Carew Tower
Cincinnati, Ohio   45202

Members of the American
Institute of Certified
Public Accountants

December 1, 1976

The Board of Directors
Multi-Products, Incorporated
Cincinnati, Ohio   45212

Gentlemen:

This is to confirm our conversation of November 30, 1976, regarding the examination of the financial statements of Multi-Products, Incorporated, for the year ended December 31, 1976.

The examination will be made in accordance with generally accepted auditing standards and will include all procedures considered necessary for the rendition of our opinion regarding the fairness of the financial statements.

Our examination will include (1) a study of the system of internal control, (2) proper tests of the accounting records and other financial records, to the extent considered necessary, (3) the preparation of the federal income tax return, and (4) a review of the accounting system in operation.

Our fees for this examination are on the basis quoted to you earlier in writing.

In accordance with our agreement, you are to have customer statements ready for mailing on the morning of January 5, 1977; we will insert our confirmation requests and control the mailing. Also, you are to prepare a general ledger trial balance not later than February 1, 1977, together with schedules of prepaid insurance, fixed assets, and related depreciation accumulations.

We are to complete the examination not later than April 15, 1977.

Very truly yours,

Richard W. Bennett

Richard W. Bennett

RWB:JH

After the preliminary arrangements have been completed, a letter of confirmation (Illustration 4–1) (or a contract) should be sent to the client.

In either a new or a repeat examination, an auditor will prepare an engagement memorandum. This is retained in the auditor's permanent file. The purpose of an engagement memorandum is to initiate the work preparatory to the audit, to guide the auditor's firm personnel, and to cover all points discussed with the client during the preliminary arrangement. See Illustration 4–2.

A Client's Preparation for the Auditor. Many auditors request that the client prepare certain data and schedules prior to the start of the examination. If the auditor requests that the applicable data and schedules listed below be prepared prior to the start of the examination, time and money will be saved—*and the preparation of the following items properly is an internal function and not an external audit function.*

1. Trial balances
   a) General ledger, factory ledgers, private ledgers.
   b) Accounts receivable and accounts payable.
2. Cash
   a) Returned bank checks and bank statements.
   b) Bank reconciliations.
   c) Schedules of cash items in transit.
   d) Confirmation request to be mailed by the auditor.
3. Receivables
   a) Statements to customers, to be verified and mailed by the auditor.
   b) Aging schedules for receivables.
   c) Notes receivable and schedules of the notes.
4. Investments
   a) Schedules, by types, including current-year purchases and sales, and interest received and interest accrued.
5. Inventories
   a) Original inventory-count data.
   b) Inventory price schedules and total summaries.
   c) Sales price schedules.
6. Prepaid expenses
   a) Schedules of all prepaid items.
7. Fixed assets
   a) Schedule showing agreement of control and subsidiary records.
   b) Schedules of additions to and deductions from fixed assets, and all supporting documents.
   c) Analyses of depreciation accumulations, showing charges and credits.
   d) Analyses of repair and maintenance accounts.

Illustration 4–2

BENNETT AND BENNETT
Engagement Memorandum

Case No. *888*   Date *December 1, 1977*   Prepared by *Richard W. Bennett*

1. Client Name	*Multi-Products, Incorporated*
2. Address	*2525 Floral Avenue, Cincinnati, 45212*
3. Telephone	*631–2740*
4. Type of Business	*Hardware accessories manufacturing*
5. Conference with	*William B. Johnson, President*
6. Date and Place of Conference	*November 30, 1976; client's office*
7. Confirmation Letter Sent	*December 1, 1976*
8. Address the Report to	*The Board of Directors and Stockholders*
9. Period to Be Covered	*January 1, 1976, December 31, 1976*
10. Type of Examination	*General; system and internal control examination*
11. Statements to Be Prepared	*Usual; income tax returns*
12. Report Copies	*4 complete; 8 short-form*
13. Account to Be Charged	*Multi-Products, Incorporated*
14. Fee Basis per Seven-Hour Day	*Regular*
15. Estimated Man-Hours	*150*
16. Place of Audit	*2525 Floral Avenue*
17. Records Are in Charge of	*Eilene Hite*
18. Audit to Start	*January 5, 1977*
19. Report to Be Finished	*April 15, 1977*
20. Type and Date of Organization and Charter Number	*Ohio corporation; May 1, 1952; 64823*
21. Capital Stock Listed? Where?	*Not listed*
22. Registrar and Transfer Agent	*None–None*
23. Attorneys	*Tilbury and Tilton*
24. Name of Bank(s)	*First National*
25. Assigned to: Partner	*Richard W. Bennett*
Senior	*James Swaisgood*
Staff Assistant	*Nelson Woodruff*
26. Comments	*Investigate January 1, 1976 inventories*

  8. Current liabilities
- *a)*   Statements from creditors.
- *b)*   Schedules of notes and any collateral given.
- *c)*   Copies of all current-year tax returns prepared by the client.

  9. Long-term liabilities
- *a)*   Copies of bond indentures.
- *b)*   List of bond owners, if there is no trustee.
- *c)*   Schedules of interest payments and accruals.
- *d)*   Canceled bonds retired during the current period.

10. Corporate capital
- *a)*   Schedules of ownership of capital stock, by name and number of shares, if there is no transfer agent.
- *b)*   Analyses of charges and credits made to each noncapital stock proprietorship account during the year.

11. Profit and loss
- *a)*   Labor summaries and overhead distribution summaries.
- *b)*   Schedules of actual manufacturing expenses.
- *c)*   Analyses of expenses and revenues, as indicated by the auditor.

12. Miscellaneous
- *a)*   Copies of contracts, leases, and so on.

Initial Audit Actions. When an audit is started, it is important that client time is not wasted. Therefore the auditor in charge of an engagement should have assignment schedules prepared for himself and for all firm members who will participate in the engagement.

Without regard to the rank of the various members of an accounting firm, the following constitutes a listing of the work to be done in the early stages of an audit. The listing below is *not* intended to constitute a sequential order.

Examine the systems of internal control and internal audit.

Prepare—or prove—a general ledger trial balance.

Count cash on hand.

Prepare bank statement reconciliations.

Prepare a schedule of all books and records.

List notes receivable and notes payable.

Confirm receivables and payables.

Age receivables.

Examine articles of incorporation and amendments thereto, or the articles of copartnership.

Examine the code of regulations (bylaws) or the annual alterations thereto.

Examine the minutes of meetings of stockholders, directors, or partners.

Verify the accuracy of inventory records.

Verify security transactions.

Prepare insurance schedules.

Charging a Client

In order to change a client properly, an auditor must maintain time records for each member of his staff, for each client. Three commonly used methods of charging follow.

The Per Diem Basis. In this method the auditor establishes a daily or hourly charge rate for each member of his staff (or for each staff category), based upon a normal number of hours (assume seven) per day. Within one accounting firm the same per diem rate may not be used for all clients.

Today, the use of a per diem rate is only *one* factor in computing charges. Other factors include importance of the work, complexity, and results accomplished.

The Flat-Fee Basis. A flat fee, agreed to by the client and the auditor, is prearranged, provided unforeseen circumstances do not develop during the course of the examination.

The Maximum-Fee Basis. In this method, per diem rates or rates per hour are used, with the understanding that the cost of the engagement is not to exceed a prearranged maximum, provided unforeseen circumstances do not develop.

AUDIT WORK PAPERS

Objectives of Work Paper Preparation. A review of recent court cases involving the liability of CPAs for negligence, fraud, and conspiracy to defraud, and a review of the advice of legal counsel of the Institute and that of other attorneys definitely will indicate the importance of proper work paper preparation.

The initial statement may be made that the objectives of preparing audit work papers are to serve as the bases for audit decisions. Audit work papers constitute a record of the work the auditor considered necessary, how the work was performed, and the audit conclusions. Audit work papers are composed of all data compiled during the course of an independent audit and during the process of internal auditing. These data are in support of auditing standards and procedures followed and adhered to during the examination. Thus work papers support the scope and opinion in the audit report. If an audit program and internal control questionnaire are well designed, audit work papers will be logically and completely developed as any audit proceeds.

The normal approach to an audit is via an examination of internal control, the preparation of audit work papers, the examination of evidence, and the testing of transactions and tracing them through the records. The records may range from those manually prepared, machine prepared, and electronically prepared. In many instances, the start of the preparation of work papers may precede the examination of internal control, and the examination of evidence may lead to the preparation of work papers. An auditor no longer initially plunges directly into the detail of the composition of a client's accounts and remains preoccupied therewith. Audit work is professional, and a professional approach is used.

There are no "standard" forms for audit work papers. Each work paper should be designed to fit the audit situation under consideration. Any work paper of the prior year should serve only as a guide to the form of work paper to be designed for the current year. If the form of any work paper for the prior year is blindly followed, there will be no improvement in the contents of the work paper and there will be no improvement or advancement in the method of collecting audit evidence.

Purposes Served by Audit Work Papers

Audit work papers prepared by an auditor serve as the connecting link between the audit report and the client's records and data. In a sense, they constitute proof of the validity of the client's records and the audit report. Work papers also indicate the extent of reliance on the systems of internal control and internal audit, as indicated by comments concerning internal control and internal audit appearing on the various work papers. They also serve the auditor as sources of data reference in the oral discussion of business matters with the client. For years subsequent to their preparation, work papers assist an auditor in the solution of questions arising from various taxing units and government regulatory bodies. In the relatively rare event of legal action, work papers serve the auditor as proof of defense of position in cases involving negligence and fraud.

Another purpose of audit work papers is to provide a firm partner or a manager a basis for review of the field work of other firm members. The work papers serve as a guide for subsequent audits of the same client. Finally, if the records of a client are stolen, lost, burned, or altered, complete work papers will prove of value in record reconstruction.

Contents and Ownership

Briefly, the work papers accumulated in an audit engagement will include a pencil copy of the report and the financial statements; trial balance work papers; audit adjustments; schedules and analyses of assets, liabilities, capital, revenues, and expenses; confirmation data; a copy of the articles of incorporation (or copartnership) and amendments thereto; organization charts; excerpts from bylaws; copies of contracts; copies of lease agreements; copies of the minutes of meetings of the board of directors and the stockholders; reconciliations; tax returns; audit programs and internal control questionnaires; and many others, to be developed as this book progresses.

The work papers accumulated during the course of an independent audit are the property of the auditor. The ownership has been established by the court case of *Ipswich Mills* v. *Dillon* (260 Mass. 453), in 1927. There is no objection to an auditor giving a copy of any work paper to a client; however, a client cannot demand and receive work papers, thereby leaving the auditor with none.

In a court case, work papers may be offered by an auditor in evidence to establish the fairness of his opinion and the propriety of his audit. Also, they may be offered in evidence by a plaintiff to support his allegations. A court order can force an auditor to divulge the contents of his work papers.

Several jurisdictions have statutory laws specifically vesting work paper ownership in the accountant.

PRINCIPLES OF WORK PAPER PREPARATION

Skill and experience are necessary in the preparation of adequate work papers. In the preparation of work papers, if an auditor adheres to all accounting principles and to all auditing standards and procedures, and then submits his work papers to another accountant—and if the latter can prepare an audit report—the work papers have withstood all tests of excellent preparation.

The principles underlying the preparation of work papers by the auditor may be set forth as follows:

1. They must be competently prepared from the point of view of proper inclusion of material data.
2. Irrelevant (nonmaterial) data should not be included.
3. Data suporting any item in the report should be included.
4. Data which might (even remotely) be used in the future should be included.
5. Data necessary for the support of the correctness of the records and transactions should be included.
6. All work papers should be neatly prepared and must be accurate mathematically.
7. The work must be prepared ready to be filed on "sign-off" day.
8. All work papers must be dated and initialed.
9. Each work paper should contain a concise statement of the work performed in connection with the preparation of that paper.
10. The "suggestions for next year" should be better than those for last year.

During the course of an audit, all work papers must be protected, controlled, and then preserved. Responsibility for the preparation of each work paper must be allocated to each person engaged in the audit.

In order to identify responsiblity of preparation, as each individual work paper is completed, it must be signed and dated by the person preparing it. When a supervisor or a manager or a partner reviews each work paper, he will sign and date it.

Deficiencies in Work Papers

Audit work papers should be free of *all* deficiencies. However, deficiencies sometimes do exist. A *few* of these deficiencies (which really are deficiencies in the audit) are set forth below:

1. Lack of evidence that the system of internal control was investigated and was found to be adequate or inadequate.
2. Failure to note the clearance of points raised earlier in the audit.
3. Failure to describe the review of accounts not analyzed.
4. Negligence in indicating the auditing procedures followed.
5. Failure to cross-index audit adjustments.
6. Incomplete data for report preparation.
7. Omission of pricing bases for assets.
8. Failure to indicate a survey of depreciation policies.
9. Failure to obtain client certifications for inventories, liability inclusion, and future commitments.
10. Failure to indicate the work performed regarding transactions occurring after the balance-sheet date.
11. Failure to include notations regarding the closing of tax matters of prior years.
12. Failure to indicate a comparison of original cost and current market value or replacement cost for assets—when necessary.
13. Failure to clear noncash items from cash funds.
14. Failure to assemble and analyze confirmation request replies.

Audit Code Legend

During the course of an examination, an auditor will use many symbols or tick-marks of various shapes and sizes—and perhaps colors—both in the records of the client and in his personal work papers. Within each firm of accountants the tick-marks may or may not be standardized. If standardized, each mark has the same meaning for all of the firm members. A partial audit code legend is presented below:

√ Use in records of original entry to indicate comparison with an invoice or other appropriate document.

ʌ̣ Place under vertical totals to indicate footing.

√/ Place opposite amounts in ledger accounts to indicate the tracing of postings from records of original entry.

— Place under an amount in a record to indicate the last cur-rent-period item examined.

· In the check record, place beside each outstanding check amount to be listed in the bank reconciliation.

⊙ In the check record, place beside each amount for which the paid check was compared.

S Use in the trial balance to indicate that a schedule is to be prepared.

$ When the schedule, above, is completed, place a slant line through the S.

∧ When a comment has been investigated and accepted, or adjusted and accepted, use this inverted check mark.

There are many additional code legends. Frequently, more than one code legend is used in one place—for example, √ and ʌ̣.

A Complete Set of Work Papers

Chapter 1 contains an audit report for Multi-Products, Incorporated. All following work paper illustrations in this book bearing the title of Multi-Products, Incorporated, are for the same company and are in support of the audit report. If the internal control questionnaires of the appropriate following chapters, and the appropriate audit procedures to follow, and all Multi-Products, Incorporated, work papers were removed from the book, they would constitute a complete file for the examination of the financial statements of Multi-Products, Incorporated. (Purposely —due to differences of opinions of accountants—some cross-references and some audit comments in the work papers are omitted.)

All illustrations that are not a part of the Multi-Products, Incorporated, work papers bear the title, "The Blank Company."

Trial Balance Work Papers

Early in an audit, general-ledger trial balance work papers should be started. They cannot be completed until the audit is finished. Trial bal-ance work papers are started early in the examination in order to promote familiarity with the accounts, and in order to serve as a guide during the course of the examination. If a general-ledger trial balance is prepared early in the course of an audit or if an auditor uses a client-prepared trial balance, it may be said that he is working backward from client data to underlying supporting evidence.

The trial balance work papers for Multi-Products, Incorporated, are presented in Illustration 4–3. This work paper *is completed* in order to prevent repetition in a later chapter, and in order to show the completed product.

If desired, asset, liability, proprietorship, revenue, and expense accounts each could be placed on a separate sheet. This is advisable if the number of ledger accounts is large, or if functional sections of an audit are to be assigned to several staff members.

The Work Paper Number column refers to the individual work papers which are in support of the item in the trial balance. The Audit Adjustments columns are for the adjustments prepared by the auditor—not those prepared by the client. The Report Reclassification Data columns are used by the auditor to group or separate similar items for financial statement preparation purposes and to transfer balances within the work papers. For example, a client may charge sales returns directly to the Sales account, but if the total of the sales returns is to be shown separately in the income statement, the auditor would prepare a reclassification entry charging Sales Returns and crediting Sales. As another example, debit balances might exist in accounts payable and an auditor might prepare a report reclassification entry charging Accounts Receivable—Vendors and crediting Accounts Payable.

Leading Schedule Work Papers

Schedules are prepared in order to develop desired information and thereby reach audit decisions. A leading schedule, also known as a summary or top schedule, is one that summarizes similar or related items. (See Chapter 11 for examples of leading schedules for the fixed assets of Multi-Products, Incorporated.) Normally, the totals appearing on a leading schedule correspond with class totals in the financial statements.

Supporting Schedules

Supporting schedules—or analyses—substantiate, or carry the detail of, each item appearing in a related leading schedule. (See Illustration 11–9, Chapter 11.) On each supporting schedule there must be recorded—

1. The detail of the periodic debits, credits, and adjustments.
2. Audit adjustments and explanations thereof—if audit adjustments are required.
3. Questions raised concerning the item scheduled.
4. The conclusions reached for the item being scheduled.
5. A concise recital of the procedures followed in the examination.

Illustration 4–3

MULTI-PRODUCTS, INC.

Working Trial Balance: Assets, Liabilities, Capital, December 31, 1976

Work Paper No.	Acct. No.	Account Name	Balance per Audit December 31, 1975 Dr.	Balance per Audit December 31, 1975 Cr.	Clients' Records December 31, 1976 Dr.	Clients' Records December 31, 1976 Cr.
1		Petty cash fund	2000		2000	
2-3		First National Bank, checking	77602		48352	
4		Accounts receivable	186528		326176	
5		Allowance for doubtful accounts		17448		6406
6-7		Trade notes receivable	44000		74000	
6		Accrued interest receivable			690	
10		Cash surrender value life ins.	7926		7926	
18		Sinking fund investments	113050		116500	
12-13-14-18		Raw materials inventory	258294		259488	
15-18		Work-in-process inventory	111212		120604	
16-18		Finished goods inventory	166706		170880	
17-18		Factory supplies	12496		8700	
19		Prepaid insurance	9724		8926	
20		Land	90000		100000	
21		Building	840000		872400	
22		Accumulated depr., building		127892		145340
23		Machinery	558560		579560	
24		Accumulated depr., machinery		193952		251908
25		Office equipment	49300		53300	
25		Accumulated depr., office equip.		32986		38316
26		Patents	34000		34720	
27		Trade accounts payable		33728		69752
28		Notes payable, bank				40000
29		Income tax withheld		16428		19248
29-30		F.I.C.A. tax liability		730		1250
29		Federal unemployment tax liability		1756		2196
31		State unemployment tax liability		2842		3188
29		Accrued workmen's comp. insurance		1304		
27		Accrued interest payable		11200		8300
AJE		Accrued miscellaneous taxes		18534		20650
		Provision for federal income taxes	160000	187324	180000	
35		Bonds payable		500000		400000
36		Common stock		800000		800000
38		Paid-in capital		200000		200000
37		Retained earnings		452336		575274
37		Dividends	80000		100000	
		Net income		202938		
		Totals	2801398	2801398	3064222	2581828

Work Papers for Audit Adjustments

Audit adjustments are recorded in the following three places:

1. On the supporting schedule for the accounts being adjusted.
2. On the trial balance work papers.
3. On the audit adjustments work papers.

	Initials	Date
Prepared By	RW	2-27-77
Approved By	CF	2-28-77

Audit Adjustments Dr.	Cr.	Balance Sheet December 31, 1976 Dr.	Cr.	Report Reclassification Data		
	① 580	1420		A⟩ Cash on hand and in bank		49772
		48352		A⟩		
② 7 132	③ 4200	327300		B⟩ Receivables, gross	327300	
	④ 1808			Allowance	17690	
④ 1 808	⑤ 13092		17690	B	309610	
		74000		B Notes	74000	
		690		B⟩ Accrued interest	690	384300
⑥ 3 224		11150				
		116500				
⑦ 5 000		264488		C⟩		
		120604		C⟩ Inventories		562582
		170880		C⟩		
	⑦ 2090	6610		C⟩		
		8926				
		100000				
		872400				
⑧ 1 148			144192			
		579560		Accumulated depreciation		428480
⑨ 5 936			245972			
⑩ 720		54020				
			38316			
	⑪ 6130	28590				
	⑫ 5000		74752			
			40000			
			19248			
			1250			
			2196	Other liabilities		56380
			3188			
	⑬ 1548		1548			
			8300			
			20650			
		180000	201904	Federal income tax liability (AJE 15)	21904	
			400000	H: Current portion	-100000	
			800000			
			200000			
			575274	I⟩ Retained earnings	746284	
		100000				
			271010	I⟩ Net before taxes	472914	
24 968	34448	3065490	3 065490			

In normal journal entry form, the auditor writes up each audit adjustment on separate work papers entitled "Audit Adjustments." A full explanation must accompany each adjustment. Each adjustment is cross-indexed to its related supporting schedule. (Purposely, in order to save searching time for the reader, each adjustment is *not* cross-indexed to its related supporting schedule.) The adjustments are numbered consecu-

Illustration 4–3—Continued

MULTI-PRODUCTS, INCORPORATED

Working Trial Balance: Revenues, Expenses, December 31, 1976

Work Paper No.	Acct. No.	Account Name	Balance per Audit December 31, 1975 Dr.	Cr.	Clients' Records December 31, 1976 Dr.	Cr.
8		Sales		4 167 186		4 902 322
		Cost of Sales	2 985 164		3 569 110	
		Transportation-out	22 530		26 004	
33		Sales salaries	164 282		173 800	
		Travel expense	13 506		9 848	
		Advertising	80 460		91 062	
		General selling expense	36 842		34 412	
33		Administrative salaries	337 500		359 578	
25		Depreciation of office equip.	4 850		5 330	
5		Uncollectible accounts expense	8 436			
		Office supplies	5 350		4 280	
33		Office operating expense	12 572		15 304	
10-19		Insurance expense	9 160		9 292	
		Professional services	13 000		16 000	
29		Miscellaneous taxes	22 614		35 654	
29		F.I.C.A. tax expense	19 244		25 050	
29		Federal unemployment tax	1 908		2 196	
29		State unemployment tax	17 448		19 776	
29		Workmen's compensation insurance	2 468		1 418	
10		Life insurance expense	5 124		5 124	
6-10		Interest and dividend income		4 134		5 450
23		Profit and loss–fixed assets		1 400	3 840	
3-27-29		Interest expense	20 000		18 300	
		Totals, this page	3 782 458	4 172 720	4 425 378	4 907 772
		Totals, preceding page	2 801 398	2 801 398	3 064 222	
		Grand total	6 583 856	6 974 118	7 489 600	
		Net income before income taxes	390 262			
			6 974 118	6 974 118		
		Federal income taxes	187 324			
		Net income after income taxes	202 938			
			390 262			

tively, and the numbers should correspond with those in (1) the trial balance work papers and (2) the supporting schedules.

A copy of the audit adjustments is submitted to the client, to be formally journalized and posted by the client. (See Illustration 4–4 for the adjustments prepared by the auditor in the examination of the records of Multi-Products, Incorporated.) Report reclassification entries are not submitted to a client because they are used only by the auditor.

Extractions from Minutes Records

If the auditor can obtain a copy of the minutes of the meetings of stockholders, directors, important committees, and partners, he should

	Initials	Date
Prepared By	RW	2-27-77
Approved By	EF	2-28-77

Audit Adjustments Dr.	Audit Adjustments Cr.	Income Statement Dr.	Income Statement Cr.	Report Reclassification Data	Amount
(3) 4200	(2) 7132		4 905254	J: Detail for cost of sales:	
(7) 50	(8) 1148	3 570296		Inventories, January 1	536212
(7) 2090	(9) 5936			Raw materials purchased	2 525548
(11) 6130				Transportation-in	23372
		26004			3 085132
		173800		Inventories, December 31	555972
		9848			2 529160
(14) 1770		92832		Direct factory labor	674102
	(14) 1770	32642		Indirect factory labor	204600
		359578		Depr. of building	16300
		5330		Depr. of machinery	52020
(5) 13092		13092		Building maintenance	14470
(7) 368		4648		Machinery maintenance	20970
(7) 162	(10) 720	14746		Heat and power	24684
		9292		Factory supplies expense	24460
		16000		Patent amortization	9530
		35654			
		25050		Cost of sales	3 570296
		2196			
		19776			
(13) 1548		2966			
	(6) 3224	1900			
			5450		
		3840			
		18300			
29410	19930	4 437790	4 901704		
24968	34448	3 065490	3 065490		
54378	54378	7 503280	7 976194		
		472914			
		7 976194	7 976194		
		201904*			
		271010			
		472914		* See AJE 15	

mark in them the items that have a bearing on the audit. If the auditor is forced to extract data from the minutes records, he should extract only those data having a bearing on and related to the audit. Examples of data to be extracted include dividend declarations, fund borrowing and related interest rates, authorizations to acquire fixed assets, authorizations to increase or decrease or change the capital structure, pension plan authorizations and changes, and so on.

The minutes should be examined for periods subsequent to the date of the financial statements up to the date of concluding the audit, because events after the date of the balance sheet may have an effect on the fair presentation of the financial statements.

Illustration 4–4

MULTI-PRODUCTS, INCORPORATED
Audit Adjustments, December 31, 1976

AJE 1		
Office Operating Expense	162	
Cost of Sales (Machinery Maintenance)	50	
Office Supplies	368	
Petty Cash		580
To charge December, 1976, petty cash disbursements to 1976 operations.		
AJE 2		
Accounts Receivable	7 132	
Sales		7 132
Goods shipped to M Co.; not billed.		
AJE 3		
Sales	4 200	
Accounts Receivable		4 200
Returns, F Company, 1976		
AJE 4		
Allowance for Doubtful Accounts	1 808	
Accounts Receivable		1 808
To charge off the following accounts:		
B Company $58.00		
N Company 550.00		
U Company 1,200.00		
$1,808.00		
AJE 5		
Uncollectible Accounts Expense	13 092	
Allowance for Doubtful Accounts		13 092
Allowance increased; see Work Paper 4.		
AJE 6		
Cash Surrender Value of Life Insurance	3 224	
Life Insurance Expense		3 224
Adjustment of cash surrender value; see Work Paper 8.		
AJE 7		
Cost of Sales (Factory Supplies Expense)	2 090	
Factory Supplies Inventory		2 090
Supplies inventory adjusted to $6,610.		

Agenda Sheets

Unfinished audit matters, questions that require additional investigation, notations for items to be included in the audit report, and recommendations to be made to the client are placed on so-called Agenda sheets. As each item later is cleared, it should be ticked off on the agenda sheet.

Illustration 4–4—Continued

	Initials	Date
Prepared By	RW	2-27-77
Approved By	EF	3-29-77

AJE 8						
Accumulated Depreciation of Building	1	148				
Cost of Sales (Depreciation of Building)				1	148	
Correction, Work Paper 20.						
AJE 9						
Accumulated Depreciation of Machinery	5	936				
Cost of Sales (Depreciation of Machinery)				5	936	
AJE 10						
Office Equipment		720				
Office Operating Expense					720	
To capitalize on adding machine						
charged to expense.						
AJE 11						
Cost of Sales (Patent Amortization)	6	130				
Patents				6	130	
To adjust the Patents account to						
conform to the policy of total						
amortization at December 31, 1978.						
AJE 12						
Raw Materials Inventory	5	000				
Trade Accounts Payable				5	000	
Unrecorded invoice.						
AJE 13						
Workmen's Compensation Insurance	1	548				
Accrued Workmen's Compensation Ins.				1	548	
Accrual, last half of 1976.						
AJE 14						
Advertising	1	770				
General Selling Expense				1	770	
Distribution correction.						
AJE 15						
Provision for Federal Income Taxes	21	904				
Federal Income Tax Liability				21	904	
Remaining 1976 tax liability. Income						
tax for 1976, $201,904.00 (See Ill. 4-1)						
less amount paid--$180,000.00--during						
1976. See our file copy of the return						
(which is not in this text due to						
changing laws, code regulations, and						
rates.)						

Indexing Work Papers

Work papers must be indexed and cross-indexed. Indexing may take place either during or at the conclusion of an audit. Four methods of indexing are shown in Illustration 4–5. Method 4 is followed for Multi-Products, Incorporated, to the extent necessary for that company.

Illustration 4–5

	Method			
1	*2*	*3*	*4*	*Audit Report and Financial Statements*
1	A	AA	1	Audit Program and Internal Control Questionnaire
2	B	BB	2	Agenda
3	C	CC	3	Abstracts of Minutes
4	D	DD	4	Trial Balance Work Papers
5	*E*	*EE*	5	Audit Adjustments
5–1	E–1	EE–1	6	Audit Adjustments
5–2	E–2	EE–2	7	Audit Adjustments
6	*F*	*101*	8	Cash Summary
6–1	F–1	101A	9	Cash in Bank (First National)
6–2	F–2	101B	10	Bank Confirmation
6–3	F–3	101C	11	Petty Cash Fund
6–4	F–4	101D	12	Payroll Fund
7	*G*	*102*	13	Accounts and Notes Receivable and Related Allowances
7–1	G–1	102A	14	Accounts Receivable
7–2	G–2	102B	15	Notes Receivable
7–3	G–3	102C	16	Allowance for Doubtful Accounts
7–4	G–4	102D	17	Confirmation Data
8	*H*	*103*	18	Inventory Summary
8–1	H–1	103A	19	Raw Materials
8–2	H–2	103B	20	Work in Process
8–3	H–3	103C	21	Finished Goods
8–4	H–4	103D	22	Inventory Certificate
8–5	H–5	103E	23	Inventory Test Schedule
8-6	H–6	103F	24	Inventory Pricing Schedule
9	*I*	*104*	25	Prepaid Expense Summary
9–1	I–1	104A	26	Prepaid Insurance
9–2	I–2	104B	27	Interest Paid in Advance
10	*J*	*105*	28	Long Term Investment Summary
10–1	J–1	105A	29	Bonds
10–2	J–2	105B	30	Stocks
11	*K*	*106*	31	Fixed Asset Summary
11–1	K–1	106A	32	Office Equipment
11–2	K–2	106B	33	Factory Equipment
12	*L*	*107*	34	Depreciation Accumulation Summary
12–1	L–1	107A	35	Accumulated Depreciation of Office Equipment
12–2	L–2	107B	36	Accumulated Depreciation of Factory Equipment
13	*M*	*108*	37	Intangible Assets Summary
13–1	M–1	108A	38	Patents
14	*N*	*201*	39	Current Liability Summary
14–1	N–1	201A	40	Accounts Payable
14–2	N–2	201B	41	Taxes Withheld
14–3	N–3	201C	42	Federal Income Taxes
14–4	N–4	201D	43	Certificate of Liabilities

Illustration 4–5—Continued

Method				
1	*2*	*3*	*4*	*Audit Report and Financial Statements*
15	*O*	*251*	44	Bonds Payable
15–1	O–1	251A	45	Letter to Trustee
15–2	O–2	251B	46	Trustee's Certificate
16	*P*	*276*	47	Capital Summary
16–1	P–1	276A	48	Common Stock
16–2	P–2	276B	49	Paid-In Capital–Excess over Stated Value
16–3	P–3	276C	50	Retained Earnings
17	*Q*	*301*	51	Sales and Sales Returns
17–1	Q–1	301A	52	Sales and Sales Returns, Product 1 (Store 1)
17–2	Q–2	301B	53	Sales and Sales Returns, Product 2 (Outside Salesmen)
18	*R*	*401*	54	Direct Material Cost
19	*S*	*501*	55	Direct Labor Payroll Summary
19–1	S–1	501A	56	Direct Labor, Department 1
19–2	S–2	501B	57	Direct Labor, Department 2
20	*T*	*601*	58	Manufacturing Overhead Summary
20–1	T–1	601A	59	Supervision
20–2	T–2	601B	60	Factory Taxes
20–3	T–3	601C	61	Rent
20–4	T–4	601D, etc.	62	Etc.
21	*U*	*701*	63	Selling Expense Summary
21–1	U–1	701A	64	Salesmen's Commission
21–2	U–2	701B	65	Traveling Expense
21–3	U–3	701C	66	Sales Office Expense
21–4	U–4	701D, etc.	67	Etc.
22	*V*	*801*	68	Administrative Expense Summary
22–1	V–1	801A	69	Officers' and Office Salaries
22–2	V–2	801B	70	Depreciation of Office Equipment
23	*W*	*901*	71	Other Expense Summary
23–1	W–1	901A	72	Interest Expense
23–2	W–2	901B	73	Sales Discount
24	*X*	*951*	74	Other Revenue Summary
24–1	X–1	951A	75	Interest and Dividend Revenue
24–2	X–2	951B	76	Miscellaneous

Filing Audit Work Papers

Audit work papers commonly are divided into (1) the permanent file and (2) the current file.

The Permanent File. Normally, the permanent file includes data and all papers retained over two years. The purposes of the permanent file are as follows:

1. To provide a financial history of the business.
2. To provide reference for recurring items.
3. To reduce work paper preparation for items that have not changed since the preceding examination.
4. To segregate and organize specialized data for subsequent audits, for tax examinations, for changes in capital structure, and so forth.

The contents of the permanent file are as follows:

1. A general information sheet, similar to that appearing in Illustration 3–3.
2. A copy of the latest articles of incorporation and amendments thereto; a copy of the code of regulations; for a partnership, a copy of the partnership agreement.
3. Copies of trust agreements, important contracts, pension plans, profit-sharing plans, union agreements, and so forth.
4. Copies of securities registration statements and stock-listing applications.
5. Copies or *important* excerpts of the meetings of stockholders, directors, and major committees.
6. Organization charts.
7. A chart of accounts.
8. A copy of the client's current accounting manual.
9. Engagement memorandums.
10. Internal control questionnaires and audit programs.
11. Copies of federal, state, and local tax returns—for as long as necessary.
12. Lists of plants, offices, and stores.
13. Schedules of noncurrent accounts.
14. Copies of audit reports.

At least the following items should be removed from the permanent file and *destroyed:* monthly financial statements not needed at the completion of an annual audit, outdated descriptions of client procedures, outdated flow charts, superseded documents, and obsolete client forms.

The Current File. The current file consists of all papers, data, and correspondence accumulated during the dates intervening between fiscal periods. The current file will contain at least the following:

1. Engagement memorandum—current and next engagement.
2. Internal control questionnaire and audit program.
3. Correspondence.
4. New contracts, charter changes, minutes extractions, and so on.
5. Trial balance work papers.
6. Leading and supporting schedules.
7. Audit adjustments, and perhaps closing and reversing entries.
8. Notes on unfinished work—agenda sheets.
9. The audit report, financial statements, and tax returns.
10. Time and expense reports.

Periodically, the following items may be moved from the current to the permanent file: charter changes, changes in the code of regulations, minutes, contracts, correspondence, tax returns, and special items.

Preservation of Audit Records

Among accountants, there is no rigid uniformity of agreement in regard to preserving or destroying audit records. If audit records are destroyed in accordance with the expiration of the period of legal liability, local and federal statutes of limitations should be consulted. For variations in practice, see *Management of an Accounting Practice* (*MAP 19*) issued by the AICPA in 1963. The following preservation schedule represents the practices of one national firm of certified public accountants for a continuing client:

1. Retain permanently:
   a) A typed copy of each audit report.
   b) The up-to-date internal control questionnaires and audit programs; destroy all that are not current.
   c) Work papers necessary to validate a client's financial statements.
   d) Summaries of fixed assets and related depreciation accumulations.
   e) Analyses of all capital accounts.
   f) Tax returns; data in direct support of tax returns may be destroyed after final clearance with the taxing authorities; clearance notices should be retained.
   g) In-force data filed with the SEC.
   h) Correspondence judged to be of a permanent nature.
   i) Active contracts and trust agreements.
   j) Up-to-date lists of key personnel.
   k) The current accounting manual, chart of accounts, organization chart, plant lists, articles of incorporation and amendments thereto, and samples of stock certificates and active bonds.
2. Retain for 10 years:
   a) Copies—or excerpts—of minutes.
   b) Detailed analyses of fixed assets.
   c) Detailed analyses of revenue and expense accounts.
   d) Expired contracts.
   e) Reports prepared by affiliated accountants.
3. Retain for five years:
   a) Agenda sheets.
   b) Engagement memorandums and time expense reports.
   c) Bank reconciliations and the related confirmation requests replies.
   d) Trial balances of receivables and payables.
   e) Confirmation request replies for receivables and payables.
   f) Analyses of prepaid expenses and deferred credits.
   g) Inventory data.
4. Retain for two or three years:

    a)   Routine correspondence.

    b)   Extra copies of typed reports.

    c)   Rough-draft reports.

SUGGESTED ADDITIONAL READING

Statement on Auditing Standards No. 1, Section 338.

QUESTIONS

1.   *a*)   After preliminary arrangements are made with a client, would it be proper to confirm accounts-receivable balances prior (assume one month) to the close of the fiscal period? Present reasons for your answer.

    b)   What might be some (if any) of the advantages in the audit process if the procedure in (*a*) was followed?

2.   Prepare an engagement letter which differs from Illustration 4–1 in the text. Make either your own assumptions or those given by your instructor.

3.   *a*)   As an audit progresses, the auditor obtains data from several sources. These data and other materials are incorporated in the work papers. List six general classifications of the content of work papers which are normally prepared in the course of an annual audit and give an example of each classification. In classifying the content, consider the source of evidence and the auditor's activities.

    b)   Prepare a list of types of work papers you would expect to find in an ordinary annual audit.

                                                      (AICPA, adapted)

4.   Are all audit adjustments prepared by an auditor submitted to the client for transcription into its records?

5.   *a*)   In an audit work paper, why is a brief recital of the work performed of importance?

    b)   What are the purposes of a work paper entitled "Notes to Be Cleared"?

6.   A small manufacturing company is your client. Describe a method of filing your work papers, taking into consideration everything from your formal report to the most insignificant—but necessary—memorandum.

7.   *a*)   What are the ultimate objectives in preparing audit work papers?

    b)   For what purposes are audit work papers prepared and preserved?

8.   At the conclusion of an engagement, the client demands your work papers. What position will you take?

9.   At the conclusion of an audit, you submitted to the client a work paper containing the audit adjustments necessary for the correction of the accounts. The client admitted their correctness but refused to record them in his accounts. What would be the effect of this refusal (*a*) on the audit report and (*b*) on the succeeding audit?

10. You are to audit the financial statements of a company for the year ended December 31, 1976. The company manufactures and sells special-order machinery. The company was incorporated January 3, 1970. The records have never been examined by an independent accountant.

For the accounts listed below, prepare an outline of the work you would perform with respect to the balances of these accounts as of January 1, 1976, based upon the application of recognized principles of accounting. The accounts are:

a) Inventories.

b) Machinery (and the related accumulated depreciation).

c) Accounts Payable.

11. After the first annual audit, a client asked why it was necessary to retain all the work papers prepared during the course of the examination. What answer would you give?

12. Name the informational categories which should be maintained in the permanent file of work papers rather than in the file of work papers for the current annual examination of the records of a corporation.

PROBLEMS

1. You are meeting with the board of directors of the Spring Company to arrange your firm's engagement to examine the company's financial statements for the year ending December 31, 1976. One executive suggested that the work be divided among three audit personnel so that one would examine assets, a second would examine liabilities and capital, and the third would examine revenue and expense accounts, in order to minimize time, avoid duplication of effort, and reduce interference with company operations.

Advertising is the company's largest expense, and the advertising manager suggested that a member of your staff whose uncle owns the advertising agency which handles the company's advertising be assigned to audit the advertising expense account. The staff member has a thorough knowledge of the complex contract between the company and the advertising agency.

a) To what extent should a CPA follow a client's suggestion for the conduct of a audit? Discuss.

b) List and discuss the reasons why audit work should not be assigned solely according to asset, liability and capital, and revenue and expense categories.

(AICPA, adapted)

2. You have been engaged to examine the financial statements of Kalb, Inc., for the year ended December 31, 1976. The former CPA firm declined to accept the engagement because a son of one of the CPA firm's partners received a material amount of Kalb common stock in exchange for engineering services rendered to Kalb, Inc., in 1976. The CPA firm's partner whose son received the stock has never participated

in the Kalb audit. Another of the CPA firm's 20 partners would have been in charge of this engagement.

In the past the audit report was discussed at the annual stockholders' meeting. Because of the shortage of time before the stockholders' meeting early in 1977, Kalb directors are willing to accept (*a*) your report containing unaudited financial statements and (*b*) your final report after the audit is completed. At a later date the client would like to receive (*c*) A report containing a forecast of the corporation's operations for 1977 and 1978.

a)   Should the former CPA of Kalb, Inc., have declined the examination for the year ended December 31, 1976? Discuss.

b)   Discuss the issues involved in the client's request that you render unaudited financial statements prior to the rendition of your final report.

c)   What are the issues involved for a CPA in rendering a report containing forecasts of a client's operations? Discuss.

(AICPA, adapted)

3.   You have been engaged to examine the financial statements of Reef, Inc., for the year 1976. The accountant who maintains the financial records has prepared all financial statements since the organization of the company, January 2, 1974. You discover numerous errors in these statements. The client has asked you to compute the correct income for the three years 1974 through 1976 and to prepare a corrected balance sheet as of December 31, 1976.

In the course of your examination you discover the following:

(1)   Sales taxes collected from customers is included in the Sales account. When sales tax collections for a month are remitted to the taxing authority on the 15th of the following month, the Sales Tax Expense account is charged. All sales plus sales taxes for 1974 through 1976 were $495,430, $762,200, and $924,940, respectively. The totals for the Sales Tax Expense account for the three years were $12,300, $21,780 and $26,640.

(2)   Furniture and fixtures were purchased January 2, 1974, for $12,000 but none of the cost has been charged to depreciation. The corporation wishes to use the straight-line method for these assets which have been estimated to have a life of ten years and no salvage value.

(3)   In January 1974 installation costs of $5,700 on new machinery were charged to Repairs Expense. Other costs of this machinery of $30,000 were correctly recorded and have been depreciated using the straight-line method with an estimated life of ten years and no salvage value. Current estimates are that the machinery has a life of 20 years, a salvage value of $4,200 and that the sum-of-the-years-digits method would be most appropriate.

(4)   An account payable of $8,000 for inventory purchased on December 23, 1974, was recorded in January 1975. This inventory not included as such on December 31, 1974.

(5)   Inventory costing $6,550 was not included in the December 31, 1975, inventory, and inventory costing $2,180 was included twice in the December 31, 1976, inventory. The periodic inventory method is used.

(6)   A check for $1,895 from a customer, on account, was received December 30, 1974, but was recorded January 2, 1975.

(7)   Dividends of $2,500 have been declared near the end of each calendar quarter since the corporation was organized, and the accountant has consistently recorded all dividends at the date of payment which is the 15th of the month following declaration.

(8)   At December 31, 1974, sales catalogues advertising a special January 1975 sale were on hand but their cost of $1,360 was included in Advertising Expense for 1974.

(9)   When the 500 shares of outstanding stock having a par value of $100 were initially issued on January 2, 1974, the $55,000 cash received was credited to the Common Stock account.

(10)   The corporation has used the direct write-off method for bad debts. Accounts written off during each of the three years amount of $1,745, $2,200, and $5,625, respectively. The corporation has decided that the allowance method would be more appropriate. The estimated balances for the Allowance for Doubtful Accounts at the end of each of the three years are: $6,100, $8,350, and $9,150.

(11)   On January 2, 1975, $100,000 of 6 percent 20-year bonds were issued for $98,000. The $2,000 discount was charged to Interest Expense. The corporation records interest only on the interest payment dates of January 2 and July 1.

(12)   A pension plan adopted January 2, 1976, includes a provision for a pension fund to be administered by a trustee. The employees who joined the corporation in 1974 and 1975 were given credit for their past service. A payment of $25,000 for the full amount of these past service costs was made into the fund immediately. A second payment of $15,000 was made into the fund near the end of 1976. However, actuarial computations indicate that pension costs attributable to 1976 are $16,600. The only entries applicable to the pension fund made during 1976 were debits to Pension Expense and credits to Cash. The corporation wishes to make the maximum annual provision for pension cost in accordance with generally accepted accounting principles.

Prepare a work paper showing the computation of the effects of the errors upon income for 1974, 1975, and 1976, and upon the balance sheet as of December 31, 1976. The work-sheet analysis should be presented in the same order as the facts are given with corresponding numbers.

(AICPA, adapted)

4.   You have been assigned to complete the examination of the 1976 financial statements of a client because the senior and a staff accountant who started the engagement were hospitalized. The engagement is about

one half completed, and the audit report must be delivered in three weeks in accordance with your firm's agreement with the client. You estimate that by utilizing the client's staff to the greatest possible extent you can complete the engagement in five weeks. Your firm cannot assign an assistant to you.

The work papers show the following status of work on the audit:

(1)   *Completed:* Cash, fixed assets, depreciation, mortgage payable, and stockholders' equity.

(2)   *Completed except as noted later:* Inventories, accounts payable, tests of purchase transactions, and payrolls.

(3)   *Nothing done:* Trade accounts receivable, inventory receiving cutoff, price testing, accrued expenses, unrecorded liability test, tests of sales transactions, payroll deduction tests, observation of payroll distribution, review of operations, preliminary audit report, internal control investigation, minutes, tax returns, procedural recommendations for management, subsequent events, supervision, and review.

Your review discloses that the staff accountant's work papers are incomplete and were not reviewed by the senior. For example, the inventory work papers contain only incomplete notations, incomplete explanations, and no cross-references.

a)   What standards of field work were violated by the senior who preceded you? How were the field work standards you listed violated?

b)   In planning your work to complete this engagement you should examine work papers and schedule certain work as soon as possible and also identify work which may be postponed until after the audit report is submitted to the client.

(1)   List the areas on which you should work first, that is, for your first week, and for each item explain why it deserves early attention.

(2)   State which work could be postponed until after the report is rendered to the client and present reasons why the work may be postponed.

(AICPA, adapted)

5.   You have been engaged to prepare corrected financial statement figures for Hows, Inc. The records are in agreement with the following balance sheet:

HOWS, INC.
Balance Sheet
December 31, 1976

Assets		*Liabilities and Capital*	
Cash	$11,000	Accounts payable	$10,000
Accounts receivable	11,000	Notes payable	3,000
Notes receivable	13,000	Common stock	20,000
Inventory	25,000	Retained earnings	27,000
	$60,000		$60,000

A review of the records indicates that the following errors and omissions had not been corrected during the applicable years:

December 31	Inventory Overstated	Inventory Understated	Prepaid Expense	Prepaid Income	Accrued Expense
1973	$ —	$6,000	$900	$ —	$200
1974	7,000	—	700	400	75
1975	8,000	—	500	—	100
1976	—	9,000	600	300	50

The net income according to the records is: 1974, $7,500; 1975, $6,500; and 1976, $5,500. No dividends were declared during these years, and no adjustments were made to retained earnings.

Prepare a work sheet to develop the corrected net income for the years 1974, 1975, and 1976, and the adjusted balance sheet items as of December 31, 1976. (Ignore income taxes.)

(AICPA, adapted)

6. Tom Zero, a retailer, kept poor records. You are to prepare an income statement for the year ended December 31, 1976. Support your statement with the necessary work papers and computations. Use the accrual method.

Inventory purchases were paid for by checks, but the costs of most other items were paid out of cash receipts. No record was kept of cash in bank or of sales. Accounts receivable were recorded only by keeping a copy of each invoice, and this copy was destroyed when the customer paid. Weekly, all cash on hand was deposited in the bank.

Zero started business January 2, 1976, with $10,000 cash and a building which cost $27,000, of which $6,000 was the value of the land. The building had an estimated useful life of 25 years and an estimated salvage value of $1,000. By analyzing the bank statements, it was possible to ascertain the following information:

Total deposits, $163,400 (excluding original investment of $10,000 cash and land, and building of $27,000).

Bank balance, December 31, 1976, $12,100.

Checks paid by the bank in January 1977, but dated in December 1976, amounted to $3,500. Cash on hand, December 31, 1976, $1,590.

An inventory taken on December 31, 1976, showed $18,000 at cost. Unliquidated customers' invoices totaled $1,270, but $170 of that amount is not collectible. Unpaid supplier's invoices for merchandise amounted to $5,500. During the year, Zero borrowed $10,000 from his bank but repaid by check $5,100, including $5,000 principal. He had taken $9,600 from the cash collections to cover personal expenses. Business expenses paid in cash were as follows:

Advertising	$ 500
Part-time help	3,600
Supplies	925
Utilities	680
Taxes	675

Store fixtures with a list price of $7,000 were purchased on January 5, 1976, on an installment basis. During the year, checks for the down payment of $1,000 and all maturing installments totaled $5,700. At December 31, 1976, the final installment of $1,500 remained unpaid, plus interest of $50. The fixtures have an estimated useful life of ten years and an estimated salvage value of $1,000. Use a full year in computations for depreciation; the straight-line method is to be followed.

5

Evidence; Original Record Examination; Statistical Sampling

EVIDENCES, TRANSACTIONS, AND ORIGINAL RECORDS

Original evidences refer to such data as purchase requisitions, purchase orders, vendors' invoices, receiving reports, paid checks, sales orders, sales invoices, cash register tapes, punched paper tape, duplicate bank-deposit tickets, minutes of directors, and so on. As pointed out earlier, evidence may be in existence at the time an audit is started, it may be created during the course of an audit, or it may be the result of logical deduction. See preceding chapters for the types of audit evidences.

Original records refer to all journals and ledgers, punched cards, and all other financial and nonfinancial documents that have an effect on the financial accounting. The examination of original evidences and records of original entry has a direct effect on the verification of all financial statements, because account balances are the result of entries made in the records of original entry. The examination of original evidences and original records must adhere to recognized audit procedures—to be developed in this chapter.

The examination of evidence, transactions, and original records involves detailed work which must be performed. Prior to the examination of original records and underlying evidences, the system of internal control must be evaluated and an internal-control questionnaire should be prepared. Then an audit program for the examination of original records and underlying evidences should be developed. Many audits are approached (after the examination of internal control) by the examination of original evidences and original records, simply because this constitutes a logical work-flow approach.

In auditing, it is a recognized practice to examine evidence in support of financial transactions; consequently the assumption is to the effect that recorded financial data are in a condition which may be verified. On the assumption that an examination of a portion of the transactions and their recording will reveal a given percentage of error, an examination of *all* transactions and their recording should reveal approximately the same percentage of error. Therefore, if internal control is satisfactory, the examination of transactions and their recording is limited to a portion of the total. Testing is a recognized auditing standard. If an auditor is not satisfied with the results of his test for any given array of data, he must extend the amount of the testing until he is satisfied or until he is convinced that errors exist which are of sufficient magnitude to force him to disclaim an opinion.

SAMPLE SELECTION AND TESTING

The purposes of sampling and testing are (1) to arrive at conclusions concerning the acceptability or nonacceptability of a population, (2) to assure the accuracy of conclusions regarding any area of the financial records, (3) to serve as a basis regarding an audit decision concerning the fairness of the presentation of the financial statements, and (4) to accelerate an audit operation.

Sampling is based on the theory of probabilities. In using statistically designed samples, an auditor must exercise judgment in defining and establishing the areas of accounts, entries, and documents from which he will select his samples. Also, a preaudit decision must be made regarding the percentage of error to be tolerated in any sample; if the results of a sample examination exceed the established percentage of error, additional samples must be drawn and tested until the population is accepted or rejected.

Characteristics of a Sample. Every sample must be adequate, representative, and must show stability.

An adequate sample is one which contains a sufficient number of items to show the same examination results that would be found if another sample—or other samples—of the same size were selected from the same population.

A representative sample possesses characteristics similar to all of the data in the particular population. In accordance with the theory of probability, a sample selected at random assumedly should be sufficiently representative of the population.

A sample shows stability when the results of examining the sample remain the same even if the sample size is increased.

Three problems arise in determining the size of a sample; they are: (1) the extent of error to be allowed in the results of the sample test, (2) the precision desired in estimating the extent of error through the sampling process, and (3) the risk of being misled by the sample data.

Types of Samples

In auditing there are several types of samples, each of which is briefly discussed in the following sections. In using *any* sample plan, there must be specified in advance (1) a satisfactory quality level for the data being examined, (2) the established satisfactory quality level's risk of leading to the rejection of a satisfactory population, (3) an unsatisfactory quality level for the data being examined, and (4) the established quality level's risk of being led to the acceptance of an unsatisfactory population.

Judgment Sample. A *judgment* sample is one wherein the items (of a population) to be examined are selected on the basis of the auditor's judgment. For example, after surveying the inventory purchases, an auditor believes that the month of March is representative of those purchases; therefore, vendors' invoices and all related data and entries for the month of March are examined. As another example, an auditor might decide to verify the original data and the recording of every 25th sales invoice.

Block Sample. A *block* sample is one selected on the basis of consecutive time, with a total verification of all items in the block. For example, one month's cash disbursements may be examined; one week's payroll calculations may be verified. The block may be selected on the basis of judgment, or it may be selected at random.

Unrestricted Random Sample with Replacement. An *unrestricted random sample with replacement* is one in which each item in a population has an equal chance of becoming a part of the sample selected. All remaining items have an equal chance of being chosen as the second item in the sample, and so on, until the sample total is accumulated. When an unrestricted random sample is selected, there must be no preference or lack of preference which would tend to include or exclude any datum in the population. Many accounting data are good for random sampling, and a random sample is a good sample if the data are subject to random selection. The unrestricted random method of selecting a sample may be used for verification of inventory count-and-price sheets, paid checks, sales invoices, and for many other items.

For statistical analysis, only unrestricted random samples can be used because the limits of errors in making final decisions can be computed statistically. Acceptable and unacceptable error limits must be established in advance of the examination in order to determine the acceptance or rejection of the results of the sample. If the examination results of a sample are unsatisfactory, additional samples may be selected until an acceptance or rejection level is reached. As already stated, in order to apply mathematical formulas to a sample, that sample must be random, it must be free from predetermined prejudice, and it must be representative of the population. Therefore, all items in the population must be homogeneous. This basic principle is applicable to the majority of accounting data and transactions; there are exceptions, as indicated by the inconclusive results emanating from a random sample of general journal entries.

Various methods may be used in selecting an unrestricted random sample. One method is to use a published table of random numbers. When selecting a random sample from a table of random numbers, it is necessary that all items in the population be numbered and that all items are available for possible selection. In many cases, the items in the population already bear serial numbers—prenumbered sales invoices or paid checks and the like. A beginning number in a random number table is selected as a starting point; and in accordance with the predetermined number of items to be selected, the random numbers necessary to complete the sample are determined. Random numbers may be selected from a random number table in any order and in any direction within the table—consecutively, every second number, every third number, crosswise, or in any other predetermined systematic pattern. When random numbers are used in selecting a sample, all items in the population must be assigned numbers in sequence.

Accounting population items normally not bearing assigned numbers are entries in any type of journal, postings, footings, extensions on invoices, and extensions on inventory count-and-price sheets. How to apply random number selection to consecutively unnumbered items may be illustrated as follows: A cash receipts record contains 30 full pages for the year under examination. Each page is 25 lines deep with one entry per line; this represents 750 cash receipts debits for the year. The preaudit decision was that 10 percent or 75 items are to be examined in detail. Seventy-five random numbers are selected from a random number table. One drawn number is 352; this would be the second item on cash receipts journal page 15 ($352 \div 25$ items = 14 pages + 2 lines) or ($25 \times 14 + 2 = 352$).

Every nth item may be the basis for selecting a sample—not totally random. For example, from a sales invoice population of 3,000 items, 150 items (5 percent) are to be examined for complete verification. Then, from a random number table, on the basis of a sampling ratio of 5 percent, a number between 1 and 20, inclusive, is drawn; if this number is 4, the sample will be drawn as item 4, 24, 44, 64, etc., of the sales invoices.

Unrestricted random samples may be drawn on the basis of a single sample, a double sample, a multiple sample, or a stratified random sample. A single sample involves the drawing of only one sample. A double sample plan exists when only a portion of the entire sample is drawn and examined; if the examination results are satisfactory, the remainder of the sample is not drawn; if the examination results are not satisfactory, the remainder of the sample is drawn and examined. A multiple sample is an extension of the double sample. A sample is divided into two subsamples; the first subsample is drawn and examined, and immediately thereafter a decision is reached whether to accept or reject the population, or to continue sampling. A stratified random sample is one selected on the basis of subdivisions of the population into subclasses. From *each* subclass, a single random sample is drawn and examined. The results of the examination of all of the subclasses are combined, and a conclusion may be formed regarding the quality of the population. Stratified random sampling is applicable to the examination of any items when those items may be subdivided by dollar-size, product, type of customer, and so on. For example, stratified random sampling applied to the confirmation of accounts receivable may be illustrated as follows:

Account Balance	Total Dollars	Confirmation Requests (percentage)	Confirmation Requests (dollars)	Dollar Amount Confirmed	Percentage Confirmed
$ 0.01-$ 99.99 ..	$124,800	5%	$ 6,240	$ 4,492	72%
100.00- 499.99 ..	63,000	10	6,300	5,040	80
500.00- 999.99 ..	113,400	25	28,350	26,648	94
1,000.00- 9,999.99 ..	89,600	75	67,200	40,320	60
10,000.00-largest	191,000	100	191,000	156,620	82
	$581,800		$299,090	$233,120	80%

Sampling for Attributes

A variable is a characteristic which may vary within a range of values and would probably be represented numerically. An accounts receivable control account balance would be an example of a variable. Attributes are usually associated with the rate of occurrences of certain specific characteristics of a population. The percentage of the client's sales invoices that contain extension errors is an example of an attribute.

Certain steps must be followed in order to sample attributes successfully:

1. The sampling objectives must be defined.
2. The size of the sample must be determined.

Illustrations 5–1 and 5–2 are so constructed that they represent cumulative binomial distribution and assume that an unrestricted random sample will be drawn with replacement. If these tables are to be used by the auditor, he will be required to be precise in the definition of the sampling problem. He must therefore establish the upper precision limit, the required confidence level, and the estimate of the sample occurrence rate if he is to arrive at a satisfactory sample size.

Looking at Illustrations 5–1 and 5–2 more closely, it can be seen that round numbers are infrequent in the precision limit percentages. Since the auditor would think in round numbers, he would select the number closest to his set precision limit percentage which would give him the

Illustration 5–1
DETERMINATION OF SAMPLE SIZE
Percentage of Occurrences in Sample; Reliability (confidence level): 95 Percent

Sample Size	1	2	3	4	5	6	7	8	9	10	12	14	16	18	20	25	30	35	40	45	50
50						0	0	0	0	2.0		4.0	6.0	8.0	10.0	14.0	18.0	22.0	26.0	32.0	36.0
60					0	0	0	1.7	1.7		3.3	5.0	6.7	8.3	10.0	15.0	18.3	23.3	28.3	33.3	38.3
70					0	0	1.4		2.9	2.9	4.3	5.7	7.1	10.0	11.4	15.7	20.0	24.3	28.6	34.3	38.6
80				0	0	1.2		2.5		3.8	5.0	6.2	8.8	10.0		16.2	20.0	25.0	30.0	35.0	40.0
90				0	0		2.2		3.3	4.4	5.6	6.7	8.9	10.0	12.2	16.7	21.1	25.6	30.0	35.6	40.0
120			0	.8	.8	1.7	2.5	3.3	4.2	5.0	6.7	8.3	10.0	11.7	13.3	17.5	22.5	27.5	31.7	36.7	41.7
160		0	.6	1.2	1.9	2.5	3.1	3.8	5.0	5.6	7.5	8.8	10.6	12.5	14.4	18.8	23.8	28.1	33.1	38.1	43.1
240		.4	.8	1.7	2.5	3.3	4.2	5.0	5.8	6.7	8.3	10.0	11.7	13.8	15.4	20.0	24.6	29.6	34.6	39.2	44.2
340	0	.6	1.2	2.1	2.9	3.5	4.4	5.3	6.2	7.1	8.8	10.6	12.4	14.4	16.2	20.9	25.6	30.6	35.3	40.3	45.3
460	0	.9	1.5	2.4	3.3	3.9	4.8	5.7	6.7	7.6	9.3	11.1	13.0	14.8	16.7	21.5	26.3	31.1	36.1	40.9	45.9
1000	.4	1.2	2.0	2.9	3.8	4.7	5.6	6.5	7.4	8.4	10.2	12.1	14.0	15.9	17.8	22.7	27.5	32.4	37.4	42.3	47.5

more conservative results. For example, using the 95 percent confidence level table and desiring a 5 percent precision limit and a 3 percent occurrence rate, he would select the 3.5 percent as his occurrence rate and a sample size of 460. Thus, if the occurrence rate selected does not appear in the table, he would move down to the next higher value.

ILLUSTRATION. To continue with the preceding sales invoice problem where a sample size of 120 sales invoices was established, the auditor would

Illustration 5–2
DETERMINATION OF SAMPLE SIZE
Percentage of Occurrences in Sample; Reliability (confidence level): 90 Percent

Sample Size	1	2	3	4	5	6	7	8	9	10	12	14	16	18	20	25	30	35	40	45	50
50						0	0	0	2.0	2.0	4.0	6.0	8.0	10.0	10.0	16.0	20.0	24.0	30.0	34.0	38
60					0	0	0	1.7	3.3	3.3	5.0	6.7	8.3	10.0	11.7	16.7	21.7	25.0	30.0	35.0	40
70					0	0	1.4		2.9	4.3	5.7	7.1	8.6	11.4	12.9	17.1	21.4	25.7	31.4	35.7	41
80				0	0	1.2		2.5		3.8	5.0	6.2	7.5	10.0		17.5	22.5	27.5		36.2	
90				0	0		2.2		3.3	4.4	6.7	7.8	10.0	12.2	13.3	17.8	22.2	27.8	32.2	36.7	4
120		0	0	.8	1.7	2.5	3.3	4.2	5.0	5.8	7.5	9.2	10.8	12.5	14.2	19.2	24.2	28.3	33.3	38.3	4
160		0	.6	1.2	2.5	3.1	3.8	5.0	5.6	6.2	8.1	10.0	11.9	13.8	15.6	20.0	25.0	29.4	34.4	39.4	4
240	0	.4	1.2	2.1	2.9	3.8	4.6	5.4	6.2	7.1	8.8	10.8	12.5	14.6	16.2	20.8	25.8	30.8	35.4	40.4	4
340	0	.9	1.5	2.4	3.2	4.1	5.0	5.9	6.8	7.6	9.4	11.2	13.2	15.0	17.1	21.8	26.5	31.5	36.2	41.2	4
460	.2	.9	1.7	2.6	3.5	4.3	5.2	6.1	7.2	8.0	9.8	11.7	13.7	15.4	17.4	22.2	27.0	32.0	37.0	41.7	
1000	.5	1.3	2.2	3.1	4.0	4.9	5.9	6.8	7.7	8.7	10.6	12.5	14.4	16.4	18.3	23.2	28.0	33.0	37.9	42.9	

now use an unrestricted random sample procedure to select the 120 sales invoices to be audited for extension errors. His audit of these sales invoices reveals the following extension errors:

$$
\begin{aligned}
\text{Invoice No. S6321} \ \ldots \ \ & 10 \text{ items @ } \$10 = \$110 \\
& 5 \text{ items @ } 20 = \ 110 \\
\text{Invoice No. S7943} \ \ldots \ \ & 5 \text{ items @ } 20 = \ 10
\end{aligned}
$$

Since the auditor is seeking to determine the percentage of sales invoices containing errors, he has found two invoices that contain errors. As far as sampling the attribute of sales invoices containing errors is concerned, he is not interested with the size or value of the error in this procedure. The auditor must now evaluate the results to determine whether or not he can state with 95 percent confidence that the population does not contain an occurrence rate of sales invoices containing extension errors in excess of 5 percent.

Illustrations 5–3 and 5–4 are available to answer this problem. These tables can be found in *Supplementary Section 2—Sampling for Attributes* as published by the AICPA's Professional Development Division.

Taking Illustration 5–3 and going down the Sample Size column to 120 and across the page to the 10 percent Precision (upper limit) Percentage column, it will be seen that a number of sales invoices (6) could contain errors. Since two invoices were found to contain errors, the auditor can state with confidence that the population does not contain an occurrence rate of sales invoices containing errors in excess of 5 percent.

Today many CPA firms have computer programs developed which assist in more rapidly selecting the unrestricted random numbers, determine

Illustration 5–3
EVALUATION OF RESULTS
Number of Occurrences in Sample; Reliability (confidence level): 95 Percent

Sample Size	Precision (upper limit) Percentage																				
	1	2	3	4	5	6	7	8	9	10	12	14	16	18	20	25	30	35	40	45	50
						0				1	2	3	4	5		7	9	11	13	16	18
				0				1			2	3	4	5	6	9	11	14	17	20	23
				0				1		2	3	4	5	7	8	11	14	17	20	24	27
			0			1		2		3	4	5	7	8	9	13	16	20	24	28	32
			0			1	2	3		4	5	6	8	9	11	15	19	23	27	32	36
			0	1	2	3	4	5		6	8	10	12	14	16	21	27	33	38	44	50
		0	1	2	3	4	5	6	8	9	12	14	17	20	23	30	38	45	53	61	69
		1	2	4	6	8	10	12	14	16	20	24	28	33	37	48	59	71	83	94	106
	0	2	4	7	10	12	15	18	21	24	30	36	42	49	55	71	87	104	120	137	154
	0	4	7	11	15	18	22	26	31	35	43	51	60	68	77	99	121	143	166	188	211
	4	12	20	29	38	47	56	65	74	84	102	121	140	159	178	227	275	324	374	423	473

Illustration 5–4
EVALUATION OF RESULTS
Number of Occurrences in Sample; Reliability (confidence level): 90 Percent

Sample Size	\multicolumn{21}{c}{Precision (upper limit) Percentage}

Sample Size	1	2	3	4	5	6	7	8	9	10	12	14	16	18	20	25	30	35	40	45	5
50					0				1		2	3	4	5		8	10	12	15	17	1
60			0					1		2	3	4	5	6	7	10	13	15	18	21	2
70			0		1			2		3	4	5	6	8	9	12	15	18	22	25	2
80		0		1		2		3	4		5	6	8	9	10	14	18	22	25	29	3
90		0		1	2			3	4		6	7	9	11	12	16	20	25	29	33	3
120		0		1	2	3	4	5	6	7	9	11	13	15	17	23	29	34	40	46	5
160		0	1	2	4	5	6	8	9	10	13	16	19	22	25	32	40	47	55	63	7
240	0	1	3	5	7	9	11	13	15	17	21	26	30	35	39	50	62	74	85	97	10
340	0	3	5	8	11	14	17	20	23	26	32	38	45	51	58	74	90	107	123	140	15
460	1	4	8	12	16	20	24	28	33	37	45	54	63	71	80	102	124	147	170	192	21
1000	5	13	22	31	40	49	59	68	77	87	106	125	144	164	183	232	280	330	379	429	47

the sample size, offer a choice of confidence levels, accept selected error rate in the universe, recognize the desirable sample reliability selected, and immediately indicate the sample size, and print out the unrestricted random numbers to be used.

Stratified Random Sampling

In many respects, stratified random sampling is similar to the technique of unrestricted random sampling. The primary difference is that the population is divided into two or more groups, each of which is sampled separately and then combined to give an estimate of the total population value.

ILLUSTRATION. Your client is a manufacturer of sewing machines and it has been decided to take a stratified random sample to estimate the total inventory in the hands of the franchised dealers. It is desired to have a precision of 8,000 sewing machines at the 95 percent confidence level. On the basis of data obtained from the prior audit, the following information is developed:

Stratum	Number of Dealers	Amount of Variance from Mean
1 (1 to 9 sewing machines)	10,000	16
2 (10 to 19 sewing machines)	1,500	49
3 (20 to 29 sewing machines)	500	81
4 (30 to 39 sewing machines)	300	144

The auditor desires the greatest precision in this situation so he chooses the optimum sampling method. (Proportional sampling method could be used, but this would require more samples.)

The first step is to determine the total number of dealers whose inventory will be taken. This may be illustrated as follows:

Σ = sum of
n = total sample size
Nh = number of dealers in specific stratum
Sh^2 = variance from mean in each stratum in the past
V = desired total variance $(4,000)^2$
nh = number of dealers in each stratum that will be audited

$$n = \frac{(\Sigma Nh \cdot Sh)^2}{V + (\Sigma Nh \cdot Sh^2)}$$

Nh	$Sh = \sqrt{Sh^2}$	$Nh \cdot Sh$
10,000	$\sqrt{16} = 4$	40,000
1,500	$\sqrt{49} = 7$	10,500
500	$\sqrt{81} = 9$	4,500
300	$\sqrt{144} = 12$	3,600
12,300		58,600

Nh	Sh^2	$Nh \cdot Sh^2$
10,000	$\sqrt{16}$	160,000
1,500	$\sqrt{49}$	73,500
500	$\sqrt{81}$	40,500
300	$\sqrt{144}$	43,200
12,300		317,200

$$n = \frac{(58,600)^2}{(4,000)^2 + 317,200} = \frac{3,433,960,000}{16,317,200} = 211 \text{ dealers}$$

After determining the size of the dealer sample, the auditor must calculate the number of dealers to be audited in each stratum nh. This is done as follows:

$$nh = \frac{Nh \cdot Sh}{58,600} \times 211$$

$Nh \cdot Sh$		nh
40,000	$\dfrac{40,000}{58,600} = 68\% \times 211 =$	143

$$10,500 \qquad \frac{10,500}{58,600} = 18\% \times 211 = \qquad 38$$

$$4,500 \qquad \frac{4,500}{58,600} = 8\% \times 211 = \qquad 17$$

$$3,600 \qquad \frac{3,600}{58,600} = 6\% \times 211 = \qquad 13$$

$$\overline{58,600} \qquad\qquad\qquad\qquad\qquad\qquad \overline{211}$$

The inventory was then taken, based upon an unrestricted random selection of the dealers in each stratum, and the following results were obtained.

Stratum	Mean Sewing Machines per Dealer in Each Stratum	Actual Sewing Machine Variance from Mean in Each Stratum
1	4	14
2	9	38
3	25	85
4	36	130

New symbols must now be established for determining actual audit results.

Yh = mean sewing machines per dealer in each stratum.
Si^2 = actual sewing machines variance from mean in each stratum.
N = Total inventory.

The estimate of the total sewing machine inventory would be calculated as follows:

$$N = Yh \cdot Nh$$

Stratum	yh	Nh	N
1	4	10,000	40,000
2	9	1,500	13,500
3	25	500	12,500
4	36	300	10,800
			$\overline{76,800}$

It is now desirable to determine the precision attained; in other words, $\sqrt{V}$ must be calculated.

$$V = \Sigma Nh \cdot (Nh - nh) \cdot \frac{Si^2}{nh}$$

$$\sqrt{V} = \text{precision obtained}$$

Stratum	Nh	nh	Si^2	$Nh-nh$	$\dfrac{Si^2}{nh}$	$Nh \cdot (Nh\text{-}nh) \cdot \dfrac{Si^2}{nh}$
1	10,000	143	14	9,857	.10	9,857,000
2	1,500	38	38	1,462	1.00	2,193,000
3	500	17	85	483	5.00	1,207,500
4	300	13	130	287	10.00	861,000
	12,300	211				14,118,500

$$V = 14,118,500$$
$$\sqrt{V} = 3,757$$

It can be seen that the requirements of 95 percent confidence level of 8,000 sewing machines, $\pm$ 4,000, were met.

The final requirement would be to determine if the auditor over or under sampled. The following calculation must be made so that the auditor can be assured the inventory figure arrived at is reliable. Therefore,

$$n = \frac{(\Sigma Nh \cdot Si^2)}{V + (\Sigma Nh \cdot Si^2)}$$

Stratum	Nh	Si	$Si = \sqrt{Si^2}$	$Nh \cdot Si$	$Nh \cdot Si^2$
1	10,000	14	3.74	37,400	140,000
2	1,500	38	6.16	9,240	57,000
3	500	85	9.21	4,605	42,500
4	300	130	11.40	3,420	39,000
				54,665	278,500

$$n = \frac{(54,665)^2}{(4,000)^2 + 278,500} = \frac{2,988,262,225}{16,278,500} = 184$$

The auditor could have sampled 184 dealers rather than 211, or he has over-sampled by 12+ percent.

Systematic Sample

A systematic sample is prepared by selecting every nth item beginning with a random start. This procedure does not require a sample of a given size, nor does it require that every possible sample of that size is equally likely to be drawn. The auditor can also vary the sample interval if he so desires. The auditor's knowledge of the population being sampled would be a significant factor in using this sampling technique upon which he would base a conclusion.

Cluster Sample

Instead of drawing individual sample items, the auditor (in cluster sampling) would select groups of contiguous sample items. For example, using a random number table, select two pages within the check register and audit all checks on those pages. A possible disadvantage to this method is that a group of contiguous checks might be for similar expenditures and therefore the sample may not provide adequate coverage of the range of expenditures.

Selection of Sampling Method

The sampling method that produces the desired results with the least work and at a minimum of cost should be used in the examination of any area. Each audit problem has its own peculiarities, and unnecessary procedures should not be adopted which will produce no better results in the measurement of data quality than are obtainable by the use of simpler plans.

The amount of sampling and testing in any area is dependent upon the system of internal control and internal audit, the relative importance of any item, and the preaudit determined acceptance quality levels. In sampling and testing, it is desirable to establish the reliability of the greatest possible dollar values in any accounting area. Random sampling of any kind usually produces a better "pattern" than does block sampling, provided the data in the population are easily subject to random sampling. There is no reason for not using a block sample if the block is representative of the population. Also, a combination block and random sample may be used; for example, a sales register may be examined for one solid month, combined with a simple random sample of sales invoices for the remaining 11 months of the year, accompanied by tracing the random-selected sales in voices into the sales register.

MECHANICAL FEATURES OF AUDITING

The mechanical and routine features of an audit are centered principally in the examination of transaction data and the recording of those data in the accounting records. Mechanical and routine work is necessary in order to obtain reliable evidence and proof of accuracy. Mechanical and routine features primarily involve proof of extension accuracy, proof of footing accuracy, proof of posting accuracy, vouching and verification of transactions, preparation of reconciliations, and analyses of accounts.

Proof of Extension Accuracy

Proof of extension accuracy involves multiplications on invoices, payroll records, and other vouchers. The objective of proving extension accuracy should be that the largest possible dollar accuracy is proved with a minimum of work. Prices and quantities must be expressed in the same units. To illustrate: If 120 items priced at $1 per dozen were extended as

$120, the error would be $110; or if ten dozen items priced at $1 each were extended as $10, the error would be $110. Also, misplaced decimal points will result in incorrect extensions.

In testing the accuracy of the extensions on sales invoices and vendors' invoices, the auditor may select every (assume) tenth invoice; or he may select all invoices in excess of a stated amount—$500 or $1,000. He might then scan the extension accuracy of every (assume) 20th invoice showing a total of less than $500.

In testing the accuracy of extensions on payroll calculations, the auditor may select the complete periodic payroll data for approximately 10 percent of the total number of employees, followed by scanning the extension accuracy for *not more* than an additional 5 percent. Or he may select payroll data at random for all employees for a number of weeks of the year and prove the accuracy of extensions.

In testing the accuracy of inventory extensions, the auditor may decide to verify all extensions of $1,000 or more, followed by random tests of approximately 10 percent of the extensions of $1,000 or less. Or he may select every fifth item on an inventory count-and-price sheet, or on a computer printout. By the examination of both large and small extension amounts, errors that overprice an inventory will be revealed in the examination of large amounts and errors that underprice an inventory will be revealed in the examination of small amounts.

Proof of Footing Accuracy

Proof of footing accuracy involves vertical and horizontal additions. Depending upon the system of internal control, records of original accounting entry should be footed for one, two, or three nonconsecutive months of the year. The month or months may be varied each year. Another plan is to foot the last page of all journals for all months of the year on the theory that if dishonesty exists, the pages bearing totals to be posted will be altered. In footing, many auditors omit the cents columns on the premise that the cents columns will vary from $0.00 to $0.99, that the average will be $0.50, and that if a page is 40 lines deep, the maximum error could not exceed a few dollars.

There is no substitute for the proof of footing accuracy. If an employee suspects the test plan of the auditor, he may risk fraudulent practices in the months or on the pages which he believes the auditor will not prove, with the hope that the fraud will not be discovered. Consequently, the auditor should not indicate the pages or periods footed.

Each general-ledger account not to be analyzed should be footed, and the account balance should be extracted. This is necessary in order to determine account balance accuracy, in order to detect malpractices, and in order to tie together journals and ledgers. To illustrate: A person stole $1,000 from total cash sales of $10,000 in the last month of the year. The cash receipts record for the month was debited for $10,000, and sales were credited for $10,000; the postings were made to the two general-ledger accounts in the same amount—$10,000. The cash and the sales general-ledger accounts then were underfooted $1,000 each. Therefore, the bank reconciliation will appear to be proper. Only by footing the accounts could the fraud be discovered.

Proof of Posting Accuracy

Posting accuracy should be verified in the same proportion as original record footings are proved. The postings are traced from the records of original entry to the ledger accounts or, if desired, from the accounts to the records of original entry.

Two persons working together speed up the work of proving posting accuracy if one person with a journal calls journal data to the person with the ledger.

Corrections of postings are placed on the audit adjustment work papers. If there is a tendency to ignore the postings of small amounts to incorrect accounts, the total of the incorrect account postings and their total materiality and significance on the financial statements must be judged. If an auditor is in doubt concerning the correction of incorrect account postings, he should follow the policy of correction.

Examination of Vouchers Supporting Transactions

The purposes of examining original evidential papers and data supporting transactions are:

1. To determine that the vouchers are properly authorized and approved.
2. To determine that the vouchers are for proper purposes.
3. To determine that the amounts of the vouchers are correct.
4. To determine that the vouchers are properly entered in the records.

In the examination of vouchers and all underlying documents, the objective of the auditor is to verify the largest possible dollar amount of any set of data. Even though he will not examine all of the vouchers, an auditor should request access to all vouchers of each class.

The following schedule shows the various types of vouchers and the normally related records of original entry:

Voucher Name	*Probable Original Record*
Journal voucher	General journal
Minutes (directors and stockholders)	General journal; cash records
Duplicate bank deposit tickets and/or customer remittance lists	Cash receipts records
Paid bank checks	Cash disbursements records
Petty cash vouchers	Cash disbursements (or vouchers payable) records

Payroll checks . . . . Payroll records
Expense reports . . . . Cash disbursements (or vouchers payable)
        records
Creditors' invoices . . . . Purchase records; voucher register
Creditors' debit memorandums   Purchase returns record; voucher register
Sales invoices . . . . Sales records (or journals)
Customers' debit memorandums . . . . Sales returns records

AUDIT PROGRAM FOR VOUCHER EXAMINATION

An audit program for the examination of original evidential papers may be introduced as follows:

1. Examine the system of filing each class of voucher.
2. Account for all numbers for consecutively prenumbered documents.
3. Decide upon a sample: unrestricted random, block, or combination, in accordance with the data to be examined—their type, quality, importance, and filing.
4. Draw the sample and all related data.
5. Compare the date, name, and amount of each sample voucher with the corresponding data appearing in the original accounting record.
6. Verify the numerical computations on the sample vouchers.
7. Verify approval for accounting record entry, payment, receipt of goods, or other purposes.
8. Examine voucher distribution for correct department or account classification.
9. Investigate "duplicate" vouchers in order to determine that duplicate accounting entries were not made.
10. Reconcile minutes of the board of directors with the accounting entries arising therefrom, in accordance with the vouchers.
11. Trace each document in the sample to its record of original accounting entry—individually or summarized— and tick off.

Sample Selection

For *illustrative purposes only,* assume that a test program requires an examination of approximately 17 percent (2 months out of 12) of one type of voucher—for example, sales invoices. Normally, *if internal control is satisfactory, a 17 percent examination of routine transactions is high;* but for illustrative purposes *some* assumption must be made, and this sample size is not intended for universal use. It is then decided that—

1. If a block sample is to be used:
   Select the vouchers for two nonconsecutive months. The two months may be selected at random; or use the last month of the fiscal year

and draw the other month at random. Then examine and authenticate the sample items in accordance with items 5–11, above.

2. If an unrestricted random sample is to be used:
    Draw a random sample of 17 (exactly, 16⅔) percent of the vouchers, based upon a table of random numbers; or if a random number table is not used, start with an *n*th number selected at random (from a deck of cards, for example) and continue in that sequence until the total sample is drawn. Then examine and authenticate the sample items in accordance with items 5–11, page 147.

3. If a combination block and unrestricted random sample is to be used:
    Select the vouchers for one month (assume the last) of the period, plus a random sample of 7 percent of the vouchers from the remaining 11 months. Then examine and authenticate the sample items in accordance with items 5–11, page 147.

The techniques of the preceding methods of sample selection are applicable to *any type of original documentary data.* In accordance with the predetermined plan of sample selection, the auditor draws the sample to be verified. The client is *not* informed of the sample selected, and the auditor consequently locates all papers of a particular type from which the sample will be drawn and examined.

INTERNAL CONTROL FOR SALES AND SALES RETURNS

Cash Sales. Proper internal control over cash sales involves separation between the duties of making sales and receiving cash. Cash sales made by each business organization pose a different problem for purposes of internal control. Preferably, a salesperson should not receive cash but should either prepare a sales ticket or ring the amount of the sale on a register. The person who receives the cash then rings the amount on a separate register; the daily totals of the two registers should be in agreement. If a salesperson prepares a sales ticket, one copy is given to the customer, one is given to the cashier, and one is retained by the salesperson. Thus a cross-check is obtained between the sales force and the cashiers. In many instances the salesperson records the sale on a visible cash register, which ejects a receipt to be given to the customer; the customer may pay the salesperson or a central cashier. If goods sold bear a removable tag, the total of the daily removed tags should equal the total of the cash register readings or the sales slips for the same day.

Credit Sales. Credit sales may or may not involve the preparation of sales orders. If a sales order is prepared, it must be approved by the sales and the credit department. If a sales order is not prepared, a sales invoice is immediately prepared: One copy is given to the customer, and one copy is sent to the accounting department. Later, when the customer remits, the salesperson must not be permitted to receive the remittance. If merchandise is to be shipped, a copy of the sales order (or the invoice) is sent to the shipping department, which compares the merchandise with the sales order (or the invoice), adds necessary transportation charges, and returns its copy of the sales order (or invoice) to the billing department, together with a copy of the shipping report.

The billing department prepares the final sales invoice. The original is sent to the customer. A copy may be filed with the customer's order, and another copy is sent to the accounting department.

Sales Returns and Allowances. Neither the accounting department nor the cashier should approve credits for returns and allowances. Returned sales should be routed through the receiving department or an adjustment department. False credit memorandums may result in cash thefts. Credit memorandums for returned goods must be accompanied by authorizations to the receiving department to accept the items.

An internal control questionnaire in Illustration 5–5 is established for

Illustration 5–5

INTERNAL CONTROL QUESTIONNAIRE
Sales and Sales Returns

	Yes	No	Not Appli-cable	Remarks
Company_____ Period Covered_____				
1. Are sales orders properly controlled?				
2. Are orders from customers approved by the sales department?				
3. Are orders approved by the credit department?				
4. Is the credit department independent of the sales department?				
5. Are sales orders consecutively prenumbered by the printer?				
6. Are all sales orders accounted for?				
7. Are sales orders matched with sales invoices?				
8. Are back orders properly controlled?				
9. Are shipments made on proper authority?				
a) Are shipping advices prenumbered?				
b) Are shipping advices matched with the items of sales invoices?				
c) Does the billing department receive a copy of the shipping advice directly from shipping?				
10. Is there simultaneous preparation of the following:				
a) Invoice?				
b) Shipping advice?				
c) Inventory requisition?				
11. Are sales invoices consecutively prenumbered by the printer?				
12. Are voided sales invoices retained?				
13. Are all sales invoices accounted for?				
14. Are sales invoices examined for:				
a) Credit terms granted?				
b) Quantities billed versus quantities shipped?				
c) Prices, extensions, and footings?				
15. Are sales proved independently of the accounting department?				
16. Is merchandise from returned sales properly handled?				
17. Are receiving reports prepared for sales returns?				
18. If receiving reports are prepared, are they matched with credit memorandums and approved?				

Illustration 5–5—Continued

	Yes	No	Not Appli-cable	Remarks
19. Is the preparation of credit memos properly controlled to prevent unauthorized sales returns debits and receivable credits?	___	___	___	_____
20. Are the classes of sales indicated below controlled and recorded in the same manner as regular charges sales:				
a) Cash sales?	___	___	___	_____
b) C.O.D. sales?	___	___	___	_____
c) Sales to employees?	___	___	___	_____
d) Scrap sales?	___	___	___	_____
21. Is it possible to match unit sales with inventory record credits:				
a) By the use of a perpetual inventory?	___	___	___	_____
b) By the use of the retail method?	___	___	___	_____
22. Is there an adequate check on transportation allowance:				
a) By reference to terms of sale?	___	___	___	_____
b) By comparison with rate schedules and transportation bills?	___	___	___	_____

Prepared by_____   Reviewed by _____
Date _____   Date _____

sales and for sales returns and allowances. In the questionnaire, the answer "yes" is indicative of proper internal control. A "no" answer indicates improper control, which should be explained in the "Remarks" section, and which may be the basis of a management letter to the client recommending necessary changes.

AUDIT PROGRAM FOR SALES AND RETURNS

An audit program for sales and sales returns records may be as follows:

SALES RECORDS:

1. Prove footings and crossfootings for two nonconsecutive months.
2. Trace postings to controls and subsidiaries, for item 1, above.
3. Compare duplicate sales invoices with entries in the sales record:
    a) For two nonconsecutive months—or
    b) For the last month of the period, plus a random sample, so that the total comparison equals a 17 percent test, approximately—or
    c) By selecting a random sample which will equal an approximate 17 percent test.
4. Compare sales invoices with sales record entries and with shipping records for the last week of the period to determine that sales billed were shipped and that goods shipped were billed.

5. Investigate sales cutoff for the last day of the year.
6. Ascertain shipment date for sales dated the last day of the year.
7. Verify prices, extensions, approvals, and totals on the sample invoices; item 3(a), (b), or (c).

SALES RETURNS AND ALLOWANCES RECORDS:

1. Prove record footings and crossfootings for two nonconsecutive months, including the last, and trace the related postings to controls and subsidiaries.
2. Compare credit memos with entries in the returns and allowances records for two nonconsecutive months (or follow item 3(b) or (c), under "Sales Records").
3. Trace returned goods to receiving records and to inventory records in accordance with item 3(a), (b), or (c), under "Sales Records."

In the examination of sales records and sales returns and allowances records, and the underlying data, the following points are of importance:

1. Sales record entries must be supported by customers' orders, copies of invoices, register tapes, or original sales slips as used in retail stores.
2. Money from cash sales must be recorded as it is received.
3. Invoices must be sequentially numbered and properly controlled.
4. Customers should be charged for agreed transportation costs.
5. Sales records must be promptly closed at the end of the period.
6. Unshipped but recorded end-of-the-period sales must not be included in inventory.
7. Sales returns and allowances credit memorandums must be properly authorized, approved, and recorded.

The major objective in examining sales data is to ascertain that all revenues which should be received have been recorded as received or receivable. During the course of an examination, the auditor should control all duplicate copies of invoices (or sales tickets or cash register tapes) in order to prevent substitution of original data.

The sales cutoff point should be for all sales made through the last day of the period. Normally, a sale is concluded when merchandise is shipped or service rendered. Therefore, for a few days prior to the close of the period and for a few days of the subsequent period, sales invoice dates should be compared with shipping records, bills of lading, and credits to inventory accounts.

INTERNAL CONTROL FOR PURCHASES

Purchases of services may be authorized by the personnel department for factory, store, and office employees; and by the board of directors for executive employees, lawyers, certified public accountants, and other specialized services. Regardless of the type of service, proper internal control requires that the authority to purchase be vested in a central source.

Proper internal control for the acquisition of assets demands that purchasing be segregated from receiving, and from the recording of the purchase and the subsequent payment. A separate purchasing department (or person) should have exclusive power to place purchase orders for assets—after the orders have been originally properly authorized and then properly approved. The following steps are involved in proper internal control of purchases.

The Purchase Requisition. The department or person requesting an item should send a properly approved requisition to the purchasing department. The purchase requisition opens the operations of the purchasing department for the acquisition of the item requested.

The Purchase Order. After approval by the properly designated official, the purchasing department places a purchase order with a vendor in conformity with company policy concerning quality, price, quantity, packing, and shipping. The number of copies of a purchase order depends upon the internal operating organization of a company. The original is sent to the vendor, and the purchasing department retains a copy; copies may be sent to the accounting department, to the receiving department (with or without quantities), and to the department originally requisitioning the item. When filing a placed purchase order, the purchasing department should attach the original purchase requisition. Purchase orders should be consecutively prenumbered, and all numbers should be accounted for; if a placed purchase order is canceled or is not accepted by the supplier, all copies should be recalled and filed.

Receiving. All items purchased should be delivered to a centralized receiving department where they are counted (or weighed, etc.) and inspected for specifications. The receiving department then prepares a receiving report, one copy of which is sent to the purchasing department, one may be sent to the accounting department, and one retained by the receiving department. A receiving department should not accept any item without proper authorization by the purchasing department.

Vendors' Invoices and Payment. Vendors' invoices may precede or follow receipt of the items ordered. Prior to approval of a vendor's invoice, the purchasing department should compare the invoice with the purchase order and with the receiving report. After approval of the vendor's invoice, the purchasing department should send the invoice to the accounting department, preferably with a copy of the receiving report. The accounting department should compare the invoice with its copy of the purchase order and verify invoice extensions and footings. The invoice then is filed in the Open Accounts Payable file. Prior to paying an invoice,

Illustration 5–6

INTERNAL CONTROL QUESTIONNAIRE
Purchases and Purchase Returns

	Yes	No	Not Appli- cable	Remarks
Company _____ Period Covered _____				

1. Is there an organized purchasing department?
2. Is the purchasing department independent of:
   a) The receiving department?
   b) The shipping department?
   c) The accounting department?
3. Are all purchase orders executed in writing?
4. Are all purchase orders sequentially prenumbered?
5. Are purchase orders properly approved for:
   a) Price?
   b) Quantity?
   c) Supplier?
   d) Authorization?
6. Does the accounting department receive directly:
   a) A copy of the purchase order?
   b) A copy of the receiving report?
7. Does the receiving department obtain copies of purchase orders for authority to accept incoming items?
8. Are receiving reports sequentially numbered?
9. Is the sequence of numbers checked by the accounting department?
10. Does the receiving department retain a copy of reports?
11. Does the purchasing department receive a copy of the receiving report?
12. Is the accounting department notified of returns to vendors?
13. Are shipping reports prepared for items returned to vendors?
14. Are the shipping reports in Question 13 matched with credit memorandums from vendors?
15. Does the accounting department match invoices with:
    a) Purchase orders?
    b) Receiving reports?
16. Are invoices properly approved for:
    a) Prices?
    b) Extensions and footings?
    c) Transportation charges?
    d) Payment?
17. Are invoices stamped to prevent duplicate payment?
18. Are creditors' statements compared by the accounting department to the open accounts payable?
19. Prior to approval for payment, are all documents related to invoices assembled in one place?
20. Are items purchased for the convenience of employees routed in the regular manner?

Prepared by _____   Reviewed by _____
Date _____   Date _____

the invoice and all supporting documents must be approved by the person in charge of authorizing cash disbursements.

An audit program for purchase and purchase returns records is presented below:

AUDIT PROGRAM FOR PURCHASES AND PURCHASE RETURNS

An internal control questionnaire is presented in Illustration 5–6 for purchases and purchase returns.

PURCHASES:

1. Prove original entry record footings and crossfootings; trace the totals to the general ledger for two nonconsecutive months.
2. Examine vendors' invoices and related vouchers and compare with entries in the purchase record (or voucher register) for—
   a) Two nonconsecutive months, as in item 1, above—or
   b) The last month of the period plus a random sample, the total of which will equal approximately 17 percent of the annual total —or
   c) A random sample of approximately 17 percent.
3. Verify extensions in accordance with item 2(a), (b), or (c), above.
4. Trace postings to creditors' accounts for the last month of the period.
5. Examine receiving records for the last week of the period and trace the receipt of the goods to the purchase records.
6. Determine the propriety of the cutoff at the last day of the period.
7. Watch for incorrect account distributions.

PURCHASE RETURNS AND ALLOWANCES:

1. Prove footings and crossfootings in the returns and allowances records and trace the totals to the general ledger for the test period.
2. Examine returns and allowances memorandums and compare with entries in the returns and allowances records for—
   a) Two nonconsecutive months—or
   b) The last month of the period plus a sample, the total of which will equal approximately 17 percent of the annual total—or
   c) A random sample of approximately 17 percent.
3. Trace debit postings to creditors' accounts for the last month of the period.
4. Examine shipping records for the last week of the period to ascertain that debits entered in creditors' accounts were represented by goods returned.
5. Determine the propriety of the cutoff at the last day of the period.

In the examination of purchase records, returns and allowances records, and all underlying data, an auditor must ascertain that purchase record entries are supported by properly authorized and approved purchase orders, receiving reports, and vendors' invoices, and that credits for returns and allowances are supported by proper memorandums from vendors. Purchase and purchase returns records must be properly closed at the end of the period to include all goods purchased through the last day and to exclude goods returned through the last day. The name, date, and amount of each invoice and related vouchers should be compared with the same items appearing in the purchase record.

The auditor must examine invoices and related vouchers for proper price, extensions, totals, and evidence of the receipt of goods or services. Each invoice and its related vouchers should bear evidence of approval for payment. As the auditor examines creditors' invoices and related documents, he must ascertain that paid items are so stamped so that they may not be presented for payment more than one time, and "duplicate" invoices must be investigated.

One of the most important phases of the examination of inventory acquisitions is to ascertain that all items purchased through the last day of the period are entered by proper debit and credit, and—if not sold—are included in inventory. Items in transit, to which the client has title, also should be included in inventory and in payables. Invoices received for goods which have not been received should be recorded and included in inventory if the client has title. Goods received for which an invoice has not been received should be included in inventory, and a liability set up for them.

INTERNAL CONTROL OF CASH RECEIPTS

The operation of a system of internal control for cash receipts must result in assurance that all cash receipts are recorded as such and that all cash receivable is received. At this point the reader is referred to the section entitled "Errors and Fraud" in Chapter 3, and to the handling of cash and credit sales earlier in this chapter.

It is fundamental that the receipt of cash and its recording be separated. When cash is received by mail, the mail must be opened by a person who (1) is not the cashier, (2) does not have access to the accounting records, and (3) does not have access to cash funds. If the cashier opened the mail, access to cash is available and so is the opportunity to manipulate accounting records. If the person who opened the mail had access to the accounting records, cash thefts would be easy. If a cash fund custodian opened the mail, theft would be possible by fund manipulation.

Mail remittances should be listed in detail. One copy of the remittance list should be sent to the cashier for entry in the cash records and for preparation of the bank deposit. Another copy should be sent to the accounting department for entry in the general ledger and the receivables ledger. Another copy is sent to the treasurer for comparison with the controlled duplicate bank deposit tickets. The remittance list serves as a deterrent to theft—particularly through the lapping process—because the cashier does not have access to the accounts receivable and the accountant does not have access to the cash.

If the person who opens the mail steals money, the remitting customers will complain when they receive repeat billings. If the cashier steals money, the records must be altered, and that person is exposed to detection by the auditor. If a cashier and the bookkeeper work in collusion, the original remittance list will vary from the detail of the bank deposit. Thus the possibilities of fraud are reduced if there is separation between the functions of receiving cash and of recording the cash receipts.

In any business organization, all cash receipts should be cleared through one central point. Cash should be deposited intact. Disbursements should not be made from receipt money but should be made by check or from specific funds. Banks should be instructed, in writing, to accept checks and other cash items for deposit only. Branches may deposit locally, but a branch should not be permitted to make cash disbursements from its cash receipts.

An internal control questionnaire for cash receipts is presented in Illustration 5–7.

AUDIT PROGRAM FOR CASH RECEIPTS RECORDS

An audit program is presented below for the examination of cash receipts records:

1. Prove footing and cross-footing accuracy in the original-entry records for two nonconsecutive months of the year; vary at least one of the months each year.
2. In accordance with item 1, above, trace the postings to the general ledger accounts and the subsidiary accounts.
3. Trace cash receipts from original data (such as register tapes, invoices, etc.) to the cash receipts original accounting record:
   a) For two nonconsecutive months—or
   b) For the last month of the period plus a random sample, whereby the sum of the two equal approximately a 17 percent test—or
   c) By selecting a random sample of original data which is approximately equal to a 17 percent test.
4. Compare total daily cash receipts with bank deposits in accordance with item 3, above.
5. If necessary, prove the total annual recorded receipts with the total of the bank deposits, adjusted for items in transit.
6. Determine that the cash receipts cutoff is proper.

Illustration 5–7

INTERNAL CONTROL QUESTIONNAIRE
Cash Receipts

			Not	
Company _____	Yes	No	Appli-	Remarks
Period Covered _____			cable	

1. Are bank accounts properly authorized by the board of directors?

2. Is the mail opened by a person:
   a) Who does not prepare the bank deposit?
   b) Who does not have access to accounts receivable or the general ledger?

3. Does the person who opens the mail list the receipts in detail?

4. Are the listed mail receipts compared with the accounting records by an independent person?

5. Are cash receipts deposited daily and intact?

6. Is cash sales money proved against the totals of invoices, register tapes, inventory release tickets, etc.?

7. Is the proof in Question 6 prepared by a person who does not have access to the cash?

8. Are cash receipts from miscellaneous sources independently controlled?

9. Does a person other than the person who prepares the bank deposit make the deposit?

10. Is the bank-stamped duplicate deposit ticket returned to a person other than the one who prepared the deposit?

11. Are bank-stamped duplicate deposit tickets compared with the cash receipts record?

12. Are persons bonded who handle cash or cash transactions?

13. Are returned customer checks delivered to a person other than the one who prepared the bank deposit?

14. Is it impossible for employees to redeem dishonored customer checks?

15. Are noncash negotiable securities in the custody of a person other than the one responsible for cash receipts?

16. Does any person in the cashier's department (answer "No," for proper control):
    a) Prepare sales invoices?
    b) Maintain the sales records?
    c) Have access to the accounts receivable ledger?
    d) Have access to customers' statements?
    e) Authorize credit extension?
    f) Approve discounts, returns, or allowances?
    g) Sign notes payable?
    h) Participate in collection duties?
    i) Prepare, sign or mail checks?

Prepared by _____   Reviewed by _____
Date _____   Date _____

One of the principal objectives of the auditor in examining cash receipts records is to determine that all cash receipts have been recorded and that all cash which was receivable has been received. If all sales are made on open account, the total annual net debits to receivables should equal the total cash receipts, after adjusting for returns, allowances, and discounts, and after considering the difference between the receivables balance at the beginning and at the end of the year. Where sales are for both cash and credit, remittance lists, corrected cash register tape totals, and paid invoice copies should be traced to the cash receipts records in accordance with the test pattern [item 3(*a*) or (*b*) or (*c*)] set forth in the audit program. Then the same receipts entries should be traced to bank-deposit tickets and to the bank statements. Daily, the bank deposit should equal the total of the remittance lists, corrected cash register tapes, and invoice copies. In order to obtain a total annual "tie-up" between bank deposits and recorded receipts, the total of the cash debits is compared with the total of the bank deposits. In this way, cash manipulations could be detected in the months not tested.

Entries in the cash receipts record may agree with bank statement deposits, but the cash deposited might be less than the amount received. If duplicate deposit tickets are not controlled, they should be footed, because they may be underfooted to agree with an understated cash receipts debit; this would result in a bank balance larger than the Cash account balance and thereby lay the groundwork for the execution of fraudulent disbursements.

An auditor must be certain that cash debits of the last day of the period actually are deposited in the bank; this is accomplished by examining the bank statement of the following month. Also, bank deposits for the last several days of the period must be matched with cash debits in order to detect an attempt to cover a cash shortage by depositing money in the bank and not making an accounting entry. A lapse of more than one day plus holidays may lead to the discovery of lapping. If cash receipts are deposited and no entry is made near the end of the period, the entry will be made early in the next period—and again the Cash account balance will be in excess of the bank balance.

Cash receipts for several days after the end of the period should be traced to the bank statement. If cash received in the new period was entered as of the end of the prior period, the auditor should reverse the entry to prevent an inflated year-end cash position.

Entries for cash receipts and cash disbursements must be properly cut off at the end of the period. All cash received and all cash disbursed through the last day of the period must be entered in the cash records before they are closed. If cash receipts were entered on remittance lists and held until the succeeding period, those receipts would be disclosed when bank reconciliations were prepared.

If cash investments made by owners near the end of a period are withdrawn early in the subsequent period, the obvious intent is to "window-dress" the balance sheet. In order to adhere to recognized auditing standards in the preparation of financial statements, the auditor should not permit "window dressing."

Cash receipts records must be examined to determine that sales discounts and transportation allowances are not overstated, accompanied by theft of an equivalent amount from cash receipts, in order to conceal the overstated discounts or allowances. To detect this type of fraud, remittance lists are compared with cash debit entries; and if the cash debit entry is less than the amount on the remittance list, fraud has occurred. If a customer took a discount in excess of the regularly allowed amount, or if a customer took a discount after the discount period and if the client did not object, there is no action to be taken.

Lapping is practiced in connection with the accounting for customer remittances. The person practicing lapping will be certain that the cash bank balance agrees with the cash ledger account balance—thereby preventing a surprise cash count resulting in disagreement between the book balance and the bank balance. Consequently, the guilty person always is certain that the *total* of each deposit ticket equals the *total* of the recorded receipts. However, the *detail* of the deposit will not agree with the *detail* of the credits to accounts receivable. If a person guilty of lapping decided to reduce his shortage, a personal check or currency must be deposited in the bank. To detect lapping, the *detail* of the bank deposit tickets must be matched with the *detail* of the entries in the cash receipts records. If a bank deposit is not recorded in the cash receipts records, lapping is indicated. Later an entry may appear in the cash receipts records, and no matching amount will appear on a deposit ticket.

INTERNAL CONTROL OF CASH DISBURSEMENTS

The validity of cash disbursements must be established by satisfactory evidence of authority to disburse. It is necessary to separate such duties as (1) approval of vendors' invoices, (2) recording of payables, (3) preparation of checks, and (4) control of checks already prepared.

All disbursements, with the exception of those from cash funds, should be made by check, in order automatically to obtain a receipt. Checks should be drawn payable to the order of a person or a company. Authorized signatures should be on file at the depositary banks, supported by proper authorization to the bank to honor only those signatures.

The basis of check preparation should be properly authorized and supported by properly approved invoices, vouchers, and other necessary documents. All paid invoices, vouchers, and other documents must be ineradicably stamped "Paid" so that they cannot be presented again for payment. Unused vouchers must be controlled to prevent false preparation and false payment. Purchase returns and allowances must be verified to determine that the net payment is not for an excess amount. Purchase discounts must be verified to determine that they are properly computed and that the payment check is not for an amount smaller than the underlying documents—thereby opening the way for the theft of an equivalent sum from cash receipts.

The person who disburses checks should have no connection with the preparation of underlying documents authorizing the disbursements. The last person signing checks should detach all supporting documents and return them to their proper place—the accounting department, the accounts payable department, and so on.

Bank-paid checks should not be returned to the cashier or to a bookkeeper. After bank statements are reconciled, paid checks may be returned to a bookkeeper. All checks—used and unused—must be accounted for. Paid checks may be compared with original invoices and other documents in order to detect alteration or substitution. Checks issued for the transfer of funds between banks should be traced for evidence of kiting.

The internal control questionnaire in Illustration 5–8 adheres to satisfactory standards of internal control for cash disbursements made for any purpose except payroll disbursements.

AUDIT PROGRAM FOR CASH DISBURSEMENTS

With the exception of petty cash and payroll disbursements, the following audit program is applicable to the examination of cash disbursements records:

1. Prove the accuracy of footings and crossfootings in the records of original entry for two nonconsecutive months; vary at least one of the months each year.
2. Trace the postings, from item 1, above, to the general-ledger accounts and to the subsidiary-ledger accounts.
3. Trace original invoices and other vouchers to the disbursements records:
   a) For two nonconsecutive months—or
   b) For the last month of the period plus a random sample, whereby the sum of the two will equal approximately a 17 percent test —or
   c) Select a random sample of original data which will equal approximately a 17 percent test.
4. Compare bank-paid checks with entries in the cash disbursements record, and tick off, in accordance with the test in item 3, above.
5. Account for all check numbers.
6. Ascertain that original invoices and supporting documents are stamped "Paid."
7. If necessary, prove the total annual recorded disbursements with

Illustration 5–8

INTERNAL CONTROL QUESTIONNAIRE
Cash Disbursements (Except Payroll)

	Yes	No	Not Appli- cable	Remarks
Company_____ Period Covered _____				

1. Are all checks prenumbered by the printer?
2. Are spoiled checks properly retained?
3. Are voided checks mutilated to avoid reuse?
4. Are unused checks properly controlled?
5. Is a check protector used?
6. Are all checks made payable to a person or a company?
7. Are persons who sign checks prohibited to:
   a) Have access to petty cash?
   b) Approve cash disbursements?
   c) Record cash receipts?
   d) Post to the ledger accounts?
8. If used, are signature machines properly controlled?
9. Are persons who sign checks properly authorized to do so?
10. Have banks been instructed not to cash checks payable to the order of the company?
11. Are all checks signed only after they are prepared?
12. When checks are presented for signatures, are accompanying invoices and other necessary papers also submitted?
13. Are invoices and other accompanying papers stamped "Paid" at the time the accompanying checks are signed?
14. Is it impossible to present an invoice or voucher for payment two or more times?
15. Do two different persons prepare checks and approve invoices?
16. Are bank accounts reconciled at least once each month?
17. Are bank statements and paid checks delivered directly to the person who prepares the recon- ciliation?
18. Is the person preparing the reconciliation:
    a) Prevented from signing checks?
    b) Prevented from handling cash?
    c) Prevented from recording cash transactions?
19. Does the person preparing the reconciliation:
    a) Account for all check numbers?
    b) Examine signatures?
    c) Examine endorsements?
    d) Examine payee's name?
20. Are interbank fund transfers promptly recorded?
21. Are improperly endorsed checks returned to the bank for correction?
22. Are long-outstanding checks properly followed and controlled?

Prepared by_____   Reviewed by _____
Date _____   Date _____

bank statement totals, adjusting for outstanding checks and items in transit.
8. Watch for proper cutoff.

Cash disbursements record examination may involve the use of a voucher register, in which case the cash disbursements record is merely a check register. Or cash disbursements record examination may involve the use of a disbursements record in which expenses and asset acquisitions are debited; in the latter case the audit procedures are similar to those set forth earlier in this chapter for purchases. Entries other than debits to accounts payable—recorded in a disbursements record—must be examined for authenticity of invoice, approval for payment, and correctness of the recorded amount.

All checks made payable to the order of "Cash," "Bearer," banks, officers, and payroll should be listed and investigated; and the endorsements should be examined. The purpose for which each such check was prepared should be understood, and the check should be traced to the accounting records. No valid reason exists for checks made payable to the order of "Cash" or "Bearer." However, checks *are* so prepared; and the auditor must investigate the authorization for, purpose of, and the accounting entries for such checks.

Checks drawn payable to the order of banks normally will represent interest payments or loan principal repayments. When totaled, interest payment checks serve as a partial proof of interest expense.

Checks may be drawn payable to the order of named company officers, for salary advances, travel expenses, or personal account withdrawals. Personal account balances should be approved in writing by the persons involved. In connection with nonpayroll checks issued to officers—or any other employee—the auditor must examine the records for the first several days of the subsequent accounting period, because an officer or other employee may be indebted to his company; and at the end of the current period, may issue a personal check to eliminate the indebtedness. Immediately after the close of the period, a new company check may be issued to the same person. In such cases the auditor must reverse the year-end entries. This eliminates the obvious intention to alter the balance-sheet cash position.

The total of the checks drawn payable to the order of a Payroll account should be compared with the net cash payroll credit according to the payroll records.

Kiting of checks has been explained. Checks representing interbank transfer of funds must be traced to *both* cash receipts and cash disbursements records—before and after the close of the period. There should be a debit to one bank account and a credit to another bank account *when the transfer was made*. If kiting exists, there will be a deposit in one bank and no accounting entry because the bank balance was less than the cash ledger account balance. Paid checks and checks returned after the close of the period because of insufficient funds should *not* be returned to any person who has the opportunity to overstate a bank balance temporarily through the deposit of a fictitious check. Consequently, when funds are transferred between banks, the cash credit must be matched with a bank deposit—according to an independently obtained bank statement. Also, the detail of the confirmed duplicate deposit tickets (obtained directly from the bank) should be compared with entries in the cash receipts records.

Paid Check Examination. The examination of paid checks should adhere to the following plan:

1. On the work papers of the prior period, tick off the then-outstanding checks cleared in the current period.
2. Obtain access to all paid checks properly arranged.
3. Account for all checks issued during the current period.
4. Compare check date with the disbursement entry date.
5. Compare the name of the check payee and the amount of the check with the corresponding name and amount in the cash disbursements record.
6. Watch bank-paid dates on checks issued close to the end of each month to ascertain if clearance time is proper and to prove that checks written were properly recorded.
7. Examine checks for proper signatures.
8. Scrutinize endorsements and investigate multiendorsements, especially if the last is that of a company employee.
9. Investigate all checks made payable to the order of "Cash" or "Bearer."

As checks are traced to disbursements records, each should be marked, and a tick-mark should be placed opposite the item in the cash disbursements record in order to indicate examination of evidence. Unticked entries in the disbursements record represent outstanding checks to be used in the bank reconciliation. If checks are not supported by proper documents—invoices and so forth—the auditor cannot be certain of the propriety of the checks.

AUDIT PROGRAM FOR PETTY OR OTHER CASH FUND DISBURSEMENTS

The following audit program is presented for cash fund disbursements. The examination of the fund is set forth in Chapter 6.

1. Select a sample of the fund reimbursement vouchers and the accompanying individual expenditure vouchers. The size of the sample is dependent upon the importance of the size and activity of a fund

compared with other assets and/or other operations, and upon the internal control of a fund and its activities.

2. Prove extensions and footings on the sample reimbursement vouchers.
3. Prove the total of the individual expenditure vouchers with the total of each reimbursement voucher selected.
4. Trace reimbursement voucher data to the cash disbursements record.
5. Examine each selected individual expenditure voucher for date, approval, amount, and account to be charged.
6. Examine the propriety of ledger account distributions as indicated by the selected reimbursement vouchers.

Proof of the accuracy of extensions and footings on the reimbursement vouchers and proof of the total of the individual expenditure vouchers with each reimbursement voucher total are necessary procedures; if the reimbursement voucher was for a larger amount than the sum of the individual vouchers, the difference could have been stolen. If the entry prepared when the fund was reimbursed is for an amount larger than the reimbursement voucher, the difference could be stolen.

Cash funds should be operated under the imprest system. Vouchers should be consecutively prenumbered by the printer. A separate cash voucher should be prepared for each individual disbursement. Each cash voucher should be prepared in ink, should be properly dated, should show the account name and/or number to be charged with the disbursement, should contain any necessary explanations, should be properly approved, and should be signed by the fund custodian and the recipient of the money. When possible, original invoices should be attached to the applicable fund vouchers.

Cash funds should be used for business operating purposes only. A surprise recount of the cash funds may reveal antedated or postdated checks which were not present when the fund originally was counted. Fund cash shortages must be properly approved, and should be charged to a fund cash shortage general-ledger account.

AUDIT PROGRAM FOR A GENERAL JOURNAL

A suggested audit program for a general journal follows:

1. Obtain access to all documents authorizing and supporting entries in the general journal.
2. Trace amounts appearing on each document to the journal.
3. Determine the equality of debits and credits for each entry.
4. Prove posting accuracy by tracing to the ledger accounts involved.

Journal vouchers may be used instead of a general journal, but the audit program does not change. General journal or journal voucher entries may or may not be supported by underlying documents. If supported, the entries will arise from actions expressed in minutes of the board of directors' meetings, letters from collection agencies, contracts, requests from company officials, and so on.

Each general journal or journal voucher entry should contain a full explanation—which must be understood by the auditor. Entries reducing asset accounts should be particularly investigated in order to ascertain that fraud has not occurred and that accounting principles have been correctly applied. To illustrate: A collectible account receivable might be charged off to the allowance for doubtful items, and the collected amount stolen; the entire proceeds from the sale of a fixed asset might be credited to the asset account, without proper recognition of any gain or loss on the disposition. An auditor should prevent resubmission of data by placing a code legend on the entry and on the applicable document.

AUDIT PROGRAM FOR A GENERAL LEDGER

In connection with the examination of a general ledger, the auditor will prepare a trial balance at the end of the period, and will prove the footing and balance accuracy of all accounts not to be analyzed.

Prior to taking a current-period trial balance, the auditor should determine that all records have been posted for the period. Many clients, with or without the request of their auditors, journalize and post period-end adjusting entries. These two operations save time for the auditor and also prevent the possibility of manipulation after the auditor has released the ledger.

Postings to the general ledger were proved in connection with the audit programs for records of original entry. The auditor should place a tick-mark after each posting involved and after the last posting for the year so that additional postings may be detected.

The auditor should determine whether or not the client has recorded the audit adjustments of the prior year. If the client inadvertently recorded prior-period audit adjustments in the current period, entries correcting these are the first to be made in the current audit so that the beginning trial balance will agree with the prior-period audit work papers.

MACHINE-PREPARED RECORDS AND AUDIT PROCEDURES

Automation may be described as the performance of control functions by machinery. The auditing standards applicable to records produced by electronic equipment are the same as those applicable to records maintained in ink, journalizing and posting machines equipped with programming bars, and by punched card equipment. Thus, the objectives of audit and control do not change. For the audit of electronically produced data and records, only the examination procedures will be altered—and in the majority of instances, these alterations will not be too great. The "storage unit" constitutes one of the greatest changes. The auditor should not be surprised if he asked to see the accounts-payable file and was handed a magnetic tape, a disk pack, or was informed that the information requested is stored in a computer many miles away.

In general, data processing has advanced in the following stages:

1. Readable hard-copy original data are prepared, converted to machine-sensible form, and then processed.
2. Readable hard-copy original data and machine-sensible form data are prepared simultaneously. This may be illustrated by the typing of a sales invoice and the simultaneous paper-tape punching of the sales invoice data for machine processing.
3. Readable hard copy will not exist, and the original data are prepared only in machine-sensible form. This may be illustrated by the insertion of an employee's key in a time clock, with the time transfer being made directly on magnetic media.

At the present time, hard-copy originating data are frequently available from which the auditor may proceed to test and follow through the processing to the printout point; or he may work from the printout point back to the available hard copy.

The auditor must remember that the five component parts of electronic data processing equipment are input, storage, arithmetic processing, control, and output. If an audit program is designed with these points, functions, and operations in mind, an auditor should experience no more difficulty than in an examination running from original documents, to a journal, to a ledger, to a trial balance, to the financial statements.

Auditing procedures are affected by the presence of a computer, in terms of the two following major phases of an audit examination: (1) the evaluation of the system of internal control and (2) the evaluation of the records produced by the EDP system.

If the auditor is to deal effectively with EDP systems, he should have computer knowledge and capability at two levels: (1) a basic working knowledge of computers and computer-based data processing sufficient to adequately review the system of internal control, to conduct proper tests of the system under audit, and to objectively evaluate the quality of the records produced; and (2) the ability to use the computer, when necessary, in making the tests desired.

Internal Control Examination.   Basic to an audit of the records and data prepared with electronic equipment is the assurance of adequate internal control; the first intensive work of the auditor will constitute a review of the control procedures. In a study of internal control, the auditor should investigate (1) the controls established outside the data processing center and (2) the controls built into the equipment. System designers will prepare flow diagrams which show the basic operations to be performed; these should be studied for internal control features.

Electronic data processing equipment strengthens internal control because it normally provides for internal control features built into the equipment, and at the programming stage, and in the form of self-proof devices and automatic stoppage of the equipment if an error is found. The theory, purpose, and results of internal control do not change, but the mechanics of examining the system do change to parallel the programming and the work flow through the equipment.

There are several types of program controls—or checks—built into or incorporated in every data processing program. The auditor should ascertain that a client is availing itself of the opportunity effectively to use these controls and checks. Also, the auditor should make use of these controls and checks in examining the operation of the system. A few of the controls and checks incorporated in a data processing program are proof figures, sequence checks, self-checking numbers, check points, cross-footing balance checks, limit check, reverse multiplication, record count, and hash totals. When duplicate arithmetic circuits are in operation, all arithmetic computations are prepared twice—simultaneously and independently. In the course of an audit, the results may be compared for proof of accuracy.

The effectiveness of the controls within the equipment may be tested by following through a series of transaction data—or a comprehensive understanding and testing of the program itself should be obtained.

Flow diagrams normally show the type of information recorded at the input stage, its progress through each procedure, and the contents of the output—all of which may be held on magnetic tape, punch cards, disk pack, or storage facilities of a remote service center. The determination of the extent to which controls are built into the computer programs and the testing to determine if they are operative will require different techniques, depending on the circumstances.

It has been a common practice for an organization making changes in data processing methods to seek the help of its auditing firm in designing the changes. In this way the auditor can review the control features and point out probable weaknesses and, in addition, provide for audit trails and the safeguarding of files.

Internal control of electronic equipment may be further illustrated by using accounts receivable and related sales procedures as follows:

1. The computer center should account for the serial numbers of all invoices. These should be verified by the receivables department.
2. Copies of all invoices should be routed directly to the accounts-receivable department.

3. Summarized invoice totals should be submitted to the accounting department by the computer center without routing through the accounts-receivable department.
4. There should be independent internal investigation to determine that all sales orders shipped are billed.
5. If perpetual inventories are maintained, the computer center should prepare inventory control credits for items sold and inventory control debits for returned merchandise.
6. Master tape changes for product prices should be independently approved by the sales department.
7. The computer center should produce a printed record of all changes in prices, item numbers, and item descriptions, which should be authorized by and verified by the sales department.
8. An authorized person, outside the data processing center, should verify a printout of the master register for changes.
9. Exceptions to master tape prices should be followed up by a person outside the computing center.
10. If shipments are made to customers not appearing on the master tape, an outside person should follow up the transactions for propriety.

Audit tests should be made of all items and procedures set forth above, plus the testing of other control features peculiar to the operations of any given client. Each section of the investigation should be repeated each year because with the advances in electronic data processing, controls, and procedures change rapidly. An auditor cannot assume that a control or procedure currently in effect will not be altered in the near future.

Internal control can be greatly improved through the separation of duties of individuals. Recognizing the principle of separation would require the data processing functions to be divided as follows: (1) system analysis and design, (2) programming, (3) computer operation, and (4) internal auditor or control section.

A Client's Documentation of the Data Processing System. Also basic to an audit of the records and data prepared with EDP equipment is the assurance that the client has adequate documentation of the data processing system. Documentation consists of documents and records which clearly set forth the system and procedures for carrying out the data processing tasks. It is the means of communicating the essential elements of the EDP system and the logic built into the computer programs. The auditor should determine whether or not the client's documentation will at least serve the following purposes:

1. Provide a valid basis for a satisfactory evaluation of internal control.
2. Supply the computer operator with complete and current operating instructions.

3. Provide answers to all questions relating to the operation of the computer program.
4. Can serve as a good basis for review of the present system and evaluation of proposed system expansion.
5. Be so complete that revisions will be easily performed.
6. Provide the best instruction for new personnel.

A careful examination of the preceding points illustrates why the examination of a client's documentation is vital to the completion of an EDP system audit.

Since the computer run is the basic unit on which documentation is based, the run manual must be inspected in detail so that the auditor has an understanding of the runs and their interrelationship. The run manual is prepared by the systems analyst and/or programmer and consists of the complete description of the program or programs used for a data processing run. This manual is an important corporate record and should be given fireproof storage. In order to prevent its loss or alteration, a control copy should be stored outside the processing center. Further auditing should reveal that access to the run manual is restricted to the systems and programming personnel, and under no condition should the machine operators have access to this manual.

The following should be found in the run manual and inspected in detail by the auditor:

1. Problem definition—should present formally and clearly the problem to be solved. Also, it should set forth the part of this program in relation to the total data processing system.

2. System description—should support the problem definition by indicating the general outline of the program computer and noncomputer, and how it relates to the EDP system of which it is a part. Here the auditor will find the system flow charts, record formats, activity codes, and how the control function, if involved, is to be handled.

3. Program description—covers the details which document the computer program portion of the system only. This is one of the most important sections of the run manual as it consists of the program flow charts; decision tables used in testing the program together with a complete description of these tables; a listing of all working storage areas; sense switches, if any, which permit alteration of the program flow; a complete description of program modification or "patches"; and program listing, which serves as a backup in case the source deck or disk pack is lost or destroyed.

4. Operating instructions—contains all information required to run the program by the computer operator including changes which are listed as separate instructions.

5. Listing of controls—summarizes the controls, inside and outside, and the procedures associated with a program. Such things as checks on the

accuracy of input data, checks on batch controls, programmed error detection, and checks on the accuracy of output are provided for in this section of the run manual.

6. Acceptance record—consists of copies of input and output test data as it relates to the original test and any subsequent changes. Here the auditor would also find who was responsible for initiating the change as well as the person responsible for making the change.

Proper documentation can be invaluable to the auditor when a review of internal control and methods of testing indicates that computer-based tests should be used. Further, it can eliminate much of the detailed work associated with writing a program or developing test data. He will also find that the time needed to develop an audit approach will be reduced.

Equipment Malfunctions. It is desirable for the auditor to have a general understanding of built-in hardware control features. This will aid in understanding the working of the equipment, why it is reliable, and to evaluate the effectiveness of machine checks.

Since a computer system consists of electronic elements and mechanical parts, there can be a malfunction of either part. Electronic elements are controlled by electrical pulses and failure of an electronic element may lead to an error. A mechanical part failure may occur when there is a malfunction of the read/write units that are most frequently associated with input/output and file storage equipment. Warped cards or an improperly balanced disk pack can cause mechanical errors.

Equipment Controls. A *redundant character check* is frequently used for the sole purpose of detecting an error that may occur. This type of check involves the addition of a character to determine if an error has taken place when moving of data in the system is involved. It assists in determining whether the transfer has been correctly made by repeating the redundant character.

If the auditor wishes to verify whether or not the equipment has been activated without testing the actual results, he will perform an *echo check*. This may involve sending a command to activate an input or output device to perform an operation and the device responding that the command is being followed.

Another equipment check is the *validity check*. This may involve an instruction of increasing the pay rate for a certain class of employee before the memory system has been updated.

One other step may be taken by the auditor to determine the extent of a client's equipment controls, and that is to perform an *equipment check*. This involves checking the computer for proper operation without checking the results of operations. This is not a positive check as the equipment may be functioning properly, but incorrect information could be processed and the results obtained would be meaningless.

The auditor may find it necessary to develop equipment controls dealing with specific pieces of the EDP system. Such controls might involve the central processor, card reader, card punch, printer, direct access storage devices, and any other hardware of the EDP system.

Operating reports and computer logs will greatly aid the auditor in determining to what extent he will be concerned about the possible existence of errors in the data processing equipment. Because an auditor can usually rely upon the equipment and the hardware controls for detecting errors, he should devote more attention to the procedures for handling errors and making certain that they have been handled properly.

Input/Output Controls and the Audit. It is necessary that the auditor realizes the importance of input errors and how they can occur. One of the most common errors is incorrectly recording data at the point of inception, for example, when (a) raw material is requisitioned for processing, or (b) raw material is recorded as being requisitioned. An error can be created when a keypunch operator is converting data to machine-readable form. Because of difficulty in reading a 7,000 figure, a keypunch operator may punch 9,000. A source document may be lost in handling. The bank may lose a deposit ticket, and it cannot be determined to whom the overage belongs. Finally, there may be errors in processing the data by the computer. A wrong program used to process the data may run, but the results are incorrect. An auditor may locate the input errors by reviewing the output and comparing it to source documents. This would involve the auditor in inspecting error corrections in order to eliminate the introduction of new errors or the accumulation of uncorrected errors in an error correction account. The frequency and type of errors encountered at the point of input and output will aid greatly in determining the nature and extent of the audit work.

AUDIT RETRIEVAL PACKAGES

Because of the expanding automated environment, the computer is becoming increasingly involved in the overall audit process. With more material being processed, files are becoming larger and processing is becoming more sophisticated. Therefore, these data bases are being extensively used for internal decision making as well as facilitating the audit process.

In the not too distant past, the auditor was presented information as a result of the client's programs or it was obtained for him through specially written programs. Under such unfavorable conditions, the auditor would frequently receive more information than he needed or the special programs were difficult to justify economically.

It is therefore clear that an auditor needed something to provide a means, on short notice, whereby a wide variety of specific information could be retrieved from computerized records and enable him to perform the needed audit procedures.

As a result, all large CPA firms have developed audit retrieval packages which usually consist of prewritten computer programs that can be linked together and accurately adapted by the auditor to the requirements of his audit program.

These retrieval packages are used to:

1. Perform mathematical computations.
2. Select samples.
3. Search and retrieve items that have audit significance from a large mass of data.
4. Make file comparisons and at the same time merge and/or sort data.
5. Summarize and report selected data.
6. Print and/or punch out results in the required audit format.

In order for the preceding results to be obtained, retrieval packages recognize the complexity of design and the magnitude of computer systems configurations. All retrieval packages have certain common objectives as follows:

1. To provide computer-based audit independence for the auditor.
2. To provide immediate access to data generated and stored by a variety of computer systems and at various locations.
3. To utilize the speed of a computer system, and thereby reduce routine clerical analyses.
4. To execute major segments of an audit through the computer.
5. To increase and improve the range of statistical and analytical techniques necessary for comprehensive auditing.
6. To minimize the requirements for a high degree of computer-technological expertise on the part of the auditor.
7. To direct the auditor's talents into more advanced auditing techniques.

The following examples demonstrate the basic applications of retrieval packages:

1. A client has an inventory of 50,000 items and the auditor needed to know the structure of this inventory. Therefore, the auditor's program has certain criteria established, such as: slow turnover (units), unusual cost/selling price relationship (dollar value), last purchase/requisition date (obsolescence). This program would provide the auditor with several types of materials necessary for the proper valuation of inventory.
2. A client has used 100,000 purchase vouchers during the year. Since all vouchers were prenumbered, the auditor can generate a random number basis of selection rapidly, determine a satisfactory sample

size, establish the desired statistical confidence level, and print out the desired voucher information in numerical sequence.

3. A client has used 25,000 sales invoices during the year and each invoice has a minimum of 20 extensions. The auditor would follow procedure 2, above and satisfy himself of the accuracy of the client's sales invoices.

4. In observing a physical inventory, an auditor will test-count inventory items. The next step is to compare these selected items with the client's inventory records in order to identify discrepancies. To facilitate this comparison, the auditor will punch his information into cards or tape and then, using the retrieval package, match his findings against the client's complete file. Quantity differences and cost and price extensions will be printed out at the same time. If the auditor has set his precision limits, the print-out will be listed for the auditor's further examination.

All retrieval packages are aimed at harnessing the speed of the computer to aid an auditor in improving the quality of his work and to require less time. In addition, an auditor will achieve greater reliability in certain aspects of an audit, thus affording greater confidence in the audit work and reporting.

AUDIT PROBLEMS RELATING TO COMPUTER CENTERS

Many small to medium-sized organizations need certain phases of their accounting activity handled by a computer. However, it is not economically feasible for them to own the equipment, so they contract for services of a computer used by many firms. All of these computer service centers have programs already prepared or have qualified personnel that can prepare the necessary programs to meet a given requirement. The main problem the auditor faces here is that an outside organization enters into the client's scheme of processing, internal control, and record retention. However, since there is separation of persons, deliberate manipulation of these records is quite remote. Because of this arm's-length relationship, errors in data processing are often more likely to be detected. Certain audit procedures must be followed under these circumstances. The auditor must first be assured that the client has proper control over data transmitted to the processing center. This involves document count, transaction count, and a control total, such as the total of employee identification numbers. The auditor must then make certain that the client has a means of verifying the details processed by the service center such as a prelist of the amount of all account receivable invoices turned over for processing. The auditor would then determine the center's control over the master file and changes thereto, plus the control over error correction and resubmission. This is important as the issuance of instructions and data to the service center must be restricted to authorized persons.

This same care must be exercised in the return of the data to the client's personnel responsible for maintaining controls. The carrying out of these functions can be determined by the auditor through the inspection of error printouts, error log maintained by the client, and the signatures of the persons receiving the input data at the service center and output data in the client's office. The auditor should observe the operations at the service center, noting the manner in which the data are processed and inspecting the record security procedures. The final step in an audit program would be to examine for accuracy a sample of transactions processed at the service center.

Time-sharing computer service centers are now extensively used for the processing of accounting information. Here the client will have an input/output device in his own office, usually a teletypewriter with special features that adapt it to the central computer frequently located in some other city. The client will have an identification number to which only he has access, and will use this number to identify the files he wishes to use.

The system is so designed that it prevents one user from gaining unauthorized access to the files of another. Frequently a client will not only have his own data files, but all firms providing this service have developed many programs, such as a random numbers selection program, that a client has access to at a very nominal cost. It is evident that the on-line processing method used in time-sharing service is distinctly different from the method of batching data and sending it to a service center for processing. Since the auditor is seldom able to audit the control programs of the time-sharing center, a client should make certain that the information required for audit purposes can be made available. In addition, the auditor must be assured that the time-sharing service center has controls and protections that will produce the desired results.

An auditor must satisfy himself that the time-sharing center provides protection against unauthorized alteration or destruction of the client's program, and that there is provision for file reconstruction if something should happen. Further, there must be control against unauthorized use of the client's file as well as any proprietary programs. Finally, there must be complete provision for recovery from equipment failure as well as inaccurate transmission of input/output data. Having satisfied himself as to the time-sharing center's controls, he must then determine the adequacy of his client's controls over input data and the control totals, record count, and any other measures taken to insure accurate input. Since it is impractical for the auditor to obtain satisfaction about the computer center's time-sharing system by direct examination, records maintained at the service center may be tested by using printouts of the file or by running audit routines. An audit routine would involve testing a certain series or set of transactions or the development of simulated transactions which would determine the accuracy of operation of the program.

The Audit Trail and Audit Procedures

The skepticism with which the auditor greeted the introduction of the computer to the field of accounting has properly disappeared. Early programs were unsatisfactory, largely due to the lack of knowledge on the part of programmers and system designers. However, management's need of inquiry trails for reference purposes and the auditor's insistence upon maintaining adequate audit trails have completely changed the unacceptable conditions that existed originally.

Most clients have sufficient printed records, journals, and source documents, so that audit trail conditions have not changed enough to require significantly different audit procedures from those used in non-EDP systems. Undoubtedly, the best way the auditor can assure himself as to the existence of satisfactory audit trails and audit procedures is through the development of special audit computer programs. This is being widely done today, so that the auditor uses the computer to develop audit criteria and procedures for analysis and selection of records for audit as well as to analyze the transaction and master files. The auditor will not only successfully accomplish the objective of an audit, but will insure management against a system that will not provide it with the information needed to operate the business satisfactorily.

SUGGESTED ADDITIONAL READING:

Statement on Auditing Standards No. 1, Sections 320A and 320B, 330 through 332.

Statement on Auditing Standards No. 3.

American Institute of Certified Public Accountants Professional Development Division—Statistical Sampling. All sections.

QUESTIONS

1. What constitutes original records?
2. What are the purposes of sampling and testing?
3. What are the characteristics of an "adequate" sample?
4. What problems arise in determining the size of the sample to be selected?
5. Briefly describe the types of samples an auditor might use.
6. What must first be established before any sample plan can be used?
7. For detailed examination an auditor customarily selects a sample of items entered in a voucher register.
   a) What are the audit purposes of this type of vouching test?
   b) List the items for which each voucher should be examined.
8. An audit report normally includes the following statement: ". . . and accordingly included such tests of the accounting records as we considered necessary in the circumstances."

How does the auditor determine what tests of the accounting records are necessary and the extent of their testing?

9. What are the points of importance in the verification of (*a*) cash receipts, and (*b*) cash disbursements?

10. An auditor is interested in verifying transactions occurring between the balance sheet date and the date of completing his examination.

    a) Present specific examples of auditing steps to be followed and the reasons for them.

    b) As a result of matters disclosed by this additional auditing, what might be some of the effects on the audit period-end financial statements?

11. What are the major phases of an audit examination that are affected by the presence of a computer in the accounting system?

12. What basic knowledge is required of an auditor to effectively audit EDP systems?

13. Why does EDP equipment strengthen internal control?

14. What are some of the controls and checks incorporated in a data processing program?

15. How can the effectiveness of controls within the equipment be tested?

16. Why is it desirable for an auditor to assist a client in developing and changing his EDP system?

17. How frequently should the auditor review his client's system of controls?

18. In order for internal control to be effective in an EDP system, how would you divide the processing function?

19. What are audit retrieval packages?

20. What are the common objectives of retrieval packages?

PROBLEMS

1. This is the first audit of the Sample Company. The company was organized January 2, 1976. When informed by the president of the company that the

SAMPLE COMPANY
Trial Balance
December 31, 1976

	Debit	Credit
Cash in bank and petty cash	$ 32,800	
Accounts receivable	169,600	
Merchandise inventory	84,200	
Store equipment	20,800	
Accounts payable		$ 49,200
Common stock		200,000
Sales		512,800
Purchases of inventory	283,800	
Salaries	95,600	
Taxes	5,400	
Rent	13,000	
Store operating expense	56,800	
Totals	$762,000	$762,000

records were to be examined, the cashier-accountant prepared the following trial balance—and left town!

In examining the records or original entry and the ledger accounts, the following items were disclosed:

(1) The Cash debit column and the Accounts Receivable credit column in the cash receipts journal were each underfooted $4,000.

(2) An adding machine tape of the cash sales invoices for the year was $5,600 in excess of the cash sales debits in the cash receipts journal.

(3) An examination of the check record disclosed that the Cash credit column was overfooted $1,600, the Accounts Payable debit column was similarly overadded.

(4) Bank reconciliations prepared by the cashier-accountant for the first 11 months of the year were perfect. In your preparation of a bank reconciliation as of December 31, 1976, a difference of $2,800 was disclosed. The paid checks returned with the December bank statement including one check for $2,800, made payable to the order of "Cash"; this check had not been recorded.

(5) In the $2,000 petty cash fund, there was an IOU for $1,600 signed by the departed cashier-accountant.

(6) When the Store Operating Expense account was examined, it showed several charges for checks drawn payable to the order of "Cash," for a total amount of $5,600. Each check had been signed by the president, who admitted that he sometimes signed checks drawn to "Cash" because the cashier-accountant advised him that they were for petty cash fund reimbursements. The president also stated that occasionally he would sign blank checks in advance of their use.

(7) Also, when analyzing the Store Operating Expense account, one check for $8,800, made payable to the order of J. J. Boyd, bore the endorsement of J. J. Boyd followed by the endorsement of the cashier-accountant. An examination of purchase orders and vendors' invoice disclosed no J. J. Boyd. The president stated that the company had never purchased from J. J. Boyd.

(8) An examination of the payroll records showed duplicate payments to the cashier-accountant for June and July totaling $5,600 gross and also net of all taxes which should be deducted.

From the preceding data, prepare:

a) The audit adjustments necessary to correct any errors.

b) A work sheet starting with the company trial balance, then audit adjustments, and concluding with an adjusted trial balance.

c) A recapitulation of the shortages to be submitted to the insurance company which had bonded the cashier-accountant for $20,000.

2. In any statistical sampling situations, the desired precision is usually specified before any information is obtained. Precision obtained through sampling is usually expressed as a numerical quantity or as a percentage of the estimate.

a) If the estimate is $300,000 and the precision of this estimate is ± 2 percent, what are the amounts that the true value is expected to be no less than and no more than?

b)   If the estimate is $500,000 and the precision limits are $475,000 and $525,000, what is the precision ± dollar amount and percent amount?

c)   If the estimate is $220,000 and the precision of this estimate is ± $10,000, what are the precision limits?

d)   If the estimate is $400,000 and the precision of this estimate is ± 3 percent, what are the precision limits?

e)   If the estimate is $50,000 and the precision limits are $48,000 and $52,000, what is the precision dollar amount and percent amount?

3.   By using Illustrations 5–1 and 5–2 of the text, an auditor can determine the required sample size.

a)   Determine the required sample size under each of the following conditions:

	Client 1	Client 2	Client 3	Client 4
Reliability	95%	90%	95%	90%
Upper precision limit	8%	10%	30%	30%
Estimated occurrence rate	5.0%	7%	24.6%	25.8%
Sample size	?	?	?	?

b)   Determine the upper precision limit under each of the following conditions:

	Client A	Client B	Client C	Client D
Reliability	95%	90%	95%	90%
Upper precision limit	?	?	?	?
Estimated occurrence rate	10%	8%	22%	27%
Sample size	120	460	120	460

c)   Determine the reliability or confidence level under each of the following conditions:

	Client 7	Client 8	Client 9	Client 10
Reliability	?	?	?	?
Upper precision limit	18%	40%	12%	30%
Estimated occurrence rate	15%	37%	9%	22%
Sample size	340	460	460	120

d)   Determine the estimated occurrence rate under each of the following conditions:

	Client X	Client Y	Client Z	Client O
Reliability	90%	90%	95%	95%
Upper precision limit	9%	18%	16%	45%
Estimated occurrence rate	?	?	?	?
Sample size	460	340	340	90

4. Illustrations 5–3 and 5–4 of the text provide the auditor with a means of determining whether or not he can state with a definite degree of confidence that the population does not contain more than a certain predetermined percent of errors. Using Illustrations 5–3 and 5–4, answer the questions in the following situations:

a)

	Client 1	Client 2	Client 3	Client 4
Confidence level	95%	90%	95%	90%
Number of errors	30	30	87	85
Sample size	340	240	340	240
Upper precision limit	?	?	?	?

b)

	Client A	Client B	Client C	Client D
Confidence level	90%	95%	90%	95%
Number of errors	26	14	90	48
Sample size	?	?	?	?
Upper precision limit	10%	9%	30%	25%

c)

	Client 7	Client 8	Client 9	Client 10
Confidence level	95%	95%	90%	90%
Number of errors	?	?	?	?
Sample size	160	160	160	160
Upper precision limit	10%	40%	9%	40%

d)

	Client X	Client Y	Client Z	Client O
Confidence level	?	?	?	?
Number of errors	17	5	32	147
Sample size	340	80	80	460
Upper precision limit	7%	14%	50%	35%

5. The use of statistical sampling techniques in an examination of financial statements does not eliminate judgmental decisions.

   a) Identify and explain four areas where judgment may be exercised by a CPA in planning a statistical sampling test.

   b) Assume that a CPA's sample shows an unacceptable error rate. Describe the various actions that he may take based upon this finding.

   c) A nonstratified sample of 80 accounts payable vouchers is to be selected from a population of 3,200. The vouchers are numbered consecutively from 1 to 3,200 and are listed, 40 to a page, in the voucher register. Describe four different techniques for selecting a random sample of vouchers for review.

(AICPA, adapted)

6. Select the best answer for each of the following items:
   a) In performing a review of his client's cash disbursements, a CPA uses systematic sampling with a random start. The primary *disadvantage* of systematic sampling is that population items—
      (1) Must be recorded in a systematic pattern before the sample can be drawn.
      (2) May occur in a systematic pattern, thus negating the randomness of the sample.
      (3) May occur twice in the sample.
      (4) Must be replaced in the population after sampling to permit valid statistical inference.
   b) From prior experience, a CPA is aware of the fact that cash disbursements contain a few unusually large disbursements. In using statistical sampling, the CPA's best course of action is to—
      (1) Eliminate any unusually large disbursements which appear in the sample.
      (2) Continue to draw new samples until no unusually large disbursements appear in the sample.
      (3) Stratify the cash-disbursements population so that the unusually large disbursements are reviewed separately.
      (4) Increase the sample size to lessen the effect of the unusually large disbursements.
   c) In connection with his test of the accuracy of inventory counts, a CPA decides to use discovery sampling. Discovery sampling may be considered a special case of—
      (1) Judgmental sampling.
      (2) Sampling for variables.
      (3) Stratified sampling.
      (4) Sampling for attributes.
   d) Approximately 5 percent of the 10,000 homogeneous items included in Barletta's finished-goods inventory are believed to be defective. The CPA examining Barletta's financial statements decides to test this estimated 5 percent defective rate. He learns that by sampling without replacement that a sample of 284 items from the inventory will permit specified reliability (confidence level) of 95 percent and specified precision (confidence interval) of ∓ 0.25. If specified precision is changed to $\mp .05$, and specified reliability remains 95 percent, the required sample size is—
      (1) 72.
      (2) 335.
      (3) 436.
      (4) 1,543.
   e) The "reliability" (confidence level) of an estimate made from sample data is a mathematically determined figure that expresses the ex-

pected proportion of possible samples of a specified size from a given population—
  (1) That will yield an interval estimate that will encompass the true population value.
  (2) That will yield an interval estimate that will not encompass the true population value.
  (3) For which the sample value and the population value are identical.
  (4) For which the sample elements will not exceed the population elements by more than a stated amount.

f) In an examination of financial statements a CPA generally will find stratified-sampling techniques to be least appropriate to—
  (1) Examining charges to the maintenance account during the audit year.
  (2) Tests of transactions for compliance with internal control.
  (3) The recomputation of a sample of factory workers' net pay.
  (4) Year-end confirmation of bank balances.

g) A CPA's client maintains perpetual inventory records. In the past, all inventory items have been counted on a cycle basis at least once during the year. Physical count and perpetual record differences have been minor. Now, the client wishes to minimize the cost of physically counting the inventory by changing to a sampling method in which many inventory items will not be counted during a given year. For purposes of expressing an opinion on his client's financial statements, the CPA will accept the sampling method only if—
  (1) The sampling method has statistical validity.
  (2) A stratified sampling plan is used.
  (3) The client is willing to accept an opinion qualification in the auditor's report.
  (4) The client is willing to accept a scope qualification in the auditor's report.

h) As the specified reliability is increased in a discovery sampling plan for any given population and maximum occurrence rate, the required sample size—
  (1) Increases.
  (2) Decreases.
  (3) Remains the same.
  (4) Cannot be determined.

(AICPA, adapted)

7. The following situations apply to an examination by Ruth Waters, CPA, of the financial statements of Allan Manufacturing for the year ended December 31, 1976. Allan manufactures two products: Product A and Product B. Product A requires raw materials which have a very low per-item cost; Product B requires raw materials which have a very high per-item cost. Raw materials for both products are stored in a single warehouse. In 1975, Allan established the total value of raw materials stored in the warehouse by physically inventorying an unrestricted random sample of items selected without replacement.

Ms. Waters is evaluating the statistical validity of alternative sampling plans Allan is considering for 1976. Waters knows the size of the 1975 sample and that Allan did not use stratified sampling in 1975. Assumptions about the population, variability, specified precision (confidence interval), and specified reliability (confidence level) for a possible 1976 sample are given in each of the following five items. Using the responses listed below, you are to indicate in each case the effect upon the size of the 1976 sample as compared to the 1975 sample. Each of the five cases is independent of the other four and is to be considered separately. In each of the five following cases your answer will be either:

(1)   Larger than the 1975 sample size.

(2)   Equal to the 1975 sample size.

(3)   Smaller than the 1975 sample size.

(4)   Of a size that is indeterminate based upon the information given.

   a)   Allan wants to use stratified sampling in 1976 (the total population will be divided into two strata, one each for the raw materials for Product A and Product B). Compared to 1975, the population size of the raw-materials inventory is approximately the same, and the variability of the items in the inventory is approximately the same. The specified precision and specified reliability are to remain the same.

   b)   Allan wants to use stratified sampling in 1976. Compared to 1975, the population size of the raw-materials inventory is approximately the same, and the variability of the items in the inventory is approximately the same. Allan specified the same precision but desires to change the specified reliability from 90 percent to 95 percent.

   c)   Allan wants to use unrestricted random sampling without replacement in 1976. Compared to 1975, the population size of the raw-materials inventory is approximately the same, and the variability of the items in the inventory is approximately the same. Allan specifies the same precision but desires to change the specified reliability from 90 percent to 95 percent.

   d)   Allan wants to use unrestricted random sampling without replacement in 1976. Compared to 1975, the population size of the raw-materials inventory has increased, and the variability of the items in the inventory has increased. The specified precision and specified reliability are to remain the same.

   e)   Allan wants to use unrestricted random sampling without replacement in 1976. Compared to 1975, the population size of the raw-materials inventory has increased, but the variability of the items in the inventory has decreased. The specified precision and specified reliability are to remain the same.

(AICPA, adapted)

8.   Evidential matter supporting financial statements consists of the underlying accounting data and all corroborating information available to the auditor. In the course of an audit of financial statements, the auditor will perform detail tests of samples of transactions from various large-

volume populations. The auditor may also audit various types through all stages of the accounting system.

a) What are the various audit objectives associated with a sample of transactions from a large-volume population?

b) What evidential matter would the auditor expect to gain from auditing various types of transactions by tracing a single transaction of each type through all stages of the accounting system?

(AICPA, adapted)

6

Cash and Cash Transactions

APPROACH TO AN AUDIT

A definitive audit program should be prepared for each functional area —that is, audit steps should be presented so that the audit objectives are satisfied. The approach to an audit involves a review of internal control, examination of transactions and their evidential supports, and a professionally conducted review of all necessary financial data and nonfinancial information, as stated in Chapter 5. An audit primarily constitutes the examination of past events with the objective of rendering an opinion regarding the fairness of presentation of a client's financial statements. However, all audits should be performed with the thought in mind of future operations and financial condition of a business organization. Past history cannot be changed. In the communication and measurement of financial operating data, income statements may be more important than balance sheets or statements of changes in financial position. Therefore, it may appear logical to approach an audit from a revenue and expense point of view; and an audit can be approached by initially examining revenue and expense transactions and tying those transactions into related assets or liabilities. However, all revenue and expense transactions terminate in assets and their acquisition or disposition, and/or in liabilities and their incurrence or liquidation.

Traditionally and logically, in most audits balance-sheet items and their related transactions normally are considered initially, because to do so automatically correlates the examination of assets, revenues, liabilities, and expenses. When examining an asset or a liability, all related items will be examined. As an example, when auditing investment securities, there will be an examination of the authority to purchase, the price paid, dividends, interest received, interest receivable, and the amortization of premiums or discounts.

In some instances, an auditor will start with a client's financial statements or trial balance and trace the client's operations until he is satisfied with the examination of evidences and related entries. For example, in the verification of cash balances, an auditor can refer directly to cash funds, bank statements, and bank reconciliations. In examining sales, an auditor can start with sales for the year and test sales transactions until he is satisfied with the propriety of the annual sales; one or two months' sales record entries would be footed and the related invoices proved for accuracy and compared with customers' orders and shipping records. In many instances, it may be simpler and more logical to start with the audited account balance of the prior period and work forward to the client's ending balance of the current period. For example, in the examination of an office equipment account for a continuing client, an auditor can start with the audited account balance of the prior period, examine current-period evidences, and trace those evidences into the account for the current period.

CASH AUDIT OBJECTIVES

The objectives of examining cash transactions, cash funds, and cash balances in banks are to establish the validity and propriety of the cash transactions and to properly state the cash for purposes of financial statement presentation. Cash is no more valuable than any other asset of equal current market price. However, the examination of cash and cash transactions is important (1) because cash is a favorite item for theft, (2) because the majority of all business transactions involve a cash account or terminate in it, (3) because errors in any account can result in errors in cash accounts, and (4) because errors in cash accounts indicate probable errors in other accounts—principally, accounts-payable debits and accounts-receivable credits.

Normally, cash—on hand, in funds, and in depositaries—is examined and verified early in an audit. This early examination saves time because the auditor obtains a current verification and is not forced to prove year-end balances by working back to the year-end from a later date.

INTERNAL CONTROL OF CASH FUNDS

Proper internal control over cash funds—petty cash funds, cash register funds, and others—demands that the responsibility for each fund be vested in one person, that disbursements be made only after proper approval, and that the funds be safeguarded. See Chapter 3.

An internal control questionnaire for cash funds is presented in Illustration 6–1.

Illustration 6–1

INTERNAL CONTROL QUESTIONNAIRE
Cash Funds

	Yes	No	Not Appli- cable	Remarks

Company_____
Period Covered_____

1. Is the imprest system used?
2. Is responsibility for each fund vested in one person?
3. Are cash fund vouchers:
   a) Prenumbered by the printer?
   b) Required for each fund disbursement?
   c) Signed by the person who receives the cash?
   d) Filled in with numerals and spelled-out amounts?
   e) Approved by a responsible person?
   f) Properly canceled, together with supporting documents, so that they cannot be used again?
4. Does the fund custodian have access to cash receipts?
5. Does the fund custodian have access to general accounting records?
6. Are reimbursement checks made payable to the order of the fund custodian?
7. Are personnel advances from the fund properly approved?
8. Are checks cashed from the fund deposited promptly?
9. Are postdated checks in the fund?
10. When the fund is reimbursed, are the cash vouchers internally audited?
11. Is there a surprise internal audit of cash funds?
12. Are the funds reasonable in amount?

Prepared by_____   Reviewed by_____
Date_____   Date _____

AUDIT OF CASH FUNDS

Audit procedures for petty cash fund disbursements were presented in Chapter 5. The same procedures are applicable to all other cash funds. The following audit procedures are applicable to the examination of the funds proper.

When cash funds are to be counted, there should be simultaneous control over all cash and all negotiable securities in order to prevent transfers from fund to fund, from securities to cash, and from cash to securities during the course of an audit. After the contents of each cash box, safe, securities file, etc., have been counted, each item may be released to the client. Preferably, cash funds should be counted after the close of business hours in order to expedite audit operations.

A separate listing is made of the contents of each cash fund. Noncash items—such as loans—must, by audit adjustments, be transferred to receivables; expense vouchers in the fund must, by adjustment, be transferred to the proper expense accounts. Checks in cash funds must be listed and compared with the auditor's prior-period work papers in order to detect long-term borrowing.

Illustration 6–2
WORK PAPER 1

	Initials	Date
MULTI-PRODUCTS, INCORPORATED Prepared By	CF	1-2-77
Petty Cash Fund, December 31, 1976 Approved By	RW	1-11-77

	Number	Denomination	Extension	Total
Paper Currency:	44	10 00	440 00	
	46	5 00	230 00	
	137	1 00	137 00	807 00
Coin Currency	42	50	21 00	
	70	25	17 50	
	125	10	12 50	
	240	05	12 00	63 00
Total Currency				870 00

Checks:	Date	Maker	Bank	Amount	
	12-28-76	W. Alden	Silverton	250 00	√
	12-30-76	James Bly	First	175 00	√
	12-30-76	Joe Cardon	Provident	125 00	√
Total Checks					550 00

Paid Vouchers				
Number	Date	Paid to	Distribution	Amount
888	12-20-76	Plaza Hotel	Off. Operating	162 00
889	12-22-76	Natl. Reg.	Mach. Maint.	50 00
890	12-28-76	Stationers, Inc.	Office Supplies	116 00
891	12-30-76	Store Sta. Co.	Office Supplies	252 00
Total Vouchers				580 00
Total Fund				2 000 00

√ Cashed at bank, under our control.
Examined reimbursement vouchers and supporting detail
for March 10, May 15, October 21, and November 20--15%

Count witnessed by Al Garon

Return of fund acknowledged by Carl Jones

AJE 1				
Office Operating Expense			162 00	
Machinery Maintenance			50 00	
Office Supplies			368 00	
Petty Cash				580 00
To clear the December, 1976, vouchers, and to reduce				
the fund to $1,420.				

A cash fund count and listing for Multi-Products, Incorporated appears in Illustration 6–2. This is exemplary of work paper preparation for any cash fund. The handling of the auditor's adjustments should be noted, as should the use of audit code legends.

After the items in each fund are counted and listed and a work paper total is obtained, that total must be compared with the corresponding general-ledger account balance. To illustrate the necessity for this comparison: A work paper total for a fund was $500; the general-ledger account balance was $600; the fund custodian had "borrowed" $100 and had hoped that the auditor would not make the comparison.

Under control of the auditor, all checks in each fund which bear dates prior to the fund count should be deposited in the bank. The succeeding bank statement should be examined for the clearance of those checks. If the checks did not clear, the auditor should prepare audit adjustments, charging receivables or uncollectible items expense in accordance with the circumstances.

Approved postdated checks in the funds are receivables as of the financial statement date. The auditor should obtain written approval from a responsible person for all receivables, expense vouchers, and checks of employees in the funds. This is necessary as a precaution against the possibility of unauthorized items being in the funds.

An auditor should obtain confirmations directly from persons who have received advances from *any* fund. Travel expense funds may be in operation; the persons who obtained money from the funds may have spent a portion or all of the amount received prior to the close of the fiscal period. After obtaining proper confirmations, the auditor is in a position to adjust the accounts. Confirmations also are an aid in the detection of fraud, wherein one person may have stolen from a fund and may have signed the name of an innocent person to the withdrawal voucher.

If funds exist at distant locations—branch stores, for example—and if the auditor cannot visit those distant locations, caution must be exercised. The materiality of the amount of each such fund, the system of internal control, and the system of internal audit will guide the auditor in his decision either to accept or reject the fund composition. The best procedure to follow is to insist that funds that cannot be counted be reimbursed by the main office as of the close of business on the last day of the year. He also should insist that all distant fund vouchers be sent to the main office for examination.

A representative of the client should witness the count of all funds by the auditor. This procedure proves the count and frees the auditor from the possibility of suspicion of fraud. Some auditors obtain a receipt from the fund custodians; others do not.

It is not always possible to count and list fund balances exactly at the close of the year. When funds are counted subsequent to the year-end date, the fund composition must be reconciled back to the financial statement date. Assuming a financial statement date of December 31, 1976, and a fund count date of January 21, 1977, this reconciliation is accomplished as follows:

Fund count, January 21, 1977 . . . . $4,000
Add: Fund vouchers, January 1–January 21, 1977   800
                                                                  $4,800
Deduct: Fund reimbursement, January 1–January 21, 1977   800
Fund balance, December 31, 1976 . . . . $4,000

INTERNAL CONTROL OF CASH ON HAND

Internal control features applicable to undeposited cash on hand were presented in Chapter 5 in connection with cash receipts and cash disbursements. Internal control questionnaires for cash receipts and cash disbursements appear in Chapter 5. To summarize: Cash receipts should be recorded immediately; they should be controlled; and they should be deposited intact. Cash disbursements should be by check. Personnel duties should be separated for receiving cash, recording receipts, depositing, reconciling, authorizing disbursements, and disbursing.

AUDIT OF CASH ON HAND AND IN BANKS

Audit procedures applicable to cash receipts and cash disbursements were set forth in Chapter 5. An audit program for cash on hand and in banks is as follows:

The large majority of sales are made on credit; therefore, this chapter purposely deemphasizes the audit of revenues, which are treated in Chapter 7.

As stated on page 186, all cash, cash items, and negotiable securities should be controlled simultaneously at the time of counting and listing. If simultaneous control of all items is not possible, uncontrolled items should be sealed by the auditor in order to prevent transfers of items between locations.

Undeposited cash and cash items should be listed in *detail,* and the auditor must trace these items to the next bank statement in order to prove that all items subject to deposit were deposited. If expenses or other costs are paid from cash receipts, the bank deposits will be short of the cash received by the amount so spent.

The auditor should obtain, directly from the banks, confirmations of amounts on deposit as of the closing date of the fiscal period. Confirmation requests are prepared by the auditor and signed by the client. They are mailed by the auditor, together with a return envelope addressed directly to the auditor. This prevents the possibility of altering confirmation request replies. When received, the confirmation replies are compared with bank-statement balances.

It is preferable to mail confirmation requests to banks in advance of the examination of cash so that replies will be available when the cash examination is started. Confirmation requests should be mailed to *all* banks with which the client has conducted business since the date of the last audit. It is possible, for example, that a client may have closed a bank account—except for uncleared checks. The client's Cash account would show no balance, but a confirmation would show as a balance the amount of the uncleared checks.

If possible, the auditor should compare the detail of cash receipts as shown by the cash receipts record with the *detail* of the confirmed duplicate deposit tickets for the last few days of the audit period and the first few days of the subsequent period. He may mail these duplicate deposit tickets to the bank and request direct confirmation of the *detail* appearing therein, or this request may be included as a part of the confirmation procedure.

Today, very few banks compare the detail of deposit tickets with the items deposited; most banks total the deposit and compare that total with the total of the deposit tickets. Therefore, the comparison of details is almost a practice of the past. Because a bank cannot be expected to allot excessive time to examining the duplicate deposit tickets of its customers —in this case, the client of the auditor—the client should carefully control its duplicate deposit tickets by not permitting them to be returned to the cashier or the accountant. Most duplicate deposit tickets can be easily altered.

Deposits in transit must be traced to the next bank statement, or direct confirmation of deposits should be obtained from the bank. Items in transit should reach the bank in a few days at the maximum. If more than normal time elapses, it may indicate that cash has been received and charged on the records of the client and temporarily borrowed by an employee by a system of lapping. Occasionally, when a cash receipt is not deposited, the cashier will make the statement that advances for salaries or travel expenses were made from the receipts, and that the cashier is waiting for reimbursement for those items before making the deposit. Even if the excuse is the truth, the attention of the client should be called to this undesirable practice.

Cash deposits made by branches on the last day of the year but not taken up by the home office on the same day owing to transportation should be considered as home office receipts as of the last day of the period. Transit items, if not traced by the auditor, may cover fraud through kiting. Some companies carry a Cash in Transit account which is charged with cash on its way to the home office and credited when the money is received. If a customer notifies the company that he is paying a bill, no entries should be made until the cash has actually been received by the company.

One form of bank confirmation request has been prepared by the AICPA. It is designed to request not only the amounts on deposit to the credit of the client but also to request confirmation of liabilities to the bank and client collateral held by the bank. This confirmation request is prepared in duplicate; the bank returns one copy to the auditor and retains one. See Illustration 6–3 for the confirmation for Multi-Products, Incorporated.

Prior to counting the cash on hand and reconciling the bank balances, the auditor must have access to all bank statements, duplicate deposit tickets, bank paid checks, and the last client-prepared reconciliation.

Bank Reconciliations. There are many forms of reconciliations, one of which is shown in Illustration 6–4 for Multi-Products, Incorporated. When preparing a reconciliation, the auditor must refer to his preceding reconciliation and tick off checks then outstanding which have cleared in the period under examination. Illustration 6–5 is an example of a work paper which serves as a proof of cash transactions over the year-end.

Reconciliations may be prepared (1) as of a date prior to the balance-sheet date, (2) as of the balance-sheet date, or (3) as of a date subsequent to the balance-sheet date.

A bank reconciliation may be prepared as of a date prior to the balance-sheet date. Acceptable auditing procedure permits this practice only if the client reconciles its bank accounts each month, and only if the system of internal control is satisfactory. If bank balances are reconciled by the auditor as of a date prior to the balance-sheet date, the client's reconciliations must be reviewed, followed by a review of cash receipts and disbursements transactions from the date before the balance sheet to the balance-sheet date. This practice reduces year-end work pressure.

If the reconciliation is prepared as of the balance-sheet date, normal procedure is to start with the bank statement balance and work toward the client's ledger account balance. Deposits in transit at the year-end must be added to the bank statement balance, and the auditor must either confirm the in-transit items with the bank or examine a later-date bank statement sent directly to him.

The original reconciliation may be prepared as of a date subsequent to the balance-sheet date. If cash is counted and reconciliations are prepared subsequent to the balance-sheet date, the auditor must obtain *directly* from the banks the bank statements and checks cleared to that date. Assume that the cash is counted and reconciliations are prepared as of January 15, 1977, for the year ended December 31, 1976. The January 15, 1977, reconciliation will be worked back to December 31, 1976, by starting with the January 15, 1977, bank statement balance and adding debits per the bank statement and subtracting credits per the bank statement. The result would be a reconciled bank balance as of December 31, 1976. See Illustration 6–5.

Most auditors prepare a bank reconciliation as of the end of the client's year. They then prepare a later—cutoff—reconciliation; or they

Illustration 6–3

> **DUPLICATE**
> To be retained by Bank

January 2, 19 77

Dear Sirs:

Your completion of the following report will be sincerely appreciated. IF THE ANSWER TO ANY ITEM IS "NONE", PLEASE SO STATE. Kindly mail it in the enclosed stamped, addressed envelope <u>direct</u> to the accountant named below.

Report from   Yours truly,

Multi-Products, Incorporated
(ACCOUNT NAME PER BANK RECORDS)

(Bank)___**First National Bank**___   By _*Dale Linder*_
                                                    Authorized Signature

___**Fourth and Walnut Streets**___

___**Cincinnati, Ohio** 45202___

Bank customer should check here if confirmation of bank balances only (item 1) is desired. ☐

NOTE – If the space provided is inadequate, please enter totals hereon and attach a statement giving full details as called for by the columnar headings below.

Accountant   **Bennett and Bennett**
                  Carew Tower
                  Cincinnati, Ohio 45202
Dear Sirs:

1. At the close of business on __**December 31,**__ 19 76 our records showed the following balance(s) to the <u>credit</u> of the above named customer. In the event that we could readily ascertain whether there were any balances to the credit of the customer not designated in this request, the appropriate information is given below.

AMOUNT	ACCOUNT NAME	ACCOUNT NUMBER	SUBJECT TO WITH-DRAWAL BY CHECK?	INTEREST BEARING? GIVE RATE
$ 39,292.00	Checking	519-13504	Yes	No

2. The customer was directly liable to us in respect of loans, acceptances, etc., at the close of business on that date in the total amount of $ 40,000.00 , as follows:

AMOUNT	DATE OF LOAN OR DISCOUNT	DUE DATE	INTEREST RATE	INTEREST PAID TO	DESCRIPTION OF LIABILITY, COLLATERAL, SECURITY INTERESTS, LIENS, ENDORSERS, ETC.
$ 40,000.00	Nov.2,1976	Demand	4.5	-0-	Unsecured

3. The customer was contingently liable as endorser of notes discounted and/or as guarantor at the close of business on that date in the total amount of $ none , as below:

AMOUNT	NAME OF MAKER	DATE OF NOTE	DUE DATE	REMARKS
$				

4. Other direct or contingent liabilities, open letters of credit, and relative collateral, were

    None

5. Security agreements under the Uniform Commercial Code or any other agreements providing for restrictions, not noted above, were as follows (if officially recorded, indicate date and office in which filed):

None

Yours truly, (Bank) **First National Bank**

Date__**January 5,**__ 19 77   By _*Henry A Kramer*_
                                          Authorized Signature

follow through the year-end reconciliation to the cutoff date, in which case cash is not recounted. Today, many banks use the "cycle" method of issuing bank statements; in this case it may be easy to use the cycle date as the cutoff date. Also, some banks refuse to issue statements at dates differing from their normal issuance dates. Either of these procedures permits the detection of unrecorded cash debit and credit entries. Also, either of these procedures permits an auditor to tick off the majority of checks outstanding at the year-end.

The procedure in following through a year-end reconciliation to a cutoff date without preparing a complete record reconciliation may be described as follows: At a cutoff date after the balance-sheet date, request *direct* return of the cutoff (perhaps cycle) date bank statement, together with checks paid to that date. Using the cutoff bank statement and paid checks—

1. Trace year-end deposits in transit to the cutoff bank statement.
2. In the year-end reconciliation, tick off checks cleared to the cutoff date.
3. Investigate balance-sheet date entries for customers' checks returned.
4. Be certain that paid checks returned at the cutoff date were listed as outstanding at the balance-sheet date; a check may have been outstanding at the year-end but not recorded as a disbursement.
5. Account for any other items affecting the balance-sheet date reconciliation.
6. Trace to the cash debit and credit all checks drawn payable to the order of the client or to a bank, indicating fund transfers, in order to detect kiting.

If the foregoing procedure is followed, all items necessary to effect a reconciliation at the cutoff date have been traced. If a *complete* second reconciliation is to be prepared, it should not be announced in advance. A second complete cash count and reconciliation may be necessary under the terms of a surety policy, or if the client is a member of the New York Stock Exchange.

In the preparation of any reconciliation, unreturned certified checks should be listed among the outstanding checks. To complete the reconciliation, the bank charge ticket for the certified check should be deducted. The bank charge for the certified check should be accepted only as evidence that a certified check has been issued; it is not acceptable in lieu of the certified check. If the certified check charge slip is used as a paid check, the certified check is eliminated from the reconciliation— and it still may be outstanding. A few banks return paid certified checks to depositors only upon request. In this case, if the client does not request their return, both paid and unpaid certified checks remain missing. It is entirely possible that a certified check never was presented for payment by the payee.

Illustration 6–4
WORK PAPER 3

	Initials	Date
MULTI-PRODUCTS, INCORPORATED Bank Reconciliation--First National Bank, December 31, 1976	Prepared By　𝓛𝓡	1-3-77
	Approved By　𝓡𝓦	1-7-77

			Amount			
Balance per bank statement, December 31, 1976					39292	
Add: After-hour deposit, December 31, 1976#					13153	
					52445	
Deduct: Outstanding checks:						
Number	Date Paid by Bank		Amount			
3,151	12-18-76		4000	cc		
3,162	12-29-76		5000	cc		
3,167	12-29-76		1468			
3,180	12-29-76	Voided: on file				
3,195	12-30-76		1471			
3,196	12-30-76		295			
3,197	12-31-76		47			
3,198⊙	12-31-76		812			
			13093			
Less: Certified checks outstanding:						
3,151		4 000				
3,162		5 000	9000		4093	
Adjusted Balance, per audit, December 31, 1976					48352	

Confirmed by bank.
⊙ Last check issued.

Checks returned by a bank are compared with bank statement debits only in the case of unlocated error, or in the case of suspected manipulation, or in cases where persons preparing accounting entries have access to uncontrolled and unused checks. A proof of checks cleared during a period may be prepared as follows:

Proof of Checks Cleared

Balance per bank statement, January 1, 1976		$ 28,021
Add: Deposits per bank statements		170,901
		$198,922
Less: Balance per bank statement, December 31, 1976		11,700
Checks and bank debits cleared in 1976, per footed bank statement	(a)	$187,222
Outstanding checks, January 1, 1976		$　650
Add: Disbursements during 1976, per footed cash record		188,122
		$188,772
Less: Outstanding checks, per reconciliation of December 31, 1976		1,550
Checks and bank debits cleared in 1976 (agrees with (a) above)	(a)	$187,222

Illustration 6–5

THE BLANK COMPANY		Initials	Date
Bank Reconciliation--First National Bank — Prepared By		BY	1-11-77
December 31, 1976--January 10, 1977 — Approved By		RW	1-12-77

Explanation	Client Balance, Dec. 31, 1976	Verified Receipts	Verified Disbursements	Auditor Balance, Jan. 10, 1977
Per bank statement and certificate	45228	75620	70500	50348
Deposits in transit:				
December 31, 1976	3928	-3928		
January 10, 1977		5000		5000
Checks outstanding:				
December 31, 1976	-4117		-4117	
January 10, 1977			2462	-2462
Unrecorded bank charges and credits:				
Note collected by bank on January 8, 1977; entered by client on January 11, 1977.		-3000		-3000
Collection charges			-12	12
Per Records	45039	73692	68833	49898

Proof of Cash. A proof of cash may be prepared showing the reconciliation of the total cash receipts recorded with the total bank deposits for the period under examination. The proof of cash also shows the reconciliation of all checks cashed by the bank with the recorded disbursements. See Illustration 6–5.

If cash receipts were recorded and then stolen, and if the cash receipts records were underfooted and so posted, this proof of cash would not be foolproof. Therefore, original cash records must be footed to substantiate the reliability of the proof of cash.

Miscellaneous Cash Considerations. Ordinarily, a cash summary schedule is prepared. This schedule groups all underlying data from supporting schedules. When in the process of preparing reconciliations it is discovered that a customer's check which has been deposited is returned because of insufficient funds, no such account, or a closed account, an adjustment should be prepared, charging Accounts Receivable (or a special account) and crediting Cash. The auditor should request the bank to notify him directly of all unpaid checks from the balance-sheet date to the conclusion of the audit field work. This is necessary to detect kiting and to determine proper treatment of unpaid checks.

For the last few days of the period under examination and for the first few days of the subsequent period, the auditor should compare the *de-*

tail of the cash receipts record entries with the *detail* of bank-deposit tickets. The auditor may mail selected duplicate deposit tickets to the bank and request direct confirmation of the detail, or he may include this request as a part of his bank balance confirmation request, because duplicate deposit tickets can be altered easily. If the client permits duplicate deposit slips to be returned to the cashier or the accountant, internal control is not satisfactory and fraud is possible.

Undeposited checks should be compared with current remittance lists and with cash receipts record entries in order to be certain that undeposited checks have been recorded.

If issued checks remain outstanding for more than two months, the auditor should show a listing of them to the proper official of the client. If a duplicate check has been issued, payment should be stopped on the original check. The auditor must ascertain that duplicate accounting entries do not appear. Checks long outstanding should be written back to cash after payment is stopped; the credit may be to an income account or to a liability account, depending on individual preference. If long-outstanding checks are not properly followed, fraud may take place. To illustrate: A check of $200 had been outstanding for several months, and the cashier decided to appropriate $200. He eliminated the outstanding check from the outstanding list, thereby placing his bank balance $200 above his cash ledger account balance. He then prepared a check payable to "Cash" for $200 and cashed it from current cash receipts. In the cash disbursements record, he marked the check "Void." The check was deposited in the bank and destroyed when it was returned by the bank. The auditor could not find the check, but he did discover a $200 bank statement debit.

FINANCIAL STATEMENT CONSIDERATIONS FOR CASH

If cash funds contain items other than cash, the auditor will remove the noncash items—by adjustment—to their proper accounts. Therefore, in the balance sheet the cash funds will be less than the fund balances according to a client's unadjusted records. See Illustration 6–2. This type of adjustment normally is reversed as of the first day of the new accounting period. In the balance sheet, cash funds may be shown separately; or, normally, they are combined with cash in banks.

In the balance sheet, under a caption such as "Cash on hand and in banks," there should be included only unrestricted and freely withdrawable amounts, undeposited cash and cash items, and the cash balances in the various cash funds.

Bank funds restricted from free withdrawal should not be included in the caption of "Cash on hand and in banks." Restricted withdrawal may be the result of deposits in closed banks, bid deposits, deposits on contracts, funds in escrow, trust fund balances, and others. Each restricted amount should appear in its proper balance-sheet classification, together with necessary explanatory footnotes.

When compensating balances arrangements exist between a client and a bank or other lending agency, such arrangements must be fully disclosed by appropriate footnote. The SEC requires total full disclosure and total explanation of all compensating balance arrangements.

Cash in foreign banks and branches may be included in the "Cash on hand and in banks" caption, among the current assets. The cash at foreign points should be stated in domestic dollars at the rate of exchange prevailing at the balance-sheet date if the funds are unrestricted by the depositor and by governmental action. If the domestic dollar is at a discount, the appreciation should be shown in a special account entitled "Allowance for Fluctuation of Foreign Exchange." If the domestic dollar is at a premium, the loss may be charged to the allowance; if an allowance does not exist, the charge should be to an "other" expense account.

An overdraft may actually exist in a bank, or it may be only an apparent overdraft on the records of the client. If the latter, it probably is the result of paying liabilities in anticipation of cash collections to be deposited before the issued checks have cleared. If the prepared checks have not been mailed, the auditor should debit Cash and credit Accounts Payable as of the balance-sheet date.

An actual bank overdraft should be shown as a current liability. If accounts are maintained in two or more banks, an overdraft in one bank theoretically should not be offset in the balance sheet by balances in other banks. In practice, it is customary to use the principle of offset, provided the balances are freely transferable from one bank account to another.

SUGGESTED ADDITIONAL READING

Statement on Auditing Standards No. 1, Section 620.01, 620.05, 620.06.

QUESTIONS

1. What are the objectives of auditing cash and cash transactions?
2. For the audit of cash and cash transactions, outline an audit test procedure of the cash records to disclose the following irregularities.
   a) Improper cash borrowing during the period under audit which were restored prior to the end of the period, and
   b) Misappropriations of collections of accounts receivable at the close of the period by kiting or by overlapping cash receipts.
3. You have audited the financial statements of Adams, Inc., for ten consecutive years. All petty cash vouchers and original supporting data

for 1976 were destroyed in a fire on December 31, 1976. Interim audit work had not been performed. In connection with the destroyed vouchers and data, and assuming that all other records and data were intact, how would you proceed in your examination? The imprest amount of the fund was $5,000.

4. *a)* Why should an auditor review petty cash fund transactions if the fund is not material in amount and is active?

    b) You are preparing to audit the petty cash of a client whose fiscal year ends November 30. You intend to count the fund prior to the opening for business on December 1. The amount of the imprest fund is $10,000. Prepare instructions for the examination of the fund and its activities.

5. The fiscal year of Laurel, Inc., is November 30. On November 27, the company received a large check from a regular charge customer in an amount equal to 20 percent of Laurel's total assets and 40 percent of its total current assets. On November 28, Laurel mailed the check to its bank for deposit. The check never reached the bank. On December 18, the customer stopped payment on the check and issued a duplicate check to Laurel; the auditor traced this check to the bank.

    By confirmation and inquiry, the auditor was satisfied that the original check had been received and was mailed to the bank. It was impossible to determine at what point in the transmission the check was lost. Would you carry the amount of the lost check as a part of the November 30 cash in bank balance, or would you consider it to be a portion of the accounts receivable balance? Present reasons for your answer.

6. The X Company employs six salesmen. Advances for travel expenses are made to the salesmen from a special cash fund after approval by the sales manager. When a salesman returns from a trip, cash not spent is returned to the special fund custodian, who reviews the accompanying expense reports and files them. When the special cash fund is reimbursed, expenditures are classified and entered in a voucher register, a check is prepared for the net cash disbursed, and the fund is replenished.

    a) Wherein is this procedure at fault?

    b) What principle of fund control has been violated?

    c) Would the procedure be proper if the salesmen's expense reports were attached to the reimbursement voucher?

    d) Suggest a system that would afford proper control.

7. *a)* The bank balances of a certain client are reconciled by the auditor as of a date prior to the balance-sheet date. What procedures should the auditor follow to ascertain that the cash in bank is correctly stated as of the balance-sheet date?

    b) On a balance-sheet date, an audit client has a large dollar amount of undeposited checks and cash received on the last day of the fiscal period. In auditing these items, what procedures will you follow?

8. In an examination of cash an auditor watches for signs of lapping and kiting.

a)   Define (1) lapping and (2) kiting.

b)   What audit procedures would uncover (1) lapping and (2) kiting?

c)   In an examination of financial statements an auditor evaluates the quality of the accounting evidence available to him. An audit procedure that may be employed in the examination of cash is to submit duplicate deposit slips to the depository banks to be authenticated.

(1)   Discuss the reliability of authenticated duplicate deposit slips as accounting evidence.

(2)   What additional procedures are available to an auditor to verify the detail of deposits?

(AICPA, adapted)

9.   While examining the financial statements of a company, you were working in the office of the treasurer who had sole control over cash receipts and disbursements. While you were counting the cash and examining the related records, the treasurer frequently asked if he might be of assistance.

You discovered that the cash receipts record had been underfooted and that several receipts had not been deposited. What action would you take? What are the reasons for your answer?

10.   A client refused to request a bank confirmation for an auditor. He told the auditor that he knew his cashier was honest, that the bank statement gave the account balance at the close of the period, and that it would therefore be foolish to bother the bank. Do you consider the client correct or incorrect in his line of reasoning? Present reasons for your answer.

11.   In the audit of cash, what significance would you attribute to each of the following:

a)   An entry for a bank deposit appearing in the cash receipts record on May 28 but not shown on the bank statement in May?

b)   An unentered check for $2,000, drawn December 31, 1976, on the First National Bank, and a deposit of $2,000 on the same day in the Second National Bank?

c)   Offsetting items appearing on a bank statement but not appearing in the cash records?

d)   A bank statement charge for a check but no corresponding paid check?

12.   In the examination of cash and cash transactions, outline a test audit procedure of cash records to reveal the following irregularities:

a)   Improper cash borrowing during the period under review which were restored before the close of the period, and

b)   Misappropriation of accounts receivable collections at the close of the period by kiting or by overlapping receipts.

13.   Beech, Inc., operates sales stores in several cities. Each store collects its own receivables, and maintains a local bank account in which all cash from cash sales and from the collection of receivables is deposited intact daily. On Monday of each week, the banked collections of the preceding

week are transferred to the home office by a check drawn on the local bank; no other checks are drawn on the local bank account. Cash receipts and disbursements records are maintained, and copies are retained by each store; all other original accounting records are maintained at the home office.

As part of your audit, you will include an examination of cash transfers between the stores and the home office. All stores will be visited.

a)   List the purposes of the audit of the cash transfers.

b)   Name the audit procedures necessary for an examination of the cash transfers only, from each store to the home office.

14.   L.M.N., Inc., maintains bank accounts in San Diego and Chicago. All payrolls, vouchers, and invoices must be approved by proper department heads for payment; they are again approved by the treasurer, who turns them over to the cashier for check preparation. All checks require the signatures of the cashier and the treasurer. At the end of each month, the cashier obtains the bank statements and prepares bank reconciliations, and then gives the reconciliations, bank statements, paid checks, and other data to the treasurer, who reviews and approves the reconciliations. All checks are serially numbered.

The cashier embezzled $10,000 on December 17, 1976, by drawing a check payable to his own order on the San Diego bank; the counter-signature of the treasurer was forged by the cashier. The cashier did not enter the check in the disbursements record. On December 31, 1976, the cashier drew a check for $10,000 on the Chicago bank, payable to the order of the San Diego bank; the treasurer's signature was obtained by stating that funds were being transferred. The cashier then deposited the check in the San Diego bank on December 31, 1976. No entries were made in the records.

When the cashier obtained the December bank statement and the paid checks from the San Diego bank, he destroyed the check payable to himself. The treasurer did not discover the shortage.

During the course of your audit for the year 1976, which you started on January 31, 1977, you discover the embezzlement.

Describe three methods of verifying cash transactions and balances by the use of which this type of fraud should be discovered.

15.   A company maintains bank accounts in New York, Cincinnati, and Los Angeles. Fund transfers between these banks are common, depending upon the cash requirements in each city. If you were in Los Angeles, how would you proceed to verify the balance in each bank as of a common date?

16.   *a)*   On checks cleared with a cutoff bank statement, why should an auditor examine cancellation dates and bank endorsement dates?

b)   For what purposes are bank cutoff statements obtained and used?

17.   A client has several accounts in one bank. One of these accounts is restricted to weekly payroll disbursements and is operated on an imprest basis. The account should always reconcile to a zero balance; and for this reason, your client has not reconciled the account at any time during the year under review. The account does not appear in the general ledger.

In the course of the audit of the payroll, you examine all paid checks returned by the bank during the eight weeks following the balance-sheet date. Included among these are checks totaling $10,500, all of which are dated prior to the balance-sheet date. The paymaster also has on hand unclaimed payroll checks for $900 dated prior to the balance sheet. The bank statement shows a balance of $9,300 at the balance-sheet date.

Assuming that there is no fraud involved and that no errors in footing have been made, set forth three possible explanations of the situation indicated by the figures. For each explanation, set forth the procedures you would follow to determine if the explanation is correct.

(AICPA, adapted)

18. You were to audit the financial statements of a company that does not deposit its receipts intact and that pays some expenses from cash receipts. It is impossible to visit the client until January 20, 1977. However, you had requested the client to prepare a bank reconciliation as of the balance-sheet date, December 31, 1976; but the client had not complied. In fact, a reconciliation had not been prepared since December 31, 1975.

On the morning of January 20, 1977, you counted the cash on hand, which was $8,000, and you obtained directly a bank statement as of that date, which showed a balance of $33,040; there were no outstanding checks. The balance of the Cash ledger account, after work sheet posting of the receipts and disbursements from January 1 to January 20, 1977, was $44,000, thus resulting in a discrepancy of $2,960.

a) How would you proceed to account for this difference?

b) What suggestions would you offer for procedure in the future?

PROBLEMS

1. The December bank statement of Jason Company showed an ending balance of $187,387. During December the bank charged back NSF checks totaling $3,056, of which $1,856 had been redeposited by December 31. Deposits in transit on December 31 were $20,400. Outstanding checks on December 31 were $60,645 including a $10,000 check which the bank had certified on December 28. On December 14, the bank charged Jason's account for a $2,300 item which should have been charged against the account of Jackson Company; the bank did not detect the error. During December, the bank collected foreign items for Jason; the proceeds were $8,684 and bank charges for this service were $19. From the above information prepare a bank reconciliation.

2. From the information presented below:
   a) Prepare a reconciliation of the Cord Company's bank account of December 31, 1976.
   b) Prepare one journal entry to adjust the Cord Company's records to reflect the correct bank balances at December 31, 1976. In auditing the records of the Cord Company, you obtained the bank statement, paid checks, and other memorandums relating to the company's bank account for December, 1976, directly from the

bank. In reconciling the bank balance at December 31, 1976, you observed the following facts:

(A)	Balance per bank statement, 12/31/76	$146,330
(B)	Balance per Cash in Bank account, 12/31/76	91,140
(C)	Outstanding checks, 12/31/76	62,475
(D)	Receipts of 12/31/76, deposited on 1/3/77	9,555
(E)	Proceeds of bank loan, 12/15/76, discounted for three months at 5 percent per year, omitted from Cord's records	19,750
(F)	Deposit of 12/23/76, omitted from bank statement	5,300
(G)	Check from a customer, charged back on 12/22/76 for absence of signature; redeposited with signature on 1/4/77. No entry was made by the company for the charge-back or the redeposit	500
(H)	Check No. 1022 of Cork Company, charged by bank in error to Cord Company	8,210
(I)	Proceeds of note of Rattan, Inc., collected by bank, 12/10/76, not entered in cash record:	

Principal $4,000
Interest 40
Less: Collection charges 10   4,030

(J)	Erroneous debit memorandum of 12/31/76, to charge company's account with settlement of bank loan, which was paid by Check No. 417 on same date	10,000
(K)	Deposit to Cork Company of 12/5/76, credited in error to Cord Company	2,500

3. Using the numbers shown in parentheses, indicate how each separate question will affect the reconciliation at 12–31–76. (Assume you are reconciling the balance per books and the balance per bank to the correct, or adjusted balance).

(1)   Add to bank balance.
(2)   Deduct from bank balance.
(3)   Add to book balance.
(4)   Deduct from book balance.
(5)   No affect.

1. Bank service charge for December, $3 not recorded on books.
2. Checks totalling $4,150 were outstanding at 12–31–76.
3. Deposits totalling $2,650 were in transit at 12–31–76.
4. Check No. 196 dated 11–30–76 was paid by the bank in December.
5. Check No. 246 for $205 was recorded on the books as $250.
6. At 12–31–76 there was an outstanding check for $415 dated 11–5–74.
7. Ten checks dated 1–2–77 were paid by the bank on 12–31–76.
8. A check from a customer was paid by the bank in December. It had been returned earlier in December for proper endorsement and was redeposited. No entry for the return or redeposit had been made.
9. The December bank statement included the proceeds of a customer's draft collected by the bank on 12–30–76, but not recorded on the books.

10. A customer's N.S.F. check was returned by the bank.

11. An interest charge was made to the account by the bank in error.

12. A check for $392 was voided as it had a date of 2–2–76.

13. Credit memo from the bank for December was not recorded in December. It was, however, recorded in January 1977.

14. Customer's check was returned by the bank for N.S.F. It was redeposited on 1–2–77 and subsequently paid.

15. The December bank statement indicated that another firm's deposit had been credited to our account.

16. Customer's check was returned by the bank marked "Account Closed," it was then written off as a bad debt on 12–26–76.

17. Credit memo from the bank was recorded as a credit to cash on 12–15–76.

18. Deposit made on 12–21–76 was omitted from December bank statement.

19. A debit memo issued by the bank in error on 12–4–76 was corrected by a credit memo issued by the bank on the 1–31–77 bank statement.

20. A "stop payment order" was issued for Check No. 267 on 12–7–76, and no entry was made to record this instruction to the bank.

21. A check was returned by the payee uncashed because the amount was in error.

22. A customer's certified check was deposited on 12–30–76 and was paid by the bank on 1–3–77, appearing as a deposit on the January 1977 bank statement.

23. A debit memo issued by the bank for $45 was recorded as a credit to cash.

24. Applied for a bank loan on 12–4–76; the proceeds of the loan were credited to our account on 12–19–76. No entry was made on the books.

25. Another firm's check was charged to our account in error by the bank on 12–10–76.

26. The December bank statement contained a debit memo charging our account for a quarterly interest payment, which was paid by Check No. 307 on 12–31–76.

27. A deposit of $950 on 12–27–76 was credited to another firm's account by the bank.

4. From the following information, prepare a complete work paper for the checking account balance of Commercial Company.

   a) You receive directly from the bank the bank statement dated December 28, 1976 (balance $88,494), together with the cancelled checks.

   b) Checks written on the following dates, and entered in the cash disbursement journal, have not cleared the bank:

Date	Check No.	Amount
12–22 852		$ 1,146
12–25 854		1,540
12–28 855		1,137
12–29 858		10,750
12–30 859		5,250
12–31 860		3,870

c)   Confirmation received from the bank showing balance at 12–28–76 of $88,494.

d)   All checks listed as outstanding were returned as cleared with interim bank statement dated 1–15–77.

e)   Board of directors minutes of June 1, 1976, state that either J. T. Thomas, treasurer, or T. J. Quinn, controller, are authorized to sign checks.

f)   Cash receipts of December 31, 1976 in the amount of $26,200, were recorded as a deposit by the bank on January 3, 1977.

g)   The balance per the books, December 31, 1976 is $96,400.

h)   After a review of the system of internal control, January and December are selected to test cash receipts and disbursements.

i)   December bank service charges in the amount of $20 have not been recorded on the books.

j)   Debit memo with bank statement of December 28, 1976, indicates that the bank has deducted $20,000, face amount of note, plus $200 interest from Commercial's account on December 15 and was not recorded.

k)   Engagement letter indicates the audit is to be performed for the year ended December 31, 1976.

l) $25,000 borrowed for 90 days from the bank on December 31 was not recorded. Interest is at the rate of 9 percent per annum.

5.   As part of your audit of R & P, Inc., for the year ended December 31, 1976, you examine the petty cash fund for the months of January, June, and December, and counted the fund at 5 P.M. on December 31. You find the contents of the fund to be:

Unnumbered but approved December travel expense vouchers $235.13.

Employee's IOU's: J. Allen, $30; S. Dwyer, $25; W. Hughes, $50.

Currency: $20 bills, 11; $10 bills, 26; $5 bills, five; $1 bills, 31.

Coins: Half-dollars, 11; quarters, 10; dimes, 12; nickels, six; pennies, 39.

Postage Stamps: 60¢–50; 30¢–100; 10¢, four rolls of 100 each; 8¢ post cards, 100.

Cash sales tickets: No. 3500 for $146.92; No. 3600 for $209.77, No. 3700 for $32.14.

Unnumbered paid petty cash vouchers:

Dated 1976	Paid to	For	Amount
Jan. 15	Mary Jones	Attendance at professional meeting	$ 25.00

Dec. 16	Railway Express	Collect express on inventory purchase	30.00
20	J. C. Arnold	January 1977 travel advance	100.00
31	James Florist	Flowers for Mary Jones	20.00

Checks:

Date *1976*	*Maker*	*Amount*
Oct. 17	Dan E. Morgan, former employee, cannot be located	$ 20.00
Dec. 10	J. Brown, credit manager, paid on account	50.00
	Garrison & Ross, customer payment on account	456.69
	C. Cosgrove, employee, paid on account	83.10
1977 Jan. 31	Mary Jones, employee, personal use (postdated check)	100.00

Except for the check of Morgan, all checks were good as of check date. The Morgan check, following its deposit on October 20, had been returned by the bank marked "account closed."

The balance of the Petty Cash ledger account was $1,000; the fund was in charge of Mary Jones, who was not bonded.

During the audit of the January, June, and December transactions, Mary Jones often collected the proceeds of cash sales, and sometimes accepted cash from customers to apply on their accounts. Such receipts were usually turned over to the general cashier on the day of the receipt; coin and currency were mingled with petty cash monies and adjustments for these collections were made whenever petty cash was reimbursed. Reimbursements occurred irregularly, usually two or three times a month, the last reimbursement being dated December 15. These practices occurred with the full knowledge of the chief accountant.

Prepare work papers covering your examination of petty cash.

6. You started the examination of the financial statements of the Door Company on January 20, 1977, for the year ended December 31, 1976. The cash account balance as of December 31, 1976 is $12,360.

The cashier's December 31, 1976, cash reconciliation contained the following items:

Cash per ledger, December 31, 1976	$12,360
Cash per bank, December 31, 1976	13,205
Checks outstanding	1,267
Check of Witt, Inc., charged by bank in error on December 20, 1976, corrected by bank on January 7, 1977	37
Cash in transit, credited by bank on January 2, 1977	175

From January 2, 1977 to January 20, 1977, the date of your cash count, total cash receipts appearing in the cash records were $2,675. According to the bank statement for the period from January 2, 1977, through January 20, 1977, total deposits were $2,399.

The count of the cash and cash items on hand at the close of business on January 20, 1977 was as follows:

Currency and coin	$122
Expense vouchers	18
Checks of customers in payment of accounts	48
	$188

After further investigation, you discover the following:

(1)   On July 5, 1976, cash of $200 was received on account from a customer; the Allowance for Doubtful accounts was charged and Accounts Receivable credited.

(2)   On December 5, 1976, cash of $150 was received on account from a customer, Inventory was charged, and Accounts Receivable credited. Cash of $175 received during 1976 was not recorded.

(3)   Checks received from customers from January 2, 1977, to January 20, 1977, totaling $100, were not recorded but were deposited in the bank.

(4)   In the cashier's desk, there were receipts for bills paid by customers on January 14, 1977, totaling $225; these were unrecorded and undeposited. You are required:

   a)   To prepare the necessary audit adjustments for the above unrecorded or incorrectly recorded transactions.

   b)   To compute the correct bank balance as of December 31, 1976.

   c)   To compute the cash shortage as of December 31, 1976, and up to January 20, 1977.

7.   At a year-end, bank activity for all bank accounts may be reconciled with the records for several days prior to the end of the year and for several days after the year-end in order to detect kiting. If such a reconciliation can be prepared, many detailed comparisons can be avoided.

   a)   Using the data in the problem, prepare a work paper to determine kiting; and reconcile on the work paper the bank balances at the *three dates shown,* and show the bank activity for the period from December 1, 1976, to January 12, 1977.

   b)   For each time on your work paper, show, by number, and separately describe, the procedures necessary to complete the audit.

   c)   Prepare audit adjustments necessary at December 31, 1976.

TENTH COMPANY

	November 30, 1976	December 31, 1976	January 12, 1977
Balance, bank statement	$34,442	$27,502	$36,533
Balance company records	28,332	32,807	
Outstanding checks	8,824	9,731	4,672
Deposits in transit	3,500	4,000	2,500

	December 1–31, 1976	January 1–12, 1977
Receipts, cash record	$ 96,323	$29,250
Credits, bank statement	94,101	32,149
Disbursements, cash record	100,848	17,757
Charges, bank statement	101,041	23,018

The client obtained bank statements for November 30 and December 31, 1976, and reconciled the balances. Directly you obtained the statement of January 12, 1977, and the necessary confirmations. You have found that there are no errors in addition or subtraction in the client's records. The following information also was obtained:

(1)   Check No. 89 for $34 cleared the bank in December as $134. This was found in proving the bank statement. The bank made the correction on January 8, 1977.

(2)   A note of $2,000, sent to the bank for collection on November 15, 1976, was collected and credited to the account on November 28, 1976, net of a collection fee of $8. The note was recorded in the cash receipts on December 21, 1976, at which date the collection fee was entered as a disbursement.

(3)   The client records returned checks in red in the cash receipts record. The following checks were returned by the bank:

Customer	Amount	Returned	Recorded	Redeposited
M.	$327	Dec. 6, 1976	No entries	Dec. 8, 1976
N.	673	Dec. 27, 1976	Jan. 3, 1977	Jan. 15, 1977

(4)   Two payroll checks for employee's vacations totaling $550 were drawn on January 3, 1977, and cleared the bank on January 8, 1977. These checks were not entered in the client's records because semimonthly payroll summaries are entered only on the 15th and the last day of each month.

(AICPA, adapted)

7

Receivables, Related Transactions, and Credit Losses

AUDIT OBJECTIVES

The audit objectives of examining receivables are to determine (1) validity; (2) accuracy of amount; (3) collectibility; (4) the propriety of periodic sales transactions, revenue deductions, and credit losses; and (5) proper valuation for financial statement presentation.

The objectives of auditing revenues are (1) to determine the adequacy of internal controls over revenues, (2) to ascertain that all revenues earned have been recorded and that all recorded revenues have been earned, (3) to ascertain that all reductions of revenue have been properly recognized, and (4) to analyze and interpret trends in the various revenue categories by studying management-prepared comparisons, or by preparing, analyzing, and interpreting comparisons.

Fundamental to the proper audit of receivables and revenues is the necessity for an understanding of the client's products, sales policies, credit-granting policies, credit terms granted, and the organization and efficiency of the sales department and the credit department.

Credit losses arising from uncollectible receivables, the use of allowances for doubtful receivables, available sales discounts, and the interest earned on such items as notes and installment accounts receivable are all allied to the objectives of the examination of the receivables. Because fraud is possible by the manipulation of receivables and their related collection, care must be exercised in the auditing processes.

In the examination of receivables, an auditor also will examine sales, sales deductions, credit losses, and amounts earned on interest-bearing receivables. Thus the auditor will not be forced to refer back to interest-bearing receivables when examining other revenues.

Accounts receivable assume many forms, including those due within a few days, installment accounts, consignment receivables, and others. Accounts receivable may be trade or nontrade items. Notes receivable may be trade or nontrade, notes from employees, and many others. Acceptances receivable are trade items, as are bills of exchange. Notes receivable may be secured by collateral or title, or they may be unsecured.

The majority of revenue accounts are examined when the original data are audited, or when assets and liabilities related to specific revenues are audited. In accordance with the effectiveness of internal control and internal auditing, the extent of the verification of revenues and expenses may be extended or curtailed. If properly applied, internal control procedures and internal auditing procedures, as set forth in other chapters up to this point, are instrumental in reducing the detailed work necessary in any examination other than one involving fraud.

The verification of revenues and expenses is limited to tests, scrutiny, and comparisons, with detailed analyses of selected items for either the entire period, a portion of the period, or selected entries within the records. These tests and analyses should be sufficiently extensive to satisfy the auditor that the nature of the transactions is genuine, that the transactions are accurately recorded, and that account classification is proper. Thus, combined with the examination of assets, liabilities, and owners' equities, reliable financial statements may be produced.

Revenue and expense accounting must be identified with specific events. The proper determination of periodic net income is a matter of matching related revenues and the expenses of obtaining those revenues. The acceptance of a sales order eventually leads to revenue recognition. Expenses are revenue reductions made as the expense is incurred—not necessarily when cash is disbursed.

INTERNAL CONTROL OF RECEIVABLES

Internal control over receivables starts with an accepted sales order or loan approval. Thus, there is brought into existence evidence for the formation of an audit trail. Certain features regarding internal control of receivables were set forth in Chapter 3, and internal controls for sales were set forth in Chapter 5.

For proper internal control over credit sales and resultant receivables, it is necessary to divide functional duties so that there are separated responsibilities for (1) preparation of a sales order, (2) credit approval, (3) definite guidelines for credit granting, (4) release of goods to be shipped, (5) shipping, (6) billing customers, (7) invoice verification, (8) control account maintenance, (9) subsidiary account maintenance, and (10) collection of the receivables, accounting for the cash received, and controlled banking of the cash. Proper internal control of accounts receivable also requires proper accounting for returned merchandise, proper control of the returned goods, and approval for the charge-off of uncollectible items. Periodically, the receivable should be aged in order to determine the efficiency and actions of the credit and collection departments.

Thus, for internal control over accounts receivable to be proper, (1) sales must be separated from the accounting for them; (2) accounting must be separated from the receipt of cash; and (3) returns, allowances, discounts, and uncollectible charge-offs must be properly approved and separated from the cash receipts function.

The general pattern of internal control of notes receivable follows that for accounts receivable. After approval for the acceptance of notes receivable, there must be proper control of the notes and properly safeguarded collection. Proper internal control further demands that (1) the notes receivable custodian does not have access to cash or to the general accounting records; (2) a responsible official who does not have access to the notes approve note renewals, in writing; (3) charge-offs of defaulted notes be approved in writing by a responsible official who does not have access to cash or notes; and (4) proper procedures be adopted for the follow-up of defaulted notes.

Internal control questionnaires for accounts receivable, notes receivable, credit losses, and revenue related to receivables are presented in Illustrations 7–1 and 7–2.

AUDIT OF ACCOUNTS RECEIVABLE

Scheduling Accounts

Audit procedures for accounts receivable are interwoven with the examination of sales, sales returns and allowances, discounts, and uncollectible write-offs. In fact, the audit procedures for accounts receivable may easily be constructed around the examination of sales. An auditor should prepare, or obtain from the client, a trial balance of the accounts receivable. If obtained from the client—if prepared manually, mechanically, or electronically—the auditor should compare the items in the trial balance with the balance of each corresponding subsidiary account receivable. Normally, this comparison is on a sample basis. The net trial balance amount then is compared with the general ledger controlling account balance. The trial balance may be an adding machine tape, a listing by name and amount, or a listing by name and amount in the form of an aging schedule, as shown in Illustration 7–3 for Multi-Products. Time is saved if the auditor requests the client to prepare a trial balance of the accounts receivable in the form of an aging schedule.

The location of errors between the net trial balance total and the controlling account balance is a function of the client, unless the auditor is requested to locate differences. If the client reconciles controlling ac-

Illustration 7–1

INTERNAL CONTROL QUESTIONNAIRE
Accounts Receivable

Company_____ Period Covered_____	Yes	No	Not Appli- cable	Remarks
1. Are controlling accounts and subsidiary ledgers regularly balanced?				
2. Are the accounts receivable aged periodically?				
3. Are delinquent accounts reviewed by a proper official?				
4. Are uncollectible account write-offs properly approved?				
5. After write-off, is proper control exercised in the event of future collection?				
6. Are doubtful account allowances adequate?				
7. Are all credit memorandum numbers accounted for?				
8. Are credit adjustments approved by a proper official?				
9. Are customer statements prepared, or verified, by a person not having access to the cash receipts records or the accounts receivable credits?				
10. Are statements mailed by the accounts receivable department?				
11. Are statements contolled to prevent interception prior to mailing?				
12. Does the client confirm accounts receivable balances?				
13. Are differences reported by customers handled by a person other than the cashier or the accounts receivable department?				
14. Is the credit department separated from the accounts receivable record keeping?				
15. Are unusual discounts and allowances approved by a responsible person?				
16. Are the duties of the accounts receivable personnel separated from all cash receipts and disbursements functions?				
17. Are all shipments represented by invoices?				
18. Does the cash collection division operate as a check on the work of the accounts receivable department?				
19. In passing on credit terms, does the credit division have any connection with: a) The sales department? b) The accounts receivable department?				
20. Are customer credit limits properly adhered to?				
21. Are consignments-out carried as accounts receivable?				
22. If the accounts receivable are pledged as loan security, is the accounting treatment proper?				

Prepared by_____   Reviewed by_____
Date_____   Date_____

...ount balances and subsidiary account balances at least each month, ...rrors can be allocated to short periods. Many companies now prove controls and subsidiaries daily.

Footings and balances of subsidiary accounts should be tested for

Illustration 7-2

INTERNAL CONTROL QUESTIONNAIRE
Notes Receivable

Company_____	Yes	No	Not Appli- cable	Remarks
Period Covered_____				

1. Are individual notes regularly proved with the controlling account balance?
2. Is a detailed record maintained for the notes receivable?
3. Prior to acceptance, are all notes properly approved?
4. Are the amounts of partial payments noted on the reverse side of the notes?
5. Is a contingency record carried for discounted notes receivable?
6. Does the client periodically confirm notes balances?
7. Are unpaid notes properly followed?
8. Are past-due notes charged back either to Accounts Receivable or to a Dishonored Notes account?
9. Does proper approval exist for the write-off of uncollectible notes?
10. Is proper control exercised over future collections of notes charged off?
11. Does the custodian of the notes have access to:
    a) Cash receipts records?
    b) Notes receivable records?
    c) General ledger accounts?
12. If negotiable collateral is held against the notes, does the custodian have access to:
    a) Cash receipts and disbursements records?
    b) Notes receivable records?
    c) General ledger accounts?
13. Are notes receivable and related collateral kept under proper control?
14. Is more than one person required to be present when access to notes and related collateral is necessary?
15. Is notes receivable collateral adequate?
16. Is proper internal control maintained over revenue from notes receivable?

Prepared by _____   Reviewed by_____
Date _____   Date _____

accuracy. The footing accuracy and balance of the controlling account should be proved for the year under audit. If a controlling account balance is larger than the sum of the subsidiary account balances, fraud could exist by posting debits and credits to the controlling account, not posting to a subsidiary account, and stealing the remittance. At a year-end, if a theft is not in process, subsidiary account totals would agree with the balance of the controlling account. If errors exist between subsidiaries and controls which cannot be located, the control should be brought into agreement with the sum of the subsidiary account balances.

As stated in Chapter 5, the auditor must test discounts, returns, and sales allowances. The examination of sales returns records affords the auditor clues to defective, obsolete, and otherwise unsalable merchandise. This serves as a warning to watch the pricing of inventory when that section of the audit is undertaken.

Aging Schedules

An aging schedule develops an analysis of accounts receivable for the purposes of judging possible uncollectibility, ascertaining the efficiency of the credit and collection department, and aiding in providing allowances for possible uncollectible items. Aging schedules may be prepared on the basis of days past the billing date or days past maturity. It is not necessary to include in detail accounts not past due. Also, an aging schedule aids an auditor in segregating nontrade items, advances to affiliated companies, and credit balances in accounts; and the scheduling often reveals items in dispute. The day intervals used in an aging schedule depend upon the credit terms offered. If normal credit is for 30 days, 30-day intervals should be used; if credit is for 60 days, 60-day intervals should be used. Aging schedule results may be summarized effectively in the audit report by classifying totals not due and totals for each day interval past due.

During the process of examining a prepared aging schedule, the following points must be borne in mind:

1. Segregate other-than-trade accounts receivable.
2. Watch payment promptness from customers with large balances.
3. Investigate reasons for credit balances.
4. Be certain the bad debt provisions are adequate.
5. See that postdated invoices are not placed in the past-due accounts.
6. Watch for past-due balances which constantly increase; this can mean that the customer should be cut off, or it may indicate that a customer has paid his account and that the money has been misappropriated.

Aging and Examination of Installment Receivables

The time intervals in the aging schedules for installment receivables should be established in accordance with either of the following plans:

1. One installment past due, two installments past due, and so on—or
2. By months of the current year and by months of subsequent years.

If a client sells under more than one payment plan, it may be necessary to prepare an aging schedule for each plan.

The auditor must be familiar with the installment sales contracts. Notes may support the accounts. Title may pass to the customer, or it

Illustration 7–3
WORK PAPER 4

MULTI-PRODUCTS, INCORPORATED
Analysis of Accounts Receivable, December 31, 1976

Customer Name	Balance Dr.	Balance Cr.	Days from Date of Billing Under 60	Days from Date of Billing 60-120	Days from Date of Billing Over 120
A	7104 √		5400	1704	
B	58 √				58
C		640			
D	17488 √		13896	2512	1080
E	7100 √			7100	
F	24650 √		20000	4650	
G	1232 √				1232
H	11800 √		8000	3800	
I	1750 √				1750
J		1 680			
K	4820 √			4820	
L	49310 √		37244	12066	
M	3482 √			3482	
N	550 √				550
O	6780 √		6000	780	
P	6400 √		5500	900	
Q	4920 √			2440	2480
R	38924 √		17256	11892	9776
S	9858 √			9858	
T	41422 √		21428	19994	
U	13880 √				13880
V	1200 √				1200
W	2912 √			2912	
X		330			
Y	4498		2000	2498	
Z	5124			5124	
All other current balances (93). . . .	63564		63564		
	328826	2 650	200288	96532	32006
Deduct: Credit balances.	2650				
	326176 ∅				
Add: AJE 2.	7132				
	333308				
Deduct: AJE 3	4200				
	329108				
Deduct: AJE 4 (Work Paper 5)	1808				
Adjusted Balance, per audit.	327300				

√ Compared with individual ledger balances.
  Invoices for all open receivables traced to individual ledger balances.
∅ Agrees with general ledger control.
∧ Traced to cash receipts of 1977.
  Negative confirmations used for all accounts. No discrepancies reported.
  All accounts are trade receivables.
  Both the credit manager and the treasurer approve, in writing, accounts
    to be charged off as uncollectible.

may pass with a mortgage having been given by the customer, or the seller may retain title until the installment payments have been collected.

Delinquent installments should be set forth in the audit report, or in a separate communication. If governmental regulatory requirements are in effect, the auditor must determine proper adherence to those require-

	Initials	Date
Prepared By	AR	2-6-77
Approved By	RW	2-9-77

Uncollect-ible	Doubtful (Provide Allowance)	Cash Collections Date Received	Amount	Remarks
58				Damaged goods claim.
		1-7-77		Send check.
		1-7-77	1080 ∧	Always slow, but good.
		2-28-77	7100 ∧	E's credit terms.
	1232			Out of business.
		2-2-77	11800 ∧	
		1-25-77	1750 ∧	
				Use against future billings.
		2-4-77	4820 ∧	
		1-31-77	12066 ∧	
				90-day credit.
550				Disputed: client accedes.
		2-6-77	6400 ∧	
	4920			Unreliable.
		1-15-77	21668 ∧	
				90-day credit.
		1-22-77	41422 ∧	
	6940			50 percent collectible.
1 200				Bankrupt.
		1-28-77	2912 ∧	
				Use against future billings.
				90-day credit.
		1-2-2-16-77	40924 ∧	
1 808	13092		151942	46 percent of net receivables collected prior to close of audit.

		AJE 2		
		Accounts Receivable	7 132	
		Sales.		7 132
		Goods shipped to M; not billed.		
		AJE 3		
		Sales	4 200	
		Accounts Receivable		4 200
		Return by F. applicable to 1976		

ments—by the client and the customer. The auditor must investigate the propriety of the accounting methods used when chattel mortgages are foreclosed. The method of pricing repossessed goods must be examined, and the auditor must ascertain that installment receivable balances are reduced when goods are repossessed.

Prior to closing an examination, an auditor should refer to his aging schedules for all types of receivables to ascertain if past-due items unpaid at the balance sheet date were paid in the new period. Paid items should be ticked off in the schedules.

Management Reports

Management requires periodic reports of accounts receivable in order to be certain that all work relating to the receivables is being performed in accordance with company policy. The reports include:

1. An aged trial balance of the receivables. The dollar amount in each age classification should be expressed as a percentage of the total receivables. This report focuses immediate attention upon the quality of the receivables from report date to report date, and in comparison with the same report date of the prior year. This report also furnishes information regarding the effectiveness of the collection program.

2. Analyses of requests for credit, classified into those approved and those rejected. Decisions then may be made regarding the credit policy of the company—it may be proper, or too lenient, or too rigorous—and the resultant effect on profitable operations.

3. A detail of accounts charged off as uncollectible. If the causes of bad debts can be determined, decisions may be made regarding the effectiveness of credit and collection policies. Also, such analysis and proper follow-up discourages fraudulent charge-offs and premature charge-offs.

4. A listing of sales returns and allowances by customers should be prepared so that customers receiving adjustments and the person(s) granting the adjustments can be determined. This analysis would assist management in determining the effectiveness of its returns and allowance policies.

Confirmation of Accounts Receivable

Accounts receivable entries are company records only—not evidence. Therefore, where it is practicable and reasonable to do so, accounts receivable should be confirmed directly to the auditor by a client's customers. Confirmation of receivables places an auditor in a position to express a proper opinion of the receivables, and it assists in the detection of error and fraud. The Securities and Exchange Commission *requires* that the accounts receivable of brokers' customers be confirmed. When confirmation is noncompulsory, although it is a recognized auditing procedure, an auditor normally requests confirmations of a portion of the receivables total. The objective is to obtain confirmation of the largest possible percentage of the receivables dollar total by requesting confirmation of accounts indicated in items 1–8, below.

When confirmation requests are directed to selected debtors, the sample should include:

1. Accounts (large and small), active and inactive, selected on a random basis.
2. Accounts of customers who are in financial difficulty.
3. Accounts in which debits are large at the year-end.
4. Accounts turned over to collection agencies.
5. Accounts in dispute between the client and the debtor.
6. Accounts charged off during the year.
7. Accounts with credit balances.
8. Accounts written off due to sales returns, etc.
9. Accounts with zero balances.

The sample to be circularized is drawn by the auditor. If the client requests that certain customers be omitted from the list to be circularized, the auditor should investigate those accounts and extend his audit procedures.

Credit balances in accounts receivable are liabilities which may be due for payment. Credit balances also may result from selling and receiving payment, followed by the return of goods; receiving deposits; or errors in posting to subsidiary accounts. The causes of credit balances should be investigated.

Internal control of cash and receivables and the internal audit practices of a client enable an auditor to judge more effectively the amount of confirmation work necessary. Internal auditing departments commonly confirm customers' accounts receivable balances. It may develop that the independent auditor is willing to accept the results of the internal auditing department to a large extent and thereby reduce his requests for confirmations. If internal control is satisfactory, it is not totally necessary that receivables be confirmed as of the year-end date. For example, if December 31 is the year-end date, receivables could be confirmed as of November 30; this would permit time for replies to be received in December, and year-end work pressure would be reduced. Then if the auditor examined sales and cash transactions for December, he would, in effect, be ascertaining the accuracy of December 31 balances.

Receivables are confirmed by either (1) the negative method (Illustration 7–4) or (2) the positive method (Illustration 7–5). In the negative method, a communication is sent to the customer requesting reply to the auditor *only* in the event of disagreement of balances between customer and client. The weak point of negative confirmations is that if a reply is not received, there still is no evidential proof of accuracy. In many instances the auditor attaches the negative confirmation request to the latest invoice or statement to be sent to the customer. The auditor controls the mailing of the invoices or statements so that alterations cannot be made. Only the latest balance may be contained in the statement, or it

Illustration 7–4
CONFIRMATION REQUEST: NEGATIVE TYPE

PLEASE EXAMINE THIS STATEMENT

In connection with the audit of our records, the enclosed statement indicates the balance of your account at the date stated thereon.

Please examine this statement and, if you do not agree with this balance, report all differences to our auditors, Bennett and Bennett, Certified Public Accountants, Carew Tower, Cincinnati, Ohio 45202.

If you do not report any exceptions, it will be assumed that the statement is correct. This request is for information and not for payment. A business reply envelope is enclosed.

---

may contain the entire account activity for a period of time. Prior to mailing, the auditor will compare the invoices or statements with the client's accounting records.

Negative confirmations are approved by the accounting profession, especially in those situations where a client has a large number of relatively small-amount accounts—utilities, department stores, chain stores, and other clients selling directly to a final consumer.

In the positive method of confirming receivables, a communication is sent to customers, requesting direct confirmation to the auditor of the accuracy or inaccuracy of a balance. Positive confirmations offer the better method of verifying account balances—if the customer replies. Customers many times are not too willing to devote their time to completing and mailing the reply. If a reply is not received to the original positive confirmation request, at least a second request should be sent. Where positive confirmation replies are not received, the auditor should thoroughly investigate related accounts receivable. Also, an auditor should investigate confirmations returned with legitimate exceptions in order to be totally satisfied with the exceptions prior to accepting the validity and balance of the accounts receivable.

If an auditor does not confirm receivables, he should place the fact of nonconfirmation in his report, together with the reasons for omitting this recognized procedure. The reasons might include client refusal of permission, control of collections by the auditor, or the use of other audit procedures which resulted in satisfaction with the results of the examination, or a total receivable balance of nonmaterial amount.

If receivables are not confirmed, the review of internal control should be extended for sales, shipments, billing, collections, control of cash, re-

Illustration 7–5
CONFIRMATION REQUEST: POSITIVE TYPE

Date *December 11, 1976*

To: *Forest Hills, Inc.*
     Five Mile Road
     Cincinnati, Ohio 45230

Gentlemen:

Please advise our auditors, Bennett and Bennett, Certified Public Accountants, Carew Tower, Cincinnati, Ohio 45202, on the attached form, of the correctness of the balance of your account as shown by our records at the date and in the amount stated, or of any exceptions you may take thereto. A business reply envelope is enclosed. Your prompt attention will be appreciated.

Very truly yours,

Fairlane Company

(THIS IS A REQUEST FOR CONFIRMATION, NOT FOR REMITTANCE.)

- -

Bennett and Bennett
Certified Public Accountants
Carew Tower
Cincinnati, Ohio 45202

No. *46*

The amount of *$10,000* representing our indebtedness to Fairlane Company, at November 30, 1976, is correct with the following exceptions:

Exceptions (please state differences in detail, giving all pertinent dates and amounts):
Our records show a balance of $8,000. Apparently the difference is the result of a payment made by us on November 29, 1976, of $2,000.

Signed *Forest Hills, Inc.*

By *C. D. Evanor*

turns, allowances, and write-off of uncollectibles. In addition, tests of sales transactions may be extended.

In his report the auditor may summarize the results of confirmations somewhat as follows:

Date	Number of Accounts	Percentages	Amounts	Percentages
December 31 . . .	600	60	$65,600	82
November 30 . . .	250	25	9,600	12
October 31	100	10	4,000	5
Prior	50	5	800	1
Totals	1,000	100	$80,000	100

Account Validity and Accuracy

An auditor must determine that accounts receivable are valid; that is, that they are those of bona fide customers. This is necessary so that sales may not be charged to fictitious names, followed by charging a collected receivable to bad debts expense or the allowance for doubtful accounts. Confirmation requests assist in determining validity and accuracy. In addition, in connection with the examination of original records, the auditor must examine the system of charging and billing, and the separation of the duties of cash collections and the recording of credits to accounts receivable. A matching of names and amounts on remittance lists with credits to accounts receivable also aids in establishing validity.

Noncash credits to receivables must be investigated, not only because of the possibilities of fraud but also to ascertain if credit memorandums are properly approved and processed and authorization for write-off of uncollectible accounts is proper.

Collection-on-Delivery Receivables

The method of controlling and accounting for cash receipts from this source must be examined. Normally, cash from collection-on-delivery sales is received within a few days after shipment. Therefore the sale and the corresponding cash receipt should be matched. Some companies record a c.o.d. sale as a sale at the shipment date; other companies record the sale when the cash is received. In the first instance, uncollected items are accounts receivable at the balance-sheet date. In the second instance, the goods shipped must be included in the ending inventory.

Under the Uniform Commercial Code, 2–401, the passing of title is covered. The practice of recording sales at the time of shipment regardless of the seller's delivery obligations may not be in conformity with the UCC 2–402 title rules. However, if all credit sales are recorded at the time of shipment, c.o.d. sales may be recorded in the same way. The fact that possession is not given to the buyer until he pays does not mean that title has not passed. (The same is true for "layaway" sales.) Therefore, present accounting practice is to record any sale when title passes.

Consignment Receivables

Only the amount due from consignees for goods they have sold should be considered as accounts receivable. The cost-of-sales figure must include the cost of all goods sold by the consignees. The sales price of goods out on consignment but not sold should not appear as accounts receivable because the goods are to be included in the inventory of the consignor.

In those instances where consignment is merely a traditional form of sale and if returns have not been more than completed sales, the consignments may be viewed as accounts receivable if the client so treats them. The cost of such goods should be excluded from inventory.

An auditor may not realize that an account is a consignment unless he looks for small credits, or confirms the accounts, or examines correspondence, or watches for consignment reports accompanying customer remittances. In many instances, it may be necessary to wait several days after the balance-sheet date in order to obtain the year-end consignment report of a consignee.

Foreign-Customer Receivables

Receivables from customers in foreign countries must be examined for validity and collectibility. If a receivable represents a draft which is open at the balance-sheet date, proper practice dictates that a receivable does not appear because the draft may not be honored. In this case, the cost of the goods shipped would be included in the seller's inventory. Restrictions in transfers of currency should be examined.

Nontrade Receivables

Nontrade accounts receivable must be investigated for validity, collectibility, and classification as current or noncurrent assets. Nontrade receivables include—among others—amounts due from company personnel, stockholders, unpaid capital stock subscriptions, claims receivable from insurance companies and transportation companies, deposits on contracts which may not materialize, and receivables from subsidiary or otherwise affiliated companies.

The auditor should examine receivables from subsidiary and otherwise affiliated companies in order to determine the nature of the receivables; that is, whether they are due from sales, or if they are advances, expenses paid, merchandise transferred, or other assets advanced. Affiliated company accounts receivable may be current assets or noncurrent assets, depending upon the circumstances of each case. If consolidated balance sheets are prepared, affiliated company receivables are eliminated from the financial statements.

In order to determine the reason for their existence, all nontrade receivables should be analyzed even if there is no balance at the end of the year. Credits to nontrade receivables made close to the end of the year should be listed; these amounts should be scrutinized prior to closing the audit in the new period to ascertain if a debit in the new period matched a credit in the prior period. This may reveal long-term or even unauthorized borrowing by company personnel. The auditor should request direct confirmation of all loans—open and closed.

Assigned Receivables

If a client assigns receivables, they should be confirmed directly to the auditor by the assignee involved. There are several plans of assignment, and the auditor should read the agreements with the assignee to ascertain that the client is adhering to the terms of the agreements.

Each assigned receivable should be coded by the client, both in the receivables ledger and on all invoices involved. This is especially necessary if the "nonnotification" plan of assignment is in force. In the majority of assignment contracts, poor receivables must be replaced with good accounts. In accordance with the terms of the contract, customers may remit directly to the client; or they may be requested to remit directly to the assignee.

When obtaining confirmations from an assignee, the auditor should request:

1. The balance of the uncollected assigned accounts; this figure will represent the accounts receivable—except those not assigned.
2. The amount advanced by the assignee; this represents the liability of the assignor.
3. The amount withheld by the assignor; this should represent the original difference between items 1 and 2, above.

Accounting entries for assigned receivables are similar to those for discounted notes receivable, and an Assigned Accounts Receivable account should be credited for the total of the receivables transferred to the assignee. This represents the possible contingency of the assignor.

Account Collectibility and Allowances for Doubtful Items

Proof of collectibility lies in collection. An account may be confirmed, it may be valid, it may be correct—and yet it may not be collectible. Consequently, the auditor must attempt to determine collectibility so that the balance sheet does not overstate realizable amounts and so that the auditor may render an adequate opinion in his report. Aging schedules aid in determining account collectibility; however, the auditor must discuss past-due accounts with the client. In addition, the auditor must relate account balances with sales, credit terms, and material increases or decreases in receivable balances in comparison with increases or decreases in sales. To illustrate: Assume credit terms of net cash in 30 days. Then approximately one twelfth of the annual sales should be represented by accounts receivable, provided sales are fairly equally distributed throughout all months of the year. If sales were approximately $100,000 per month throughout the year and if the accounts receivable balance at the end of any one month materially exceeded $100,000, collections are slow. Noncollection losses of prior years should be compared with losses of the current year in order to ascertain an increase or a decrease in credit losses. Correspondence should be reviewed for indications of current-year losses and possible future losses. In periods of expanding sales, receivable balances normally will increase. Whether these situations will result in larger credit losses cannot easily be forecast in the transition period.

Receivables definitely known to be uncollectible should be charged to expense or to the allowance for doubtful items if an allowance is used. The auditor should examine the client's written approval of accounts charged off during the year. In establishing the allowance for doubtful receivables, judgment must be used; the allowance should be large enough to provide for all doubtful receivables—notes, accounts, and any other receivables; also, the allowance should not be excessive. Some companies experience a quite constant ratio of credit losses to sales; others do not. Illustration 7–6 sets forth a work paper for the allowance for doubtful receivables.

The following points may serve as guides in judging *definite* uncollectibility of receivables:

1. When customers have been discharged from bankruptcy and there are no dividends.
2. When customers have disappeared.
3. When collection is barred by the statute of limitations.
4. When collection agencies indicate inability to collect.
5. When items are in dispute and the client is willing to settle.

The following points may serve as guides of *possible* uncollectibility:

1. When notes are accepted for past-due accounts receivable.
2. When items are placed with collection agencies.
3. When customers are in receivership.
4. When credit customers are transferred to a c.o.d. basis.
5. When periodic debits to receivables exceed periodic credits and balances continue to increase.

Illustration 7–6
WORK PAPER 5

							Initials	Date
				Prepared By			⅃R	2-6-77
	MULTI-PRODUCTS, INCORPORATED			Approved By			RW	2-19-77
	Allowance for Doubtful Accounts Receivable, December 31, 1976							

Balance, December 31, 1975		17448		
Deduct: Accounts charged off in 1976		11042		
Balance per ledger, December 31, 1976		6406		
Deduct: AJE 4, below		1808		
		4598		
Add: AJE 5 provision		13092		
Balance, per audit		17690		
AJE 4				
Allowance for Doubtful Accounts Receivable		1808		
Accounts Receivable			1808	
To charge off the following accounts:				
B Company	$ 58			
N Company	550			
V Company	1 200			
	$1 808			
AJE 5				
Uncollectible Accounts Expense		13092		
Allowance for Doubtful Accounts Receivable			13092	
See Aging Schedule (Work Paper 4).				

6. When customers have discontinued buying and are liquidating their accounts in round amounts.
7. When answers are not received to collection letters.

Auditors must examine the records for all accounts charged off and later collected in order to determine proper accounting treatment and in order to ascertain the propriety of the chargeoff policy.

AUDIT OF NOTES AND ACCEPTANCES RECEIVABLE

Notes receivable may be classified as (1) trade notes; (2) nontrade notes; (3) notes from company personnel; and (4) notes from subsidiary and otherwise affiliated companies. Trade acceptances are bills of exchange similar to notes receivable, but they originate with the seller and do not bear interest until the maturity date. Bankers' acceptances are drafts, and a bank is the acceptor.

Internal control features applicable to notes receivable were set forth in Illustration 7–2. The same internal controls are applicable to acceptances and drafts. The auditing procedures applicable to the examination of accounts receivable are equally applicable to drafts, notes, and acceptances receivable; however, for these items an auditor has evidence in the form of an instrument signed by an outside party. Consequently, the following comments constitute a briefing of the procedures for accounts receivable, plus procedures applicable exclusively to drafts, notes, and acceptances.

The auditor should prepare or obtain from the client a schedule for notes, drafts, and acceptances receivable similar to Illustration 7–7. It should be noted that interest accruals are included in the schedule. The

Illustration 7–7
WORK PAPER 6

		Initials	Date
	Prepared By	*LR.*	2-7-77
	Approved By	*RW*	2-9-77

MULTI-PRODUCTS, INCORPORATED
Notes Receivable and Accrued Interest, December 31, 1976

Name of Maker		Date of Note	Due Date	Amount of Note	Interest Rate %	Interest Accrued 12-31-76	Interest Income 1976
Ohio Co.	√	9-1-76	2-1-77	10000 √ ∧	6	(4) 200	200
Kentucky Co.	√	10-1-76	3-1-77	6000 ∧	6	(3) 90	90
Indiana Co.	√	10-15-76	4-1-77	12000 ∧	6	(2,5) 150	150
Pennsylvania Co.	√	11-1-76	3-1-77	2000 ∧	6	(2) 20	20
Illinois Co.	√	11-1-76	4-1-77	16000 ∧	6	(2) 160	160
Michigan Co.	√	12-1-76	3-1-77	8000 ∧	6	(1) 40	40
Florida Co.	√	12-15-76	4-15-77	12000 ∧	6	(0,5) 30	30
New York Co.	√	12-31-76	5-31-77	8000 ∧	6	0 0	0
Balance per audit				74000 ∧			690
Interest earned on notes paid in 1976							1 310 ⊙
Total Note Interest, per audit							2 000

√ Examined.
√ Paid February 1, 1973, plus interest. Traced to cash receipts.
∧ Confirmed--directly.
⊙ Verified.
    All notes appear to be collectible.
    None of the notes represent renewals.
    All notes are for product sales in the normal course
    of business.

footed schedule totals should be compared with the footed general ledger controlling account balances. If the auditor obtains a schedule from the client, he must match the *detail* of each item in the schedule with the corresponding instrument—if it is available. Notes on hand should be examined for authenticity and propriety.

Postings from original records should be tested to the extent necessary to convince the auditor of the reliability and accuracy of the accounting. Notes and acceptances receivable will be on hand, or out for collection, or discounted, or pledged as collateral, or returned to the maker if paid after the balance-sheet date and prior to the examination. Whether on hand or not on hand, notes and acceptances open at the balance-sheet date should be confirmed. Positive confirmations are better than negative confirmations because it is possible to obtain more detailed data. A note

Illustration 7–8
WORK PAPER 7

	Initials	Date
MULTI-PRODUCTS, INCORPORATED — Prepared By	XR	2-7-77
Notes Receivable Confirmation Summary, December 31, 1976 — Approved By	RW	2-9-77

Positive Confirmations Mailed to:	Date Mailed 1977	Date Confirmed 1977	Amount Confirmed	Remarks
Ohio Co.	1-17	2-4	10 000	Paid 2-1-77
Kentucky Co.	1-17	1-25	6 000	
Indiana Co.	1-17	1-24	12 000	
Pennsylvania Co.	1-17	2-4	2 000	
Illinois Co.	1-17	1-27	16 000	
Michigan Co.	1-17	2-6	8 000	
Florida Co.	1-17	2-2	12 000	
New York Co.	1-17	1-24	8 000	
			74 000	

receivable confirmation summary is shown in Illustration 7–8. In the report, an auditor may indicate confirmation data.

If collateral is held, it should be inspected and noted in the notes receivable work papers. The market price of collateral as of the balance-sheet date must be ascertained in order to determine the adequacy of the collateral in accordance with the terms under which it was taken.

Notes and acceptances should be made payable to the order of the client or properly endorsed to him. Notes on hand should be inspected for amount, signatures, and witnessing when necessary. In order to judge apparent collectibility, the auditor may investigate the credit ratings of, and former experiences with, note makers and endorsers. Additional guides to collectibility may be expressed as follows:

1. For demand notes, has demand been made and rejected?
2. Have notes been offered for discount and rejected by the bank?
3. Why are certain notes past due?
4. If the client is not the payee, why did the client acquire the instrument?
5. Is an endorser's credit satisfactory?
6. Are any notes those of affiliated companies?

Past-due instruments should be charged to Accounts Receivable or to a Dishonored Notes Receivable account. Dishonored past-due instruments have lost their negotiability. If the instrument definitely is not collectible, it should be charged to expense or to the proper allowance. If a note that is past due at the balance-sheet date is collected prior to closing the audit, the cash received should be traced to the bank. Collection could be mentioned in the audit report because a post-balance-sheet-date event affected the balance sheet.

In addition to obtaining confirmations and following other prescribed auditing procedures, the auditor should trace contra entries for notes receivable debits and notes receivable credits—in order to assist in establishing note genuineness.

If notes are renewed, the renewal may indicate a possible uncollectible item. Provision for possible uncollectibility should be made. If notes are renewed, the renewal should be set forth in the accounting records, either by explanation or by a debit and a credit to Notes Receivable—with a full explanation.

Notes and acceptances discounted should be discussed with the client for the possibility of a contingency developing into a real liability. Trade acceptances are not renewable but are eligible for discount.

As in the case of accounts receivable, the auditor should observe proper executive approval for all notes and acceptances charged off as uncollectible. Also, confirmation of charged-off instruments should be obtained and correspondence for collection attempts should be examined.

Usually, an auditor will compute or verify interest income, interest received, and interest accrued on notes at the time of examining the notes. This saves repetitious reference to work papers and to client records. All interest income credits, interest expense debits, prepaid interest debits and credits, and accrued interest receivable debits and credits must be "tied up" with the instruments bearing interest.

If the allowance for doubtful accounts is not large enough to care for possible uncollectible notes, drafts, and acceptances, a separate allowance should be established or the allowance for doubtful accounts increased.

Client Representations

If an auditor requests from the client a written representation covering receivables, the certificate thus obtained should be signed by the treasurer and the credit manager. The representations should be somewhat as follows:

1. Trade accounts and trade notes receivable represent valid claims.
2. Nontrade receivables from employees, stockholders, and controlled companies are correctly and properly set forth in the balance sheet.
3. Consignments are excluded from the receivables.
4. The accounts receivable balance contains no charges for merchandise shipped after the balance-sheet date.
5. All assigned receivables are properly indicated in the records.
6. All receivables discounted are properly indicated in the balance sheet.
7. The balance of the receivables is not subject to allowances for price adjustments, liens, transportation deduction, or discounts in excess of the customary cash discount.

8. All known uncollectible receivables have been charged off at the balance-sheet date.
9. The allowance for doubtful accounts of $_____, in the opinion of undersigned, is adequate to provide for all losses in the receivables at the balance-sheet date which may result from uncollectibility.

The signed certificate is one of the auditor's work papers. The representations of the client do not reduce the responsibility of the auditor in his examination of receivables. Rather, the representations serve as a deterrent to a false statement, and they serve as some measure of protection for the auditor.

AUDIT OF REVENUES

Audit Objectives

As stated on the first page of this chapter, objectives of an audit of revenues are (1) to determine the propriety of internal controls over revenues, (2) to ascertain that all revenues earned have been recorded and that all recorded revenues have been earned, (3) to ascertain that all reductions of revenue have been properly recognized, and (4) to analyze and interpret trends in the various revenue categories by studying management-prepared comparisons, or by preparing, analyzing, and interpreting comparisons.

An important phase of any audit is assurance that all revenues earned have been recorded. The asset side of the balance sheet serves as a guide in determining sources of revenue. Assets that produce revenue may appear, and investigation may prove that no revenue or insufficient revenue is being received, or that revenue is being received and not recorded.

Summarized, an audit program applicable to revenues may be stated as follows:

1. Investigate the system of internal control.
2. Verify revenues through the audit of original records.
3. Audit by comparison.
4. Test invoice prices, extensions, footings, and discounts.
5. Test trace sales from invoices to the sales records.
6. Test foot sales records and trace to the ledger accounts.
7. Test postings to customers' accounts and to inventory records.
8. For a few days before and after the close of the period, compare sales records and shipping records.
9. Examine the accounting for prepaid transportation charges.
10. Examine the treatment of c.o.d. sales.
11. Investigate the accounting for consignment sales.
12. Examine the accuracy of the accounting for installment sales.
13. Test for inventory debits arising from sales returns.

14. Verify interest and dividend revenues.
15. Analyze sales of assets other than inventory and ascertain the correctness of recorded net gains from these sources.
16. Examine revenue accounts to determine the accuracy of related assets.
17. By reference to the type of business, prove selected revenue accounts.
18. Watch for revenue not recorded.

Sales Record Errors

The following errors result in an *understatement* of sales:

1. Errors in computing invoices.
2. Failure to record profits on sales of consigned goods.
3. Failure to record sales.
4. Crediting an account other than Sales for consummated sales.
5. Holding sales records open beyond the end of the preceding period, which act reduces sales figures for the current period.
6. Premature closing of the sales records for the current period.

The following errors result in an *overstatement* of sales:

1. Crediting Sales when another account should be credited.
2. Crediting Sales for orders taken when the goods have not been shipped.
3. Crediting the Sales account for inventory out on consignment.
4. Holding the sales records open past the closing date.
5. Premature closing of the sales records for the prior period.
6. Errors in computing invoices.

Effect of Internal Control

If internal control and internal audit of sales and the recording system are satisfactory, sales record totals should be test-verified in accordance with the predetermined test pattern. The totals should be compared with debits to Accounts Receivable and to Cash. If the system of internal control is unsatisfactory, the test should be extended to the point where the auditor is satisfied—or remains dissatisfied. An auditing of sales records serves the following purposes:

1. To determine that only sales for the period under examination are included.
2. To determine that all sales for the period under audit are included.
3. To determine that sales are correctly entered as to amount and customer.

Audit adjustments are required if sales records either are prematurely closed or are held open past the close of the period.

Revenue Transaction Verification

Illustrations 7–9 and 7–10 present work papers for analyses of sales. After selecting the sample of the sales invoices -to be examined, the following audit procedures normally are followed:

1. For the selected sales sample, unit prices on the sales invoices are compared with price lists, removed inventory tags, or formal inventory records in order to ascertain pricing correctness to customers.
2. Extensions and footings on sales invoices are proved for the selected sales sample (1, above). If sales are made only to a few customers, the percentage test will increase.
3. To determine that sales records are promptly closed, dates on invoices are compared with customer account charges and inventory credit dates.
4. The selected invoices are traced to sales records.
5. Sales record postings are traced to general-ledger accounts.

Illustration 7–9
WORK PAPER 8

MULTI-PRODUCTS, INCORPORATED

Product Net Sales Analysis for the Year Ended December 31, 1976

	Initials	Date
Prepared By	YR	2-7-77
Approved By	RW	2-7-77

Month--1976	Product A	Product B	Product C	Product D	Product E	Total
January	204896	35504	11860	10624	12928	275812
February	156964	34168	13888	11452	4868	221340
March	220080	38884	11248	11916	6248	288376
April	340904 ✓∅	66492 ✓∅	12052 ✓∅	23896 ✓∅	7476 ✓∅	450820
May	381144	87840	24496	41276	11768	546524
June	432572 ∧	107904 ∧	33040 ∧	56468 ∧	10912 ∧	640896 ∧
July	381056	96096	34364	85848	9092	606456
August	342620 ✓∅	72984 ✓∅	26516 ✓∅	68160 ✓∅	8068 ✓∅	518348
September	272880	59716	16992	40056	5696	395340
October	316644	30040	19736	27684	10512	404616
November	274896	22260	11664	19504	7684	336008
December	167882 ✓∅	15960 ✓∅	10804 ✓∅	9364 ✓∅	17708 ✓∅	220718 =
Total	3 492538 ⊙	667848 ⊙	226660 ⊙	405248 ⊙	112960 ⊙	4 905254 ⊙
Comparison with 1975:						
1975 sales	2 606270	739568	219084	380648	117928	4 063498
Increase (+) or						
decrease (-)						
1976 over 1975 +	+ 886268	-71720	+7576	+24600	-4968	+ 841756

✓ Priced, extended, and totaled 300 duplicate invoices. Errors: $96.20 in
   12 invoices. Ignore.
∅ Tested 5 percent of the postings to customers' accounts.
⊙ Footings agree with general ledger Sales account postings.
∧ Tested Sales account distributions. Ok.
= Compared invoices and shipping records from December 21 to
   December 31.

Illustration 7–10
WORK PAPER 9

THE BLANK COMPANY
Proof of Sales Accuracy, December 31, 1976

Inventory, January 1, 1976		45 712
Materials Purchased		788 691 √
Labor		165 233 ∧
Overhead		94 971
		1 094 607
Inventory, December 31, 1976		52 101
Cost of goods sold		1 042 506
Cost of Sales is 60 percent of sales price		1 041 357
Add: Actual gross profit		694 061
Computed sales		1 735 418
Difference between computed and actual		
sales of $1,735,595.		
Ignore		177
√ Traced to invoices of test months.		
∧ Distribution verified.		

6. Sales record postings are traced to subsidiary accounts receivable in accordance with the test patterns.
7. Cash sales money is traced to the bank statement.

As valid evidence of shipping dates and the proper closing of sales records, shipping records are examined. The procedure follows: For the last several days of the current period and for the first few days of the subsequent period, sales invoice dates and shipping department shipping dates are compared. If a sale was recorded and the merchandise not shipped, Sales and Accounts Receivable (or Cash) are overstated. If merchandise was shipped in the current period and entered as a sale in the next period, Sales and Receivables (or Cash) are understated.

Title to goods passes from seller to buyer in accordance with the intention of the parties and in accordance with legal requirements. Customary practice is to the effect that current-period sales include all sales made, recorded, and shipped through the last day of the period. Legally, for free-on-board shipments, title passes to the purchaser at the agreed f.o.b. shipping or destination point. For cost-including-freight shipments, title passes to the purchaser when the goods are delivered to the carrier.

The Sales account should contain credit only for those items normally held forth for sale in the regular course of business operations. Significant upward or downward fluctuations in sales of the current year compared with the prior year should be investigated for cause and for effect on net income. Fluctuations may be caused by general business conditions, inflation, price changes, product changes, strikes, fires, use of substitute products, changes in managerial efficiency, and changes in competition. An analysis of sales on a comparative basis should set forth the changes in terms of dollars and percentage.

Sales Returns and Allowances

Sales returns and allowances are audited by test and by comparison with similar items of prior years. One purpose of the examination is to obtain the reason for increases in sales returns and allowances in comparison with sales and, if possible, to suggest remedial measures. Another purpose in the examination is to ascertain the propriety of the accounts charged and credited when the original sale was made.

All credit memorandums issued to customers during the year should be accounted for to the satisfaction of the auditor. All returns and allowances should be supported by approved credit memorandums. On a test basis, credit memorandums should be traced to the proper accounts, such as sales returns, sales allowances, cash, receivables, and inventories. Tests should be made of prices, extensions, and footings on the memorandums. If sales returns and allowances journals are used, these records should be test-footed and the totals traced to the ledger accounts. Sales returns and allowances general-ledger accounts should be footed.

Credit memorandums for returned merchandise should be test-compared with both the receiving records and inventory records. Credit memorandums for sales returns not supported by receiving records constitute evidence of fraud or improper accounting. Sales returns and allowances for approximately two weeks after the close of the period must be investigated to determine that sales made during the period under examination were proper credits to that period and were not sales entries made to "window-dress" financial statements.

Installment Sales

Recognized accounting procedure is to the effect that only the gross profit portion of the total installment sales collections be recognized in the current year. The gross profit on uncollected amounts is deferred to the year of collection, and the entire annual collections must not be credited to income. Of course, this recognized method is not always used in business operations. Under any operating circumstances the auditor must be familiar with the installment sales contracts. Also, he must adequately examine the records to determine that proper and consistent accounting procedures are being followed and that customers are remitting in accordance with contract terms.

Consigned Goods Sales

When goods are consigned out, profit should not be recognized until the goods are sold by the consignee. The auditor should obtain year-end confirmations from consignees for goods sold to the year-end and for remaining inventory at that date. Consignment sales profits may be reduced by certain expenses allowed consignees, in addition to commissions, all in accordance with the agreement between the consignor and the consignee. If the consignor has billed goods shipped to the consignee at a price above cost, the remaining inventory must be reduced—at least to cost.

Goods held by a consignee are inventories of the consignor. Accounting methods are not uniform for consignors and consignees. In some cases the consignee will record the entire sales price as a sale and (1) show deductions therefrom for amounts to be remitted to the consignor or (2) show the deductions as cost of sales and expense items.

Under any given circumstance of handling goods consigned in and/or out, the auditor must—

1. Ascertain that remaining inventories appear on the records of a client consignor at no more than cost.
2. Ascertain that remaining goods do not appear as inventory on the records of a client consignee.
3. Ascertain that the client consignor has taken up all profits on out-consigned goods sold by consignees through the last day of the period.
4. Ascertain that the client consignor has reduced its profits by agreed expenses allowed consignees.
5. Ascertain that a client consignee has recorded all profits on in-consigned goods sold through the last day of the period.
6. Ascertain that a client consignee has deducted allowable expenses from remittances to consignors.

Rental Revenue

If a written rental contract is in existence, the rental revenue may be verified in accordance with the terms of the contract. The auditor should obtain or prepare a schedule of rentals by properties, tenants, and periodic rentals—making proper provisions for changes in rental rates and vacancies. The total rentals thus computed are compared with cash receipts records. Rental payments may be confirmed from tenants. If rentals are in arrears, it should be scheduled. If the landlord has accrued rentals in arrears, provision for contemplated noncollection should be made. Whether or not the landlord has accrued arrearages in rental revenue, the auditor should inquire into the possibility of collection.

If advance rental payments have been received, they should be prorated between periodic revenue and amounts received in advance. However, the Internal Revenue Service requires them to be included in periodic revenue.

Profits on Long-Term Construction Contracts

Because many long-term construction periods overlap accounting periods, profits frequently are taken up on the percentage-of-completion method. In the percentage-of-completion method, profit is recorded in the ratio of the actual cost of the partially completed project to the total *estimated* cost of the entire contract. To illustrate, assume that a contract is for $308,000, that the work completed to date has cost $200,000, and that the *estimated* cost to complete the project is $120,000:

Contract price		$308,000
Less: Cost to date	$100,000	
Estimated cost to complete	120,000	220,000
Estimated profit		$ 88,000

Of the total estimated profit of $88,000, 100/220, or $40,000, represents the amount earned in the current period.

If a contract is on a cost-plus basis, current-period profit can be determined with much greater accuracy than if the contract is for a flat price. In flat-price contracts, many companies originally estimate the gross profit on the contract and by using the estimated gross profit percentage figure bring into the records as of the end of the accounting period the estimated gross profit earned on the contract to that date.

If the "completed-contract" method is used, the excess of accumulated costs over current billings should be shown as a current asset. An excess of accumulated billings over corresponding costs is a current liability.

Profits taken up on uncompleted contracts should be verified by the auditor. Mature judgment is necessary to determine (1) the validity of the profits taken up and (2) the cost to complete the contract. If amounts are withheld by the customer—for contingencies or workmanship—the auditor must confirm the amounts, ascertain if the amounts withheld are in agreement with the terms of the contract, and attempt to ascertain the probabilities of contingencies for which the amounts were withheld.

FINANCIAL STATEMENT CONSIDERATIONS

All receivables should be shown at an amount no larger than their cash collectible worth. Proper distinction must be made between receivables to be classified as current assets and those to be classified as noncurrent assets.

If the balance of the nontrade current accounts receivable exceeds approximately 5 percent of the total, the trade and nontrade accounts should be separated in the balance sheet. Also, the nontrade accounts receivable—if material in amount—should be subdivided in a manner to disclose their origin. If the total of the nontrade accounts is not material, they may be shown together under a title such as "Other Accounts Receivable."

Receivables of significant amount from company personnel should be segregated in the balance sheet, regardless of the reason for the receivables. This segregation is necessary due to the possibilities of personal interests and due to the relation of these persons to a separate corporate entity.

Receivables from affiliated companies and other related parties should be separately set forth because of the possibility of nonconversion to cash. Whether related parties receivables are to be shown as current or noncurrent assets depends upon the circumstances of expected cash collection.

Receivables from capital stock subscriptions should be segregated in the balance sheet due to the relationship of the receivable to the corporate capital structure. If collection is anticipated within the operating cycle, this nontrade receivable should be included among the current assets; otherwise not.

If material in amount, credit balances in accounts receivable should be shown as such in the current liability section of the balance sheet. The gross total of the debit balances in the receivables will appear as assets.

Allowances for doubtful accounts and notes, and allowances for discounts, rebates, and transportation charges to be deducted, should be subtracted from the gross total of the receivables in the balance sheet. If allowances are not used or are not necessary for doubtful receivables, that fact should be indicated in the balance sheet. Allowances for discounts, rebates, and transportation to be deducted are seldom used, on the basis that the amounts normally are not material and that the amounts are fairly constant from period to period.

In the balance sheet of a conditional assignor of accounts receivable, several methods of setting forth the fact of assignment are possible; one method follows:

Accounts receivable		$250,000
Less: Assigned accounts	$80,000	
Amount withheld	24,000	56,000
Remaining equity		$194,000

If the accounts receivable are shown only at $194,000, both the fact of assignment and the contingency of $80,000 would be hidden. From the remaining equity of $194,000 would be subtracted the allowance for doubtful accounts.

Drafts, notes, and acceptances receivable must be presented in accordance with recognized principles of accounting; and the presentation must offer full disclosure of all material facts. Trade and nontrade items should be separated; in accordance with circumstances, current and noncurrent items should be separated. Trade notes and acceptances receivable not due are current assets if the collection time falls within the cycle of business operations; otherwise, they are not current assets. Notes and acceptances discounted normally are not included in the assets, and a balance-sheet footnote should set forth the dollar amount of the items discounted.

If separate allowances are used for doubtful notes, drafts, and acceptances, they should be separately deducted in the balance sheet.

As a minimum, for only modest disclosure of all material operating data, an income statement should include sales revenues, cost of sales, selling expense, administrative expense, nonoperating revenues and expenses, federal income tax, and net income. Preferably, income statements should be prepared in comparative form with the preceding year. Many corporations present stockholders with income statement data for ten consecutive years.

Sales revenue may be shown net, unless returns and allowances are material in amount. Sales revenue (whether gross or net) should not be shown net of cost of sales. If a company has several categories of revenues, preferable treatment is to the effect that each sales category be shown separately—and totaled—in order to offer full disclosure of all material facts. The SEC is moving toward product-line reporting.

Expenses of material amount should be separately set forth and not combined with other items. Such expenses normally include cost of sales, depreciation, major selling and administrative expenses, interest charges, and federal income tax.

Nonrecurring revenues and gains of material amount, and expenses and losses of material amount should be clearly set forth as such (together with applicable income tax adjustments) in the income statement in a manner which will not distort normal net income.

Full disclosure in the financial statements requires, in most instances, explicit footnotes so that the reader will know the nature of accounts and notes receivable. An illustration of this presentation, which was a part of a recent published report, is given below.

During 1973, the purchaser of a business sold by National in 1970 defaulted on its note payment due in connection with such sale. A provision for loss has

Accounts and Notes Receivable	1974	1973
Trade accounts receivable (approximately $8,700,000 and $9,700,000 pledged in 1974 and 1973, respectively	$39,933,000	$35,288,000
Notes receivable	10,301,000	12,905,000
Other receivables	6,045,000	2,912,000
	56,279,000	51,105,000
Less allowance for doubtful accounts and notes . .	(2,827,000)	(1,678,000)
	$53,452,000	$49,427,000
Current portion	$44,803,000	$38,183,000
Noncurrent portion	8,649,000	11,244,000
	$53,452,000	$49,427,000

been reflected in the accompanying 1973 financial statements for this note. In February 1974, the purchaser of a business sold in 1972 by a subsidiary of National defaulted on its note payable to the subsidiary. National and the subsidiary have guaranteed certain obligations of this business. The subsidiary provided a reserve in 1973 for losses that it may incur. Additional reserves for possible loss have been provided in 1974 for both these notes and related guarantees.

SUGGESTED ADDITIONAL READING

Statement on Auditing Standards No. 1, Section 310.03–310.08; Section 451.01, 02; Section 542.01–542.04.

Statement on Auditing Standards No. 4, Paragraphs 2, 3, 6, 7, 8, 17.

QUESTIONS

1. What are the audit objectives in examining accounts receivable?
2. How would you divide the functional duties for proper internal control over credit sales and resultant receivables?
3. Your client presents you with a printout of the accounts receivable ledger and, after making necessary adjustments, the total agrees with the general-ledger control account. What audit procedures should be followed before accepting this printout and making it a part of your working papers?
4. What points must be kept in mind when examining a client's aging schedule?
5. An observation an auditor should make is to review the client's system of management reports. What types of management reports are desirable and would indicate to the auditor that the client is knowledgeable about its accounts receivable?
6. To whom should confirmation requests be sent?
7. What is a negative confirmation? When might it be used?
8. Why should noncash credits to receivables be investigated?
9. Even though an account may be confirmed, it may be uncollectible. What audit procedures should be followed to determine collectibility or uncollectibility of the account?
10. Even though a note receivable may be confirmed, it may be uncollectible. What questions might you ask to determine collectibility?
11. A written representation should be obtained from a client. What does the representation contain and of what value, if any, is it to the auditor?
12. What purposes are served by auditing the sales records?
13. The exceptions indicated below appeared on the positive confirmation requests returned to you by customers of one of your clients, the Kern Company, in connection with an audit for the year ended June 30. Name the documents and records you would examine in investigating

Confirmation Number	Customer	Amount	Exceptions
86	Brand, Inc.	$ 6,000	Paid June 29, our Check No. 2468.
126	Dove, Inc.	4,000	Credit requested June 26.
168	Forze, Inc.	8,000	Please forward our purchase order numbers so we can check.
184	Richie, Inc.	19,200	No account on our records with Richie.
200	Tanner, Inc.	5,000	Damaged merchandise not accepted from trucking company. Please reship at once.

each exception. What is your purpose in examining the stated documents and records?

14. In response to a request for positive confirmation of its outstanding receivables, one of your client's customers—a large manufacturer whose debit balance represents approximately 40 percent of the total accounts receivable and 15 percent of the total current assets of the client—replies that its records are not maintained in a manner permitting confirmation.
    a) What additional audit procedures, if any, should be followed?
    b) What disclosures, if any, should be made in the financial statements or in footnotes thereto?
    c) What qualifications, comments, or references, if any, should be included in a short-form report in addition to the items in (*b*), above?

15. Prepare four examples of errors arising in the recording of transactions which might not be discovered during the audit of balance-sheet items and their related revenues and expenses, assuming that the audit is conducted on a normal test basis.

16. *a)* What are normal procedures in an audit of sales returns?
    b) Why should sales returns subsequent to the end of the accounting period be examined?

17. A company maintains a sales record and a sales returns record. Both records are supported by a file of prenumbered and controlled duplicate invoices and credit memorandums. Outline the audit procedures for the verification of the net sales for a year.

18. During the course of an audit, why is it important to verify sales against maintained perpetual inventory records?

PROBLEMS

1. You have been engaged for the first annual audit of Newby, Inc. Since this client has experienced only minor problems in collection of accounts receivables in the first year, you are asked (*a*) to establish procedures for determining anticipated uncollectible accounts and (*b*) to determine the basis for preparing the annual adjustive entry recognizing anticipated uncollectible accounts. Credit terms are 2/10; n/60.

2. An aging schedule for the Turner Corporation follows:

THE TURNER CORPORATION
Aging of Accounts Receivable
December 31, 1976

Customer	Balance Due	Current	Days Past Due 1-30	Days Past Due 31-60	Days Past Due 61-90	Days Past Due Over 90	Comments
J. Ashton	$ 5,500	$ 1,100	$ 600	$ 2,100		$ 1,700	Account good, customer usually pays about 90 days late.
C. Brock	2,300			2,300			Merchandise found defective—returned by customer on November 10 for credit. Inspected receiving report.
Brooks Corp.	10,500	6,200	2,000	1,300	$1,000		Account is good.
George Inc.	8,750	2,300	1,450	1,000		4,000	Merchandise worth $4,000 destroyed in transit on June 4, 1976. The carrier was billed on 7-1-76. (See Race Company and Vend Corporation.)
G. Lee	9,350	5,300	2,050	1,000		1,000	Customer billed twice in error for $1,000. Balance felt collectible.
D. Palmer	7,450	3,200	1,500	1,250	400	1,100	Account felt collectible—but "hold" being placed on any new shipments.
Race Co.	4,000					4,000	Company promises full payment.
E. Reston	3,500		3,500				Amount represents sale made by Turner of used machine.
Smith, Inc.	3,100	1,500	1,600				Paid in full on 12-29-76. Not recorded, but deposited 1-3-77.
S. Stockton	2,300	2,300					A note to Turner Corporation from S. Stockton, president.
S. W. Corp.	100	100					Received accounts payable confirmation from customer for $1,100. Investigation revealed an erroneous credit for $1,000. (See T. Vail.)
R. Williams	12,500	7,000	1,500	1,000	2,000	1,000	Will not bill until 1 January 1977. Confirmed.
T. Vail	6,400	2,000	1,800	1,600		1,000	Neglected to post $1,000 credit to customer's account.
Vend Corp.	6,000	6,000					Customer wants to know reason for receipt of $4,000 credit memo.
	$81,750	$37,000	$16,000	$11,550	$3,400	$13,800	

Accounts receivable (control) $81,750.00

a) Prepare the entry or entries to correct the subsidiary and control accounts and show the effects on Aging of Accounts Receivable schedule.

b) Prepare the entry to establish the allowance for Bad Debts (previously bad debts have amounted to 5 percent of accounts overdue for 1–90 days and 20 percent for accounts due over 90 days.)

3. You are assigned the responsibility of auditing the Trade Notes Receivable account for Ace, Inc.

a) Briefly describe the audit program you would follow.

b) Prepare the complete work paper for this account at December 31, 1976, and any related accounts based upon the notes and additional information discovered as a result of your audit. As a result of your review of the client's activities, you find that—

1. There are no other sources of interest income.
2. Interest was to be accrued on a monthly basis.
3. When any trade notes receivable are discounted, the bank deposits the net receipts in the client's checking account.

The notes given to you by the client are as follows:

Ohio Company—9/1/76–3/1/77—$10,000—6%
Kentucky Company—10/1/75–4/1/76—$20,000—6%. Principal and interest are unpaid at 12/31/76.
Indiana Company—10/1/76–2/1/77—$10,000—6%. Discounted 10/1/76 at 6%.
West Virginia Company—6/1/76–12/1/76—$40,000—6%. Note and interest paid at maturity.
A. J. White, Pres.—7/1/76–7/1/77—$10,000—6%.
North Carolina Company—7/1/76–10/1/76—$20,000—6%. Renewed 10/1/76 now due (5/1/77). Interest was paid on each note at time of renewal.

Balances of ledger accounts at 12/31/76:

#10—Notes Receivable-Trade—$60,000:	
Ohio Company	$10,000
Kentucky Company	20,000
A. J. White, Pres.	10,000
North Carolina Company	20,000
#11—Accrued Interest Receivable—$2,100:	
Ohio Company	300
Kentucky Company	1,500
A. J. White, Pres.	300
#30—Prepaid Interest—$612.00:	
Indiana Company	612
#88—Unearned Interest Income—No balance	
#110—Interest Income—$4,600	
Ohio Company	300
Kentucky Company	1,200
Indiana Company	600
West Virginia Company	1,200
A. J. White, Pres.	300
North Carolina Company	1,000

4. You are auditing the financial statements of Land, Inc., for the year ended December 31, 1976. Your examination of the accounts receivable

proves that the data presented below represent typical operations for sales, sales returns, uncollectible items, and receivables balances. Cash receipts are applied to the oldest billings. Credit terms are net cash in 60 days.

From the data:

a) Prepare an aging schedule, based upon the number of days past the transaction date.

b) Prepare the entry to charge off accounts and amounts which in your opinion are uncollectible.

c) On the assumption that there is no balance in the Allowance for Doubtful Accounts Receivable, what are your suggestions for the establishment for an allowance? What are the reasons for your suggestions? Annual sales are approximately $12,000,000.

Account No.	Dates (1976) and Transactions	Balance Dec. 31, 1976
1	Nov. 15, $6,000 sale. Nov. 25, $1,000 return. Dec. 17, $15,000 sale.	$20,000 Dr.
2	June 10, $2,000 sale. July 10, $2,000 sale. Aug. 10, $2,000 sale. Aug. 25, $2,000 cash. Sept. 10, $2,000 sale. Sept. 25, $1,000 cash. Nov. 10, $2,000 sale. Dec. 10, $2,000 sale.	9,000 Dr.
3	Dec. 20, $6,000 sale. Dec. 31, $14,000 return arising from sale of Nov. 15.	8,000 Cr.
4	Oct. 10, $7,000 advance to branch office.	7,000 Dr.
5	June 10, $12,000 sale. Customer has been paying $1,000 per month.	6,000 Dr.
6	Feb. 10, $10,000 sale. Apr. 10, $10,000 cash. July 10, $2,000 allowance for defective goods. Agreed to send check January 2, 1977.	2,000 Cr.
7	Jan. 4, $1,000 sale. Customer totally bankrupt.	1,000 Dr.
8	Sept. 5, $12,000 sale. Nov. 12, $11,000 cash.	1,000 Dr.

5. Wink, Inc., showed a balance in its Accounts Receivable control of $21,530 as of December 31, 1976. The subsidiary ledger accounts of the company appear below. Credit terms are 60 days net.

Account No. and Name	Date	Debit	Credit	Balance
1. Alder & Alden	May 31	500		500
	July 1		300	200
	7	500		700
	Sept. 1		300	400
	25	800		1,200
	Nov. 1		300	900
	Dec. 10	300		1,200
2. Bayer Bros.	Aug. 8	840		840
	Oct. 4		840	0
	Nov. 25	2,200		2,200

Account No. and Name	Date	Debit	Credit	Balance
3. Garden, Inc.	Jan. 1	12,000		12,000
(two month, 6% note)	Mar. 1		12,120	120 Cr.
(two month, 6% note)	Dec. 1	10,000		9,880
4. Jotter, Inc.	Feb. 3	1,000		1,000
	Aug. 3	1,000		2,000
5. Kraft, Inc.	Feb. 10	3,000		3,000
	Apr. 9		3,000	0
	May 4	4,000		4,000
	July 2		4,000	0
	Sept. 6	5,278		5,278
	Nov. 26	222		5,500
6. Mann Company	July 17	500		500
	Aug. 16	444		944
	Sept. 30 (open)	750		1,694
	Oct. 15		944	750
	18	600		1,350
	Dec. 20		600	750

The allowance for Doubtful Receivables before audit has a credit balance of $500. The allowance is to be adjusted to a balance determined as follows:

Accounts not due . . . . 1/2 of 1 percent
Accounts 1–60 days past due . . . .   2 percent
Accounts 61–120 days past due . . . . . .   5 percent
Accounts over 120 days past due . . . . . .   50 percent

The provision is to be based only on the trade accounts. Except where payments are earmarked, the oldest items are paid first.

From the information presented:

a)   Prepare work papers for aging the accounts receivable. In your schedule, show also the disposition and any remarks which you, as the auditor, would note.

b)   Show the adjustments necessary for the provision and also any other necessary adjustments.

6.   During the course of the audit of the financial statements of Mark, Inc., for the year ended December 31, 1976, you examined the notes receivable represented by the following items:

*Item
No.*

1.   A four-month note dated November 30, 1976, from the Avon Company, $10,000; interest rate, 6 percent; discounted on November 30, 1976, at 6 percent.

2.   A draft drawn payable 30 days after date for $15,000 by the Bark Company on the Carew Company in favor of the Gusto Company, endorsed to Mark, Inc., on December 2, 1976, and accepted on December 4, 1976.

3. A 90-day note dated November 1, 1976, from J. C. Cline, $25,000; interest at 6 percent; the note is for subscriptions to 250 shares of the preferred stock of Mark, Inc., at $100 per share.

4. A 60-day note dated May 3, 1976, from the First Company, $3,000; interest at 6 percent; dishonored at maturity; judgment obtained on October 10, 1976. Collection doubtful. (No interest after maturity.)

5. A 90-day note dated January 4, 1976, from the president of Mark, $8,000; no interest; note not renewed; president confirmed.

6. A 120-day note dated September 14, 1976, from the Stock Company, $6,000; interest rate, 6 percent; note is held by bank as collateral.

When the Company discounted a note, Interest Expense was debited for the discount cost and Interest Income was credited for the revenue.

From the information presented, prepare the following:

a)   A work sheet for the notes receivable as of December 31, 1976.

b)   All necessary audit adjustments, including entries for interest accrued and prepaid.

c)   A presentation of the notes receivable in the balance sheet as of December 31, 1976.

(Note: In computing interest, the first day is omitted and the maturity date day is included.)

7. The notes receivable of the James Corporation appear in the schedule on page 244.

JAMES CORPORATION
Schedule of Trade Notes Receivable
December 31, 1976

Name of Maker	Dated	Due	Amount	Interest Rate	Prepaid Interest	Accrued Interest Receivable	Un-earned Interest Income	Interest Income	Comments
Allen Corp.	11-1-76	4-1-77	$ 2,000	6%	$-0-	$ 20		$ 20	
Barn Inc.	10-1-76	2-1-77	5,000	6%	-0-	75		75	
Cook Co.	11-1-76	2-1-77	1,800	6%	9	-0-	$18	9	Discounted at 6% on 12-31-76.
Dean Co.	9-1-76	11-1-76	3,000	6%	-0-	-0-		30	Paid 11-1-76 and credited to Dean Co.
Evans Co.	7-1-76	10-1-76	6,000	6%	-0-	150		150	Time extended 90 days on note.
J. George (employee)	12-1-76	2-1-77	1,000	6%	-0-	5		5	
F. Hayes (officer)	11-1-76	3-1-77	3,000	none	-0-	-0-		-0-	
T. Link (officer)	11-1-76	12-1-76	1,000	none	-0-	-0-		-0-	
			$22,800		$ 9	$250	$18	$289	

The above schedule has been prepared by the company accountant and presented to you, together with the notes.

a) What is the total amount of trade notes receivable at 12–31–76?
b) What is the total amount of interest income, accrued interest receivable, prepaid interest, and unearned interest income?
c) Complete the work papers.

8

Investments and Related Revenues

AUDIT OBJECTIVES

The audit objectives in the examination of investments in securities are to (1) ascertain existence, (2) obtain evidence of ownership, (3) provide proper valuation on a basis that conforms with generally accepted accounting principles, (4) give proper revenue recognition, (5) determine the effect of related party transactions, and (6) provide adequate disclosure in the financial statements. Evidence of existence may be determined by inspection or by confirmation. Evidence of ownership may be determined from brokers' invoices, bank-paid checks, and related accounting entries. Evidence of proper valuation is determined by comparing cost (or other basic figure) with balance sheet date market quotations. Evidence for proper revenue determination is obtainable from annual dividend and interest services. Satisfactory evidence must exist that all investments are properly set forth in the records and that revenues are properly accounted for and recorded.

INVESTMENT CLASSIFICATIONS

Investment securities are classified as:

1. Temporary marketable securities—current assets.
2. Long-term investments—noncurrent assets, separately classified.

Temporary marketable securities are represented by high-grade marketable instruments, such as federal government obligations. These securities are purchased when cash is available in excess of current business requirements. When purchasing temporary marketable securities, the intention is to sell them when cash is required for operating purposes.

Temporary marketable securities must be readily marketable at a definite price.

Long-term investment securities are acquired for purposes of control, for the creation of specific funds for business-relation purposes, or for the purpose of yielding a relatively permanent source of other income. Long-term investments may or may not be readily marketable. These noncurrent asset investments include controlling or noncontrolling stock investments; bonds; debentures; mortgages; special funds, such as a sinking fund or a pension fund; loans or advances to affiliated companies; cash values of life insurance policies on personnel when the owner is the beneficiary; and fixed assets not used directly in the business.

Thus the primary distinction between temporary marketable securities and long-term investments lies in the purpose for which the investment originally was made. An owner later may change his original intention, in which case a temporary marketable security may be changed to the long-term category; or it may be decided to convert a long-term investment to cash for working capital purposes.

INTERNAL CONTROL OF INVESTMENT SECURITIES

Proper internal control of investments demands that the custodianship of the securities be separated from accounting for them. Securities must be properly controlled physically in order to prevent unauthorized use, and the securities must be registered in the name of the owner (unless unregistered coupon items exist). Purchases and sales of all investments must be made only after proper authorization—usually by the board of directors or by a finance committee. Obviously, discretion to buy or sell should not be vested in one person. Access to securities should be vested in at least two persons, acting jointly. Periodically, investment revenues should be reconciled with the amounts that should be received. A periodic physical inventory of securities should be taken by a person who has no responsibility for the control or record keeping of the securities.

Satisfactory standards of internal control may be determined from the questionnaire in Illustration 8–1.

Reports to Management

In many instances, it is desirable periodically to submit to top management—for example, the board of directors—reports setting forth the securities portfolio and its activities to date from the date of the last report. Such a report should set forth the cost of each security, its current market price, the rate of return being earned on cost and on current market price, purchases and sales of securities, gains and losses on sales, and any other important and desired data. Based upon a periodic report

Illustration 8–1

```
┌─────────────────────────────────────────────────────────────────────────────┐
│                     INTERNAL CONTROL QUESTIONNAIRE                            │
│                Investment Securities:  Temporary and Long–Term                │
│                                                                               │
│                                                           Not                 │
│  Company _____        Yes   No   Appli-  Remarks│
│  Period Covered _____                    cable         │
│                                                                               │
│   1. Are all investment documents under the contol of a                       │
│      custodian?                                                               │
│   2. Is the custodian adequately bonded?                                      │
│   3. Is an independent custodian employed?                                    │
│   4. Are investment documents kept in a safe–deposit box?                     │
│   5. To open the box, must more than one person be present?                   │
│   6. Are investment documents periodically inspected and                      │
│      reconciled with the accounting records?                                  │
│   7. Does the securities custodian have access to the                         │
│      accounting records?                                                      │
│   8. Are registered securities held in the name of the client?                │
│   9. Does the accounting department maintain an indepen-                      │
│      dent record of each investment security?                                 │
│  10. Is there proper accounting for all investment revenue?                   │
│  11. Are purchases and sales of investments properly                          │
│      authorized?                                                              │
│  12. Is proper control exercised over securities written down                 │
│      to zero?                                                                 │
│  13. Are all insurance and fidelity bonds adequate?                           │
│                                                                               │
│  Prepared by_____    Reviewed by _____           │
│  Date_____     Date _____            │
└─────────────────────────────────────────────────────────────────────────────┘
```

of this nature, management may arrive at decisions regarding investment policies and practices.

AUDIT OF INVESTMENTS IN STOCKS AND BONDS

At the simultaneous control of all cash and negotiable instruments, the auditor should prepare or obtain a schedule listing all stocks and bonds. See Illustrations 8–2 and 8–3. Work paper details should be compared with the stock certificates and the bonds, and the totals of the schedules are compared with the corresponding general-ledger account balances. A representative of the client should be present when the independent auditor has possession of the securities. If simultaneous count of cash and securities is not possible (because the securities are in a safe-deposit box), an auditor should request his client to not remove securities from the box until all cash is counted. Then a written statement should be obtained from the bank that the safety-deposit box had not been opened during the dates of the cash count. Without such a statement, control and the advantages of simultaneous count have been lost. If a securities portfolio is too large to list them in a relatively short time, the portfolio

Illustration 8–2

THE BLANK COMPANY
Stock Investments, December 31, 1976

Name of Stock	Certificate Number	Common or Preferred	Balance, December 31, 1975		
			Shares	Cost per Share	Total Cost
ABC	87 654	C	100 A	156	15600
DEF	8 642	P			
GHI	1 357	P	200 A*	51	10200
JKL	24 531	P	100 A	91	9100
MNO	369	C	100 A	54	5400
Balance, per audit ⊗					40300 A

A *Agrees with 1975 work papers.*
ø *Examined brokers' invoices.*
* *Sold 100 in 1976.*
¶ *Received 4 dividends on 100 shares, and 2 dividends*
  on 100 shares, $0.60 per share.
¶ *Received 4 dividends of $0.9375 each on 100 shares, and*
  2 dividends of $0.9375 each on 100 shares
∧ *Received 20 percent stock dividends, January 28, 1976.*
√ *Authorizations for purchases and sales inspected.*
⊙ *From Standard and Poor's Annual Dividend Record.*
≠ *Traced to cash receipts.*
  All certificates are in the name of the Blank Company.

should be broken into groups, sealed, and then examined and tabulated. Withdrawals from sealed packages must be noted by the auditor—and the packages resealed.

Securities should be registered in the name of the client or his nominee, or endorsed to the client, or endorsed in blank, or have a properly executed power of attorney attached. In listing stocks and bonds, the auditor must be certain of exact names; for example, 100 shares of Standard Oil of Indiana may have an entirely different cost than 100 shares of Standard Oil of California. In listing bonds, par denominations must be accurate—$100, $1,000, etc. When examining coupon bonds, the auditor must ascertain that all future coupons are attached.

If a client owned the same securities at the date of the last audit, the auditor should compare the detail of the composition for each stock certificate number and company name, and each bond number and name, with his work papers for the preceding year.

If stocks and bonds are held by others—brokers or banks, or if they are out for transfer—the auditor should obtain direct confirmation of those items. Securities on hand should not be released before confirmations have been obtained for items not on hand because in the interval the released securities might be placed with the confirming party.

Market Price December 31, 1976		Purchased in 1976	Sold in 1976	Profit or (Loss) on Sale	Balance December 31, 1976		Dividends Received in 1976
Per Share	Total				Shares	Lower of Cost or Market	
184	18400 ○				100	15600	9000
119	11900 ○	11800 ✓∅			100	11800	5000
48	4800 ○		4700 ✓∅	(400)	100	4800	36000 ✓
100	20000 ○	9900 ✓∅			200	19000	56250 ✓
61	7320 ○				120 ∧	5400	28800
	62420	21700	4700			56600 ⊗	2 61050 ≠

Receipt

All securities in this schedule were counted in my presence in the vault of The Central Trust Company by representatives of Bennett and Bennett, CPAs, and were returned to me intact.

Harry Kline	11:00 AM
Treasurer	1-12-77

As of the balance-sheet date, market prices should be obtained for all securities and noted in the work papers; see Illustrations 8–2 and 8–3.

Purchases and Sales of Securities

For the period under audit, authorizations for purchases and sales of securities must be examined, with directors' minutes or finance committee actions serving as the normal original authorization. Brokers' invoices (advices) are compared with the purchase and sale authorization data and then are traced to the accounting records. For investment securities sold during the period, an auditor must examine the accounts for credits of proper amount and verify the computation of gain or loss on the sales. See Illustrations 8–2 and 8–3. If securities sold can be identified specifically, the Investment account is credited for the cost—or other basic value—of the security sold. If identification is not possible, the first-in, first-out method must be used for federal income tax purposes.

If an audit is started after the close of the fiscal period, the auditor must trace sales and purchases from the date of starting the audit back to the balance-sheet date. This is necessary in order to arrive at the account composition as of the balance-sheet date.

Illustration 8–3

THE BLANK COMPANY

Bond Investments, December 31, 1976

Type and Description	Bond Numbers		Balance at Cost, Dec.31, 1975	Purchases at Cost, 1976	Sales at Cost, 1976
ZYX Co., 9%, 1987	521-2-3-4-5	⊙	4500		
WVU Co., 6%, 1996	8,9,10,11,12			5100 √	
TSR Co., 8%, 1976	19,20,21,22,23	⊙	4800		4800
QPO Co., 7%, 2001	112-3-4-5-6	⊙	5000	3000 √	
			14300	8100	4800
					√

⊙ Agrees with 1975 work paper, --and 1976 audit
√ Examined brokers' invoices.
√ Traced to cash receipts and ledger accounts.
√ Profit of $200 properly accounted for.
∅ Agrees with general ledger --and audit
⊖ Prices from Wall Street Journal, January 2, 1977.
∧ Calculations verified.
A Purchased April 1, 1976.
B Sold on July 1, 1976.
C Purchased ($3,000) December 27, 1976.
All bonds are registered in the name of the Blank Company
All coupons are clipped to date (for coupon bonds).
Examined authorizations to buy and sell.

Revenues from Securities

Revenues from stocks and bonds usually are verified by the auditor at the time of examining the securities and preparing the work papers. An internal auditor is in a position to predetermine revenue, based on his securities schedules and on dividend and interest dates and amounts. Dividends according to the auditor's work papers should be "tied up" with the client's dividend accounts. To assist in the verification of dividends, the auditor may use the various published annual dividend service booklets. In the case of many unlisted securities, the auditor should confirm dividends from brokers or directly from the paying company. The dividends computed by the auditor are traced to the client's accounting records—cash and revenue (or the Stock Investment account) —or to the securities record if a nonincome stock dividend was received. Usually, dividends are not accrued by a stockholder; but if they are accrued, the date of stock record should be followed in order to avoid showing revenue that will not be received because of the possible sale of the stock. Dividends received from controlled subsidiary companies are credited to income or charged to the Stock Investment account if the owner credits its portion of subsidiary company income to the Investment account—a practice recommended in *Opinion No. 18* of the Ac-

Sales t Sales ice, 1976	Balance, Dec. 31, 1976 At Cost	At Market Price	Interest Dates	Interest Accrued Dec.31, 1976	Interest Earned, 1976	
	4500	4750 ⊖	1-1, 7-1	225 00 ^	450 00	
	5100	5150 ⊖	4-1, 10-1	750 00 ^	225 00	A
5000 ✗	0	0	1-1, 7-1	0	200 00	B
	8000	8000 ⊖	1-1, 7-1	320 00 ^	520 00	C
5000	17600 ⌀	17900		1 295 00	1 395 00	
✓						

Receipt

All securities in this schedule were counted in my presence in the vault of The Central Trust Company by representatives of Bennett and Bennett, CPAs, and were returned to me intact.

Harry Kline	11:30 AM
Treasurer	1-12-77

counting Principles Board of the AICPA, assuming that the investor owns more than 20 percent of the stock of an investee. This is known as the equity method.

If stock dividends are received in the same class of stock as that held, revenue is not recognized. Revenue is realized and recognized for federal income tax purposes if a stock dividend is received in a class of stock other than the class held.

Bond interest received and accrued must be verified in accordance with the interest provisions of the bonds owned. Amounts received are traced to the accounting records. The total interest earned and received according to the work papers of the auditor must be "tied up" with the client's accounting records.

The auditor must verify or compute the amortization of bond premiums and discounts. Amortizations may appear as adjustments to Interest Income, or they may appear in separate accounts.

AUDIT OF INVESTMENTS IN LIFE INSURANCE

An auditor must understand the purposes for which life insurance is purchased. He must determine its adequacy for the original purpose, such as supplying funds for the acquisition of an interest of a deceased partner or stockholder, or supplying funds to cover the loss of business income in the event of the death or retirement of a key person.

The policies should be listed in work papers, in which should be included such data as the name of the insurance company, policy number, date of the policy, type of insurance, name of beneficiary, amount of the insurance, annual premiums, premium dates, accumulated dividends and interest, and cash surrender values. The policies contain all data except accumulated dividends and interest, prepaid premiums (over one year), and loans outstanding against the policies. Accumulated dividends and interest may be ascertained from accumulation notices submitted by the insurance company, or by requesting direct confirmation from the insurance companies for data not available.

Cash Values and Cash Loan Values

Insurance premiums are advance payments. In determining the amount of the insurance for asset purposes, some accountants use cash surrender values at the end of the insurance anniversary date or at the balance-sheet date; other accountants use loan values at the beginning of a policy year. While there is no uniformity of practice, apparently there is a tendency to use loan values at the beginning of a policy year.

Determination of the cash values or the loan values to be used is directly related to the proper determination of periodic expense and prepaid expenses at the year-end. Cash surrender values and loan values increase only after payment of the annual premium. Therefore, the cash surrender value or loan value immediately after the payment of an annual premium is the stated amount as of the next premium date, less the discount and the pro rata reduction for the remainder of the policy year. At the end of each month during the year the discount period is reduced and the cash surrender value or loan value is increased until at the end of the policy year the cash surrender value or loan value agrees with the amount stated in the policy. That portion of a premium not added to the policy cash surrender value or loan value is a prepaid expense to be prorated to expense equally over the year.

Cash surrender values and loan values *normally* do not exist until two premiums have been paid. Therefore, at least the first annual premium is expense. When the second premium is paid, cash surrender values or loan values are set up and income charged for that portion of the cash surrender value or loan value attributable to the payment of the first premium. In this way, all income statements and balance sheets are presented on a consistent basis.

Dividends and Interest

If dividends and interest are left with the insurance company for accumulation, the auditor must examine premium receipts from the insurance companies to determine proper accounting entries. Interest accumulations should be charged to cash surrender or loan values and credited to income because the interest is taxable income. Dividend accumulations should be charged to cash surrender or loan values and credited to a dividend account—which is nontaxable; dividends are construed as a reduction of gross premiums. See Illustration 8–4.

Policy Confirmation

Evidence for the accuracy of cash surrender values may be obtained by requesting confirmations from the insurance companies, and an auditor should request the following data:

1. Cash (surrender) or loan values—at the desired dates.
2. Accumulated dividends and interest.
3. Amount of loans on policies and interest on the loans.
4. Date to which premiums are paid.
5. Name of beneficiary.
6. Name of party paying premiums.
7. Is the policy assigned?

Both the internal and the external auditor should extract all pertinent data from the policies and retain those data to determine that the provisions of the policies are in agreement with the intentions of the insured and the parties insuring.

AUDIT OF INVESTMENTS IN FUNDS

An auditor must examine authorizations for the establishment of specific funds by reference to actions of the board of directors and by confirmations from the internal auditor. If funds are maintained by a trustee—common for sinking funds and pension funds—both the composition of the fund and the periodic revenue and disbursements must be confirmed. If there is no trustee, the auditor should verify fund contributions, income earned and added to the fund, and disbursements from the fund; and these data should be compared with the records of the client. The auditor also must determine that any underlying trust agreements are being observed. When a fund finally is used, the auditor must ascertain that it was used for the purpose for which it was authorized. See Illustrations 8–5 and 8–6.

FINANCIAL STATEMENT CONSIDERATIONS

Temporary Marketable Securities

Marketable securities, classified as current assets, are to be priced at not in excess of cost. If the securities are priced at the lower of cost or

Illustration 8–4
WORK PAPER 10

	Initials	Date
Prepared By	ꝺR	2-11-77
Approved By	RW	2-14-77

MULTI-PRODUCTS, INCORPORATED
Cash Surrender Value of Life Insurance, December 31, 1976

Balance, December 31, 1975 and December 31, 1976 7926
This balance represents the following amounts
set up at December 31, 1975:
a) Cash surrender value at the end of
the third policy year (9-30-74) 4 860
One fourth (¼) of the increase in cash
surrender value at the end of the
fourth policy year (9-30-75 to
9-30-76) [($7,380 - $4,500) ÷ 4] 360
5 220
b) Prepaid life insurance: three quarters
(¾) of the premium of the fourth
policy year ($3,608)* 2 706
7 926

AJE 6: Amounts required to adjust the account 3224
Balance, per audit 11150

AJE 6
Cash Surrender Value of Life Insurance 3 224
Life Insurance Expense 3224
To adjust cash surrender value of life
insurance as of December 31, 1976, to
agree with the amount furnished by
the insurance company at that date.
The amount furnished by the
insurance company was based on the
following calculations:
Cash surrender value at end of fourth
policy year (9-30-76) .... $ 7680
One fourth (¼) of increase in
cash surrender value at end of
fifth policy year
(9-30-76 to 9-30-77)
[($10,440 = $7,380) + 4] 764
$ 8444
Prepaid life insurance: three
quarters 75% of the premium
of the fifth year ($3,608) 2706
$11150

* The client has followed the practice, which we accept, of
including the prepaid portion in the cash surrender value.

Illustration 8–5
WORK PAPER 11

		Initials	Date
MULTI-PRODUCTS, INCORPORATED	Prepared By	ℐℛ	2-12-77
Sinking Fund Investments, December 31, 1976	Approved By	ℛ𝓌	2-14-77

Under the terms of the bond issue dated January 1, 1970 in a total amount of $1,000,000, bonds in a total of $100,000 are to be retired each July 1.

At December 31, 1976, $400,000 of bonds are outstanding.

The bond indenture provides that the company shall set aside $100,000 each six months starting July 1, 1970 (in addition to the $100,000 retirement at July 1, 1970) for the purpose of establishing a sinking fund for future retirements. Interest earned is to be added to the fund. The fund is under company control.

Balance, December 31, 1975:			113050
Added to the fund, 1976:			
January 1		100000	
July 1		100000	200000
			313050
Bonds retired and canceled, 1976:			
January 1		100000	
July 1		100000	200000
			113050
Interest earned, 1976			3450
Balance, per audit December 31, 1976			116500

market, for purposes of disclosure, the higher figure should be shown parenthetically. If current market price is below original cost, (1) the difference *may* be charged to expense, with the offsetting credit being to the Investment account; or (2) the Investment account may be carried at cost and an allowance credited for the decline (this is not customary). Then the accounts remain at proper figures for the determination of gain or loss on a sale, for federal income tax purposes. An additional argument for the latter procedure is that if market prices recover, the investment cost is not affected—only the allowance account is lowered. Modern practice is to the effect that marketable securities are carried at cost, with the higher- or lower-than-cost figure shown parenthetically.

Securities of security dealers may be priced at cost, at market, or at the lower of cost or market, with the higher figure shown parenthetically. Securities of investment companies may be carried at the lower of cost or market, with the other figure shown parenthetically. If valuation meth-

Illustration 8–6

			Initials	Date
THE BLANK COMPANY		Prepared By		
Pension Fund, December 31, 1976		Approved By		

Explanation	1973	1974	1975	1976
Balance at beginning of year	0	76125	125808	172632
Additions:				
Company expense charges	50000	30000	35000	40000
Employees' contributions	25000	30000	35000	40000
Interest: 3 percent of				
average balance	1125	3183	4824	6378
	76125	139308	200632	259010
Deductions:				
Benefits paid (below)	0	12000	23600	36700
Refunds to employees	0	1500	4400	3700
	0	13500	28000	40400
Balance at End of Year, per audit	76125	125808	172632	218610

			BENEFITS PAID		
Employee	Date	Type	1974	1975	1976
A	May 1, 1973	Annuity	3000	3690	3600
B	July 1, 1973	Death	9000	0	0
C	Mar. 1, 1974	Annuity		12000	14400
D	May 1, 1974	Annuity		8000	9600
E	July 1, 1975	Annuity			600
F	Aug. 1, 1975	Death			3100
G	Sept. 1, 1975	Annuity			800
H	Oct. 1, 1975	Annuity			900
I	May 1, 1976	Annuity			1600
J	June 1, 1976	Annuity			2100
			12000	23600	36700

ods are changed, the auditor should point out the changes—and the reasons therefor—in his audit report.

Long-Term Investments

Long-term investments in stocks of noncontrolled companies normally are carried at cost or at other basic acquisition figures. If market prices decline drastically and "permanently," the cost or other basic figure should be reduced. Long-term investments in stocks of controlled companies should be carried by using the equity method of accounting for them.

Long-term investments in bonds are carried at original cost plus amortized discount or minus amortized premium.

If securities of any category are pledged as loan collateral, the situation should be disclosed in the balance sheet.

Life Insurance

As stated earlier in this chapter, either cash values or loan values are used for pricing investments in life insurance. Life insurance investments are long-term investments, not current assets. The prepaid premium portion is a current asset. If there are loans outstanding against the policies, the amount of the loans may be shown among the liabilities; or it may be shown as a subtraction from the cash value or loan value, whichever is used. The audit report should discuss the loans because the loans may defeat the purposes for which the insurance was purchased.

Investments in Funds

Investments in funds should be set forth in the balance sheet in accordance with the intention of establishing the funds. For example, bond retirement funds and nontrusteed pension funds are not current assets.

SUGGESTED ADDITIONAL READING

Statement on Auditing Standards No. 1, Sections 332, 452.06.
Statement on Auditing Standards No. 6, Paragraphs 1, 2, 5, 9–18.

QUESTIONS

1. Prepare an internal control questionnaire for securities, both short-term and long-term, held by a medium-sized manufacturing company.

2. In the audit of any investment security, name five requisites that would lead to the rendition of an unqualified opinion regarding the securities.

3. *a)* A company temporarily invested some excess cash in U.S. Treasury Notes. In your preliminary audit work, it is ascertained that these securities were acquired at various dates during the year under examination through a brokerage firm, and that the securities are in the name of the client but are being held in safekeeping by the brokerage firm. The client company does not maintain an investment ledger. Outline the audit procedures for the securities and the related income, as reflected in the records of the client.

   b) You are conducting the first audit of the financial statements of a client. All investment securities owned as of the first of the year were sold during the year under examination. What procedures would you follow with respect to these securities? Present reasons for using the procedures.

4. An investment trust holds small minority interests in the stocks of several companies. In each of the following cases, should dividends be taken up as income, or be added to the principal of the portfolio? It is the practice of the trust to credit all ordinary dividends to income and all

gains or losses on securities sold are carried directly to income or expense.

a) X Company: A cash dividend of $1 per share on common stock, or one hundredth of a share of $100 par value preferred stock (a new issue).

b) Y Company: A dividend on common stock of one tenth of a share of $100 par value preferred stock (some preferred is outstanding).

c) Z Company: A dividend on common stock of $5 per share, payable —at the option of the stockholders—in cash or in the same common stock at a par-share value which is below the present market price.

5. Early in 1974, Rutt, Inc., had $10 million of temporarily excess cash— the result of a general business slowdown. The company invested the money in U.S. Treasury Bills, some with a maturity of 91 days, and others with a 182 day maturity. When purchased, the Bills were classified as current assets. At each maturity date, Rutt "rolled" the Bills. Throughout 1974, 1975 and 1976 the company's business had not recovered sufficiently to require any part of the $10 million for normal operating purposes, and could not forecast when it might recover. Between 1974 and the end of 1976, yields on the Bills ranged from 9.4 to 5.4 percent.

Your first audit of the financial statements of the company is for the year 1976. As of December 31, 1976, how should the Bills be classified for balance-sheet purposes? Present reasons for your answer.

6. a) To what extent should an auditor investigate a client's ownership of real estate and mortgages?

b) Why should insurance policies covering mortgaged properties be examined when a client holds the mortgage?

7. Outline the procedures for the verification of transactions in a sinking fund for the redemption of bonds; the fund is in the custody of an independent trustee.

8. You are auditing the financial statements of Kluff, Inc., for the year ended December 31, 1976. Kluff sells construction materials at wholesale. Company total assets are $4,000,000 and stockholders' equities are $2,000,000.

The company's records show an investment of $400,000 for 400 shares of the common stock of one of its customers, Tower, Inc. You learn that Tower is closely held and that its common stock, consisting of 4,000 shares issued and outstanding, has no quoted market price. Kluff has no other investments.

Examination of your client's cash disbursements reveals an entry for a check of $400,000 drawn on January 23, 1976, to E. K. Gary, who is said to be the former owner of the 400 shares of stock. Gary is president of Kluff.

a) What audit procedures would you follow in connection with the $400,000 investment in the capital stock of Tower, Inc.?

b) Discuss the presentation of the investment in the balance sheet, including its valuation.

9. Finance, Inc., one of your audit clients, is engaged—in part—in the purchase of mortgage notes. During the current audit year, you find that the company has purchased from the Town Bank mortgage notes from several individuals. Of the notes, some were purchased at par, some at a premium, and others at a discount. Each note purchased requires equal payments each month to cover both principal and interest. By agreement, each mortgagor pays fixed monthly amounts to cover insurance and property taxes. The seller of the mortgage notes continues to service them, remitting each month to Finance, Inc., the payments for taxes and insurance in escrow until the tax bills and insurance invoices are received for payment.

    a) What documents should be available to support your client's investment?

    b) Outline the steps for the audit of the transactions, including both principal and interest.

10. What type of opinion should a CPA render in each of the following cases?

    a) Ace, Inc., owns properties which have materially appreciated in value since purchase. The properties were appraised and are reported in the balance sheet at the appraised values with full disclosure. The CPA doubts that the values reported in the balance sheets are reasonable.

    b) Boss, Inc., has *material* investments in stocks of subsidiary companies. Stocks of the subsidiary companies are not actively traded in the market, and the CPA's engagement does not extend to any subsidiary. The CPA is able to satisfy himself that all investments are carried at *original cost,* and he has no reason to suspect that the amounts are not stated fairly.

    c) Cass, Inc., has large investments in stocks of subsidiary companies, but the investments are not material in relation to the financial position and results of operations of the corporations. Stocks of the subsidiary companies are not actively traded in the market, and the CPA's engagement does not extend to any subsidiary company. The CPA is able to satisfy himself that all investments are carried at original cost, and he has no reason to suspect that the amounts are not fairly stated.

    d) Dock, Inc., has material investments in stocks of subsidiary companies, and those stocks are actively traded in the market, but the CPA's engagement does not extend to any subsidiary company. Management *insists* that all investments be carried at original cost, and the CPA is satisfied that the original costs are fairly presented. The CPA believes that the client will never ultimately realize a substantial portion of the investments, but the client insists that no disclosure to this effect be made in the financial statements.

                                                                (AICPA, adapted)

11. How should each of the following be classified on a balance sheet?

    a) Bonds acquired July 1, 1976, for $104,000, and which mature April 1, 1985, for $100,000.

b)   A bond redemption fund administered by a trustee under a trust indenture agreement.

c)   Listed stock rights that are to be sold.

d)   Stock that is intended to be transferred to a supplier in cancellation of trade account payable.

e)   Cash value of officer's life insurance; the company is the beneficiary.

f)   Cash value of officers' life insurance; the premiums are paid by the company but the officers' spouses are the beneficiaries.

g)   Stock held for purposes of controlling a subsidiary.

h)   Parking lot for customers' convenience.

i)   Land acquired for an expansion program at least five years from now.

j)   Advances to a subsidiary company.

k)   United States Treasury Bills acquired to provide income for idle cash during the slack season.

l)   Accrued interest on company's own bonds held in a bond retirement fund.

m)   A fund to be used to pay current bond interest.

n)   A preferred stock redemption fund.

o)   A profit-sharing plan; the beneficiaries are salaried employees of the company administered by three company-appointed trustees.

PROBLEMS

1.   The balance of the Investment account at December 31, 1976, of Clear, Inc., is $60,000, which was a lump-sum payment for securities on July 1, 1976. In support of this balance your client gives you the following securities and their market value at the date of acquisition, July 1, 1976:

200 shares, Par $ 10, of X Company, common, $30.
400 shares, Par $100, of Y Company, 9% preferred, $60.
500 shares, Par $ 10, of Z Company, common, $40.

a)   Prepare an audit work paper to determine the correct valuation of these investments.

b)   After considering the following information, show the proper balance sheet presentation of these investments:

200 shares of X Company sold 1/5/77 for $8,000, which was the market value at 12/31/76.

400 shares of Y Company has a market value of $20,000 at 12/31/76. Due to the good rate of return, this stock was turned over to the client's profit-sharing plan on 12/31/76.

500 shares of Z Company has a market value of $25,000 at 12/31/76. These 500 shares constitute an 80% interest in the voting stock of the Z Company.

2.   The following transactions were discovered by you in your audit of the records of Linel, Inc., for the year ended December 31, 1976.

1976

a) 1/2 —Investment in 9% Equipment Bonds 10,860
          Cash in Bank   10,860
        Purchase of $10,000 of 9% equipment bonds at
        102 plus accrued interest of $450 and broker's
        fees of $210. Bonds mature 1/1/86.

b) 1/3 —Cash in Bank   450
          Interest Income   450
        Interest received on 9% equipment bonds. (This
        same entry was made when interest was received
        on July 1, 1976.)

c) 7/1 —Investment in Fast Company $8 Preferred Stock 100,200
          Premium paid on Fast Company $8 Preferred Stock .   2,000
          Cash in Bank   102,200
        Purchase of 1,000 shares of $8 preferred stock,
        par $100, at 102. Broker's fees $200.

d) 12/1 —Investment Speed Company Common Stock   50,000
          Cash in Bank   50,000
        Purchase of 5,000 shares $10 par common stock,
        market value $10 per share, which was 75% of the
        outstanding voting shares and after $1 per share
        cash dividend had been declared. No broker fees.

e) 12/31 —Cash in Bank   8,000
          Premium Paid on Fast Company preferred stock .   2,000
          Dividend Income   6,000
        Dividend received on Fast Company preferred stock.

f) 12/31 —Cash in Bank   5,000
          Investment Speed Company Common Stock   5,000
        Receipt of $1 per share dividend which had been
        declared prior to acquisition.

In reviewing these transactions with the client, you were advised that all of the investments are for an indefinite period, and for the purpose of obtaining a good rate of return on the investment as well as to control the operations of the Speed Company. It is agreed that if these purposes are to be fairly presented in the financial statements of the company, that all such investments should be carried at cost.

a) Since all the investments were carried in one account, you are to prepare the analysis of this account, and
b) To prepare the necessary audit adjustments which will properly complete the work paper and all related transactions.

3. The supervisor on the audit of PWO, Inc., has assigned you to the audit of the Long-Term Investments for the year ended December 31, 1976. He advises you that all investments are long-term and if any securities are sold, the client has sold them so that his profits will be maximized. All documents supporting the transactions were given to you by J. J. Quick, treasurer.

    As you proceed with the audit, the following transactions relate to the stocks held by the client.

1976

January 15 —	Long-Term Investments	7,164	
	Cash in Bank		7,164
	Purchase of 100 shares of common stock of Void Company (par $10) at $70 per share plus commission of 2% and transfer costs of $24. Certificate No. C16583.		

June 1 —	Long-Term Investments	40,000	
	Cash in Bank		40,000
	Purchase of Remit Company stock; below:		

Stock	Number of Shares	Cost
6% preferred, par $100, Cert. No. 888	200	$20,000
Class A Common, par $50, Cert. No. 593	200	12,000
Class B No-par value, Cert. No. 684	200	8,000
Purchased direct from company		

July 1 —	Long-Term Investments	24,552	
	Cash in Bank		24,552
	Purchased 300 more shares of Void Company common stock. Brokerage Commission of 2% and transfer costs of $72. Certificate No. C16990.		

August 1 —	Received a stock certificate from Void Company as a result of a one for one stock dividend declared 7/10/76 to shareholders as of record date 7/30/76. Certificate No. CC1952.

Sept. 1 —	Cash in Bank	20,000	
	Long-Term Investments		20,000
	Sold 400 shares of Void Company common stock at $50 per share.		

Oct. 1 —	Received stock certificate from Remit Company for a two-for-one stock split of its common stock. Declaration date 9/1/76; record date 9/20/76. Certificate No. R8888.

Dec. 1 —	Cash in Bank	5,000	
	Dividend Income		5,000
	Received cash dividends as follows:		
	Void Company common stock	$2,000	
	Remit Company 6% preferred	1,200	
	Remit Company common A	1,200	
	Remit Company no-par	600	

Prepare the necessary audit work paper covering the information that you have developed as a result of your audit. The *Wall Street Journal* of 1/2/77 gives the following closing per-share prices on stock still in the portfolio:

Remit Company 6% preferred	$75
Remit Company Class A Common	15
Remit Company Class B, no-par value	20
Void Company common	20

4. From the following information:

   a) Prepare a work sheet analyzing the Investment account for the period January 1, 1976, to September 30, 1976, showing transactions, adjustments, and final balance as of September 30, 1976.

b) Prepare the necessary audit adjustments to correct the following Investment account as of September 30, 1976, appearing in the records of the Paint Company:

Date	Explanation	Debit	Credit
1976			
Jan. 1	Balance	188,300	
31	Sold Red stock		21,364
Mar. 31	Bought White common	12,125	
June 30	Dividend on Blue common . .	10,000	
July 31	Sold Blue common		8,750
Aug. 31	Sold Green bonds		22,500
Sept. 30	Interest on Brown		
	mortgage		500

The audit work papers of the preceding year show that the account balance as of January 1, 1976, consisted of the following:

Red Company common:
    1,000 shares, purchased in June 1968, @ $20 per share . . . . $ 20,000
    2,000 shares, purchased in August 1970, @ $16 per share   32,000
    1,500 shares, purchased in May 1973, @ $22 per share   33,000
White Company common:
    2,000 shares, purchased in January 1974, @ $33 per share   66,000
Blue Company common:
    100 shares, purchased in August 1969, @ $73 per share (par $100) . . .   7,300
Green Company 5 percent bonds:
    20 bonds, $1,000 each, purchased in July 1972, @ par
    (interest dates February and August 1)   20,000
Brown Company chattel mortgage on machinery:
    5 percent, $10,000 mortgage taken in September 1975, in
    settlement of a receivable . . . .   <u>10,000</u>
                                                 $188,300

Your examination discloses the following:
(1) In January 1976, 1,000 shares of the Red Company common stock purchased in June 1973, were sold for $21,364, net of brokerage.
(2) In March 1976, 500 shares of White Company common stock were purchased at $24 per share plus brokerage, for $12,125.
(3) In June 1976, the Blue Company paid a 100 percent stock dividend —common on common.
(4) In July 1976, the Paint Company sold to its president, for $125 per share, 100 shares of Blue Company common stock, for which the president gave his check for $8,750 and a letter in which he agreed to pay the balance upon demand of the treasurer of the company.
(5) On August 1, 1976, the Green Company redeemed its 5 percent bonds at 110 plus accrued interest.
(6) In September 1976, the Paint Company received one year's interest on the $10,000 chattel mortgage of the Brown Company which it holds.

5. As auditor for Madd, Inc., you are to prepare the following:

    a) Work papers for the securities and for security transactions for the year ended December 31, 1976, including columns for the following:

        (1) Securities inventory at December 31, 1975, divided into security name, number of shares, cost, and average cost per share.

        (2) Security purchases in 1976, divided into date, shares, and amount.

        (3) Security sales in 1976, divided into date, shares, amount, average cost of shares sold, and profit or loss on sales.

        (4) Securities inventory at December 31, 1976, divided into name of security, shares, and cost.

        (5) Dividends received in 1976.

    b) Audit adjustment for all security transactions.

Marketable securities owned by the Madd Company at December 31, 1975:

Security A, 1,500 shares, at a cost of	$120,000
Security B, 1,200 shares, at a cost of	84,000
Security C, 1,000 shares, at a cost of	130,000
Security D, 800 shares, at a cost of	85,000
Security E, 1,000 shares, at a cost of	70,000
	$489,000

Security transactions for 1976 are shown in the two tables following:

Purchases	Shares	Cost
April 15	500A	$50,000
April 25	200F	15,000
July 15	300G	40,000
July 25	200D	20,000
August 15	200D	25,000
September 15	1,000G	90,000

Sales	Shares	Cost
March 10	200C	$ 30,000
April 10	1,200B	110,000
June 15	300C	50,000
August 20	1,000E	30,000
September 15	1,000A	125,000

Other data are as follows:

    (1) Cash dividends received, 1976: A, $12,000; C, $6,000; D, $5,000; and F, $1,000.

    (2) Stock dividend received on June 15, 1976; E, 100 percent.

    (3) Market price of securities at December 31, 1976: $565,000.

                                        (AICPA, adapted)

6. During the course of an audit you find an account, as follows:

Long-Term Investment—Branch Company

1976	*Debits*	
Jan. 15	Cost of 200 shares (par $100)	$36,000
Feb. 15	Received 100 shares as stock dividend, market price per share $100	10,000
	Credits	
Aug. 15	Sold 50 shares received as a dividend	6,250

Gain on Investment Transactions

	Credits	
Feb. 15	Stock dividend	10,000
Aug. 15	Cash dividend	6,000

Assuming the cost method, what audit adjustments would you make to these accounts?

9

Inventories and Cost of Sales

AUDIT OBJECTIVES

Briefly at this early stage, the audit objectives for the examination of inventories and cost of sales are to determine (1) the propriety of periodic cost of sales, and (2) the accuracy of the period-end inventories. The keynote to the determination of periodic net income rests in large measure on proper accounting for the cost of goods sold and for the remaining inventories.

NECESSITY FOR PROPER INVENTORY VALUATION

Proper accounting for cost of sales and inventories also determines the accuracy of the matching of periodic revenues and related expenses, and serves as a basis for future decisions, which decisions are primarily based upon the income statement. Therefore, the auditor should (1) observe the taking of an inventory, (2) test quantity counts, (3) ascertain that the inventory has been properly priced, (4) determine proper cutoff of purchases and sales, and (5) determine that the total of the inventories reflected in all financial statements is in accordance with recognized principles of accounting, consistently applied.

Responsibilities for Inventory Examinations and Valuation

An auditor has a dual responsibility with regard to inventories—his professional responsibility and his legal responsibility. His legal responsibility is easily exemplified by a study of recent court cases brought against auditors where inventories are involved.

Accounting and professional responsibilities are composed of (1) a study and evaluation of the system of internal control for inventories, (2) observation of the taking of the inventories, (3) testing of inventory counts, and (4) the examination and proof of accuracy of the inventories in terms of prices in order to set forth properly the inventories and the related cost of sales.

Legal responsibilities of the professional accountant emanate from the now prominent common law and the requirements of regulatory agencies, such as the Securities and Exchange Commission. For registrants, the Commission requires that audit reports shall state whether or not the audit was made in accordance with accepted auditing standards, shall state the procedures omitted, and shall set forth significant changes in the application of recognized accounting principles.

If the professional auditor does not include exceptions to accepted procedures in his report, the assumption is that all accepted procedures were followed in the examination of inventories and the inventory records. If the basis of pricing inventories has been changed from one year to the next year—for example, from Fifo to Lifo—that change must be mentioned in the report, together with the effect on net income. If full disclosure is not given in the report, it is misleading, and someone may allege injury. In general, courts in the United States have held that a professional auditor may become liable for negligence so great that it constitutes fraud—even to third parties who rely upon the auditor's report. Liability for negligence has been limited to the client in the past, but that concept lately has been breaking down, based upon some recent court cases.

INTERNAL CONTROL OF INVENTORIES

Internal control features for purchasing and receiving and for purchase returns were set forth in Chapter 5 in connection with the examination of the original records. To summarize: Adequate internal control over purchases demands authorized and approved ordering and the separation of the function of ordering from receiving, shipping, and accounting. Upon receipt of the ordered goods, the goods, related invoices, receiving reports, and purchase orders must be controlled to prevent improper usage of the goods and to prevent improper payment.

Adequate internal control of inventories is directly related to purchasing, manufacturing, and accounting for materials, work in process, and finished goods. Inventories must be safely controlled, requisitioned, and properly used. Remaining inventories must be properly controlled, counted, priced, and totaled. Each preceding element of internal control should be independent of each other element so that inventories cannot be diverted from the income-producing channels of the owner.

The internal control questionnaire in Illustration 9–1 adheres to recog-

Illustration 9–1

INTERNAL CONTROL QUESTIONNAIRE
Inventories

Company _____
Period Covered _____

	Yes	No	Not Appli- cable	Remarks

1. Are all inventories under centralized control?
2. Are safeguards against theft adequate?
3. Are perpetual inventory records maintained for all classes of inventory?
4. Are all items purchased delivered to a stores department?
5. Are deliveries from the stores department made on requisition only?
6. Are the inventory records maintained by employees who are independent of the stores personnel?
7. Are perpetual inventory records verified by physical count at least once every 12 months?
8. Are discrepancies between physical counts and perpetual records investigated, accounted for, and approved?
9. Are scrap materials inventories properly controlled?
10. Are obsolete, damaged, and slow-moving items reported to a responsible person?
11. Are goods consigned in and out accounted for properly?
12. Is inventory on hand which is not the property of the client physically segregated (if necessary) and under proper accounting control?
13. When inventories are to be counted, are written instructions prepared?
14. Are inventory counts verified by persons independent of those in charge of the inventory records?
15. After the inventory is counted, are the count tags, sheets, etc., properly controlled?
16. Is there proper cutoff of inventory receipts and disbursements?
17. In taking an inventory, is the following work independently verified:
    a) Prices applied to the count?
    b) Extensions?
    c) Footings?
18. Are persons who handle the inventories separated from:
    a) Sales billings?
    b) Recording of purchases?
19. Is insurance coverage adequate?
20. Has the method of valuing inventory been changed?

Prepared by _____   Reviewed by _____
Date _____   Date _____

nized standards of internal control over inventories. See Chapter 5, Illustration 5–6, for an internal control questionnaire for purchasing.

Pricing Inventories

The propriety of proper net income determination and proper presentation of financial condition lies in the proper costing of sales and the pricing of inventories. There are many acceptable methods of pricing a remaining inventory. This remaining inventory is carried forward as a charge to cost of sales in the succeeding accounting period.

Inventories may be priced:

1. At cost:
    a) Identified cost, which is the net acquisition price—or
    b) Derived cost, such as Lifo, Fifo, average cost, standard cost, or the base-stock method.
2. At market—replacement cost at the balance-sheet date.
3. At the lower of cost or market, either applied to each item or applied to the total of inventory classes, whichever more clearly reflects net income.
4. At sales price—which may be below the lower of cost or market.
5. Under the gross profits method.
6. Under the retail inventory method.

Under any of the preceding methods, pricing an inventory involves two problems: (1) the items to be included and (2) unit costs to be used for balance sheet purposes and for the determination of net income in the income statement. From period to period the pricing method should be consistent, but if the method is changed, the audit report must describe the change, together with the effect of the change on net income in the period in which the change was made. To illustrate: "In the year ended December 31, 1976, the company adopted the Lifo method of costing sales and pricing remaining inventories. As a result, the net income for the year 1976 was $125,000 less than it would have been had the change from Fifo to Lifo not been made. In our opinion, the change is justified, because cost of sales figures will reflect current market prices for raw material usage."

Properly pricing an inventory involves the matching of revenues and the costs of obtaining those revenues—of which the cost of the inventory sold is one part.

Inventories should not be stated at amounts greater than their cost, which is: invoice price, minus discounts allowed, plus transportation-in, plus insurance in transit, plus purchasing costs, plus testing. If an inventory remaining at the end of a period—priced under *any* method—exceeds market replacement cost at that date, the inventory should be reduced to market. If inventories are priced above current market replacement costs and if the owner is not protected by future sales contracts for those inventories, the gross profit of the period in which the inventories are sold will be reduced.

Disclose the Pricing Basis. Original cost is the starting point in pricing an inventory. In the inventory accounting records, the original acquisition cost may be lost, due to the methods used in pricing a remaining inventory and in costing sales made during the period. Compliance with recognized accounting and auditing standards demands that the basis of pricing an inventory be disclosed in the financial statements parenthetically or by financial statement footnote.

The SEC requires that the basis of determining inventory amounts in the balance sheet be disclosed, together with an indication of the method of determining the amount—Lifo, Fifo, average cost, and so forth. In applications for listing securities, the New York Stock Exchange, with regard to inventories, requires that the applicant state the practice followed in adjusting inventories to the lower of cost or market (on the basis of specific items, groups, or the entire inventory), and the Exchange also requires a statement whether market price is considered to be replacement market or selling market. A statement also is required setting forth the method of computing cost of sales—average cost, Lifo, Fifo, or other.

Two examples of inventory disclosure, taken from recent annual reports, are presented below:

Inventories: In 1973, inventories were stated at the lower of cost, generally on the first-in, first-out (Fifo) method, or market. In December 1974, the Company changed the method of inventory pricing at most of its domestic operations from the Fifo method to the last-in, first-out dollar value (Lifo) method, effective January 1, 1974, because management believes that the Lifo method provides a better matching of current costs with current revenues. The effect of this change was to decrease 1974 net earnings by $5,520,000 ($1.36 per share and $1.21 per share—fully diluted) as follows (unaudited; in thousands, except per share data):

	1974 Quarter Ended				*Year 1974*
	March 31	*June 30*	*Sept. 29*	*Dec. 31*	
Decrease in earnings due to change in Lifo method	$ 596	$1,588	$ 982	$2,354	$ 5,520
Net earnings, after restatement	2,528	3,373	3,858	1,201	10,960
Decrease in earnings per share due to change to Lifo	0.15	0.39	0.24	0.58	1.36
Net earnings per share outstanding, after restatement . .	0.62	0.83	0.95	0.30	2.70
Decrease in earnings per share—fully diluted due to change to Lifo	0.13	0.35	0.21	0.52	1.21
Earnings per share—fully diluted, after restatement . . .	0.58	0.76	0.87	0.30	2.51

It is not possible under the Lifo method to determine cumulative effects of the change on prior years.

At December 31, 1974, approximately 68 percent of inventories are stated at cost on the Lifo method and approximately 32 percent are stated at the lower of Fifo cost or market. Inventories consisted of the following (in thousands):

	December 31	
	1974	*1973*
Raw materials and supplies	$19,792	$13,205
Work-in-process.	9,009	8,165
Finished goods	16,355	12,196
	$45,156	$33,566

At December 31, 1974, inventories would have been stated at $56,487,000 if all inventories were stated under Fifo.

Inventories: Inventories comprised the following at December 31:

	($000)	
	1974	*1973*
Materials and supplies	$ 47,335	$26,382
Real estate developed and held for sale	29,778	30,747
Refined products	15,751	17,853
Raw materials—crude oil	7,432	11,755
	$100,296	$86,737

Refined products and raw material crude oil are valued at cost on the last-in, first-out (Lifo) method as of December 31, 1974, and on the average cost method as of December 31, 1973. The adoption of Lifo in 1974 was made to achieve a better matching of current costs with current revenues and to conform more closely to prevalent United States petroleum industry practice. The effect of the change was to reduce 1974 net income by $7,524,000 ($0.33 per share assuming no dilution) and fourth quarter net income (unaudited) by $2,621,000 ($0.11 per share assuming no dilution). The effect of the change on the first three quarters of 1974 is presented below. Due to the nature of the change, calculation of comparable information for 1973 is not practicable.

	Quarter Ended		
	March 31, 1974	*June 30, 1974*	*Sept. 30, 1974*
Net Income (unaudited):			
As Originally Reported:			
Amount.	$34,683	$39,232	$40,797
Per Share*	$ 1.52	$ 1.72	$ 1.78
As Restated:			
Amount.	$31,551	$39,232	$39,026
Per Share*	$ 1.38	$ 1.72	$ 1.70

* Assuming no dilution.

The excess of current replacement cost over the carrying value of inventories valued on the Lifo method approximated $14,500,000 at December 31, 1974.

Inventory Reports for Management. Inventory reports—normally internally prepared—for top management in the areas of finance, purchasing, production, and sales are a "must" because through inventory control, usage, and sale, working capital properly is used or is misused, and a periodic net income or net loss is produced. Financial management is interested in maintaining inventories at a minimum coordinate with anticipated near-future sales; thus, there will not be an overinvestment in inventories—particularly if short-term bank credit is desired. Purchasing, sales, and production executives are interested in quantities of raw materials, work in process, and finished goods in stock so that shortages will not develop and interrupt normal production schedules, and so that information is available with regard to slow-moving items.

Thus, a variety of internally prepared inventory reports should be available for the auditor to review and appraise. These reports will include: (1) inventory usage, (2) a list of purchase commitments, (3) short-term and long-term inventory requirements, (4) obsolete items, (5) inventory on markdown, (6) book inventory versus physical counts, (7) cost versus current replacement cost, and many others.

AUDIT OF INVENTORIES

Audit procedures applicable to inventories are based upon the auditor's responsibilities for—

1. Observation of the taking of the inventory, determining the quantity of the inventory, and testing the quantity.
2. Clerical accuracy of inventory calculations.
3. Pricing the inventory and determining the periodic cost of sales.
4. Miscellaneous considerations, such as determining proper insurance coverage, quality, obsolete items, scrap material procedure, and obtaining an inventory certification from the client.

Observation and Quantity Testing

Taking an inventory should be carefully planned in advance; in many instances the auditor will participate in this preinventory planning. Recognized auditing procedures include the observation of the method of taking the inventory and the testing of quantity counts and a comparison with evidence supplied by the client—count cards, count-and-price sheets, etc. In many instances involving unusual or highly specialized inventories, an auditor may request the services of a specialist. Prior to observing a client's count of the inventory, the auditor should become familiar with the client's system of ordering, receiving, storage, and issuance so that he may judge the reliability of the internal control. Test counts may vary from 5 to 20 percent of the total dollar amount of the items, depending on the system of internal control, the observation of the taking of the inventory, and the auditor's satisfaction with the results of his test-counting.

If subsidiary inventory records are maintained, the balances should be compared with count data—and with price data if the subsidiary records contain prices. Also, subsidiary inventory accounts should be compared with receiving records as an accuracy verification and as a determinant of proper cutoff. Subsidiary records should be adjusted to proper count and price, in accordance with the taking of the inventory. If kept in terms of prices, a trial balance of the subsidiary accounts should be compared with the inventory controlling account. If possible, differences should be accounted for; otherwise, the controls should be adjusted to the sum of the corrected subsidiary accounts.

Inventory cost prices should be compared with sales prices in order to determine the maintenance of a normal gross profit margin. This is particularly true for finished goods (page 281) and for inventories derived under the retail inventory method.

If an audit is started after the close of a period and if the auditor could not observe the taking of the inventory, he should begin with the inventory counts as of his starting date, add interim quantity sales, and subtract interim quantities purchased or manufactured in order to arrive at the inventory as of the balance sheet date.

Original Count and Price Data, and Inventory Summaries

Both the internal auditor and the professional auditor should compare original count and price data—count tags or count-and-price sheets— with the transcriptions to inventory summaries. Prices must be applied to proper units, such as dozen for dozen, or price per hundred to hundreds. A comparison of *not more* than 20 percent of the transcriptions should be adequate for judging the accuracy of this phase of the clerical work.

Inventory summaries or recapitulations should be tested for the accuracy of extensions, footings, and totals. The test should be extensive enough to result in satisfaction with the reliability of the reported inventory figure. Small totals should not be ignored, because if 1,000 at $0.10 ($100) should have been expressed as 1,000 items at $10 ($10,000), the error may be material.

Work Papers

Work papers for inventory quantity tests, price tests, extensions and footings, raw materials, work in process, finished goods, inventory counts,

Illustration 9–2
WORK PAPER 12

			Initials	Date
MULTI-PRODUCTS, INCORPORATED		Prepared By	Pm	1-10-7
Raw Material Inventory Summary, December 31, 1976		Approved By	LF	1-15-7

Inventory Item Number	Inventory Sheet Numbers	Quantity	Unit Cost Price	Unit Market Price	Extension at Cost	Extension Lower of C or Marke
1	1*	2716 lbs.	2.00 lb.	2.10 lb.	5432 00	5432
2	2-8 ✓	470 tons	38.40 ton	38.20 ton	18048 00	17954
3	9-17	11000 lbs.	4.00 lb.	4.00 lb.	44000 00	44000
4	18-19	8000 lbs.	4.80 lb.	4.90 lb.	38400 00	38400
5	20-24 ✓	22000	1.60 ea.	1.70 ea.	35200 00	35200
6	25-30 ✓	17500	1.50 ea.	1.54 ea.	26250 00	26250
7	31-33	10 tons	360.00 ton	380.00 ton	3600 00	3600
8	34-37 ✓	15200 lbs.	1.00 lb	.90 lb.	15200 00	13680
9	38-42 ✓	6570	4.40 ea.	4.36 ea.	28908 00	28645
10	43-44	4296	3.98 ea.	3.96 ea.	17098 08	17012
11	45	1560	7.96 ea.	7.84 ea.	12417 60	12230
12	46-49 ✓	3550	1.00 ea.	1.06 ea.	3550 00	3550
13	50-56 ✓	1948	2.18 ea.	2.22 ea.	4246 64	4246
14	57-59	299	20.40 ea.	20.60 ea.	6099 60	6099
15	60-62 ✓	890	9.20 ea.	9.20 ea.	8188 00	8188
					266637 92	264488

This summary was prepared after correcting
for pricing errors, quantity-count errors, and
errors in extensions and footing.
* This includes the items from the omitted
invoice; see AJE 12
✓ Prices tested; see Illustration 9-3.
∧ Computations verified.
All extensions in excess of $50 on all
inventory sheets were verified.
All inventory sheets (1-62) were footed.
Internal control--good.

and inventory certifications by the client are shown in Illustrations 9–2 to 9–8. These work papers should be examined and referred to during the discussions presented in this chapter.

Cutoff of Purchases and Sales

In order to arrive at a proper figure for the remaining inventory total and for the periodic cost of sales, proper purchases and sales cutoff must exist at the end of the period. All goods received up to the end of the period and goods in transit f.o.b. vendor must be included in inventory. A delayed billing from a vendor does not lead to exclusion. The auditor must compare invoices, receiving records, and inventory records to determine proper purchase cutoff. Goods in transit may be charged to Goods in Transit or to the inventory account and credited to the proper

Illustration 9–3
WORK PAPER 13

					Initials	Date
MULTI-PRODUCTS, INCORPORATED				Prepared By	PM	1-10-77
Raw Material Inventory Price Tests, December 31, 1976				Approved By	EF	1-15-77

Item of Inventory	Quantity Dec.31,1976	Unit Cost	Unit Market	Lower of Cost or Market	
No. 2	470 tons	38.40 ton	38.20 ton	17 954 00	
3	11000 lbs.	4.00 lb.	4.00 lb.	44 000 00	
5	22000	1.60 ea.	1.70 ea.	35 200 00	
6	17500	1.50 ea.	1.54 ea.	26 250 00	
8	15200 lbs.	1.00 lb.	0.90 lb.	13 680 00	
9	6570	4.40 ea.	4.36 ea.	28 645 20	
12	3550	1.00 ea.	1.06 ea.	3 550 00	
				169 279 20	
Total Inventory				264 488 00	
Percentage of Total Dollars Tested				64.0%	
Invoices were used for unit-cost price tests.					

payable. Of course, in-transit items cannot be inspected or counted until they are received.

Under customary circumstances the conversion of inventories to sales is at the time of delivery. Sales are recorded as such upon delivery to a customer or to a delivery service. Exceptions to this customary procedure arise in cases of c.o.d. sales, f.o.b. destination sales, and sight draft sales. By examining shipping records, an auditor can determine if all goods shipped through the last day of the period were charged to receivables and credited to Sales. If goods are billed to customers prior to the end of the period but shipped thereafter, those goods should be excluded from the seller's inventory only if title has passed, or if the seller is warehousing the goods for the buyer. To verify delayed shipments, the auditor must compare shipping records with sales invoices for a few days before and after the end of the period. If the goods obviously are those of the seller, they should be included in his inventory. Entries charging receivables and crediting Sales prior to the close of the period should be reversed.

Consigned Merchandise

Goods out on consignment are inventories of the consignor. An auditor should obtain confirmations for goods out on consignment, in terms of

Illustration 9–4
WORK PAPER 14

	Initials	C
MULTI-PRODUCTS, INCORPORATED	Prepared By	PM	/-e
Raw Material Inventory Quantity Tests, December 31, 1976	Approved By	CF	/-h

Item of Inventory	Client Quantity	Auditor's Quantity	Price in Inventory	Explanation
5	21000	22 000(1)	35200 00	Packed 100 to a carton; 220 cartons
6	17700	17 500(2)	26250 00	Counted individually
7	10 tons	10 tons (3)	3600 00	Weighed
11	1460	1 560(4)	12230 40	Counted
15	894	890(5)	8188 00	Counted
			85468 40	
Total Inventory			264488 00	
Percentage of Dollar-Quantity Tested			32.3%	
			Understated	Overstated
Client inventory:				
(1) 1,000 @ $1.60			1600 00	
(2) 200 @ $1.50				300 00
(3)			0	0
(4) 100 @ $7.84			784 00	
(5) 4 @ $9.20				36 80
			2384 00	336 80
Net understatement			2047 20	(corrected in Work Paper 10)

quantity and consigned prices. Goods out on consignment must be included in the consignor's inventory in accordance with the pricing
method of the consignor, regardless of the price at which the goods were
"billed" to the consignee. In many cases the auditor must debit Sales and
credit a consignment account or Accounts Receivable in order to adjust.

Goods held on consignment must be excluded from the inventory of
the consignee. If the consignee has debited an inventory account and
credited payables, the original entry should be reversed unless traditional
practice is to consider the consigned-in inventory as such, with an offsetting credit to Accounts Payable. Any period-end liability from the
consignee to the consignor for goods sold should be set up as a payable.

For goods consigned in or out, the auditor must study the consignment
contracts and examine the periodic consignment reports. Unpaid liabilities of the consignee to the consignor should be confirmed by both
parties.

Illustration 9–5
WORK PAPER 15

	Initials	Date
MULTI-PRODUCTS, INCORPORATED Prepared By	PM	1-11-77
Work-in-Process Inventory, December 31, 1976 Approved By	CF	1-15-77

Item in Process	Materials in Process	Labor in Process	Overhead in Process	Total
A ✓	5220 60○	9095 40	5181 52	19 497 52
F ✓	13131 50○	20382 20	12144 48	45 659 18
H ✓	9390 10○	15053 50	9164 20	33 607 80
I ✓	6409 80○	9737 90	5691 80	21 839 50
	34152 00	54270 00	32182 00 ✱	120 604 00 X

✓ Footings and extensions verified on all production orders.
○ Raw material requisitions traced to work-in-process records.
✱ Payroll charges compared with labor placed in process.
X Agrees with total of subsidiary work-in-process records.

Warehoused Merchandise

If merchandise in warehouses is not of material amount, the auditor should inspect warehouse receipts and obtain matching confirmations from the warehouses. Also, he should examine the client's internal control over warehoused goods. If the warehoused merchandise is of material amount in proportion to current assets or to total assets, the auditor should match warehouse receipts with confirmations and should visit the warehouse to inspect and test-count the items in the same manner as for nonwarehoused goods.

Purchase Commitments

Purchase commitments open at the end of the period should be totaled for dollars in order to determine if open commitments are reasonable in amount and are normal, or if they are excessive. If normal, the auditor should request confirmations from suppliers for partial deliveries. If excessive, the auditor should not only request confirmations for partial deliveries but also should determine if the client is protected by future sales contracts. If market replacement cost at the balance-sheet date is below the purchase commitment price and if the client is not protected by future sales contracts, a possible loss provision may be set up to recognize the difference between cost and market. Also, the situation should be described in financial statement footnotes.

If advances are made on purchase commitments, they should be shown separately among the current assets in the balance sheet. In this connection, debit balances in accounts payable should be confirmed to determine if they are advances on purchase commitments.

Inventory Quality

The responsibility of an auditor for the determination of inventory quality may be limited. Poor quality may be determined in the examination of the individual inventory records if returned sales are large and if items are slow moving. Obsolete items may be detected by the examination of individual inventory records for slow-moving items or by the shopworn appearance of the items.

When obsolescence and/or poor quality become established, the inventory should be written down. The reduction should be made to the

Illustration 9–6
WORK PAPER 16

			Initials	Date
MULTI-PRODUCTS, INCORPORATED		Prepared By	PM	1-11-77
Finished Goods Inventory, December 31, 1976		Approved By	CF	2-15-77

Item	Number of Units		Unit Cost∧	Total Cost	
A	852	Ø	11.10	9457 20	✓
B	545		5.72	3117 40	✓
C	992	Ø	25.50	25296 00	✓
D	395		17.84	7046 80	✓
E	802		20.60	16521 20	✓
F	1 477	Ø	31.50	46525 50	✓
G	567		49.60	28123 20	✓
H	670		23.12	15490 40	✓
I	771	Ø	16.82	12968 22	✓
J	231		18.68	4315 08	✓
K	150		13.46	2019 00	✓
				170880 00	

Ø Tested by count.
∧ Unit costs are from examined cost records.
✓ Net realizable value is in excess of cost.

Sales invoices and shipping records were compared for the first week of January and the last 10 days of December. The inventory was reconciled back to December 31, 1976, by taking the February 10, 1977 (date of audit) inventory, adding sales at cost price, and subtracting inventory debits from January 1, 1977 to February 10, 1977.

point where—when and if the goods are sold—a normal gross profit will be realized. Totally unsalable items should be reduced to zero. At no time should the "cost" of the inventory exceed expected realization.

Scrap Materials

If scrap materials are significant, the auditor must examine the procedures in operation for storing, pricing, and selling the scrap materials. If records of scrap materials are maintained, the auditing procedures are the same as for any other inventory. In many instances, records are not maintained. In these instances the auditor must inquire into scrap-handling procedures and ascertain that revenues from the sale of scrap are properly recorded either as sales, as other revenue, or as a reduction of cost sales.

Insurance Coverage

Many types of insurance coverage are available, and in large measure the type of inventory determines the type of insurance to be carried. For

Illustrated 9–7
WORK PAPER 17

			Initials	Date
MULTI-PRODUCTS, INCORPORATED	Prepared By		*PM*	*1-12-77*
Factory Supplies, December 31, 1976	Approved By		*CF*	*1-15-77*

Balance, December 31, 1975	12	496
Supplies purchased in 1976	18	574
	31	070
Cost of supplies used in 1976, per books	22	370
	8	700
AJE 7	2	090
Balance, December 31, 1976, per audit	6	610

The factory supplies inventory was taken by the client as of December 31, 1976, in a total amount of $8,700. Our tests show that the inventory of supplies was incorrectly computed for one item in the amount of $2,090.

AJE 7				
Factory Supplies Expense	2	090		
Factory Supplies Inventory			2	090
To adjust the supplies inventory to $6,610.				

example, only fire insurance might be carried on large-size sheet steel. The interest of the auditor lies in determining the adequacy and propriety of the insurance. The auditor must ascertain that inventories are covered, regardless of where they are located. Total coverage should be large enough to cover the cost of the inventories for fire and extended coverage. Depending upon the type of inventory, less than total cost amounts may be carried for burglary, theft, and mysterious disappearance.

An auditor must determine that the beneficiary under the policies is the owner of the goods, or a party possessing a lien against the goods. The operation of coinsurance clauses should be analyzed to be certain of the adequacy of protection. All policies should be in force; expired and nonrenewed policies should be discussed with the client. Premium refunds should be confirmed by insurance brokers and traced to the cash records and to the proper insurance accounts. When "specific" insurance coverage is purchased on increasing and decreasing inventories, the auditor must be certain that interim inventory reports have been promptly and properly submitted to the insurance brokers. This procedure is necessary so that the insurance at all times will be adequate but not excessive. Premium refunds will be made if the average of the inventory for the insurance year is less than the average insurance in force.

Miscellaneous Procedures

If inventories are pledged as loan collateral, the lender should be requested to confirm the loan, together with any restrictive withdrawal and replacement provisions.

If inventories are purchased under letters of credit, the goods withdrawn under the trust agreement should be separated from the client's inventory as the property of the bank holding the trust agreement. The auditor must determine that goods withdrawn under a trust agreement are not again pledged as loan security elsewhere.

The gross profits test may be applied to determine the reasonableness of an inventory. This test has value only when rates of gross profit remain constant from period to period.

Inventory turnover may be computed to determine if buying is excessive in advance of requirements and to determine if the inventory is disproportionately large in terms of units and in terms of sales dollars.

Inventories should be audited by comparison of quantity and price in order to determine abnormal quantity increases or decreases and slow-moving and obsolete items. In making these comparisons, cost price changes must be taken into consideration, along with changes in sales. An example follows:

Item	Quantity, December 31			Total Cost, December 31			Dollar Increase (decrease)	
	1976	1975	1974	1976	1975	1974	1976-75	1975-74
1	10,000	7,000	6,000	$10,000	$ 7,700	$ 5,400	$ 2,300	$ 2,300
2	100	9,000	12,000	1,000	90,000	100,000	(89,000)	(10,000)
3	400	420	450	800	820	900	(20)	(80)

Item 1: Sales are increasing. Cost prices are decreasing.
Item 2: Large demand. Short supply.
Item 3: Obsolete. No purchase since 1971.

The modern tendency is for manufacturing companies to consider supplies as a part of raw materials inventory—and not as prepaid expenses. Audit procedures for supplies are the same as for any other inventory, unless the supplies are of insignificant amount, in which case quantities normally are not tested. The auditor must inquire about supplies no longer needed. They should be written off the records.

Inventory Certificates

Auditors customarily obtain from the client a written representation concerning the inventories. Normally, this certification is drafted by the auditor and signed by the client. If a satisfactory certification cannot be obtained, the probabilities are that the audit report must at least be qualified. While an inventory certification does not relieve an auditor of any responsibility, it does emphasize the fact that the financial statements are management's representations. To be included in the inventory certification are representations concerning ownership, quality, quantity, pricing methods, total amounts, obsolete goods, purchase commitments, and pledged items. See Illustration 9–8.

Comments on Work in Process and Finished Goods

Work in process may be difficult to verify if adequate records of cost accumulation are not maintained. In verifying work in process, the auditor should:

1. Test debits to Work in Process for raw materials transferred.
2. Test labor debits to Work in Process.
3. Examine the method of allocating overhead and test the distribution of overhead to Work in Process.

In examining work-in-process records, extensions, footings, and totals must be verified in the same manner followed for any other inventory.

Illustration 9–8
WORK PAPER 18

CERTIFICATE OF INVENTORIES

Name of Client	*Multi-Products, Incorporated*
Period Ended	*December 31, 1976*
Name of Auditors	*Bennett and Bennett*

We believe the following statements to be true representations of the inventories as of the close of the period stated above. The inventories are classified as follows:

$$
\begin{array}{lr}
\textit{Raw materials} & \$264,488 \\
\textit{Work in process} & 120,604 \\
\textit{Finished goods} & 170,880 \\
\textit{Factory supplies} & \underline{6,610} \\
& \underline{\$562,582}
\end{array}
$$

1. All inventories, wherever located, were included in the preceding total.
2. All physical inventories were taken by actual count, weight, or measurement.
3. For book inventories, all quantities are based upon physical inventories taken at ___*November 30, 1976*___, and worked forward from that date to *December 31, 1976*, on the basis of purchases and sales records.
4. All inventories, supplies, and purchased merchandise were priced at the lower of cost or market, as applied to each item in the inventory. Costs were determined by Lifo. Market price is considered as the lower of replacement cost or net realizable amount less all costs of carrying and selling, and profits.
5. The basis of pricing the inventories is consistent with the methods followed at the close of the preceding period.
6. Purchase commitments are not in excess of the current market price as of the balance sheet date.
7. There are no sales contracts at prices below the cost of finished goods inventories.
8. All inventories are the property of the company.
9. There are no hypothecated inventories.
10. The liabilities for all items included in the inventories have been recorded as of the closing date, above.
11. No items are included in the inventories which were billed or shipped prior to the closing date.
12. All inventory is salable and in good condition.
13. The following exceptions to the printed statements are to be noted:

   No exceptions.

Date *February 12, 1977*	MULTI-PRODUCTS, INCORPORATED
	William B. Johnson
	President
	John Jones
	Treasurer

The sum of subsidiary accounts must be compared with control balances. A rough verification for work-in-process inventory follows:

January 1, 1976, inventories:		
Raw materials	$ 60,000	
Work in process	80,000	
Finished goods	120,000	$ 260,000
Costs, 1976:		
Materials purchased	$600,000	
Labor	800,000	
Overhead	400,000	1,800,000
		$2,060,000
Cost of goods sold in 1976 (from specifications,		
or from 1975 unit costs)		1,780,000
December 31, 1976, inventories—in total		$ 280,000
Deduct:		
Raw materials inventory, counted and		
priced	$ 72,000	
Finished goods inventory, counted		
and priced	104,000	176,000
Remainder: Work-in-process inventory,		
December 31, 1976		$ 104,000

There are many bases used to distribute factory overhead to Work in Process. The auditor must examine the propriety and accuracy of the method. Overapplied and Underapplied Manufacturing Overhead account balances indicate errors in costing production, unless unusual circumstances have arisen.

Repair jobs in process and fixed assets being manufactured are *not* a part of work in process. If such items are included as a part of the work-in-process total, they should be removed to special accounts.

Work-in-process accounts must be examined to be certain that finished items shipped directly to customers have been cleared from work-in-process accounts. Failure to make such clearances may be discovered by comparing old work-in-process accounts with shipping and sales records.

For finished goods the same procedures are followed as for work in process, plus the comparison of shipping records with sales records, and credits to inventory records for the last few days of the current period and the first few days of the succeeding period. When items are manufactured for stock—not for a customer order—the auditor should be alert to detect slow-moving and obsolete items. See the section of this chapter on inventory quality.

FINANCIAL STATEMENT CONSIDERATIONS

Inventory Comments in the Audit Report

In order to issue a report without qualifications, an auditor must observe all auditing procedures regarded as acceptable practice. With respect to inventories, the issuance of an unqualified report would mean that the auditor has (1) observed the taking of the inventory, (2) tested quantities, (3) examined inventory records for clerical accuracy, (4) compared the records with physical amounts, and (5) examined the pricing. Any deviations from recommended procedures should be specifically set forth in the scope section of the audit report, followed by any necessary opinion qualification.

If the auditor includes no exceptions in his report, the assumption should be that he has performed all work necessary and all work considered to be acceptable practice. If exceptions are included, they must be clearly expressed as such and must be clearly distinguished from informative comments.

If the basis of pricing the inventory has been changed during the year, such changes and their effect upon income should be explained.

If all accepted auditing procedures have been followed in connection with the examination of the inventories, it *may* be considered desirable to describe the scope of the inventory examination in a separate paragraph of the report.

Financial Statement Presentation

Inventories are classified as current assets in the balance sheet. Supplies are sometimes treated as prepaid expenses and, more normally, as inventory, particularly if the supplies are used in manufacturing. If inventories are to be used after the normal operating cycle—as exemplified by heavy construction industry materials of significant amount—they should be removed from the current asset category. Preferably, for manufacturing companies, in the financial statements, or in footnotes to the financial statements, inventories should be divided into raw materials, work in process, and finished goods—and not combined into one title.

Original cost is the starting point in pricing an inventory. Because differences in pricing methods result in different total dollar amounts, and also because the determination of total inventory amounts requires judgment, the basis of pricing the inventories—Fifo, Lifo, etc.—should be clearly set forth in the balance sheet. When the method of pricing the inventory has been changed, the financial statements should disclose and explain the change and indicate the effect of the change—if material—on net income for the period.

When financial statements are filed with the Securities and Exchange Commission, the method of determining cost and market must be disclosed (Rule 5.02, 6[b], Regulation S–X); in other than SEC practices, this disclosure is not considered necessary.

Securities and Exchange Commission Requirements. Regulation S–X, in the section pertaining to inventories in the statements of registrants, requires the following: "The basis of determining the amounts shown in the balance sheet shall be stated. If a basis such as 'cost,' 'market,' or 'cost or market, whichever is lower,' is given, there shall also be given, to the extent applicable, a general indication of the method of determining the 'cost' or 'market': for example, 'average cost' or 'first-in, first-out.'"

New York Stock Exchange Requirements. In the preparation for listing applications, the instructions of the New York Stock Exchange contain the following regulations for the pricing of inventories and the methods of computing the cost of sales:

Indicate the practice followed in adjusting inventories to the lower of cost or market; that is, whether on a basis of specific items, groups or classes, or entire inventory.

State whether "market" is considered

a) as replacement market, and whether in that event allowance is made for any decline in price of basic commodities in finished goods and work in process, or,

b) as selling market, and whether in that event allowance is made for selling expense and normal margin of profit.

State the company's practice if (*a*) and (*b*) are followed in respect of different parts of the inventory.

Describe treatment of intercompany profit on goods included in inventory.

State general method of computing cost of goods sold; that is, whether computed on basis of "average cost," "last-in, first-out," "first-in, first-out"—other.

When money is borrowed and inventory pledged as security, the amount of inventory pledged should be stated in the balance sheet, and the loan will appear as a liability. The amount borrowed on the inventory may take the form of bank loans or advances by customers, factors, and finance companies.

If inventories are written down from a higher cost to a lower replacement market and if an allowance is employed to show inventory reductions, the allowance may or may not be shown in the balance sheet; common practice is *not* to show it, but to present the inventory at the net figure.

Reductions from cost to market should be shown in the "other expense" section of the income statement, so that the cost of sales is accurately presented; many auditors believe that this procedure should be followed only if the reduction is significant and if it is nonrecurring.

Gross profit increase and decrease should be compared on an annual basis, and the percentage of gross profit earned on net sales should be computed and compared with that of prior years. A complete study should be made to determine the causes of fluctuations in gross profit and in gross profit percentage, so that causes of increased or decreased profits may be pointed out, and so that possible remedial measures may be instituted for correction of an unfavorable trend or for promotion of a desirable trend. The audit report should contain a description of the causes and effects of changes in gross profit.

It may be of interest to note here that the American Institute of Certified Public Accountants and the American Accounting Association differ in the basis that each would consider in the choice of method for assigning costs to inventory values. The AICPA in *Accounting Research Bulletin No. 43*, chapter 4, entitled "Inventory Pricing," states: "Cost for inventory purposes may be determined under any one of several assumptions as to the flow of cost factors (such as first-in first-out, average, and last-in first-out); the major objective in selecting a method should be to choose the one which, under the circumstances, most clearly reflects periodic income."

Accounting Principles Board Opinion No. 20 sets forth how changes in accounting principles should be reported in financial statements and what is required to justify such changes. *FASB Interpretation No. 1*, dealing with *Accounting Changes Related to Cost of Inventory*, enforces *APB Opinion No. 20* and stipulates that a change in composition of the cost elements included in inventory is an accounting change. Therefore, when such changes are made in the financial reporting of a company, *APB Opinion No. 20* must be followed and should lead to improvement in financial reporting and not on the basis of the income tax effect alone.

SUGGESTED ADDITIONAL READING

APB Opinion No. 20, Accounting Changes, especially paragraph 16.
Statement on Auditing Standards No. 1, Section 331.09–331.15; Section 541; and Section 542.01–.05.

QUESTIONS

1. What steps should be taken by an auditor to satisfy himself that there has been proper accounting for cost of sales and inventories?
2. If an auditor does not include exceptions to accepted procedures in his report, what could a reader of the report assume?
3. What should an auditor do if he has omitted required audit procedure?
4. *a)* What criteria might be adopted for inventory valuation?
    b) Why is so much importance attached to the satisfactory valuation of inventories by a CPA?
5. As relating to inventory, to what does a proper "cutoff" date refer?
6. Prepare the headings of a work paper to be used to test the quantity, and prices of inventory of a dry goods wholesaler.
7. What inventory pricing problems does an auditor face when valuing inventory?
8. What inventory pricing instructions would an auditor use as an audit guide?
9. What factors does an auditor consider when determining the physical inventory quantity?

10. Why is it important for management to receive periodic inventory reports?

11. Explain the effect of each of the following errors in the December 31 inventory of your client:
    a) Incorrectly excluded 100 units of Product W, valued at $1 per unit, from the ending inventory; purchase was not recorded.
    b) Incorrectly excluded 200 units of Product X, valued at $2 per unit, from the ending inventory; purchase was recorded.
    c) Incorrectly included 300 units of Product Y, valued at $3 per unit, in the ending inventory; the purchase had not been recorded.
    d) Incorrectly excluded 400 units of Product Z, valued at $4 per unit, in the ending inventory; the purchase had not been recorded.

12. For the past five years a CPA has audited the financial statements of a manufacturing company. During this period, the examination scope was limited by the client regarding the observation of the annual physical inventory. Since the CPA considered the inventories to be of material amount, he was not able to express an unqualified opinion on the financial statements of each of the five years.

    The CPA was allowed to observe physical inventories for the current year ended December 31, 1976, because the client's banker would no longer accept the audit reports. In the interest of economy, the client requested the CPA not to extend his audit procedures to the inventory as of January 1, 1976.

    What should the CPA mention in his short-form report?

13. State the effect of each of the following errors made by The Start Right Company, upon the income statement and the balance sheet of the (1) current period and (2) succeeding period:
    a) Goods being held on a consignment basis were included in the ending inventory.
    b) One thousand actual units in inventory were listed as 100.
    c) A purchase of inventory was not recorded; and even though it was on hand at the inventory date, it was not counted.
    d) A purchase of inventory was not recorded but was correctly included in the inventory count.
    e) Goods sold to a customer were not recorded as a sale. However, since they were in the warehouse they were included in the inventory count.
    f) Goods sold to a customer were not recorded as a sale. However, they were correctly excluded from the inventory count.

14. Annual earnings for Shades, Inc., for the period of 1972–76 are presented below. However, a review of the records for the company re-

Detail	1972	1973	1974	1975	1976
Reported net income (loss) .	$39,000	$40,000	$4,000	($9,000)	$30,000
Inventory understatement, end of year				8,000	
Inventory overstatement, end of year	3,000		5,600		3,200

veals the listed inventory misstatements. Calculate the correct net earnings for each year.

15. An auditor finds that a client has the following accounts on its records. How should they be reported in the client's year-end financial statements?

   a) Customer Materials on Hand for Processing.
   b) Advance Payments on Purchase Commitments.
   c) Raw Materials Reserved for Building Refurbishing.
   d) Appropriated Retained Earnings for Future Inventory Declines.

16. In an audit for the year ended December 31, 1976, you discovered the following transactions, all of which occurred near the closing date:

   a) Merchandise costing $2,000 was received on January 3, 1977. The related invoice was received and recorded on January 5, 1977. The invoice showed the shipment was made by the vendor, f.o.b. destination, on December 28, 1976.

   b) A packing case containing products regularly manufactured by the client and costing $800 to manufacture was in the shipping room when the physical inventory was taken. It was not included in the inventory because it was stamped "Hold for Shipping Instruction." Investigation disclosed that the customer's order was dated December 18, 1976. The products were shipped, and the customer was billed on January 10, 1977.

   c) Merchandise received on January 6, 1977, costing $700, was entered in the invoice register on the same day. Shipment was made f.o.b. vendor's plant on December 31, 1976. It was not included in the client's inventory, because it was not received as of December 31, 1976.

   d) A product, manufactured to the special order of a customer, was finished and in the shipping room on December 31, 1976. The customer was billed on that date; and the merchandise was excluded from the December 31, 1976, inventory although the item was not shipped until January 5, 1977.

   State whether each item should be included in or excluded from inventory at December 31, 1976, together with the reasons for your decision in each of the five cases.

(AICPA, adapted)

PROBLEMS

1. Your client is a toy manufacturer. The company closes its records each December 31. Perpetual inventory records are maintained in terms of quantities and prices. A complete physical inventory is taken each November 30. At November 30, 1976, you observed the taking of the inventory and were satisfied with the procedures followed. By testing, you were satisfied with the accuracy of the client's counts.

There were differences between the client's count and the perpetual records for about 30 percent of the items. Before adjusting the inventory records for the larger differences, of which there were about ten, the records were verified and the items were recounted. Typical examples of adjustments for the larger differences are:

Item Description	Perpetual Record before Adjustment	Perpetual Record after Adjustment
Red paint (gallons)	662	657
Cotter pins (dozens)	2,260	2,120
Wheels	6,901	6,883

The company did not make additional physical tests of inventories during 1976. For the year ended December 31, 1976, the company used inventory quantities shown by the perpetual inventory records.

In outline form, prepare an audit program setting for the procedures to be followed in your audit of inventories as of December 31, 1976. Do not include procedures unless you believe them to be essential under the stated conditions.

(AICPA, adapted)

2. A manufacturer of farm equipment has a fiscal year ending June 30. The useful life of its product is not over ten years. New models are introduced each year. An inventory of repair parts is maintained; and a price list of parts, which shows prices to dealers and retail sales prices, is published annually.

Perpetual inventory records of repair parts are maintained in quantities, and an annual physical inventory is taken. For statement purposes, the inventory is extended at current list prices to dealers and reduced to cost by application of a computed gross profit percentage figure.

You are the new CPA in charge of the annual audit of the company as of June 30, 1977. Your audit work will be reviewed and you will be questioned about each phase of the audit. In connection with the repair parts, for example, you will be asked if that inventory is included in the certificate obtained from the client.

In the audit of the repair parts, what additional questions might you be asked when your work is reviewed?

3. A client owns and operates 50 retail furniture stores. Perpetual inventory records are maintained at the central office and are kept in terms of quantity, units and unit cost, total cost, and store or company warehouse location. Store and warehouse inventories are taken by company employees on serially numbered tags. The inventory crews work in teams of two: One employee enters the description and count of the items on a perforated inventory tag; the second employee verifies the description and count and removes the lower portion of the count tag.

The removed portions of the tags are returned to the central office, where the descriptions and count are transferred to "item" inventory punch cards; the items then are priced at the lower of cost or market, or reduced for damaged merchandise and obsolete items, and by the use of data processing equipment are extended and summarized. Several weeks before the close of the fiscal period, the central office sends a copy of the inventory instructions to the auditors.

What procedure would you follow to verify the inventory under the circumstances outlined?

4. Your client, a manufacturer with a large and active inventory, takes its inventory as of the close of business on December 31 and "cuts off" as of that date. However, the inventory taking is not completed until the following January 8. Describe the auditing procedures you would follow with regard to inventories received and shipped during inventory taking.

(AICPA, adapted)

5. The information presented below relates to the final inventory of paper taken in your audit of Publishers, Inc., on December 31, 1976.

Inventory Classification	Quantity	Per Ream Cost	Per Ream Market
Report Grade	(Reams)		
Grade 1	100	$6.00	$6.60
2	30	5.00	4.60
3	20	4.80	4.80
Letter Stock (watermark)			
Grade 101	40	1.40	1.30
102	20	1.20	1.25
103	10	1.60	1.60
104	6	2.50	2.00
105	8	2.00	1.75
106	6	3.50	3.00
107	12	1.50	1.50
Letter Stock (80% rag content)			
Grade 201	16	1.50	1.00
202	8	2.00	1.75
203	14	2.00	2.50
204	6	1.50	1.50
205	10	1.60	1.40

Using the data presented above, prepare the necessary work papers setting forth the valuation of the inventory at the lower of cost or market assuming application (a) by item, (b) by classification, and (c) total inventory.

6. On December 1, 1976, the board of directors of Wilson, Inc., requests that you audit the records of the corporation for the year ended December 31, 1976. The company operates a chain of 20 retail stores; total assets are $3,600,000, and the total sales for 1976 will be approximately $16,000,000. This is the first audit of the financial statements.

In the examination of company internal control and in your discussion with corporate executives—prior to December 31, 1976—the following information is ascertained:

As of December 31, 1976, the cost price of the inventory will be approximately $2,000,000. The company does not use the retail inventory method, but all merchandise is marked accurately with both retail and coded-cost prices. The inventory policy, which has been consistent for years, is as follows: A representative from the head office visits each store on or about December 31. The store manager calls off the items in stock to the representative from the head office, stating the quantity of each item on hand and the unit cost, or an arbitrary figure which is below the marked cost. When an arbitrary figure is given, it represents the manager's opinion of the market price. Quantities and unit prices are listed on an adding machine tape, not accompanied by a description. Items to which no value is assigned are not listed. Tapes are returned to the head office, where they are extended and totaled. The total for each store is reduced 15 percent. The resulting store totals are summarized, and the adding machine tapes are destroyed.

a)   What are your recommendations for company procedure in order to express an unqualified opinion of the financial statements. Assume that other phases of the audit do not indicate any report exceptions.

b)   As to inventory, state the general program you would follow.

c)   State your position in the event that your proposals as to inventory procedures are not accepted.

7.   Based on the following data, calculate the ending inventory:

	Case 1	Case 2	Case 3	Case 4
Sales				
Cost of Goods Sold:	$100,000	$120,000	$?	$?
Beginning inventory	$ 20,000	$?	$ 60,000	$ 70,000
Purchases	80,000	80,000	?	130,000
Cost of Goods Available for Sale	$100,000	$120,000	$200,000	$?
Less: Ending inventory	?	?	?	?
Cost of Goods Sold	$?	$?	$150,000	$175,000
Gross Profit in dollars	$?	$ 40,000	$ 50,000	$ 25,000
Gross Profit in %	30	?	?	12½

10

Prepaid Items and Related Expenses

PREPAID EXPENSES AND DEFERRED CHARGES: AUDIT OBJECTIVES

The objectives of the auditor are to ascertain that the dollar amounts of prepaid expenses and long-term deferred charges are determined in accordance with generally accepted accounting principles, and that their amounts are reasonable when viewed from the point of future benefits to be derived.

Preliminary Considerations

Proper determination of periodic net income involves the matching of revenues and related expenses by the proper timing of charging those expenses against revenues. In accounting, it has been customary to consider prepaid items as the commonly known "prepaid expenses." However, future-period items should be thought of as including all assets of which a portion of the cost will be charged against revenues of future periods—such as inventories, depreciable fixed assets, amortizable intangible assets, and the customary prepaid expenses and long-term deferred charges.

Proper income statements include that portion of all prepaid items chargeable against the revenues of the current period. Proper balance-sheet disclosure of prepaid items is a result of determining the portion of the prepaid items chargeable against periodic revenues, and the remaining amounts are chargeable against the revenues of future periods.

In this chapter, both the customarily known short-term prepayments and long-term deferred charges are considered. Short-term prepaid items are classified as current assets in accordance with recognized accounting principles consistently applied. Current assets include those that will be consumed during the normal operating cycle of the business. Short-term prepayments usually represent expenditures for services and supplies which are not consumed at the balance-sheet date but which will be consumed in the next few accounting periods in the sales process of converting products or services into receivables and cash. Usually, short-term prepayments are not material in amount.

Long-term deferred charges arise from services and items acquired, but long-term deferred charges will be converted into expense over a period of time longer than the normal operating cycle; and long-term deferred charges do not represent items recoverable in the sales-to-receivables-to-cash process. Examples of long-term deferred charges include plant rearrangement costs, and unamortized bond discount—in the event that item is not viewed as a bond payable valuation account.

INTERNAL CONTROL OF PREPAID ITEMS

Proper internal control over short-term prepayments demands that the items be periodically reviewed to determine that they are in force and that they are stated in proper amount. Internal control also must provide for authorized use and for control over available refunds.

Proper internal control over long-term deferred charges demands a periodic review of the items to determine that they are stated in proper amount and to determine that unamortized amounts still remain as long-term deferred charges. Normally, long-term deferred charges originally are established by top-level authority.

An internal control questionnaire for short-term prepaid items and for long-term deferred charges is presented in Illustration 10–1.

AUDIT OF PREPAID ITEMS AND RELATED EXPENSES

By the examination of documentary evidence and accounting records, an auditor must ascertain that amounts carried forward as prepaid items —prepaid expenses and deferred charges—actually are chargeable to periods and to operations beyond the end of the current fiscal period. Methods of amortization for each item must be in accordance with accepted accounting principles. The methods of amortization normally are on a time basis, a revenue basis, or an inventory basis.

Short-term prepaid expense examination primarily involves test calculations of amounts prepaid and amounts to be charged to current-period expense. Long-term deferred charge examination requires mature judgment for the proper allocation of costs to expense.

Dollar amounts of short-term prepayments and long-term deferred charges must be determined in accordance with the application of ac-

Illustration 10–1

INTERNAL CONTROL QUESTIONNAIRE
Prepaid Expenses and Deferred Charges

	Yes	No	Not Appli-cable	Remarks
Company_____ Period Covered_____				

1. Are capitalized items properly authorized?
2. Is amortization properly authorized or otherwise supported?
3. Are lump-sum charge-offs properly authorized?
4. When prepaid items are purchased, is the company policy uniform with regard to charges to assets and charges to expense?
5. Are supplies inventoried?
6. Is the insurance program reviewed at least annually to determine:
   a) That the insurance is in force?
   b) That the insurance is adequate?
7. Is all insurance carried through one broker?
8. Are insurance premium payments compared with insurance policies and brokers' bills?
9. Are all insurance policies under the control of a person who does not have access to cash disbursements?
10. Are any claims pending at closing date?
11. Are premium refunds properly accounted for?
12. Do all insurance policies name the company as beneficiary?
13. Do you consider amortization to be proper for:
    a) Prepaid expenses?
    b) Deferred charges?
14. Are original debits to deferred charge accounts proper items to be deferred?
15. Do you consider deferred charges to be proper debits?
16. Do you consider deferred charges in the balance sheet to be of proper amount?

Prepared by _____   Reviewed by_____
Date _____   Date _____

---

cepted accounting principles. Amounts not considered beneficial to future periods and amounts not properly chargeable to the future should be charged to current expense. Questionable items should not appear as assets.

Work papers should be designed for each item in a clear and concise manner. Documentary evidence of original acquisition must be examined, and all *material* amounts should be traced through the records. Confirmations should be obtained for certain items, such as service and rental deposits.

Prepaid Insurance Premiums. Insurance policies should be scheduled in a manner that will portray all pertinent data, as in Illustration 10–2. If an insurance register is maintained, original policies should be compared with the data in the register. Audit work papers of the preceding examination are compared with the work papers of the current period in order to note new policies and policy cancellations. When examining the policies, the auditor should determine that the client is the beneficiary. If properties are mortgaged, the mortgagee will hold a policy; in this case, confirmations should be obtained. If paid checks exist in payment of insurance premiums and if the policies are not on hand, a lien evidently exists against the insured assets.

After determining the amount of prepaid insurance and the periodic insurance expense for each policy, the auditor should compare his amounts with those of the client. Necessary audit adjustments should be made. Normally, the straight-line method of prorating insurance premiums is used. A word of caution is in order at this point: Audit time should not be used in verifying inconsequential amounts.

Premium refunds are traced to the cash records and the proper insurance accounts. Refunds result from policy cancellations and from excess specific coverage. Correspondence from insurance brokers should be examined.

In order to judge the adequacy of insurance coverage, the coverage under each type of insurance should be compared with the present market prices or present sound values of insured assets. Coinsurance clauses should be examined. Fidelity bonds should be reviewed from the point of view of the adequacy of coverage for persons handling or having access to money, checks, securities, and accounting records.

Payrolls are the basis for workmen's compensation insurance and liability insurance. In some states, these types of insurance are not prepaid, in which case there will be a liability accrual. In other states a deposit is required. If current-period costs are deductible from the deposit, this represents a prepaid amount, from which should be deducted accruals to the balance-sheet date. In other states, premiums for the last state period constitute a prepaid amount for the succeeding period. When the next state period ends, the premiums for that period are computed. The result might be a prepaid amount, or it might be a liability if the premiums for the second period exceeded those of the first period.

In order for the auditor to further determine the accuracy and validity of the in-force insurance, a confirmation request may be sent to all insurance companies involved.

Supplies. If they are of material amount, prepaid costs of this nature should be test-counted in the same manner used in the examination of any inventory. If not material in amount, accepted practice permits these items to be charged to expenses as they are acquired. A comparison of office supplies expense accounts from year to year serves as evidence of the propriety of accounting for these items. Large expense increases may serve as an indication that supplies were purchased and charged to expense and that material amounts remained at the end of the fiscal period.

Prepaid Rent and Lease Costs. An examination of rental and lease

Illustration 10–2
WORK PAPER 19

MULTI-PRODUCTS, INCORPORATED

Prepaid Insurance, December 31, 1976

Company	Policy Number	Type	Coverage
Eastern	EX1246	Fire and extended--building	
Western	WZ4358	Fire and extended--machinery and fixtures	
Northern	NW9874	Fire and extended--inventories	
Southern	SE3579	Use and occupancy	
Planet	PL2468	Money and securities	
National	NA5791	Open-stock burglary	
Standard	ST5241	Auto liability	
Shell	SV4590	Public liability	
Buckeye	BO6142	Elevator liability	
Ohio	CV7444	Steam boiler	
Pittsburgh	PL3232	Payroll robbery	
New York	NV8878	Water damage	
Union	VS1245	Sprinkler leakage	
Fidelity	FO8642	Blanket position bond	

⊙ Agrees with general ledger, and audit
√ Calculations verified.
∧ Examined payment data.
  Examined all policies.
  Notices of return premiums were traced to cash receipts.
  Each coverage appears to be adequate.

Distribution of Insurance Expenses, 1976

Item	Policies Above	Policies Expired in 1976	Total
Manufacturing	5 890	1 632	7 522
Selling	508	156	664
Administrative	874	212	1 086
	7 272	2 000	9 272 ⊙

agreements and their payment requirements will reveal the necessity for establishing prepaid expenses for these items. Accounts for prepayments are analyzed to determine their correctness and the correctness of the periodic rent expense. If necessary, prepaid amounts may be confirmed with the lessor. If a lessee is required to bear the cost of property taxes, those taxes should be charged to a prepaid expense account—if paid in advance—and prorated over the proper periods. If the taxes are paid after incurrence, they should be periodically accrued.

Some leases require that money be deposited with the lessor as a guaranty. This deposit may be returned to the lessee at the expiration of the

	Initials	Date
Prepared By	PM	2-14-77
Approved By	CF	2-16-77

| | | Term | | | Expense | Period Prepaid | Prepaid |
Amount	Years	From	To	Premium	1976	(Months)	12-31-76
840000	3	2-1-75	2-1-78	6 480	2 160 ✓	13	2 340 ✓
650000	3	4-1-75	4-1-78	4 968	1 656	15	2 070 ✓
600000	1	9-30-76	9-30-77	1 104	276	9	828 ✓
100000	1	7-1-76	7-1-77	216	108	6	108 ✓
40000	3	5-1-76	5-1-79	1 152	256	28	896 ✓
30000	3	4-1-76	4-1-79	1 512	504 ✓	15	630 ✓
200000	1	5-1-76	5-1-77	96	64	4	32 ✓
100000	3	11-1-74	11-1-77	648	216	10	180 ✓
100000	1	7-1-76	7-1-77	200	100	6	100 ✓
80000	1	5-1-76	5-1-77	1 200	800 ✓	4	400 ✓
60000	1	7-1-76	7-1-77	540	270	6	270 ✓
20000	1	7-1-76	7-1-77	480	240	6	240 ✓
20000	1	6-1-76	6-1-77	120	70	5	50 ✓
50000	3	6-1-75	6-1-78	1 656	552 ✓	17	782 ✓
					7 272 ✓		8 926 ✓

lease, or it may be applied to rentals of final periods, or it may be pro-rated over periodic rents. If the deposit is to be returned at the expiration of the lease, the amount is not a prepayment; it is a noncurrent asset deposit. In the other two situations the remaining amount is a prepaid expense. If a bonus is paid to obtain a lease, the amount of the bonus is a prepaid item to be amortized over the life of the lease.

If leased properties are subleased, the sublease revenue may be credited to Rent Expense. For adequate disclosure, it is preferable to credit sublease revenue to an independent revenue account. If a rent agreement calls for a fixed amount plus a percentage of some item—such as sales—the auditor must extend his examination of sales revenues.

Improvements to leased properties constitute a part of the cost of the lease, but they are fixed assets. Costs of improvements, alterations, and rearrangements should be amortized over their expected life or the life of the lease, whichever is shorter.

Taxes Paid in Advance.   Certain taxes are paid in advance, others are paid currently, and some may not accrue. For many taxes, the tax period may not coincide with the fiscal period of the taxpayer. This results in prepayments or accruals. The auditor must verify or reasonably test all tax computations and compare his computations with tax bills and client-prepared tax returns. Payments are traced to the accounts and to the cash disbursements records.

Work papers for taxes should include at least the following data:

1. Type of tax—real property, personal property, intangibles, franchise, sales tax, federal income tax, etc.
2. Tax period and the date the tax is payable.
3. The basis of the tax levy.
4. Amount of the tax.
5. Amount prepaid.
6. Amount accrued.
7. Tax expense for the period under examination.
8. If overdue, the date the tax becomes a lien on assets.

Ordinarily, franchise taxes and personal property taxes are paid in advance—for the privilege of conducting business. In jurisdictions where sales taxes are in effect, it may be a requirement that sales tax stamps be purchased in advance. In this case, the remaining stamps are prepaid items. In many cities and states, local income taxes—at least partially—are payable in advance. However, a few taxes still result in accruals or in amounts withheld. In the accounting records, the commonly accepted method is to accrue property taxes each month for the fiscal period of the taxing authority.

Many corporations today are recognizing accumulated income tax prepayments that arise as a result of intercompany profits in inventories and provisions for inventory obsolescence. The Accounting Principles Board in its *Opinion No. 11* concludes that the deferred method of tax allocation provides the most realistic approach to interperiod tax allocations and the proper presentations of accumulated income tax prepayments in financial statements. This interperiod tax allocation is a procedure whereby the tax effects of current timing differences are deferred currently and allocated to income tax expense of future periods. Full disclosure of this practice would require the amount being shown as the last item in the current asset section of the balance sheet plus a fully descriptive footnote explaining the nature of the account.

The AICPA has issued the following statement regarding real and personal property taxes:

Unlike excise, income, and social security taxes, which are directly related to business events, real and personal property taxes are based upon the assessed valuation of property as of a given date, as determined by the laws of a state or other taxing authority. For this reason the legal liability for such taxes is generally considered as accruing at the moment of occurrence of some specific events, rather than over a period of time. It has generally been held that the taxes become a liability at the point of time when they become a lien. The Internal Revenue Service, however, holds that such taxes accrue on the assessment date.

Interest Deducted in Advance. Interest deducted in advance is a prepaid expense. Usually, it is scheduled in the work papers for notes payable or notes receivable discounted. In any event, prepaid interest must be calculated; and interest entries are traced through the original records to the accounts. When loans from banks are confirmed, the date to which interest has been paid may also be confirmed.

Dues and Subscriptions Paid in Advance. These items normally occur annually. It is common practice to charge these costs to expense upon incurrence. Usually, they are not material in amount, but if they are material, the advance payments as of the balance-sheet date *may* be set up as prepaid items.

Salary and Other Personnel Advances. Salary advances are prepaid expenses. If salary advances have been charged to current-period expense, audit adjustments must be prepared. Loans to employees are not salary advances. Loans to employees occur frequently, often with the provision that the loan shall be repaid by deducting an agreed amount per pay period from each salary check. The auditor must investigate the circumstances of each advance and classify the advance as a prepaid expense or as a loan to employees.

Advances to company personnel for traveling expense or other purposes should be confirmed directly to the auditor. Audit adjustments must be prepared for expended portions of each advance. Control over expense advances should be the same as the control over imprest funds and their operations.

Deferred Compensation Plans. Many corporations today have deferred compensation plans that are covered by insurance policies. Under these plans the corporation will carry life insurance on its key executives; the company will be the beneficiary. However, these policies will furnish the funds to pay the designated parties in the deferred compensation plan agreement for the designated number of years. Since the company is the beneficiary, the premiums paid are charged to retained earnings; and upon receipt of the value of the policy, the liability for the deferred compensation plan be set up. Under these conditions, payments under the agreement will be charged to the liability account. However, this is a deductible expense for federal income tax purposes and will be so recognized.

In order for the tax return and the company records to be reconciled, the Retained Earnings reconciliation on the tax return will show the amount of deferred compensation plan agreement paid each year. Since this type of policy as well as other life insurance policies naming the company as beneficiary are significant, the auditor must review these policies thoroughly and prepare schedules for them. It would also be desirable to directly confirm the existence of such policies. Particular attention must be given to the designated beneficiaries on such policies. If someone other than the company is the beneficiary, premium payments must be considered as an additional compensation to the employee. If the employee designates someone other than the company to be the beneficiary, the auditor would determine the extent of the prepaid compensation and make the necessary adjustment.

Deposits. If required deposits are made with organizations such as airlines, utilities, deposits on bid contracts, etc., they may be refundable at termination. In this case, original documentary evidence should be examined, amounts traced to the accounts, and confirmations should be obtained from the service or other organizations. If interest is allowed on deposits, the auditor should verify the interest and trace it to the accounting records. If deposits are not refundable, they are expenses—to be charged off in the period of making the deposits or to be amortized over a few fiscal periods.

Prepaid Selling Expenses. These include advance payments on commissions and advertising.

To audit commissions paid in advance, there must be familiarity with the arrangements covering employment and the method of remuneration. Sales reports and commission agreements must be examined and compared with commissions earned. The amount earned is compared with withdrawals by the salesmen to determine the existence of a prepaid amount or an accrued amount. If prepayments or accruals are material in amount, confirmations should be obtained from the salesmen.

The auditor must be certain that salesmen for whom prepaid commissions are carried forward still are either employees or independent contractors of the client. Prepaid commissions for ex-employees or ex-contractors should be written off because the probabilities of recovery are remote. If commissions earned to the end of a period are less than the amount advanced, and if the salesman starts each new period with unearned amounts canceled, the difference is not prepaid and should be charged to expense.

To verify advertising expenses paid in advance, the auditor should analyze the Advertising Expense account, relate the expense to existing advertising contracts, and verify prepaid amounts. Normally, advertising expenses paid in advance are composed of advertising materials, such as calendars and gift materials. These items should be inventoried periodically and prorated to expense in accordance with their usage.

Properly, there is today no tendency to charge the cost of large advertising campaigns to asset accounts. Whether an extended advertising campaign—television, newspapers, or magazines—will produce additional net income cannot be foretold at the time of advertising. Also, there are no definite future periods to be benefited. Therefore, all advertising costs should be charged to expense of the period in which the advertising takes place.

Future Business Expenses. Future business expenses include such items as promotion costs, exploitation costs, experimental costs, and research and development costs. Normally, the proper determination of periodic net income demands that these items be charged to expense upon incurrence.

If a company's products are of a seasonal nature, where certain expenses are paid in advance of that season and wherein it is possible to match the revenues and the expenses, it may be the practice of the company to defer the expenses paid in advance until the revenue season arrives.

The auditor must be certain that these costs have in the past benefited the revenue season, and probably will do so in the future, before he approves of their appearance as items paid in advance. Each individual case must be studied, and mature judgment must be exercised in arriving at a decision. The auditor must verify the authorizations for these expenditures and trace their payment through the accounting records.

Companies that regularly maintain experimental, promotion, and product development departments usually charge all applicable costs to periodic expense. This is proper because the costs constantly recur and because—at the time of experimentation and product development—there is no assurance of future-period revenue production.

Research and Development Costs

Expenditures for research and development currently amount to over $30 billion annually. Consequently, the need for proper recognition of these costs, in a uniform manner, in financial statements is understandably emphasized by the issuance of *Statement No. 2* by the Financial Accounting Standards Board. (*Statement No. 2* amends *Opinion No. 17*, of the former Accounting Principles Board.) This statement defines research and development as follows:

Research is planned search or critical investigation aimed at discovery of new knowledge with the hope that such activity will be useful in creating a new product, process or service or improving a present product, process or service.

Development is the translation of research findings or other knowledge into a new or improved product, process or service capable of commercialization, including the conceptual formulation, design and testing of product, process or service alternatives and the construction of prototypes and pilot operations related to the new or improved product, process or service.

It further discusses the types of activities included in the above definitions and the nature of financing these activities. The cost elements that the auditor should look for are (*a*) materials and facilities, (*b*) personnel, (*c*) intangibles purchased from others, (*d*) contract services, and (*e*) indirect costs. The conclusion is that all research and development costs not directly reimbursable by others should be charged to expense as incurred due to the general lack of measurable future benefits at the time such costs are incurred. Since research and development costs are of such importance, the following disclosures, according to *Statement No. 2*, shall be made in financial statements:

a) The summary of significant accounting policies shall indicate that all research and development costs not directly reimbursable by others are charged to expense when incurred. (Also see *APB Opinion No. 22*.)

b) Disclosure shall be made of each of the following amounts (when applicable) for each period for which financial statements are presented: Total research and development costs incurred during the period (including $xxx for research and development conducted in behalf of the enterprise of others) .... $XXXXX

Less amount of total research and development costs incurred during the period which is directly reimbursable by others XXXXX

Non-reimbursable research and development costs incurred and charged to expense during the period .... $XXXXX

If not otherwise clearly set forth on the income statement, the amounts and classifications in the income statement of the "non-reimbursable research and development costs incurred and charged to expense during the period" shall be explicitly disclosed. In addition, all research and development costs not directly reimbursable by others which had been capitalized prior to the effective date of *Statement No. 2*, shall be written off as a prior period adjustment. Further, the prior period adjustment shall recognize any related income tax effect.

Plant Rearrangement and Alteration Costs. The objective of rearranging factory machinery and equipment and store equipment is to effect an increase in net income through the medium of more efficient operations and expense reductions. If the current period cannot reasonably absorb such costs, they may be capitalized as deferred charges to future operations. At the time of rearrangement, there is no assurance that future periods will be benefited. Therefore, if possible, these costs should be charged against current-period revenues.

The auditor must verify rearrangement costs for their correctness and for their propriety as debits to deferred charge accounts. The costs should be traced through the cash disbursements records. Any deferred amount must be prorated to expense (1) on the basis of a proportionate amount per year, or (2) on the basis of a selected amount per year which is large enough to amortize the costs over a very few years.

Alterations made to rented properties should be amortized over the life of the lease or the life of the alterations, whichever is shorter. Alterations made to newly purchased property are a cost of the property, to be added to the initial purchase price. This is true because the cost of an asset is its purchase price plus all costs necessary to place the property in desired usable condition. The auditor must analyze fixed asset accounts for newly purchased properties and also must analyze related expense accounts to be certain that the capitalization policy is proper.

Unamortized Bond Discount and Issuance Costs. Bond discount and bond issuance costs must be verified in order to ascertain that the account originally was correctly charged with only discount and issuance costs. In accordance with the recognized method used to amortize the bond discount and issuance costs, the auditor must compute the periodic amortization and compare his computations with those of the client. The correctness of the remainder thereby is ascertained.

Bond discount and issuance costs normally are amortized by the straight-line method or by the bonds-outstanding method. Normally, the bonds-outstanding method is employed in connection with serial bonds. In any event, the total discount and issuance costs are to be amortized over a period no longer than the life of the bonds. If bonds are callable at a date prior to maturity, the amortization period should be from the issuance date to the call date. If the bonds are eligible for call and retirement at a premium, the periodic amortization charges thereby are increased.

Bonds of corporations usually are sold in entirety to a broker, bank, underwriter, or syndicate, at a price below that at which the issue will be offered for public sale. The purchaser of the entire issue then disposes of the bonds to the investing public at a price above the purchase price, thereby permitting the marketing agency a profit. To the discount granted the underwriters are added legal fees, appraisal costs, and any other costs necessary to issue the bonds. The total of the issuing costs and the discount should be prorated over the bonds during their outstanding life, or in accordance with the retirement plans. Under another plan of marketing, the underwriting syndicate will agree to market the bonds as the agent of the corporation. This method avoids risks to the syndicate, since the syndicate will contract to sell the bonds for a commission expressed as a percentage of the sales price.

If bonds are issued in exchange for property, discounts do not arise unless the situation is obviously one indicating property values received substantially below the par of the bonds or when bonds of the same issue are selling for cash at a discount.

In order to understand all circumstances surrounding a bond issue, underwriting syndicate contracts and trust indentures must be examined for such items as retirement premiums, call dates, refunding features, conversion privileges, and other contents.

Some accountants treat unamortized bond discount and expense as deferred charges, and other accountants treat these items as a liability valuation account—which is the better theoretical procedure. The items may be shown as deferred charges (1) because the bond liability is at least par, and (2) because periodic operations must absorb the amortized discount and expense, and the periodic interest.

A bond issue may be retired prior to the maturity date. If the bonds are not refunded, any remaining unamortized discount and expense should be charged off. The charge should be set forth separately in the income statement—with a complete explanation. If a bond issue is partly retired, determination must be made that the unamortized discount and expense applicable to the retired portion are charged off.

Bonds may be refunded prior to maturity. There is no uniformity of treatment for the unamortized discount and expense or for any redemption premium on the refunded bonds. *Accounting Research Bulletin No. 43*, chapter 15, sets forth three methods of disposing of the unamortized balance:

1. Write off the unamortized discount, issue cost, and redemption premium applicable to the original issue to Retained Earnings (no longer a good practice) or to income at the time of refunding.
2. Defer the unamortized premium or discount and other costs applicable to the original issue, and amortize them over the remaining life of the original issue just as if refunding had not occurred.
3. Defer the unamortized premium or discount and other costs applicable to the original issue, and amortize them over the life of the new bond issue.

The original contract is terminated upon refunding. Therefore, the author believes that remaining unamortized amounts should be charged off at the time of refunding (item 1, above). *Accounting Research Bulletin No. 43* recommends that item 2, above, be followed. Thus, *Bulletin No. 43* supports the advocates of the now antiquated "current-operating-performance" type of income statement. The Securities and Exchange Commission permits charges to income or to Retained Earnings.

FINANCIAL STATEMENT CONSIDERATIONS

In the balance sheet, prepaid expenses are current assets. This is in accordance with the concept of a current asset. Usually, prepaid expenses are totaled and shown as one item; however, if any items are material in amount, they *should* be shown separately. Long-term deferred charges should be separately disclosed in the balance sheet—a rarity in published annual reports to stockholders. Assuming that future periods will be benefited, and in order properly to match current-period revenues and expenses, prepaid expenses and deferred charges should be neither understated nor overstated. Inconsistency of treatment from year to year defeats the objectives of proper financial statement comparison and analysis. This is especially true when financial statements are prepared each month.

SUGGESTED ADDITIONAL READING

Statement on Auditing Standards No. 1, Section 400, Paragraphs 410.02 and 420.02.

QUESTIONS

1. Regarding prepaid items, what features of the system of internal control would indicate to the auditor that a client is following satisfactory procedures?

2. How could an auditor determine the adequacy of insurance coverage?

3. As a result of the audit of the insurance policies of a client, you find the following:

Covered	Amount Insured	Audit Value
Raw Materials	$ 10,000	$ 50,000 (Lifo)
Finished Goods	40,000	10,000 (Lifo)
Machinery	100,000	50,000 (net of depreciation)
Delivery Equipment	30,000	70,000 (net of depreciation)
Total	$180,000	$180,000

What comments and recommendations, if any, would you make?

4. Your client has leased a warehouse for a five-year period for $2,400 a year plus an advance deposit of $1,200, which will be refunded at the end of the lease if the warehouse is in satisfactory condition. The lease is cancellable by either party on 30-days notice. What would be your financial statement presentations of these facts at the end of the first year?

5. Your client has moved into a new office building and the rental contract requires that the area is to be finished by your client. The following expenditures were made in connection with the lease agreement:

    a) Fee paid to rental agency . . . . $ 1,200
    b) Cost of completing interior (walls, floor, etc.) 120,000
    c) Advance deposit which will be used as the final
        year's rent 3,600
    d) Term of lease . . . . 10 years
    e) Life of interior items . . . . 20 years

What would be your financial statement presentation of these facts at the end of the first year?

6. Define (*a*) research and (*b*) development.

7. What actions would you take in the event that you found—in a first audit —an account entitled Deferred Experimental Costs which is five years old and has never been credited?

8. Explain how an examination of insurance policies might disclose—
   a) Inventory pledged as collateral to a loan.
   b) The disposition of fixed assets without entries in the records?
   c) Possible premium refunds.
   d) Inadequate insurance coverage.

9. Atlas, Inc., issued $2,000,000 of 40-year, 6 percent bonds, at 90. The bonds were issued 25 years ago, and the Company amortized 2½ percent of the bond discount at the end of each year. At the beginning of the current year, Atlas purchased $600,000 of the outstanding bonds at 80 and canceled them. In the course of the audit, you discover that the un-amortized discount on the $600,000 of bonds for the remaining 15 years, amounting to $22,500, has been credited to income.
   a) What is the correct procedure for the $22,500?
   b) What course would you take if the company insisted upon showing $22,500 as income?

10. The accounts of a television manufacturer include the items listed below as prepaid expenses at December 31, 1976.
    (1) Traveling expenses of salesmen incurred in 1976 but applicable to merchandise to be delivered in 1977, $5,250.
    (2) Direct-mail advertising copy to wholesalers, applicable to the 1977 line of merchandise, $13,900.
    (3) That portion of the office expense judged to be applicable to ob-taining orders for 1977 delivery, $10,500.
    Should each of these items be treated as prepaid expenses? Present reasons for your answers.

11. A retail store leased its premises on January 1, 1976, for a period of 10 years at an annual rental of $50,000. The company expended $100,000 altering the store; it was estimated that the alterations would have a life of 20 years. The company charged the $100,000 to an account en-titled Leasehold Improvements and showed it as such in the balance sheet at December 31, 1976.
    In January 1977 you were asked to audit the records of the store for the year ended December 31, 1976. What adjustments would you recommend, assuming the lease will not be renewed?

12. Model, Inc., incurs large selling expenses in the late summer and early fall season of each year for major amusement model toys for spring season sale. All sales and manufacture take place according to contract, each model toy being different so far as accessories are concerned; standard accessories are not manufactured in advance of contract. The company closes its records as of December 31 of each year. Order cancellation seldom occurs. Model requests your advice regarding the deferment of

these selling expenses until the following year, in which the sale takes place.

PROBLEMS

1. Prepare the audit adjustments and explanations for the following situations you find in the records of Court, Inc., which closes its accounts December 31, 1976.

    a) *December 1, 1976:*
        Advertising Expense   12,000
        Cash   12,000
        Records payment of 1977 advertising contract.
    b) Balance of Office Supplies Expense 12/31/76   5,000
        Balance of Office Supplies on Hand 12/31/76   500
        Inventory value of Office Supplies 12/31/76   750
    c) *June 1, 1976:*
        Prepaid Insurance   1,800
        Cash   1,800
        Payment of 36 month policy for fire loss on
        inventory.
    d) Balance of Factory Supplies Expense Account 12/31/76   3,300
        Physical inventory of factory supplies 12/31/76   1,100

    e) On May 1, 1976, a three-year subscription to the *Trade Journal* for $180 was mailed in but not paid. Subscriptions Expense was charged for the entire amount.
    f) On September 1, 1975, paid 36 month premium of $3,600 on fire and extended coverage on building. No premium amortization has been recorded to date and the full amount remains in the Prepaid Insurance account.
    g) Signed a 10-year lease for a new warehouse; closing cost of $1,200, paid July 1, 1976, effective date of lease, was charged to Rent Expense.
    h) Paid annual dues of $1,200 on September 1, 1976, to the Chamber of Commerce and charged Dues Expense.
    i) Subscribed to Building Reports on April 1, 1976, agreeing to pay two equal semi-annual installments of $720 each. The first payment was charged to Prepaid Dues and the second charged to Dues Expense.
    j) Vacation advances of $6,000 were made on December 15, 1976, and charged to Vacation Expense. Of this amount $3,000 applies to vacations starting January 1, 1977.

2. You are examining the financial statements of Atom, Inc., retail enterprise, for the year ended December 31, 1976. The client presented you with an analysis of the Prepaid Expenses account balance of $30,900 at December 31, 1976 as shown below.
    Additional information includes the following:
    (1)   Insurance policy date:

Type	Period Covered	Premium
Fire	12/31/76 to 12/31/77	$1,000
Liability	6/30/76 to 6/30/77	9,500

    (2)   A postage meter was delivered in November and the balance due was paid in January. Unused postage of $700 in the machine at December 31, 1976, was recorded as expense at time of purchase.
    (3)   Bond discount represents the unamortized portion applicable to bonds maturing in 1977.

ATOM, INC.
Analysis of Prepaid Expenses Account
December 31, 1976

Description	Balance
Unexpired fire insurance	$ 750
Unexpired liability insurance	4,900
Utility deposits	2,000
Purchase of postage meter, one half of invoice price	400
Bond discount	3,000
Advertising of store opening	9,600
Amount due for overpayment on purchase of furniture	675
Unsaleable inventory—entered June 30, 1976	8,300
Contributions from employees to employee welfare fund	(275)
Book value of obsolete machinery held for resale	550
Funds delivered to New Front Stores with purchase offer	1,000
Total	$30,900

(4)   The $9,600 paid and recorded for advertising was for the cost of
an advertisement to be run in a monthly magazine for six months,
beginning in December 1976. You examined an invoice received
from the advertising agency and extracted the following description: "Advertising services for store opened in November 1976
.... $6,900."

(5)   Atom has contracted to purchase New Front Stores and has been
required to accompany its offer with a check for $1,000 to be held
in escrow as an indication of good faith. An examination of paid
checks revealed the check has not been returned from the bank
through January 1977.

Assuming that you have examined acceptable underlying evidence,
prepare a work sheet for the necessary adjustments, corrections, and
reclassifications of the items in the Prepaid Expenses account.

3.   P. A. R., Inc., is a market research company and has engaged you to audit
its financial statements for the fiscal year ending October 31, 1976. In
reviewing the insurance program, you discover that the company carries
five $25,000 life insurance policies on its chief officers. Further investiga-
tion reveals that the company is the beneficiary of these policies with the
proceeds to be used to purchase each person's stock upon deaths. The
following information is obtained from the company records and from
direct correspondence with the insurance company:

Policy No.	Insured	Annual Premium	Dividends	Period Covered
899. . . .	Officer #1	$462.75	$184.75	6/2/76–6/2/77
887. . . .	Officer #2	428.00	168.50	5/28/76–5/28/77
954. . . .	Officer #3	407.50	159.75	5/28/76–5/28/77
969. . . .	Officer #4	380.00	148.25	3/4/76–3/4/77
797. . . .	Officer #5	439.00	173.25	3/4/76–3/4/77

An examination of the entries for payment of the premiums revealed that the company is accumulating the dividends and pays the full annual premiums.

Correspondence with the insurance company provides the following:

Policy No.	Cash Value	Loan @ 5%	Accrued Interest to 10/31/76
899	$5,569.21	$4,130.00	$ 86.07
887	5,127.20	3,775.00	80.75
954	4,856.05	3,560.00	76.15
969	4,462.20	3,250.00	107.31
797	5,305.06	3,895.00	128.61

The general ledger of P. A. R. shows a balance of $22,787.75 in the Cash Value of Life Insurance account. The Prepaid Insurance account contains the gross annual premium, and the Dividend Income account contains the amount of the dividends on these policies. The total of the loans $18,610.00, is found to be in the Notes Payable Bank account. No recognition has been made of the accrued interest on these policy loans.

Prepare all necessary journal entries at October 31, 1976, to correct the client's records.

4. As of December 31, 1976, the Insurance Expense account on the records of the Tilt-Light Company has a debit balance of $4,622. A Prepaid Insurance account is not carried; all premiums are charged to expense as they are incurred.

Based upon the examination of the following policies, prepare (a) an

Insurance Company	Policy No.	Coverage	Policy Date	Expiration Date	Total Coverage	Premium
State	101	Fire and extended, factory building	7/ 1/75	7/ 1/78	$100,000	$ 648
State	102	Fire and extended, factory building	8/16/76	8/16/79	250,000	1,728
Buckeye . . .	103	Fire and extended, office building	2/ 1/72	2/ 1/77	25,000	300
Buckeye . . .	104	Fire and extended, office equipment	10/ 1/73	10/ 1/78	27,000	480
Oldtown . . .	105	Fire, merchandise	5/ 1/76	5/ 1/77	310,000	444
Mutual	106	Comprehensive, delivery equipment	8/ 1/76	8/ 1/77	25,000	600
Acme	107	Inside theft and burglary	11/ 1/76	11/ 1/79	20,000	450
Northern . .	108	Employee fidelity	3/ 1/76	3/ 1/79	*	900
State	109	Workmen's compensation	9/ 1/76	9/ 1/77	†	‡

* Position on 3/1/79 is $30,000.
† Payroll at $0.25 per $100; the payroll from 9/1/76 to 8/31/77 is $302,400.
‡ Deposit of $756 made on 9/1/76.

insurance schedule and (*b*) the adjustment entry or entries properly to set up the prepaid insurance.

5. The audit for the year ending December 31, 1976, of the Storm Company revealed that the present balance of Prepaid Insurance account consisted of the following policies. All insurance premiums were charged to this account.

Policy No.	Company	Type Coverage	Dollar Coverage	Policy Date	Expiration Date	Amount of Premium
43S	A	Fire and extended—bldgs.	$100,000	8/1/75	8/1/78	$1,872
6574	B	Fire and extended—bldgs.	150,000	2/1/76	2/1/79	2,736
7711	C	Product liability	100,000	7/1/74	7/1/78	768
013	D	Fire and theft—inventory	65,000	8/1/76	2/1/79	360
5V3	E	Medical—officers	100,000	6/1/75	6/1/77	1,200
006	F	Delivery equipment	50,000	11/1/76	11/1/77	240
995	G	Blanket position bond	30,000	2/1/75	2/1/77	480
112	H	Construction bonding*	100,000	4/1/76	4/1/77	195
W53	C	Term insurance on key personnel	75,000	5/1/75	5/1/79	2,160
1001	B	Officer's life†	50,000	9/1/76	9/1/77	120
662	I	Officer's life‡	50,000	9/1/76	9/1/77	120

* For construction of hospital to insure that Storm will complete the project.
† Beneficiary is company.
‡ Beneficiary is officer's wife.

(1)   Prepare an Insurance Schedule for 12–31–76, showing in addition to the above information, the amount prepaid and the expense for the year.

(2)   Prepare journal entries to record the proper amount of expense for 1976 and create the correct balance of Prepaid Insurance.

11

Fixed Assets and Related Expenses

AUDIT OBJECTIVES

Briefly, the audit objectives in the examination of fixed assets are:

1. To verify the existence of the fixed assets.
2. To verify the ownership of the fixed assets.
3. To examine and fully disclose the valuation methods used.
4. To verify the propriety of fixed asset transactions for the audit period.
5. To evaluate the propriety of the depreciation program.
6. To review and evaluate the internal control of fixed assets.

GENERAL COMMENTS

An auditor should possess as much knowledge of the fixed assets of a client as he possesses of that client's current—or any other—assets. He should understand the nature, functions, uses, and operational results of fixed assets so that he will be in a good position to express an opinion of the fairness of the presentation of financial statements.

Fixed assets include business land, land improvements, buildings, machinery, factory equipment, tools, delivery equipment, certain leased assets, office equipment, and returnable containers. Excepting land, all of the preceding are subject to depreciation. Fixed assets also include oil deposits, timber stands, mineral properties, and others—all subject to depletion.

Properly, and in accordance with recognized principles and practices, fixed assets usually are originally recorded at net acquisition cost. Additions and improvements increase the basic cost of fixed assets. Repairs and

311

ordinary maintenance do not add to fixed asset worth in excess of original cost and do not extend the life of fixed assets beyond originally estimated life; therefore, repairs and maintenance costs are periodic expenses.

Original net acquisition costs plus additions and improvements are amortized over the estimated useful business life of a fixed asset by the process of depreciation or depletion. Depreciation is the systematic allocation of the cost of fixed assets to expense over the useful business life of the assets to the owner. Profits prior to depreciation must be at least large enough to recover the cost of the fixed assets; otherwise, operations are not profitable or are not as profitable as possibly anticipated.

On rare occasions, exemplified primarily by extractive industries properties, original cost obviously may be too low a figure for purposes of fair presentation. In these occasions, accepted practice apparently is to the effect that "discovery values" may be used in the depletable fixed asset accounts. The offsetting credit should be to a permanent capital account. Also, in rare events, appraised amounts or nominal amounts may appear in fixed asset accounts. If any basis other than cost is used for disclosing the gross amount of a fixed asset, the financial statements must clearly set forth that other base. Because inflation is rampant today, much has been appearing in current literature to reflect inflationary factors in the financial statements—but no conclusions have been reached; also it must be remembered that deflation normally follows inflation.

Depreciation charges must be systematic and must be consistently applied from period to period. This statement does not mean that depreciation rates and amounts cannot be changed for good cause. They should be changed if original useful life was incorrectly established and when such factors as obsolescence or inadequacy enter the picture after asset acquisition. Proper accounting requires that fixed assets be carried in properly segregated control accounts; cost allocations to depreciation should be carried in properly segregated accumulated depreciation accounts.

INTERNAL CONTROL OF FIXED ASSETS

Internal control is equally applicable to *all* assets—even though in the past, internal control of only current assets was primarily stressed. The objective of internal control of fixed assets is to obtain maximum operating efficiency from the money invested in those assets.

Proper internal control of fixed assets may be expressed as follows: Fixed assets should be acquired only upon proper authorization. Fixed assets should be controlled physically. A controlling account should be established for each group, supported by subsidiary records. Retirements and sales of fixed assets should be properly authorized, and the accounting department should be notified of all sales and retirements. Fixed assets should be inventoried periodically—every two or three years. Easily transferable small fixed assets should be under the control of as few persons as possible. If possible, small transferable fixed assets should be allotted specific locations.

Satisfactory standards of internal control of fixed assets are set forth in the internal control questionnaire shown in Illustration 11–1.

Illustration 11–1

INTERNAL CONTROL QUESTIONNAIRE
Fixed Assets

Company _____
Period Covered _____

	Yes	No	Note Applicable	Remarks
1. Are fixed asset acquisitions properly authorized and approved by the board of directors, or by the committee or person to whom the board of directors has delegated this authority?				
2. Are fixed asset acquisitions originated by requisition or appropriation that shows:				
a) Probable cost?				
b) Description of the asset?				
c) Accounts to be charged?				
d) Reason for the acquisition?				
3. Do idle plant facilities exist? (See Question 2.)				
4. Are the costs of constructed fixed assets accumulated by work order?				
5. If the answer to Question 4 is "yes," are actual and probable costs compared? (See Question 2.)				
6. Is a work-order system used for major repair jobs?				
7. Is the policy sound for differentiation between capital and revenue expenditures?				
8. If the client constructs fixed assets for his own use by using his regular employees, are the costs properly controlled through:				
a) Payroll records?				
b) Disbursement records?				
9. Is each general ledger controlling account supported by detailed plant records?				
10. Are the detailed plant records balanced (at least annually) with the control accounts?				
11. Periodically, is an inventory of fixed assets compared with the detail plant records?				
12. Are individual fixed assets tagged, or otherwise identified, and related to the subsidiary ledgers?				

AUDIT OF FIXED ASSETS

An audit of fixed assets varies greatly from an audit of current assets. Current assets are of short life, while fixed assets are of long life. Therefore, an audit of fixed assets does not directly affect working capital or revenues. Consequently, proper cutoff for fixed asset purchases has no

Illustration 11–1—Continued

13. Are fixed assets priced at:
    a) Cost?
    b) Appraisal?
    c) Other?
14. Does the client:
    a) Use accumulated depreciation accounts?
    b) Credit the asset accounts directly?
15. Is written approval required prior to the sale of fixed assets?
16. Is written approval required prior to scrapping a fixed asset?
17. When transfers of fixed assets are made from one department or plant to another department or plant:
    a) Are transfers properly authorized?
    b) Is the accounting department notified?
18. Does the client periodically study the fixed assets for purposes of determining adequate insurance?
19. Is the depreciation policy consistent from year to year?
20. Are accumulated depreciation accounts:
    a) Adequate?
    b) So large as to result in a "secret" reserve?
21. Have depreciation rates been accepted by the Internal Revenue Service?
22. When assets are sold or otherwise retired:
    a) Are accumulated depreciation accounts properly adjusted and charged?
    b) Are asset accounts properly credited?
    c) Is useful life properly related to the accumulated depreciation and the depreciation policy and rates?
23. Are fully depreciated assets, still in use, included in the asset accounts?
24. Are small tools properly safeguarded and kept in specific locations?
25. Are returnable containers:
    a) Properly accounted for?
    b) Properly safeguarded?
    c) Properly inventoried?

Prepared by _____   Reviewed by _____
Date _____   Date _____

effect on net income; errors in cutoff of fixed asset acquisitions will be revealed when liabilities are examined.

In general, audit procedures for all fixed assets are similar. The extent of the examination of fixed assets is dependent partially on whether the engagement is a first audit or a repeat engagement. In an initial audit of a company that has been in operation for more than one year, the auditor must perform an amount of work sufficient to convince him that the fixed asset figures are properly portrayed. This may involve the examination of records and evidence in the form of contracts, invoices, deeds, etc., of years prior to the current year. The opinion of the auditor must be as reliable as though he had conducted the audit in prior years.

In an initial audit the problems of the auditor are to ascertain the propriety of the gross carrying value of each fixed asset, and to ascertain the propriety of accumulated depreciation and—if used—depletion accumulations. The propriety of the gross carrying value of a fixed asset is dependent upon (1) the proper recording of initial cost or other basic acquisition figure, (2) the proper distinction between capital and revenue charges, and (3) the correctness of recording sales, retirements, and traded fixed assets. The propriety of net carrying value is dependent upon the accuracy of gross carrying values minus the propriety of depreciation charged off and the correctness of recording dispositions of fully depreciated or partially depreciated assets. Therefore, in an initial audit the auditor must review the past accounting for fixed assets, related expenses and depreciation, and dispositions. He may partially rely upon the reports of preceding auditors, if the reports are available. Good judgment must be exercised in a first examination so each fixed asset transaction is not traced back to its inception; reasonable tests of accuracy should suffice. An examination of reports from the Internal Revenue Service is of assistance in ascertaining the propriety of accounting for fixed assets.

In a repeat engagement the fixed asset balances as of the beginning of the year should be compared with the work papers of the prior year. Then, additions to and deductions from fixed asset accounts must be verified for the year under examination, with inspection and verification of underlying data such as authorizations, invoices, and paid checks. Related expense accounts must be analyzed to determine that assets have not been charged to expense. Also, the accuracy of the periodic depreciation expense charges must be verified.

For fixed assets, accepted accounting thought is to the effect that historical costs are proper and that current replacement costs are not proper. This position also was taken by the APB and by the Study Group on Business Income of the American Accounting Association. However, the Study Group on Business Income and the Committee on Accounting Concepts and Standards of the AAA recommend the preparation of *supplementary* financial statements to reflect fixed assets and depreciation charges on a current-cost basis—preferably original cost adjusted to current prices.

Occasionally, appraisal figures will be reflected in fixed asset accounts. The reasons for recording the appraisals may or may not be justifiable. If appraisals have been recorded, the auditor (1) must ascertain that depreciation in the income statement is based on the appraised amounts, (2) must clearly set forth original costs in the financial statements, and (3) must fully disclose the facts of the appraisal in his report.

When fixed assets are constructed, the cost should include such items as material costs, labor construction cost, cost of permits, premiums for workmen's compensation insurance—and for buildings, the cost of easements, architects' fees, and construction sheds. In the opinion of the authors, financing costs represented by interest paid during construction, bond discount or premium amortizations during the construction period, and property taxes during construction should not be added to the cost of the fixed asset. They are not usual and reasonable costs incurred in asset construction.

In summary form the scheduling of fixed assets is as follows:

Balance, January 1, 1976, per audit	$20,000
Cost of acquisitions in 1976 (in detail)	10,000
Total	$30,000
Deductions in 1976 (in detail)	8,000
Ledger balance, December 31, 1976	$22,000
Audit adjustments (in detail)	2,000
Balance per audit, December 31, 1976	$24,000

Fixed Assets Acquired in Noncash Transactions. When fixed assets are acquired in noncash transactions, the current market price of the item transferred should be charged to the asset acquired as its basic acquisition figure. Fixed assets acquired by gift should be recorded either at the cost to the preceding owner if that figure represents current market price or at the current market price ascertained by competent appraisal. If fixed assets are acquired in exchange for unissued or treasury capital stock, the fixed assets should be recorded at the market price of the stock so given. If the *par* of the stock given exceeds the market price of the assets acquired, the difference should be charged to the Discount on Capital Stock account.

If investment securities are exchanged for fixed assets, the price of the fixed assets should be determined by reference to the market price of the investment securities given in exchange.

Depreciation Considerations and Decisions

With regard to depreciation, an auditor should be concerned about its accuracy, consistency, and adequacy. There are many methods of computing depreciation, including the straight-line method, the working hours method, the unit production method, the composite life method, and various declining amounts methods. The straight-line method and the declining amounts methods are the methods commonly used. Illustration 11–2 sets forth the results of three different methods, assuming an asset costing $220,000 new, with an estimated salvage value of $20,000, and an estimated life of ten years.

Theoretically, a rate slightly greater than double the straight-line rate would be required to depreciate the asset to the residual amount of $20,000. Therefore, in order that all methods may amortize the full depreciable base of the asset, under the double-declining-balance method the

Illustration 11–2
COMPARISON OF DEPRECIATION METHODS

Year	Straight-Line, 10% of Cost, Less Salvage	Sum-of-Years-Digits	Double-Declining Balance, Rate 20% of Remaining Balance
1	$ 20,000	$ 36,363	$ 44,000
2	20,000	32,727	35,200
3	20,000	29,091	28,160
4	20,000	25,455	22,528
5	20,000	21,818	18,022
6	20,000	18,182	14,418
7	20,000	14,545	11,534
8	20,000	10,909	9,228
9	20,000	7,273	7,382
10	20,000	3,637	5,906
Total Depreciation	$200,000	$200,000	$196,378

curve may be straightened out at about mid-life; the balance then is written off in equal amounts over the remaining service life, thus bringing the total depreciation up to $200,000.

An auditor must be familiar with the latest regulations of the U.S. Treasury Department; for example, the new Asset Depreciation Range, the removal of the "reserve ratio test" under ADR, etc.

Many persons object to accelerated depreciation on the basis that it merely offers a relief from current taxes, deferring larger amounts of taxes to later periods. However, if a company acquires new assets with reasonable consistency, taxes might be permanently deferred and capital gain advantages may accrue.

Gains and losses on the disposition of fixed assets are partially dependent upon company policies with regard to the timing of the depreciation, as exemplified below:

A Company: Depreciation is computed from the exact date of acquisition to the exact date of disposition.

B Company: Depreciation at the annual rate is computed on the period-opening balance of the account, and acquisitions and dispositions are ignored.

C Company: Depreciation at the annual rate is computed on the period-closing balance of the acount, and acquisitions and dispositions are ignored.

D Company: Depreciation at the annual rate is computed on the period-opening balance of the account, plus or minus one half of the annual depreciation on *net* acquisitions or dispositions during the year.

E Company: Depreciation at the annual rate is computed to nearest end of the month on assets disposed of or acquired.

Depreciations schedules may be prepared separately, or they may be prepared on the same work papers with the related asset or group of assets. An auditor must verify the client's depreciation computations or independently compute the depreciation. In the verification of depreciation, the objectives of the auditor are (1) to ascertain the adequacy of the periodic charge based upon the useful life of the asset to the business, and based upon the propriety of the estimated salvage value; (2) to ascertain the propriety of the total accumulation viewed from the point of useful asset life and asset adequacy; (3) to determine the consistency of the application of depreciation methods in accordance with recognized principles of accounting; and (4) to determine that accumulated depreciation and related asset accounts have received proper entries when assets are sold, exchanged, retired, or destroyed.

If fixed assets have been appraised during the current period, entries for the revaluations must be verified. The auditor must then ascertain that the periodic depreciation charge will be large enough to match the total depreciable amount at the end of the estimated life of the asset. Appraisal reports are examined from the point of view of competency, propriety, and reasonableness.

Management Reports

Periodically, top management should receive internally prepared reports on all fixed assets. The reports should be designed so that operating efficiency may be judged, so that decisions may be made for future capital expenditures, the disposition of assets, and so that the effect of any decision on net income may be determined. Asset additions and retirements should be included in the report.

Management reports for proposed acquisitions of fixed assets should be designed so that at least the following questions may be answered:

1. Will the new fixed assets add net income sufficient to justify the cost?
2. Will expenses be reduced by acquiring the new assets?
3. Will the new fixed assets add to diversification by adding new product lines?
4. In bringing the new assets into normal use, what will be the dollar amount of start-up expenses?
5. How many years will be required to recover the cost of the new assets via the increase in cash flow?

6. How are funds for new fixed assets to be raised—from long-term borrowing, from issuance of additional capital stock, from net income and cash generated by depreciation, or from cash now available?
7. Would it be more desirable to buy, build, or lease?

Land

The auditor must obtain satisfactory evidence of land ownership by the examination of purchase contracts, deeds, guaranty policies, tax bills, and other documents supporting the purchase authorization. All pertinent vouchers are traced to the financial records. Valuations shown in the Land account must be in conformity with the method of acquiring the land and also must be in accordance with generally accepted principles of accounting. Land is peculiar in that it is one asset always publicly registered as to ownership. The auditor must ascertain that the land is recorded in the name of the client—if the client is the owner. The auditor should obtain a confirmation of ownership from the client's attorney or from the title guaranty company (only one time). Normally, the auditor does not examine public records. In the confirmation from the attorney or title guaranty company, the auditor should obtain information concerning liens or assessments against the land.

The cost of land includes the purchase price, option costs, title examination fees, clearing costs, filling and drainage costs, liens assumed, and commissions to brokers if paid by the purchaser. Additional costs, preferably shown in a Land Improvement account—primarily because the items are depreciable—include parking lots, special assessments for sidewalks, streets, sewers, and other long-term improvements. If the worth of the land is not increased by these nontransitory costs, they should be charged to expense. All transitory costs should be also charged to expense. For federal income tax purposes, special land assessments are capital expenditures—and this may be one place where tax accounting and financial accounting do not coincide. If capitalized special assessments are paid on the installment plan, the auditor must ascertain that the Land account or the Land Improvement account has been charged for the entire assessment cost and that a liability account exists for the unpaid portion. Interest on installments is to be charged to expense.

The Land account may be scheduled in a manner similar to Illustration 11–3. Each charge and credit must be traced to the underlying records and documents, such as contracts, invoices, and paid checks.

Minutes of meetings of the board of directors should be examined for authorization to purchase land. If the land was paid for in cash, paid checks should be traced to the disbursements records and to the Land account. If land has been written up above cost, because of permanent increases in market prices and because original cost is now considered to be too low reasonably to reflect worth, the auditor must examine appraisal reports and authorizations to increase the Land account; and must trace the offsetting credit to the proper permanent capital account.

Land may be acquired upon which structures are located. If these structures are demolished immediately, the cost of the demolished structures and net demolition costs constitute land costs. If at a date after acquisition it is decided to demolish the structures because of a change from original intention, the cost of demolition plus the undepreciated cost of the structures normally constitutes an expense charge.

In his permanent file the auditor will retain important data from purchase contracts and deeds. These data will include registration dates, recording data such as deed book and page number, confirmations of ownership from attorneys and title companies, notes on existing mortgages and their cancellation, and plot sketches.

Illustration 11–3
WORK PAPER 20

MULTI-PRODUCTS, INCORPORATED	Initials	Date
Land, December 31, 1976	Prepared By CF	2-8-77
	Approved By RW	2-9-77

Balance, per audit, December 31, 1975		90 000 ∧
December 10, 1976, purchased adjoining		
land (25'x700') from James Balmo✓z		10 000
Balance, per audit, December 31, 1976		100 000∧✓
∧ Land is carried at cost. See letter from		
attorney, in permanent file, for		
original purchase.		
⊙ Contract examined.		
✓Confirmed by Jones and Jones, lawyers.		
z Purchased for parking lot purposes.		
✓ Traced to cash disbursements records.		

Buildings

The building accounts and their related depreciation accumulation accounts should be scheduled in a manner similar to Illustrations 11–4 and 11–5. For the period under examination, each charge and credit to the building accounts should be vouched thereto by examining underlying documents such as architects' invoices, contracts, and paid checks, and tracing them through the original records. Approval of debits and credits must be in conformity with recognized principles of accounting. Proper distinction must exist between capital and revenue charges. In a first examination the auditor may review the records of prior years in order to establish the propriety of the building accounts. Related expense accounts of prior years must be examined to ascertain proper distinctions between capital and revenue expenditures.

In addition to an analysis of the periodic charges and credits to the building accounts, the work papers should contain such data as the following: excerpts of authority to purchase or construct, necessary notes from purchase contracts and other vouchers connected with the acquisition or construction of buildings, the auditor's opinion concerning the propriety of the client's distinctions between capital and revenue charges, necessary notes on tax bills, and insurance coverage.

Illustration 11–4
WORK PAPER 21

		Initials	Date
MULTI-PRODUCTS, INCORPORATED	Prepared By	PM	2-9-77
Building, December 31, 1976	Approved By	RW	2-9-77

Balance, per audit, December 31, 1975					840 000	
June 30, 1972: Brick office						
addition					32 400	⊙
Balance, per audit, December 31, 1976					872 400	
√ Approved by action of the board						
of directors, February 10, 1976.						
⊙ Vouched to invoices and to cash						
disbursements.						

The auditor must determine that owned buildings are in the name of the client. An examination of rents received and tax payments serves as partial proof of ownership. Liens against owned buildings should appear in liability accounts.

Improvements to leased buildings should be scheduled in a manner similar to the analysis schedule for buildings. The auditor must verify the periodic charges and credits to the Leasehold Improvement account, and must determine that the amortization of these costs is being made over the life of the lease or the improvement, whichever is shorter. See Illustration 11–6.

In connection with depreciation, the responsibilities of the auditor in-

Illustration 11-5
WORK PAPER 22

	Initials	Date
Prepared By	Pm	2-9-77
Approved By	Rw	2-9-77

MULTI-PRODUCTS, INCORPORATED

Accumulated Depreciation of Building, December 31, 1976

Balance, per audit, December 31, 1975			127892	
1976 company addition: 2 percent of				
$872,400 12 months			17448	
Balance per ledger, December 31, 1976			145340	
Deduct: AJE 8, below			1148	
Audit balance, December 31, 1976			144192	
AJE 8				
Accumulated Depreciation of Building		1148		
Cost of Sales--Depreciation of Building			1148	
Depreciation, 1976:				
$840,000 - $40,000 at 2 percent				
for 12 months	$16000			
$32,400 - $2,400 at 2 percent for				
6 months	300			
Total depreciation	$16300			
Recorded by company	17448			
Adjustment	$ 1148			

clude the verification of the periodic depreciation charge and the accuracy of the total provision, both being provided for in accordance with accepted principles of accounting, consistently applied. After verifying the period depreciation charges and the total accumulations, the auditor should review the net book value from the point of view of the general condition of the asset. Perhaps depreciation rates and amounts have been too low or too high, and a suggested revision may be in order.

Debits and credits in the accumulated depreciation accounts must be traced to the original records, or vice versa. If assets have been sold, there must be determination of the accuracy of the charge to the accumulation accounts and determination of the proper resultant gain or loss.

Charges to accumulation accounts appear only (1) when extraordinary repairs are made which extend life beyond the originally estimated life, (2) when assets are retired, sold, or otherwise disposed of, and (3) when correcting entries are made. Gains and losses on dispositions must be verified. Fully depreciated assets still in use should not be removed from the accounts.

Illustration 11–6

THE BLANK COMPANY
Leasehold Improvements
December 31, 1973–76

		Amortization			
Explanation	*Original Cost*	*1973*	*1974*	*1975*	*1976*
1973 improvements . . .	$42,000√	4,200	4,200	4,200	4,200
1974 improvements . . .	13,086√		1,454	1,454	1,454
1975 improvements . . .	7,808√			976	976
1976 improvements . . .	4,784√				684
	$67,678	4,200	5,654	6,630	7,314

√ Verified expenditures.
Lease dated January 2, 1973; 10 years.
Termination date: December 31, 1982.

If buildings produce rental revenue, the auditor should verify that revenue; this may be in the nature of a test. All expenses related to owned buildings should be reviewed for propriety and reasonableness.

Machinery, Equipment, Tools, Office Equipment, Delivery Equipment

The auditing procedures for these assets follow the same pattern as the procedures applicable to buildings. Each account is separately scheduled, together with its related accumulated depreciation as shown in Illustrations 11–7, 11–8, and 11–9. Authorizations for acquisition of fixed assets, purchase orders, vendors' invoices, and paid checks should be traced through all records of origin into the proper account in order to ascertain the propriety and accuracy of the debit.

The proper cost of a fixed asset is its *net* cash invoice price, plus transportation charges, installation costs, and any other costs necessary to place the asset in condition for the use of the purchaser. Vendors' allowances for defective items should be credited to the proper asset account—not to income. Rearrangement and alteration costs were treated in Chapter 10.

When examining *sales* of fixed assets, the auditor should obtain evidence of authority to sell, a copy of the invoice, and evidence of the correct recording of the cash receipt. Entries removing a fixed asset and its related accumulation for depreciation must be reviewed, together with the verification of the accuracy of gain or loss on the sale.

In the verification of *exchanges* of fixed assets, an auditor should examine the authorization to exchange and all related invoice copies. After

Illustration 11–7
WORK PAPER 23

		Initials	Date
MULTI-PRODUCTS, INCORPORATED	Prepared By	PM	2-10-77
Machinery, December 31, 1976	Approved By	CH	2-11-77

Balance, per audit, December 31, 1975			558560
Additions, 1976:			
January 5, 1976: Milling Machine		16000 ✓	
July 1, 1976: Broaching Machine No.2		20000 ✓	
Total additions			36000
Deductions, 1976:			594560
July 1, 1976: Broaching Machine No.1 at cost			15000 ✓
Balance, per audit, December 31, 1976			579560
✓ Vouchers examined.			
✓ Cost	$15000		
Depreciation to July 1, 1976	7160		
Book value, July 1, 1976	$ 7840		
Sold for cash of	4000 ∧		
Loss on sale	$ 3840 ⊙		
∧ Vouched to cash receipts.			
⊙ Transactions examined.			

determining any profit or loss on the exchanges, cash receipts or disbursements are traced to the original records. Audit adjustments frequently are necessary when fixed assets are exchanged. When fixed assets are exchanged for similar fixed assets, the requirements of federal income tax regulations must be taken into consideration, particularly with regard to the recognition or nonrecognition of gains and losses arising from the exchange.

When fixed assets are *retired* without sale, journal entries should exist or be prepared transferring the asset and its related depreciation accumulation from the active accounts. If a fixed asset is retired and scrapped, a net loss may result; the auditor must verify all entries. If a fixed asset is retired and not physically disposed of, the retired asset may be charged to a Retired Assets account, and a new accumulated depreciation may be set up, to which is transferred the credit balance in the active accumulated depreciation account.

Related Expense Accounts

A thorough examination and analysis must be made of all expense accounts related to fixed assets. Normally, there are maintenance and repair accounts. Capital expenditures must not be charged to expense.

Illustration 11–8
WORK PAPER 24

	Initials	Date
Prepared By	PM	2-10-77
Approved By	RW	2-12-77

MULTI-PRODUCTS, INCORPORATED

Accumulated Depreciation of Machinery, December 31, 1976

Balance, per audit, December 31, 1975			193952	
Added by company in 1976			57956	
Balance per general ledger December 31, 1976			251908	
Deduct: Correction, AJE 9			5936	
Adjusted balance, December 31, 1976			245972	
Depreciation computation:				
$558,560 - $54,560 estimated salvage				
at 10 percent for 6 months	25200			
$543,560 - $53,160 estimated salvage				
$558,560 - $15,000 = $543,560 at				
10 percent for 6 months	24520			
$16,000 - $2,000 estimated salvage				
at 10 percent for 12 months	1400			
$20,000 - $2,000 estimated salvage				
at 10 percent for 6 months	900			
Total 1976 depreciation	52020			
Recorded by company	57956			
Reduction, per audit	5936			
AJE 9				
Accumulated Depreciation of Machinery	5936			
Cost of Sales--Depreciation of				
Machinery		5936		

Where is the line of demarcation between capital and revenue expenditures? The answer depends upon materiality, company policy, adequate continuous maintenance, and propriety in the application of accounting principles. The following statements may be made:

1. A capital expenditure for an asset implies that the life of the asset will extend beyond the current period.

2. Ordinary repairs, maintenance, and part replacements which do not extend the life of the asset beyond its originally estimated life are expense charges.

3. Extraordinary repairs, maintenance, and part replacements which do extend the life of the asset beyond its originally estimated life are capital charges—to be made to the asset account or to the allowance for depreciation account.

4. Additions, betterments, and improvements are capital asset charges.

Illustration 11–9
WORK PAPER 25

						Initials	Date
MULTI-PRODUCTS, INCORPORATED					Prepared By	Pm	2-10-77
Office Equipment and Accumulated Depreciation, December 31, 1976					Approved By	RW	2-22-77

Year	Additions (Assets)	Deductions (Assets)	Balance December 31 (Assets)	Additions (Accumulated Depreciation)	Deductions (Accumulated Depreciation)	Balance December 31 (Accumulated Depreciation)	Book Value December 31
1967	33,630	0	33630	1680	0	1680	31950
1968	6,800	0	40430	3702	0	5382	35048
1969	1,300	1000	40730	4058	250	9190	31540
1970	2,600	0	43330	4202	0	13392	29938
1971	4,200	500	47030	4516	400	17508	29522
1972	900	0	47930	4748	1680	20576	27354
1973	1,200	330	48800	4836	330	25082	23718
1974	1,000	1500	48300	4854	1300	28636	19664
1975	1,600	600	49300	4850	500	32986	16314
1976	4,000 Λ	0	53300	5330 √	0	38316	14984
	720 Λ⊙	0	54020	0	0	38316	15704

√ Calculation verified.
Λ Examined invoices.
⊙ AJE 10.

	AJE 10						
Office Equipment					720		
Office Operating Expense						720	
To set up as an asset the adding							
machine charged to expense.							

Insurance

Insurance policies covering fixed assets are reviewed to determine the adequacy of the protection. If the client has rented equipment or assets being purchased on an installment contract, the insurance requirements of the contracts are examined and compared with the adequacy and type of insurance carried. Insurance policies also are evidence of ownership.

Small Tools

Small tools include such items as portable drills, reamers, files, gauges, and many others. Proper accounting for small tools requires that they be treated in the same manner as inventories, that they be properly recorded in asset accounts, that they be properly controlled physically, and that they be charged to expense as they are used—either via depreciation or via direct expense debits. Normally, an accumulated depreciation of small tools is not used. An accumulation is not necessary if the inventory method—properly applied—is used, and if the tools periodically are properly counted and priced by competent personnel.

If periodic small-tool costs are not significant in amount, if tool purchases are relatively constant from year to year, and if the tools have a normal life of less than one year, common practice is to charge the cost of the tools to expense as they are purchased.

In many cases the audit of small perishable tools is difficult. After examining the internal control and the internal audit of small tools, the auditor should exercise care to ascertain that all tools—useful for more than one year—are properly reflected in asset accounts at the end of the year, and that they are not charged to expense in total at the time of purchase and permitted to remain as expense charges. After scheduling tool purchases and usage, the auditor should verify tool inventory records, pricing, extensions, and totals. Test counts are made on the same physical basis as those used for inventories.

Patterns, Dies, Electrotypes

Patterns, dies, electrotypes, and special-job tools usually possess only a negligible residual value after the purpose for which they were designed has been fulfilled. Unless the life of these assets definitely can be projected over firm production contracts, or unless company experience definitely indicates an asset life acceptable to the auditor, their costs should be charged against the initial production. An original production run is no indication of a repeat order or of a desire to produce additional items. Automobile roof dies may be changed annually. Production from patterns may never be repeated. The majority of books never enjoy more than a first printing; the bookplate electrotype costs cannot be deferred to future hopes. In other words, nonproductive asset costs should not be permitted to accumulate in asset accounts.

Returnable Containers

If a company owns returnable containers, a variety of accounting situations may be encountered. Customers may or may not be required to make deposits for containers. If deposits are required, they may be below, above, or at the cost of the container. In the event of nonreturn the container owner may realize a profit or may incur a total or partial loss.

Containers are fixed assets, and many of them are costly. They should be handled on the basis of the control exercised over any fixed asset or any item of inventory. The auditor should start with the physical quantity of the containers at the beginning of the year, add the number of containers purchased, and subtract the number of containers discarded and the number not returned. Thus, he will arrive at a container physical inventory at the end of the year. The resultant figure is verified by counting the containers on hand and adding to that figure the containers in the hands of customers who are expected to return them. The total cost of the container inventory should be depreciated on a basis coordinate with the useful business life of the item. Container deposits made by customers may be test-confirmed. Liability accounts exist when customers make deposits, and this liability must be reconciled with the containers in the hands of customers. If the liability is greater than the billed price of the containers out with customers, remittances are in order. If the liability is less than the billed price of the containers out, provisions for loss should be made.

Equalization Allowances

A company may create maintenance equalization allowance by periodic—monthly—charges to expense and credits to the allowance account. When ordinary repairs, maintenance, and part replacements are incurred, the costs thereof are charged to the allowance account. The auditor must determine that any balance remaining in the allowance at the end of the fiscal year is closed back to the related expense account. While the theory of short-term expense equalization may be followed, expense charges of one year should not result in the distortion of net income.

Extractive Industries Assets

Fixed assets constructed on extractive industries land do not differ from any other fixed asset. The auditor must ascertain if the cost of such fixed assets is being amortized over the estimated life of the asset or the life of the extractive operation, whichever is shorter. For example, in a logging operation, assume that it was the intention to cut the timber stand and move on to another location. Houses erected for the loggers should be depreciated over the estimated time to complete the logging if the life of the workers' quarters exceeds the logging time. If fixed assets constructed on extractive industries properties are to be moved to another site, depreciation should be over the life of the movable fixed asset.

Wasting asset properties are subject to depletion caused by the physical removal of ores, gas, oil, timber, and other resources. The cost or discovery value of the wasting asset should be prorated over the estimated life of the operation. The auditor relies on the reports of technical experts in the estimates of quantities. If the land has an estimated residual value after the operation is completed, that estimated residual worth should be deducted from original cost or discovery value—and the net difference prorated to periodic depletion charges. At best, depletion charges are estimates, subject to review as operations proceed. Computations for depletion charges are verified by examining production records. While the periodic depletion charge is to income, the charge really is an asset cost—inventory.

If an extractive industries company plans to acquire additional properties after present properties are exhausted, it may establish funds for future land purchases. In this event the auditor should verify computations for the additions to the fund—usually based on units extracted or on units extracted and sold.

The dividend policies of extractive industries companies must be examined to determine if original capital is being returned to shareholders —and that the shareholders are so informed.

FINANCIAL STATEMENT CONSIDERATIONS

In the balance sheet, each related group of fixed assets should be shown separately—preferably at cost less accumulated depreciation. Both cost and the accumulated depreciation provision should be set forth. If a basis other than cost is used, cost should be indicated parenthetically or by footnote.

In the income statement, depreciation of fixed assets should be shown by related groups, properly classified as manufacturing, administrative, or selling expenses. If fixed assets have been appraised upward or downward in the records, the depreciation in the income statement should be on the basis of the appraisal figures, with depreciation based on cost also indicated.

Land owned for business purposes should be segregated in the balance sheet from land held for investment or contemplated future use. Other fixed assets owned but used for other than business purposes should appear in the balance sheet as investment assets or other assets. Abandoned fixed assets should be shown separately.

If fixed assets of material amount are fully depreciated and are still in use, both the full cost (or other basic figure) and the total accumulated depreciation should appear in the balance sheet in order to put the reader of the balance sheet on notice that fixed assets are contributing to net income while there is no depreciation charge. The accumulated depreciation account should not be closed to the asset account. If assets are discarded, both the allowance and the asset account should be closed.

The basis of pricing small perishable tools should be set forth in the balance sheet if the tools are material in total or in relationship to other fixed assets.

If fixed assets are in the process of construction at the balance-sheet date and if their amount is significant, they may (a) be shown separately or (b) be included with the proper group totals, with the dollar amount of the construction in process shown parenthetically.

If fixed assets are partially paid for, the entire cost should appear as assets and a liability should exist in the records. The determination of existing liabilities of this nature is possible by comparing invoices for assets purchased with the asset accounts. In many types of installment contracts, title remains with the vendor until full payment has been made. Depreciation on assets partially paid for should be computed on the full contract cost price.

If fixed assets are being constructed by the company which will use them, fixed assets accounts should contain all costs incurred up to the end of the period. Unpaid costs incurred should appear as liabilities.

At the end of a fiscal period, when purchase commitments exist for fixed assets, they should be shown by explanatory footnote, if material in amount or unusual in nature.

If fixed assets are being leased by the client and if the amount is significant, full disclosure of this fact must be made in a footnote, and the amount of liability that would result if the lease were broken must be specifically stated. In connection with leases, also see *Opinion Nos. 1, 5, 27,* and *31* of the APB. In 1973, the SEC began requiring footnote disclosure of lease obligations. The FASB is now recommending that the same basic reporting criteria be applied to both lessors and lessees. Separate accounting and reporting requirements are proposed for leveraged leases, which are leases in which the cost of the leased property is financed through long-term debt. A further recommendation, applying to so called "capital leases" would have the lessee show the equipment on the balance sheet as an asset, and the obligation to make rental payments would be shown as a liability. Certain criteria will have to be met in order for such classification and these will be established by the FASB.

SUGGESTED ADDITIONAL READINGS

Statement on Auditing Standards No. 1, Section 330.01–.15.

QUESTIONS

1. In connection with the review of plant additions, a CPA ordinarily would take exception to the capitalization of the cost of:
   a) Major reconditioning of a recently acquired secondhand floor scale.
   b) Machine operator's wages during a period of testing a new roof.
   c) Room partitions installed at the request of a new long-term lessee in the office building.
   d) Maintenance of an unused stand-by plant.

2. In connection with an audit of the fixed assets of a manufacturing company, what are the general procedures by which an auditor may be satisfied (a) that all of the owned assets are recorded, and (b) that the amounts at which the assets are recorded are proper? Explain how each procedure will assist in satisfying the auditor, and whether the procedure is applicable to (a) or (b). Ignore depreciation.

3. Snow, Inc., was organized July 1, 1976, with an authorized capital of 150,000 shares of common stock. One half of the stock was sold for cash at $90 per share, and the other half was given in payment for a fully equipped building and a land site. During the course of your audit for the six months ended December 31, 1976, you noted that the fixed asset accounts involved were charged for a total of $10 million and that the Common Stock account was credited for $10 million. In view of the fact that the board of directors may use any valuation it desires, do you consider the fixed assets correctly charged?

4. *a)* A company built a fixed asset for its own use. It used its regular employees to construct the asset. This work was done during a period of the year when normal manufacture was low. The asset cost $100,000, which did not include generally proratable factory overhead, but did include overhead applicable to this construction. If the asset had been built under contract, it would have cost $110,000; the company wants to capitalize the asset at $110,000 and asks your advice. Is the request reasonable and satisfactory?

   b) Assume that the client insisted that the asset be placed in the records at $110,000. Prepare the entry to put the asset in the records and the entry to show depreciation at the end of the first year, assuming no scrap value and a life of 25 years, under the straight-line method.

5. *a)* What are the objectives of an audit of fixed assets?

   b) A client asked that you explain to him the difference between the estimated life of an asset and its useful business life. Explain the difference.

6. *a)* In an initial audit, to what extent should an auditor be concerned with depreciation provisions of prior years?

   b) In an initial audit, would you be willing to place your entire confidence in a deed as evidence of land ownership? Explain.

7. What are some general principles which will guide you in ascertaining if the depreciation provisions have been too large or too small for office equipment, machinery, and buildings? Would a flat rate of depreciation and a blanket accumulation for depreciation be satisfactory for these three assets?

8. In connection with an annual audit of the fixed assets of a manufacturing company, what are the general procedures by which the auditor may satisfy himself (*a*) that all owned assets are recorded and (*b*) that the amounts in which the assets are recorded are proper and in accordance with accepted accounting principles? Explain how each procedure will assist in satisfying the auditor, and whether the procedure is applicable to (*a*) or (*b*). Ignore depreciation.

9. In the course of the audit of the financial statements of Ginger, Inc., an analysis of the Building account showed the following debits and the reasons therefor:

   a) A fee of $20,000 paid to a firm of engineers for advice and plans for the rearrangement of machinery. The advice was not followed.

b) Title examination fees of $5,000 for a prospective land purchase for a contemplated plan for acquiring a land site for another factory.

c) Major roof reconstruction at a cost of $20,000. The roof was constructed of the same materials as the original roof, which also cost $20,000.

d) Cost of moving machinery from the second floor to the first floor, $3,000.

e) Cost of floor repairs for the places from which the machinery in (*d*) was moved, $1,000.

What is your position with respect to the propriety or impropriety of each of the preceding entries?

10. Gardens, Inc., is a closely held corporation engaged in the business of purchasing and subdividing large tracts of land and installing paved streets and utilities. The corporation does not construct buildings for the buyers of the land and does not have any affiliated construction companies. Undeveloped land is leased for farming until the corporation is ready to begin developing it.

The corporation finances its land acquisitions by mortgages; the mortgagees require audited financial statements. This is your first audit of the corporation, and you have started the audit for the year ended December 31, 1976.

Your preliminary review of the records has indicated that the corporation would have had a highly profitable year except that the president was reimbursed for exceptionally large travel and entertainment expenses.

a) The corporation has three tracts of land in various stages of development. List the audit procedures to be employed in the verification of the physical existence and title to the three tracts of land.

b) The president of the corporation asked you to prepare a report that will contain only the balance sheet and states that he will remove the income statement and the statement of changes in financial position from your report before submitting it to the mortgagees if you refuse to prepare a report containing only the balance sheet.

(1) Would accepted auditing standards permit the preparation of an audit report containing only a balance sheet? Discuss.

(2) What would be your response to the president's threat to remove the income statement from your audit report? Discuss.

(AICPA, adapted)

PROBLEMS

1. In prior years, the Robb Manufacturing Company used an accelerated depreciation method for its depreciable assets for both federal income tax and financial reporting. At the beginning of 1976 the company changed to the straight-line method for financial reporting. As a result, depreciation expense for the year was $200,000 less for financial reporting than for income tax purposes, an amount which you consider to be material. The

company did not use interperiod income tax allocation in 1976. Taxable income for 1976 was $600,000. Assume that the income tax involved was $96,000.

a) For financial statement presentation:

(1) Describe the effects of the accounting change on the Robb 1976 balance sheet, income statement and funds statement. Cite specific amounts in your answer.

(2) Explain what disclosure of the accounting change should be made in the 1976 financial statements.

b) For the audit report:

(1) Assuming that the financial statement disclosure is considered to be adequate, discuss the effects that the change in depreciation methods should have on the audit report.

(2) Assuming that the financial statement disclosure of the change in depreciation methods is not considered to be adequately informative, discuss the effects on the audit report.

(3) Discuss whether the audit report should indicate approval of the change in depreciation methods.

(4) Discuss the effects on the audit report of the failure to use interperiod income tax allocation.

(AICPA, adapted)

2. On July 15, 1976, your client, Harry Crow, sold his apartment building to Mary Miller. The escrow statement follows:

	Crow, Seller		Miller, Buyer	
	Charges	*Credits*	*Charges*	*Credits*
Sales price		$250,000	$250,000	
Paid directly to seller	$ 10,000			$ 10,000
First mortgage assumed by buyer	106,000			106,000
Purchase money mortgage	84,000			84,000
Prorations:				
Real estate taxes		250	250	
Insurance adjustment		200	200	
Interest		300	300	
Fees:				
Escrow	100		100	
Title insurance			790	
Attorney	40		60	
Revenue stamps			550	
Funds deposited in escrow account:				
July 14, 1976				52,250
Items paid from escrow account:				
Commission to realty co.	15,000			
Remit:				
Harry Crow	35,610			
Total	$250,750	$250,750	$252,250	$252,250

Crow's accounting records are maintained on the cash basis. When you undertake the September 30, 1976, quarterly audit for your client the following information is available:

(1) A "Suspense" account was opened for money received in connection with the sale of the property.

(2) The apartment building and land were purchased on July 1, 1972, for $225,000. The building was being depreciated over a 40-year life by the straight-line method. Accumulated depreciation has been consistently recorded on Crow's records for assets purchased or sold during the year. No depreciation has been recorded for 1976.

(3) The contract of sale stated that the price for the land on which the building was built was $25,000, the cost recorded on Crow's records.

(4) The purchase money mortgage payments are $1,000 per month plus accrued interest. The first payment was due August 1, 1976.

You are requested to prepare the audit adjustments to record the sale on Crow's records.

(AICPA, adapted)

3. From your examination of the financial statements of the Joan Company as of December 31, 1976, certain information is presented as follows:

Building

Date	Explanation	Debit	Credit	Balance
12-31-75	Balance	100,000		100,000
7-1-76	New air conditioner ...	17,510	1,510	116,000
9-1-76	Insurance recovery		2,000	114,000

Accumulated Depreciation, Building

Date	Explanation	Debit	Credit	Balance
12-31-75	Balance: 15 years at 4 percent of $100,000		60,000	60,000
12-31-76	Annual depreciation ...		4,440	64,440

On June 15, 1976, the company's old air conditioner was badly damaged by lightning. The air conditioner was replaced by a new and more efficient unit. The company received $2,000 as an insurance adjustment under the terms of its policy for damage to the air conditioner.

The invoice from Ferris Air Conditioning, Inc., dated July 1, 1976, and charged to the Building account by Joan, follows:

List price. New air conditioner	$17,000
Sales tax: 3 percent of $17,000	510
Total including installation	$17,510
Less: Allowance for old air conditioner, to be removed at the expense of Ferris	1,510
Net Invoice price	$16,000

While examining the preceding expenditure, you ascertained that the terms included a 2 percent cash discount which was properly computed and taken. The sales tax is not subject to discount.

A review of subsidiary records disclosed that the replaced air conditioner was installed when the building was constructed at a cost of $10,000, and charged to the building account. According to its manufacturer the new air conditioner should be serviceable for 15 years.

In computing depreciation for retirements, the Joan Company consistently treated a fraction of a month as a full month.

Prepare the audit adjustments for entry on the records of the Joan Company. The accounts have not been closed. Show computations.

4. For $300,000, Pepper, Inc., purchased land upon which was located a building. Legal fees for the contract of sale and title examination were $3,000. The records of the seller showed the following:

Land $150,000
Building   300,000
Accumulated depreciation, building   270,000

Pepper, Inc. immediately razed the building and realized $4,500 from the sale of building materials. Six months were necessary to construct a new building, which cost $900,000. Taxes during the construction period amounted to $3,000. In order to build the building, it was necessary for Pepper to borrow $300,000 for a period of two years, giving a first mortgage on the land and building. The interest rate on the loan was 6 percent. Insurance during construction was carried by Pepper. Premiums were $7,500 for a five-year period. An executive of the company spent the entire six months conferring with architects and contractors. His salary is $120,000 per year.

The client requests that you determine the proper cost (a) of the land and (b) of the building.

5. Beyer, Inc. computes depreciation on its plant assets on the basis of units of production. The plant asset balance at January 1, 1976 was $2,500,000 and the accumulated depreciation at that date was $790,000, leaving a balance of $1,710,000 to be charged off through depreciation. It was then estimated that, starting on January 1, 1976, 1,900,000 units would be produced over the remaining useful life of the plant assets. In 1976, 220,000 units were produced.

No change occurred in the Plant Asset account or the Accumulated Depreciation account, except for the 1976 depreciation, until January 1, 1977. On that date, a fully depreciated item of equipment which cost $160,000 was retired and scrapped. On the same date, new equipment costing $248,000 was placed in service. It was then reestimated that, as a consequence, there would be produced 2,000,000 units over the remaining useful life of the plant assets from January 1, 1977. The production was 250,000 units in the year 1977.

Prepare journal entries, with explanations, to record the effect of the foregoing retirement and addition of equipment, and for depreciation for the years 1976 and 1977.

6. Explo, Inc., manufactures chemicals and delivers its products in returnable drums. In order to avoid losses by failure to return drums, a charge of $200 per drum is billed to customers. Most customers remit cash only for the price of the contents and return the drums for credit. Occasionally, the amount charged for the drums is also remitted; in some instances, these drums are never returned for credit.

You are summoned by the company to supply the following:

a) In journal entry form, show how the following transactions should be recorded in the accounts of the chemical company:
  (1) Original purchase of drums.
  (2) Drums billed to customers.
  (3) Drums returned by customers.
  (4) Drums not recoverable from customers, and for which the charges cannot be collected.

b) What accounts should be kept in the general ledger, and how should they be shown in the balance sheet?

c) What verifications can be made to prove the balances in these ledger accounts?

7. In May, 1977, the IRS requested one of your new clients, Inter, Inc., to furnish a depreciation schedule for its trucks. The schedule was to set forth additions, retirements, depreciation, and other data for the three-year period January 1, 1974, to December 31, 1976.

The following data were compiled by the client, who then summoned you for assistance:

Item	Date Purchased	Cost
Truck No.:		
1	January 1, 1971	$ 4,000
2	July 1, 1971	3,600
3	January 1, 1973	2,400
4	July 1, 1973	2,000
Balance, January 1, 1974		$12,000

The Accumulated Depreciation for Trucks account, previously adjusted by a revenue agent to January 1, 1974, and entered in the ledger, had a balance on that date of $4,880, representing depreciation on the four trucks from the dates of purchase, based on a five-year life. No charges had been made to the accumulated account prior to January 1, 1974.

Transactions from January 1, 1974, to December 31, 1976 follow:

(1) Truck No. 1 was sold for $500 cash on January 2, 1974. The company debited Cash and credited Trucks, $500.

(2) Truck No. 3 was traded for truck No. 5 on January 2, 1975. The company paid the truck dealer in full by giving truck No. 3 and $760 cash. The cash market price of truck No. 5 was $2,100. The company debited Trucks and credited Cash, $760.

(3) On July 1, 1976, truck No. 4 was wrecked and was sold as junk for $50 cash. Inter, Inc., received $300 from the insurance company. The company debited Cash $350, credited Miscellaneous Income $50, and credited Trucks $300.

(4) Truck No. 6 was acquired new on July 1, 1974, for $6,000 cash, and was charged to the Truck account.

Entries for depreciation had been made each December 31 as follows: 1974, $2,400; 1975, $2,150; and 1976, $2,500.

Prepare work papers setting forth:

a)   The accumulated depreciation, by individual trucks, at January 1, 1974. Depreciation is to be calculated by the straight-line method, from the date of acquisition to the date of disposition.

b)   The correct depreciation, by individual trucks, for the year ended December 31, 1974, 1975, and 1976.

c)   A schedule of the trucks and proper accumulated depreciation for each truck as of December 31, 1976.

d)   All entries necessary to correct the company's records from January 1, 1974, to December 31, 1976.

e)   The effect on net income for 1974, 1975, and 1976, arising from depreciation adjustments and all other errors made by the Company in its truck accounting. The effect of income tax regulations on gain or loss on trades is to be taken into consideration. All trucks remaining at December 31, 1976, were in active use.

12

Intangible Assets

CLASSES OF INTANGIBLE ASSETS

Intangible assets represent exclusive privileges to a product, a process, or a location; they do not represent claims against others. The exclusive privilege may be granted by a government, as in the case of patents or copyrights; it may be granted by an owner, as exemplified by leaseholds or licenses or franchises, or it may be created, as sometimes exemplified by goodwill. An intangible asset that does not produce income is *worthless*. Therefore, an auditor must satisfy himself as to the carrying value of each intangible asset viewed from the point of its income-producing ability. Also, there must be satisfaction that intangible assets are reflected in the records in accordance with recognized principles of accounting and that amortization is in accordance with recognized principles of accounting. Normally, an auditor will find documentary evidence available for examination in connection with his examination of intangible assets.

Intangible assets commonly have been classified as—

1. Those with an existence limited by law, agreement, or the nature of the asset.
2. Those without a specified term of limited existence, accompanied by no indication of a limited life when they were acquired.
3. The excess of a parent company's investment in the capital stock of a subsidiary over its equity in the net assets of the subsidiary as shown by the latter's records at the date of acquisition—insofar as that excess would be treated as an intangible asset in the consolidated financial statements of the parent and the subsidiary. This type of asset may represent intangibles of 1 or 2, or be a combination of both.

Intangible assets with a limited existence include:

338

1. Patents.
2. Leaseholds.
3. Copyrights.
4. Fixed-term franchises.
5. Licenses.
6. Goodwill, if there is evidence of limited existence—and normally such evidence will come into existence.
7. Organization costs.

The cost of intangible assets of this class should be amortized systematically against income over the period benefited.

Intangible assets without clear evidence of limited existence at the time of development or acquisition include:

1. Trademarks and trade names—if they are continuously used.
2. Secret processes and formulas—if they continue to be *totally* secret (and this seldom occurs).
3. Perpetual franchises, if a contract is not broken, or if a governmental unit does not interfere.
4. Goodwill, if there is no evidence of limited existence (normally there is evidence of such limitation).

The preceding intangible asset classification and valuation are in accordance with *Accounting Research Bulletin No. 43*, chapter 5.

The cost of intangible assets of this class many times have been carried continuously unless it has become evident that they have become worthless, or unless it becomes evident that their existence has become limited. Normally existence is limited. In accordance with *Opinion No. 17* of the former Accounting Principles Board of the AICPA, *all* intangible assets should be amortized to expense over a period not to exceed 40 years. If totally worthless, the entire remaining cost should be charged to expense.

Recognized accounting principles are to the effect that any intangible asset originally should be stated at cost of acquisition. However, an auditor will encounter many instances in which other-than-cost figures are used to place intangible assets in the accounts.

AUDIT OBJECTIVES

In general, an auditor must verify the source, cost, appraisal figures (if used), and the amortization of intangible assets. More specifically, the objectives in examining intangible assets are as follows:

1. To determine that evidence is proper for authorization to acquire, sell, license, or charge off any intangible.
2. Determination of the valuation base used for each intangible asset.
3. Ascertainment of the propriety of amortization policies.

4. To determine that revenues from intangible assets are properly accounted for and properly controlled.
5. To determine the nature of contractural agreements, if any, that relate to intangible assets.
6. To determine that full disclosure exists in the financial statements for intangible assets and their amortization.

INTERNAL CONTROL OF INTANGIBLE ASSETS

Internal control of intangible assets involves the propriety of their original recording in the accounts, proper amortization, and proper retention in the accounts. Internal control may be important for certain intangible assets and of no particular significance for others. For example, in the examination of patents and any existing licensing contracts, it is important to study the system of internal control for the distribution of research and development expenses, and the control over revenues arising from the licensing contracts. In the verification of goodwill, the examination of internal control may be limited to ascertaining that charges and credits to the account are proper and were authorized by the board of directors or other appropriate body, and that they are in accordance with *Opinion Nos. 9* and *17* of the APB. Satisfactory standards of internal control are indicated in the internal control questionnaire for intangible assets in Illustration 12–1.

Illustration 12–1

INTERNAL CONTROL QUESTIONNAIRE Intangible Assets				
Company _____ Period Covered _____	Yes	No	Not Appli- cable	Remarks
1. Are all purchased intangibles properly recorded?	___	___	___	___
2. Are intangible assets originally priced at cost?	___	___	___	___
3. Are other-than-cost figures ever originally used?	___	___	___	___
4. Is the amortization policy proper?	___	___	___	___
5. Is the amortization policy consistent from year to year?	___	___	___	___
6. Are worthless intangibles written out of the accounts?	___	___	___	___
7. Are additions to and deductions from intangible assets properly authorized?	___	___	___	___
8. Are the opinions of the FASB and the SEC being followed?	___	___	___	___
9. Do accepted accounting principles govern the recording of expenditures for additions to intangible assets?	___	___	___	___
Prepared by _____ Date _____	Reviewed by _____ Date _____			

AUDIT OF INTANGIBLE ASSETS

Each intangible asset should be analyzed by starting with its audited balance as of the beginning of the year; add additional costs incurred during the year, subtract deductions and amortization, and conclude with the audited balance at the end of the year. Then underlying evidential papers for additions are examined and traced through the records to the ledger accounts. Evidences in support of deductions are treated in the same manner, followed by verification of the periodic amortization. Audit adjustments may be necessary, particularly after discussing with the client the remaining business usefulness of each intangible asset. See Illustration 12–2 for patents.

Underlying evidence of ownership is examined in order to establish validity, ownership, and privilege grant. The underlying evidence will

Illustration 12–2
WORK PAPER 26

		Initials	Date
MULTI-PRODUCTS, INCORPORATED	Prepared By	EF	2-25-77
Patents, December 31, 1976	Approved By	RW	2-27-77

Cost, January 2, 1970		54 760
Amortization, 6 years (1970-1975 inclusive)		20 760
Balance, December 31, 1975		34 000
January 3, 1976, cost of Patent No.4682741		4 120 ✓
		38 120
December 31, 1976, amortization per company		3 400
December 31, 1976, balance per general ledger		34 720
Less AJE 14, below		6 130
December 31, 1976, balance per audit		28 590
✓ Examined patent letters and invoices.		
By action of the board of directors,		
dated December 15, 1976, all patent costs		
are to be amortized by December 31, 1979,		
because it is believed that the useful life		
will not extend beyond that date. Therefore,		
the December 31, 1976, balance before		
amortization must be amortized over 1976,		
1977, 1978 and 1979 (four years).		
One quarter of $38,120	9 530	
Company amortization	3 400	
AJE 14	6 130	
AJE 14		
Cost of Sales (Patent Amortization		
Expense)	6 130	
Patents		6 130

include purchase contracts, patent letters, franchise grant contracts, copyright registrations, trademark registrations, formula registrations, leasehold contracts, organization cost evidences, correspondence, and other data. All necessary copies of contracts and other data become a part of the permanent file of the auditor.

The auditor must be certain that debits to intangible asset accounts are legitimate. Improper debits are exemplified by capitalizing a deficit in Retained Earnings, and by charging start-up expenses to Goodwill. There are many other illustrations. The Securities and Exchange Commission requests the opinion of the certifying accountant concerning the source and reasonableness of the valuations placed upon the intangible assets of a registrant.

The auditor's responsibilities for proper net carrying value of each intangible asset include the determination of proper amortization and the investigation of the income productivity of the asset. Verification must be made of the method and the correctness of amortization. Verification then must be made of all nonamortization credits to intangible asset accounts; these credits must be properly authorized, and the auditor must trace the offsetting debit. If it is determined that an intangible asset possesses no remaining useful value, it should be charged to expense.

Auditing procedures applicable to specific intangible assets are discussed on the following pages.

Patents

A patent is an exclusive privilege granted by a government. It gives the owner the right to manufacture or otherwise benefit from the results of an invention or a process. In the United States, patents are granted for a period of 17 years.

In examining patent accounts, the auditor should schedule each patent. The schedules should set forth a full description of the patent, the date acquired, and the cost. See Illustration 12–2. Each debit to the Patent account much be vouched, and debits for items other than direct patent costs must be *thoroughly* investigated and understood. Patent letters are examined; and if necessary, confirmations of the existence and validity of the patents may be obtained from the attorney for the owner.

If purchased, patents should be recorded at cost. When patents are developed by a company, (1) all development costs, experimental costs, patent fees, legal fees, and other costs necessary to obtain the patent may be charged to the Patent account; or (2) all of these costs may be charged to expense—which is a commonly followed practice in companies that are continually developing patents. At the time of developing and obtaining a patent, there is no knowledge of income-producing ability.

To appear as an asset, a patent should be income producing. Inactive and nonproductive patents should be eliminated. Consequently, an auditor must determine income productivity by examination of sales records, related expenses, and resultant net income from the sale of patented items.

Patent cost should be amortized over 17 years or useful life, whichever is shorter. Most patents do not enjoy a 17-year productive life. The auditor must critically analyze amortization policies for patents and discuss amortization policies with the client, viewed from the points of present income productivity and estimated future productive life. If the auditor is of the opinion that a company's amortization policy is proper, a statement to that effect may be placed in the audit report. If the auditor is of the opinion that the amortization policy is improper, a statement to that effect should be placed in the audit report, and the certification should be qualified, if necessary—and it probably will be necessary. Nonincome-producing patents should be written out of the accounts, by charges to expense.

Each debit in the Patent account should be related to the cost of that patent. Charges to a Patent account that are not allocable to that patent should be removed from the account.

Costs of lawsuits won in defending patent-infringement suits *may* properly be added to the cost of the patent. If an infringement suit is lost, the cost of defense and the remaining cost of the patent should be removed from the Patent account. The auditor should examine concluded litigation; he should inquire about contemplated litigation and, if necessary, report thereon.

If, after a patent has expired, income continues to result from the sale of the item formerly patented, the Patent account should *not* be restored; neither should a Goodwill account be set up because of the continuing revenue.

Leaseholds

A lease conveys the right to use property for the period of the contract. A lease differs from outright ownership because of the limitations placed upon the disposition and use of the leased property and because of the possibility of a limited period of use.

There are many types of leases, but for audit purposes leases may be divided into several types or classes: (a) those that represent only the right to use property for the period of the contract, (b) those that represent the right to use property for the period of the contract and then acquire the property at the termination of the contract or during the life of the contract, and (c) leveraged leases.

A lease contract of the first type will appear as an asset only if advance payments have been made, or if the original lessee capitalized his anticipated savings to be derived under a sublease—and this latter situation rarely occurs. This type of lease should be given full disclosure in the financial statements, or in footnotes, regarding the rights and obligations under the contract.

A lease contract of the second type includes the right to purchase the leased property; and if the purchase privilege is effective at the termination of the contract, the amount to be paid for acquisition normally is only a nominal amount. This type of lease (usually long term) has rapidly increased in popularity as a method of financing the acquisition of future property rights, and normally the intention of the lessee is to take title to the property at the termination of the lease. In such situations the total discounted amount of future rent payments (excluding payments to cover taxes and expenses other than depreciation) to be made by the lessee should appear as an asset because the lease permits the acquisition of future property rights and because the normal intent to purchase exists. The total amount owed under the lease should appear as a liability, properly divided between current and long term; the liability will be reduced as payments are made to the lessor. Thus, rental costs will not appear in the income statements of the lessee, but asset depreciation costs and interest costs will appear.

A lease transaction of the third type exists when the cost of the leased property is financed by long-term debt and would be recorded on the books of the lessor and lessee as an asset and a liability.

As yet there is no published uniformity of thought or practice regarding the capitalization of leases and their related liabilities within financial statements. The Securities and Exchange Commission (Rule 3–18[b]) requirements are as follows: "Where the rentals or obligations under long-term leases are material, there shall be shown the amounts of annual rentals under such leases with some indication of the periods for which they are payable, together with any important obligation assumed or guarantee made in connection therewith. If the rentals are conditional, state the minimum annual amounts."

In general, the SEC has interpreted the disclosure required by Rule 3–18 to apply to leases extending more than three years from the balance sheet date. The Commission does not permit the showing of leases as assets and liabilities in the balance sheets of registered companies; however, it does advocate the use of footnotes and will permit the showing of leases "short," that is, as memorandum figures within the balance sheet.

If leases and their related obligations are capitalized and shown in a balance sheet, either "short" or as a part of the total dollar amount of assets and liabilities, the presentation may be as shown at the top of page 345.

For additional information regarding the reporting of leases and sale-and-lease-back transactions in financial statements, the reader is referred to *Accounting Research Study No. 4*, and *Opinions Nos. 5, 7, and 31*,

Assets:
  Right to use leased building, at discounted amount of related
    rental obligations . . . . $_____
Current Liabilities:
  Current portion of lease obligation . . . . $_____
Long-Term Liabilities:
  Rental obligation under lease, discounted at __ percent, payable
    in semiannual installments of $___ , through December 1985,
    less $___ due within one year . . . . $_____

issued by the APB of the AICPA. (See Chapter 11 for present FASB thinking.)

In defining leases that should be capitalized, *Opinion No. 5* uses terms such as "material equity," "equivalent to installment purchases of property," which have not been interpreted with uniformity. The FASB intends to clarify these terms, specify the method of amortizing leased assets, and determine whether capitalization rules apply to short-term as well as long-term leases. *Opinion No. 7* provided that under certain circumstances, a lessor must treat a lease as a sale; but *Opinion No. 5* permits the lessee to treat the same lease as other than a purchase. Therefore, the lessee would not be required to capitalize the leased property on its balance sheet. It has been proposed that additional information regarding lease agreements would make financial statements more meaningful to the readers of such statements. The FASB is seeking to ascertain what type of information might be required to do this and how the data should be presented in the statements. Differing views have been expressed as to the elements to be used in the calculation of lease commitments. Among the controversial points are: the present value of rental payments versus the sum of rental payments; primary term of the lease as opposed to primary term plus all renewal terms; gross amount of rental payments or the net amount, after deducting real estate taxes, operating expenses, and other proper expenses; the interest rate to be used in the calculation.

Normally, under leases of the first type, a lessee assumes all costs except taxes and insurance. However, under leases of the second class and the "sale-and-lease-back" agreements popular today, a lessee commonly assumes *all* costs except mortgage indebtedness payments.

By reference to minutes of the board of directors or other appropriate body, an auditor should ascertain that proper authorization exists for entering into a lease agreement. Advance payments and the amortization of advance payments must be verified. The advance payments may, in accordance with the terms of the contract, be prorated over the life of the lease; or they may be applied to final rentals.

In examining lease contracts of any type, there should be obtained such data as names of parties; properties involved; terms of the contract; renewal clauses; cancellation clauses; advance deposit payments, if any; periodic rental; rent payment dates; and all provisions for insurance, taxes, and maintenance. The auditor may desire direct confirmation of these data from the property owner or a sublessor, if full data are not otherwise available to him.

All entries in leasehold accounts should be traced to the original records, and underlying evidences traced to the records. If a sublease exists, the auditor must verify the rental revenue from the sublessee.

Improvements to leased properties are fixed assets and should be depreciated over the life of the lease or the life of the improvement, whichever is shorter. If a lease contract contains a renewal clause, advance payments and improvement costs should be amortized over a period no longer than the original lease, because at the date of executing the original lease, there is no assurance that the lease will be renewed.

Copyrights

Copyrights are granted for 28 years and are renewable once. Most copyrighted items do not enjoy an income-producing life of 28 years. Therefore, the auditor must examine sales records of copyrighted items and compare gross and net income with the unamortized cost of the matching copyrights. The safest procedure is to charge copyright costs, in total, to a first production or a first printing.

When obtained originally from the government, copyrights are negligible in cost and should be charged to expense. If a copyright is purchased from a present owner, the auditor must verify cost and amortization, investigate obsolescence, and determine income productivity. If necessary, remaining costs should be written off.

If copyrights are placed in accounts at amounts in excess of cost, the auditor must investigate the offsetting credit, examine amortization policies, and disclose the other-than-cost basis in the financial statements.

Franchises

Franchises may be of limited life, or they may be perpetual. They may be irrevocable or revocable by the grantor. They may be obtained gratis, or for a periodic fee, or for a flat sum. Commissions regulating public utilities frequently specify the expenditures chargeable to the Franchise account and prescribe the method of amortization to be followed.

The auditor must read and understand each franchise in order to be familiar with the terms of the grant, including restrictions imposed, fees or rentals, specific contingencies, rate clauses, revocable features, and service and maintenance provisions. Data from the franchise become a part of the permanent file.

If acquired by purchase, the Franchise account is analyzed and verified for cost and for amortization. If there is no franchise cost, periodic rentals are compared with the contracted rentals. If a public-utility commission specifies the expenditures chargeable to the Franchise account and specifies the method of amortization, the auditor must examine the account to determine that all requirements are fulfilled. If revocable contract features might lead to cancellation, Franchise account costs should be amortized over a period not in excess of the legal life. Franchise accounts may be credited directly for amortization, or an accumulation for amortization may be established.

Licenses

License or royalty contracts commonly are granted under patents and copyrights. If a licensee paid a flat sum to obtain a license, that cost should be amortized over the life of the license or the period of anticipated income production, whichever is shorter.

In addition to determining the proper costs of licenses and the proper amortization of those costs, the auditor must verify the licensee's payments to the grantor, if payments are on the basis of production or sales.

Organization Costs

Organization costs include legal and accounting fees for incorporation, state incorporation charges, security registration and listing fees, recording fees, amounts paid to promoters, and capital stock sales commissions. Organization costs terminate when the corporation is ready to begin business. Organization costs may be amortized to income for federal income tax purposes, if incurred after August 16, 1954; the minimum amortization period is 60 months.

The auditor must determine that charges to the Organization Cost account represent only items applicable to *original* organization. The account should be analyzed, and all charges thereto should be traced to approved minutes of the meetings of directors or of stockholders. The propriety and amount correctness of all charges must be verified. The method of amortization must be understood. When cash disbursements are charged to the account, those charges must be evidentially supported by invoices and paid checks.

Some people still view the Organization Cost account as a nonamortizable permanent "asset." Most accountants are of the opinion that organization costs should be amortized as rapidly as possible.

Reorganization Costs. Capital structure reorganization costs, including capital stock issuance underwriting costs incurred after original incorporation, may be treated as deferred charges—if the cost is material, if future periods are to be benefited, and if the current period cannot reasonably absorb the charge. Otherwise, these costs should be charged against current-period income. At the time of reorganization, any remaining balances in an original Organization Cost account should be charged off, because the effect of a reorganization is to afford a fresh start.

The auditor should verify capital structure reorganization costs and examine the underwriting contracts. He also must examine entries relating to stock issues, compare remittance statements received from underwriters with cash receipts records, and verify cash disbursements.

Trademarks and Trade Names

A trademark normally applies to a product or a brand name. A trade name applies to a business. Normally, trademarks are registered with the U.S. Patent Office, although they are valid under common law if they remain in continual use. The U.S. Patent Office registration period is 30 years for both trademarks and trade names—renewable indefinitely for similar periods.

Trademarks and trade names should be carried at cost and need not necessarily be amortized if they remain in continual use. If the intention is to discontinue use, the cost should be amortized. If discarded, all remaining costs should be written from the accounts. Income production from trademarks and trade names never should be capitalized under a goodwill—or any other intangible asset—account.

In auditing trademark accounts, registration letters are examined. The auditor should then verify charges and credits to the accounts. If the items are carried above cost, the auditor should fully disclose the situation in the company's financial statements.

Secret Processes and Formulas

These items, if purchased, should be carried at cost, properly amortized. Additional profits should not be capitalized. The auditor must confer with the client, not only to determine ownership but also to determine security. If client-developed, the items preferably should be charged to expenses.

Goodwill

Fortunately, arbitrary goodwill amounts seldom appear in financial statements today. Goodwill is the least liquid of all assets; it cannot independently be disposed of by sale or any distribution method. In accordance with recognized principles of accounting, goodwill should be placed in the accounts only when it is purchased, and at the price paid for it. The price paid may be represented by the price paid which is in excess of the purchase price over the net capital of an acquired company. Or the price paid may be represented by the issuance of capital stock in excess of net capital, particularly when two or more companies merge. In a merger, a goodwill account may be created due to differences in the earning power of the companies entering the merger. The use of no-par-value stock in such instances avoids the creation of a Goodwill account.

In the audit of goodwill, it is necessary to ascertain how the amount of the Goodwill account was determined. To accomplish this objective, the auditor should (1) examine the minutes of meetings of the board of directors, (2) examine agreements to purchase other business organizations, (3) examine cash disbursements records, and (4) examine the allocation of lump-sum purchases of assets when goodwill may be involved. The audit report should explain the derivation of goodwill amounts; should contain a description of the origin of the goodwill; and should set forth amortization policies, if any.

Market prices of fixed assets fluctuate. Goodwill fluctuates in value due to fluctuations in sales and in net income. If goodwill originally was established by purchasing it and recording it at cost, it should be amortized. If goodwill no longer is valuable as an asset, it should be written off the records—either by the establishment of a reasonable amortization policy or by a total charge to expense. The reasons for a total immediate elimination should be disclosed in financial statement footnotes and in the audit report.

The American Institute of Certified Public Accountants in its *Accounting Research Study No. 10*, entitled "Accounting for Goodwill," provided some specific recommendations. In August 1970 the Accounting Principles Board of the AICPA issued *Opinion No. 17*, entitled *Intangible Assets*, which drastically altered *Accounting Research Study No. 10*. The following excerpts are from *Opinion No. 17*.

The conclusions of this *Opinion* modify previous views of the Board and its predecessor, the Committee on Accounting Procedure. This *Opinion* therefore supersedes the following Accounting Research Bulletin (*No. 43*, Chapter 5) and *Opinion No. 46* of the Accounting Principles Board:

The Board concludes that a company should record as assets the costs of intangible assets acquired from others, including goodwill acquired in a business combination. A company should record as expenses the costs to develop intangible assets which are not specifically identifiable. The Board also concludes that the cost of each type of intangible asset should be amortized by systematic charges to income over the period estimated to be benefited. The period of amortization should not, however, exceed 40 years.

The cost of an intangible asset, including goodwill acquired in a business combination, may not be written off as a lump sum to capital surplus or to retained earnings nor be reduced to a nominal amount at or immediately after acquisition (ARB No. 43, Chapter 5 and APB Opinion No. 9).

The cost of goodwill and similar intangible assets is therefore essentially the same as the cost of land, buildings, or equipment under historical-cost based accounting. Deducing the cost of an asset from stockholders' equity (either retained earnings or capital in excess of par or stated value) at the date incurred does not match costs with revenue.

Intangible assets acquired singly should be recorded at cost at date of acquisition. Cost is measured by the amount of cash disbursed, the fair value of other assets distributed, the present value of amounts to be paid for liabilities incurred, or the fair value of consideration received for stock issued as described in paragraph 67 of APB Opinion No. 16.

Intangible assets acquired as part of a group of assets or as part of an acquired company should also be recorded at cost at date of acquisition. Cost is measured differently for specifically identifiable intangible assets and those lacking specific identification. The cost of identifiable intangible assets is an assigned part of the total cost of the group of assets or enterprise acquired, normally based on the fair values of the individual assets. The cost of unidentifiable intangible assets is measured by the difference between the cost of the group of assets or enterprise acquired and the sum of the assigned costs of individual tangible and identifiable intangible assets acquired less liabilities assumed. Cost should be assigned to all specifically identifiable intangible assets; cost of identifiable assets should not be included in goodwill. Principles and procedures of determining cost of assets acquired, including intangible assets, are discussed in detail in paragraphs 66 to 89 of APB Opinion No. 16, "Business Combinations."

The Board concludes that the straight-line methods of amortization—equal annual amounts—should be applied unless a company demonstrates that another systematic method is more appropriate. The financial statements should disclose the method and period of amortization. Amortization of acquired goodwill and of other acquired intangible assets not deductible in computing income taxes payable does not create a timing difference, and allocation of income taxes is inappropriate.

A company should evaluate the periods of amortization continually to determine whether later events and circumstances warrant revised estimates of useful lives. If estimates are changed, the unamortized cost should be allocated to the increased or reduced number of remaining periods in the revised useful life but not to exceed 40 years after acquisition. Estimation of value and future benefits of an intangible asset may indicate that the unamortized cost should be reduced significantly by a deduction in determining net income (APB Opinion No. 9, paragraph 21). However a single loss year or even a few loss years together do not necessarily justify an extraordinary charge to income for all or a large part of the unamortized cost of intangible assets. The reason for an extraordinary deduction should be disclosed.

FINANCIAL STATEMENT CONSIDERATIONS

Financial statement considerations have been enumerated in preceding sections of this chapter. To summarize: Intangible assets should be separately classified in the balance sheet. The basis of valuation should be fully disclosed. The methods of amortization should be set forth in the financial statements and explained in the audit report.

QUESTIONS

1. What must an auditor verify when performing an audit of intangible assets?

2. Why is the audit of intangible assets important to the entire audit?

3. How may intangible assets be classified?

4. In accordance with recognized principles of accounting, how should intangible assets be valued?

5. What is involved in the internal control of intangible assets?

6. What underlying evidence should an auditor require in order to establish the validity, ownership, and privilege grants of intangible assets?

7. In accounting for goodwill, what are the specific recommendations of the AICPA that must be adhered to?

8. The Hopeful Company develops and carries out an extensive and costly advertising campaign on behalf of new products and charges the amount above its average yearly expense to goodwill. Do you approve?

9. When acquiring a business, what should be considered in determining the existence of goodwill?

10. Prepare an internal control questionnaire for patents for a large patent-holding company. Do not follow the internal control questionnaire for intangible assets presented in the text.

11. A obtained a patent on February 1, 1973, and immediately assigned it to B. The contract provided that B would pay A a royalty of $2 for each unit produced in accordance with the A patent and installed in B machinery delivered to any point outside the plant of B.

    On February 1, 1973, B paid A $1,000 in advance royalties. Thereafter, no royalty payments or statements of royalties earned were received by A. The efforts of A to obtain information resulted in a statement by B that the $1,000 advance was in excess of the royalties earned.

    In 1976, A asks you to determine the facts. Outline a program to ascertain the amount of the royalty due or overpaid to A under his contract with B, assuming that the company granted you access to all records.

12. During the course of a periodic audit of a beverage manufacturer you find a new account in the general ledger with the title "Formulas and Processes." This account has a debit balance of $100,000, supported by the following entry:

    Formulas and Processes 100,000
        Common Stock 100,000
    To record issuance of stock at par to John Doe for
    secret formulas and processes which are not patentable.

    a) Describe the procedures you would follow in connection with this new account.

    b) If the only information which you could obtain was to the effect that the formula was in the safe-deposit box, that the manufacturing process was broken up so that the employees could not put the formula together in proper processes and proportions without the supervision of the factory manager, and that the $100,000 represented the value of the stock at the market, which was also par, would you be willing to issue an unqualified opinion?

13. After a newly organized corporation has started operations, may any charges be made to the Organization Cost account? Explain your answer.

14. a) The Copyrights account of a publishing company has a debit balance of $40,000. What would be your procedure in connection with the audit of this item?

    b) In your opinion, when should copyrights appear as assets?

15. a) If you were auditing the records of a privately owned public utility, to what would you devote particular attention when you were investigating the Franchise account and the franchises?

    b) You were auditing the records of a local public utility for the first time. During the inspection of the franchise, you noticed a clause whereby the grantor municipality may revoke the franchise at its option. What factors would guide you in arriving at your decision as to the correct amount of periodic amortization, assuming that a lump sum had been paid for the franchise?

16. A client incurred material expenses in obtaining a trademark. The client requests your advice as to whether (a) the trademark cost should be amortized over a period of years, (b) the cost should be permanently capitalized, or (c) the cost should be charged to expense at incurrence. What advice would you offer, and why?

PROBLEMS

1. The major cost of processing beans by Lima, Inc., is the cooking time of 38 mintues. As competition increased, the company carried on continuous research, over the past five years, in an attempt to improve processing of this product. Since no improvement was developed during this period, costs incurred were periodically charged to cost of sales. Near the end of the fifth year, the company developed a blanching and sharp-freezing process which was patentable.

   The board of directors of the company had various suggestions as to how this patentable cost should be recognized on its financial statements. The suggestions follow:

   a) The write-off of the research costs had resulted in material misstatements of incomes, retained earnings, and restriction of dividends over the past five years.

   b) If the "cost" of the new patent is not correctly stated on the balance sheet, a valuable revenue-producing asset will be concealed and financial position will be misstated.

   c) Failure to set up the "cost" of the new patent will cause the incorrect matching of costs and revenues.

   You, the auditor, are to prepare an analysis of these proposals to be presented to the board of directors.

2. Trout, Inc., developed a new fishing reel that was patented. The following costs were incurred:

Materials and supplies	\$ 3,000
Salaries of persons working on reel	12,000
Overhead allocation, approved by you, the auditor	4,400
Market research incurred in determining desirable	
features which were built into the reel	2,700

The patent was granted on January 2, 1972. Due to its advanced design, management believes the beneficial life of the asset will be 17 years.

During the latter part of 1975, the Company incurred legal fees in the amount of \$4,200 in successfully protecting the patent.

On February 2, 1974, the company purchased a patent on a spinning rod for \$18,000. The patent had been granted one month earlier. However, due to changing styles, management expects an improved rod to be developed within six years.

a) Prepare the journal entries, for each patent, through 1976.

b) Briefly explain your reason for the entries.

3. You are asked to prepare goodwill computations from the following data and listed approaches:

Budgeted average annual earnings over the next	
five years	\$ 40,000
Budgeted average future value of net tangible	
assets over the next five years	300,000

Prepare calculations under each of the following assumed conditions:

a)   Goodwill is to be equal to earnings capitalized at 10 percent over budgeted average of net tangible assets.

b)   Goodwill will be equal to excess earnings capitalized at 20 percent; normal earnings rate for the industry, 10 percent.

c)   Goodwill will be equal to five years of excess earnings, normal earnings rate for the industry is 10 percent.

4. An analysis of a Patent account of a company is as follows:

Date	Explanation	Debits	Credits
Jan. 2, 1972	Basic patent cost	50,000	
Dec. 31, 1972	Patent cost	20,000	
Dec. 31, 1973	Patent cost	18,000	
Dec. 31, 1974	Patent cost	16,000	
Dec. 31, 1975	Patent cost	28,000	
Dec. 31, 1976	Patent cost	30,000	
		162.000	

An analysis of the Profit and Loss account shows net income transferred to Retained Earnings at the close of each of the following years:

1972	\$ 63,000
1973	81,000
1974	99,000
1975	117,000
1976	135,000
	\$495,000

No amortization has been taken on the Patent account. All expenditures since January 2, 1972, have been in connection with the basic patent.

The sales manager receives a salary of $20,000 per year plus a 10 percent commission on net income prior to the commission but after the salary.

a) Prepare audit work papers for the adjustment of the Patent account so that it will be completely amortized by December 31, 1981.

b) Prepare audit work papers for the adjustment of the annual net income so that the sales manager will be credited with a commission of 30 percent for all years, instead of his salary and commission just indicated. In the work papers, show the adjusted net income for each of the ten years after patent amortization and after the new arrangement for the sales manager.

5. Since your prior audit of New Parts, Inc., a manufacturer of machinery, which has a calendar-year closing, the company has undertaken a program of leasing to its customers machines which it manufactures.

The client has recorded the leased machines in a separate ledger, and the client's employees provide you with the following facts in regard to the leased machine program:

(1) Term of lease—ten years.

(2) Rental due—semiannual installments in advance.

(3) Expense—lessee to pay all taxes levied, freight, and handling charges.

(4) Lessee may terminate lease at end of fifth year or any years thereafter during the term of the lease by giving lessor proper notice.

(5) Lessee agrees to exercise proper care and repair of the machines.

(6) Lessee may elect to purchase machine at end of any year at the following prices: First year, 90 percent of list price; second year, 80 percent of list price; third year, 70 percent of list price; and so forth.

(7) Five machines were leased during the current year.

The company uses the straight-line method of depreciation.

a) Prepare an audit program to cover adequately this portion of the assets of the company and the related income and expense accounts.

b) State your balance sheet treatment of the asset.

c) Describe your recommended treatment of the rental income.

(AICPA, adapted)

6. The Blair Company was incorporated January 3, 1975. The corporation's financial statements for its first year's operations were not examined by a CPA. You have been engaged to examine the financial statements for the year ended December 31, 1976, and your examination is substantially completed. The corporation's trial balance appears at the top of the following page.

BLAIR COMPANY
Trial Balance
December 31, 1976

	Debit	Credit
Cash	$ 11,000	
Accounts receivable	42,500	
Provision for doubtful accounts		$ 500
Inventories	38,500	
Machinery	75,000	
Equipment	29,000	
Accumulated depreciation		10,000
Patents	85,000	
Leasehold improvements	26,000	
Prepaid expenses	10,500	
Organization expenses	29,000	
Goodwill	24,000	
License No. 1	50,000	
License No. 2	49,000	
Accounts payable		147,500
Deferred credits		12,500
Capital stock		300,000
Retained earnings, January 1, 1976	27,000	
Sales		668,500
Cost of goods sold	454,000	
Selling and general expenses	173,000	
Interest expense	3,500	
Extraordinary losses	12,000	
Totals	$1,139,000	$1,139,000

The following information relates to accounts which may require adjustment:

(1)   Patents for Blair's manufacturing process were acquired January 2, 1976, at a cost of $68,000. An additional $17,000 was spent in December 1976 to improve machinery covered by the patents and charged to the Patents account. Depreciation on fixed assets has been properly recorded for 1976, in accordance with Blair's practice, which provides a full year's depreciation for property on hand June 30 and no depreciation otherwise. Blair uses the straight-line method for all depreciation and amortization.

(2)   On January 3, 1975, Blair purchased two licenses, which were then believed to have unlimited useful lives. The balance in the License No. 1 account includes its purchase price of $48,000 and expenses of $2,000 related to the acquisition. The balance in the License No. 2 account includes its $48,000 purchase price and $2,000 in acquisition expenses, but it has been reduced by a credit of $1,000 for the advance collection of 1975 revenue from the license.

In December, 1975 an explosion caused a permanent 60 percent reduction in the expected revenue-producing value of License No. 1; and in January 1977 a flood caused additional damage which rendered the license worthless.

A study of License No. 2 made by Blair in January 1976 revealed that its estimated remaining life expectancy was only ten years as of January 1, 1976.

(3)   The balance in the Goodwill account includes (*a*) $8,000 paid December 30, 1975, for an advertising program which it is estimated will assist in increasing sales over a period of four years following the disbursement; and (*b*) legal expenses of $16,000 incurred for incorporation on January 3, 1975.

(4)   The Leasehold Improvements account includes (*a*) the $15,000 cost of improvements with a total estimated useful life of 12 years which Blair, as tenant, made to leased premises in January 1975, (*b*) movable assembly line equipment costing $8,500, which was installed in the leased premises in December 1976, and (*c*) real estate taxes of $2,500 paid by Blair in 1976, which under the terms of the lease should have been paid by the landlord. Blair paid its rent in full during 1976. A ten-year nonrenewable lease was signed January 3, 1975, for the leased building which Blair used in manufacturing operations.

(5)   The balance in the Organization Expenses account properly includes costs incurred during the organizational period. The corporation has exercised its option to amortize organization costs over a 60-month period for federal income tax purposes and wishes to amortize these costs for accounting purposes.

Prepare a work sheet to adjust accounts which require adjustment. Also prepare formal adjusting entries.

A separate account should be used for the accumulation of each type of amortization and for each prior period adjustment.

(AICPA, adapted)

13

Current Liabilities and
Related Costs and Expenses

GENERAL CONSIDERATIONS

Current liabilities are those which are to be liquidated within the operating cycle of the business—commonly considered to be not longer than one year. The liquidation of current liabilities ordinarily requires the use of current assets.

An auditor must obtain satisfactory evidence that current liabilities are properly recorded, that unrecorded liabilities do not exist, that revenues received in advance are properly allocable to future periods, and that their amortization is proper. The extent and nature of contingencies must be ascertained; proper disclosure of their existence must be made in accordance with the materiality of the items.

If liabilities are misstated, such misstatement probably will be on the overstated side—unless a company wishes to show a better financial condition than is proper, in which case liabilities will be understated. Therefore, an auditor must ascertain not only that all recorded liabilities are correct but also that all liabilities are recorded which should be included in the financial statements.

AUDIT OBJECTIVES

The objectives in examining current liabilities are (1) to evaluate the system of internal control over the liabilities, (2) to determine the propriety of their processing and payment, (3) to obtain satisfactory evidence that all authorized current liabilities have been properly recorded as of a balance-sheet date, and (4) to properly present the current liabilities in the balance sheet.

INTERNAL CONTROL OF CURRENT LIABILITIES

Internal control over liabilities was set forth in Chapter 5, in connection with original record examination. Summarized, internal control over current liabilities and related asset acquisitions and expense incurrences involves the points of—

1. Ascertaining proper authorization for the creation of the liabilities.
2. Ascertaining that unauthorized liabilities are not recorded and paid.
3. Ascertaining that all proper liabilities are recorded promptly.
4. Ascertaining that proper authorization exists for liability liquidation.
5. Ascertaining that the period-end cutoff is proper.

Entries in accounts payable records should be properly authorized by an internal system of requisition, purchase, receiving, purchase order and invoice approval, approval for payment, and payment.

Notes payable should be prenumbered by the printer. They should be controlled in order to prevent unauthorized use. Paid notes should be marked "Paid" and properly mutilated to prevent reuse. Persons maintaining notes payable records should be divorced from personnel who prepare and sign notes, and from persons who accept cash. Credits to Notes Payable should be supported by properly recorded minutes of the board of directors or a properly designated committee.

Accrued expenses should be approved by properly authorized personnel because the accrued items later will be liquidated in cash.

Entries for contingencies must be properly approved, and proper records must be maintained for contingencies—such as notes receivable discounted, accounts receivable assigned, product guarantees—all of which may revert to the category of real liabilities.

Satisfactory standards of internal control of current liabilities and contingencies are indicated in the questionnaire in Illustration 13–1.

Management Reports

Periodic internally prepared reports for all current liabilities should be prepared so that top management may be cognizant of current liabilities, the changes therein from period to period, the cost of borrowing, and future cash requirements. Also, if a dishonest employee had thoughts of issuing an unauthorized account or note payable, he will reconsider his intentions if he realizes that management reviews current liabilities.

For accounts payable, these internally prepared reports may set forth the accounts payable balance according to the preceding report, plus the payables added and minus the payables liquidated, the available discounts lost, concluding with the current accounts payable balance.

For notes payable, reports may be arranged in sections, as follows: (1) the detail of outstanding notes as of the preceding report; (2) payments of principal and interest made in the current period; (3) the detail of notes issued (or renewed) in the current period; (4) the detail of notes outstanding at the close of the current report data; and (5) the accrued and/or prepaid interest thereon.

AUDIT OF CURRENT LIABILITIES

Accounts Payable

The extent of testing the accuracy of accounts payable is dependent upon the reliance on the system of internal control. If internal control over

Illustration 13–1

INTERNAL CONTROL QUESTIONNAIRE
Accounts Payable

	Yes	No	Not Appli-cable	Remarks

Company _____
Period Covered _____

1. Is there a proper system of requisitioning, purchase order placement and approval, receiving, invoice approval, and approval for payment?
2. Are subsidiary accounts payable records (or unpaid vouchers) reconciled with the controlling account at frequent intervals?
3. Are vendors' invoices verified for accuracy prior to entry?
4. Are vendors' statements compared with recorded accounts payable?
5. Are accounts payable adjustments properly approved?
6. Are debit balances in Accounts Payable properly reviewed and followed?
7. Is there a procedure whereby invoices are paid within the discount period?

Notes Payable

1. Are note transactions controlled to prevent unauthorized borrowings?
2. Does the board of directors or a committee authorize borrowing on notes?
3. Do the records of the board or appropriate committee specify the institutions from which money may be borrowed?
4. Do the records of the board or appropriate committee designate the officers authorized to sign notes?
5. Are unissued notes properly safeguarded?
6. Are notes payable recorded in a note register or other organized record which shows:
   a) The amount of the note?
   b) Maturity date?
   c) Interest dates?
   d) Principal payments?
   e) Interest payments?
7. Is the person who maintains the note register authorized to sign notes or checks?

Illustration 13–1—Continued

INTERNAL CONTROL QUESTIONNAIRE
Notes Payable

Company_____ Period Covered_____	Yes	No	Not Appli- cable	Remarks

8. Are proper records maintained for collateral pledged as loan security?
9. Does the client promptly meet its obligations at maturity?
10. Are detailed note records regularly reconciled with the control account?
11. Are paid notes properly canceled and preserved?
12. Are short-term obligations expected to be refinanced?

Revenues Received in Advance

1. Are all cash receipts entered when received?
2. Are all coupons, tickets, merchandise orders, etc., serially numbered and properly controlled?
3. Are used items in Question 2 properly canceled?
4. Is there adequate review of the transfer of deferred credits to proper revenue accounts?
5. Are there escrow accounts?

Contingencies

1. Does the client properly record possible liability for:
   a) Notes receivable discounted?
   b) Accounts receivable assigned?
   c) Accommodation endorsements?
   d) Product guarantees?
   e) Contract guarantees?
   f) Losses arising from sale and purchase contracts?
2. Do pending lawsuits exist?
3. If the answer to Question 2 is "yes," is proper provision made therefor, if necessary?
4. Are purchase contracts reasonable?
5. Do lease agreements contain stipulated loss values?

Prepared by_____   Reviewed by_____
Date_____   Date_____

accounts payable is satisfactory and if the number of accounts payable is large, a test of the accuracy of not more than 10 percent of the items normally is adequate. Liabilities unrecorded at the end of the period—but properly includable—must be brought into the records. Liabilities applicable to the subsequent period must not appear as such at the balance sheet date.

Work papers for accounts payable may take a variety of forms, one of which is shown in Illustration 13–2. In the work papers, trade and nontrade accounts payable must be separated and separately totaled for proper presentation in the balance sheet. The totals of the accounts pay-

Illustration 13–2
WORK PAPER 27

MULTI-PRODUCTS, INCORPORATED
Trade Accounts Payable
December 31, 1976

	Initials	Date
Prepared By	PM	2-12-77
Approved By	RN	2-14-77

Company	Balance	Not Due	Past Due	Remarks
A	33362 ✓	33362		
B	11352 ✓	11352		
C	9510 ✓	9100	410	In dispute
D	3180 ✓	3180		
E	7856 ✓	7856		
F	4492 ✓		4 492	Lawsuit:
				defective
	69752 ⊙	64850	4 902	goods
AJE 12: Unrecorded invoice				
	5000	5000		
Audit balance, December 31, 1976	74752 *	69850	4 902	

* To balance sheet

✓ Confirmed.
⊙ Agrees with general ledger
   Examined receiving records for the last 7 days of 1976.
   Cash disbursements for 1976 were examined for 1977 purchases.
   Voucher record of 1977 was examined for 1976 purchases.
   Unpaid items (above) compared with invoices and receiving records.
   All accounts payable are trade items.

AJE 12

Raw Material Inventory			5 000	
Trade Accounts Payable				5 000
Unrecorded invoice.				

able, by classes, as shown in the work papers are compared with the corresponding controlling account balances. If discrepancies exist, a search must be made for the errors. If the controlling account balance and the sum of the subsidiary account balances are in agreement, errors still may exist. The controlling account balance should be proved by tracing postings to the account and by extracting the account balance.

Internal company vouchers must be compared with original invoices received from vendors. The accuracy of the tested invoices must be examined for name, date, quantity, prices, extensions, footings, totals, approval, and mutilation—if paid. The invoices and their corresponding internal company vouchers then are traced to the original medium of recording. This examination should not exceed 10 percent of the invoices, unless this sample proves to be inadequate. If differences exist between invoices and amounts entered in accounts payable, such differences must be investigated; and the auditor must be satisfied with the explanation of the difference, or the accounts must be adjusted.

Debit entries in Accounts Payable arise from cash disbursements records or from returns and allowances records; the debits from all sources should be traced to the accounts payable for not more than 10 percent of the debits. If checks have been prepared—but not mailed—and entered as debits to Accounts Payable and credits to Cash, the auditor should reverse the entry in order to show a proper balance-sheet date position for cash and for accounts payable.

Month-end statements received from creditors should be compared with accounts payable balances in order to assist in the determination of unrecorded liabilities.

Accounts payable balances should be confirmed. The confirmation test-request should include active accounts, plus all accounts payable with debit balances, old balances, questionable items, items not readily understood, and in all cases where internal control is not satisfactory. Differences between confirmed amounts and accounts payable balances must be reconciled. If vendors render periodic statements and if the auditor can open these statements as they are received, it may not be necessary to request confirmations because the auditor has obtained direct evidence.

If long past-due accounts payable balances exist, an examination into the cause of nonpayment should be made. Unpaid balances may be the result of disputes, in the final determination of which the auditor may assist; or they may be the result of improper accounting, or of improper cash forecasting. If past-due accounts payable bear interest, the auditor should accrue the interest and direct the client's attention to the matter.

The auditor must search for unrecorded liabilities because they must be revealed. To accomplish this, invoices and receiving records should be compared for several days prior to the end of the period in order to determine that all liabilities are properly included for the period under examination. Invoices on hand at the end of the period but not entered as credits to Accounts Payable must be examined, and audit adjustments prepared if they should have been entered. To determine if unentered invoices should be recorded, the auditor must compare the invoices with purchase orders, receiving records, and inventory records. If the invoices should *not* be entered in the period under examination, the items purchased should *not* be included in inventory. If purchased items have been received toward the close of the period and if the invoices have not been received, a liability exists as of the close of the period.

Also, in his search for unrecorded liabilities, the auditor will examine entries for the new year to determine that none of them belong in the period under audit. Purchase records, receiving records, files of paid and unpaid invoices, and cash disbursements records are examined for from seven to ten days of the subsequent period to determine the period of proper inclusion as liabilities. The longer the time interval between the end of the accounting period and the examination of the liabilities, the better are the chances of determining that all liabilities were recorded as of the end of the period. Failure to include liabilities in the proper period may be intentional or unintentional—but in all cases the preceding examination must be made. The examination is accomplished by tracing the cash disbursements to the original invoice data and judging the period applicability of the invoice. If an item included as a credit to a liability in the new period should have appeared in the prior period, adjustments must be made. As a result of his adjustments, the auditor must exercise care to ascertain that an item is not included as a liability in both the period under examination and the subsequent period. Also, credit memorandum entries should be traced to the proper period of credit. When examining invoices, their distribution to proper accounts should be scrutinized.

As indicated in Chapter 5, cash discounts should be tested for accuracy of computation and for accuracy of recording in order to detect possible fraud by discount manipulation. If available discounts are not being taken, the attention of the client should be called to the situation, together with an indication of the dollar amount of the discounts lost.

If merchandise has been *received* on a consigned basis, consignment contracts and accounting records are examined to determine the existence of unrecorded liabilities for consigned goods already sold. Confirmation requests should be sent to all consignors, and the replies should be reconciled with the consigned goods sold and the consigned goods inventory.

Notes Payable

Schedules for notes payable appear in Illustrations 13–3 and 13–4, including interest expense, and interest prepaid and accrued. Normally, interest computations are placed in the work papers for the related liability. If an internal auditor has prepared a schedule similar to Illustration 13–4, the independent auditor must prove the accuracy of the schedule or adequately test items therein. The general ledger controlling account balance must be proved by extracting the balance. The notes payable totals according to the subsidiary schedule are compared with the balance of the controlling account. If the two amounts do not agree, the following search should be made:

1. Look for postings to an incorrect controlling account.
2. Examine the note stubs, the duplicate copies of notes, or the other evidence of unentered partial payments.
3. Investigate entry correctness when notes receivable are discounted.
4. Examine the correctness of entries made when notes and interest are paid at maturity.

Illustration 13–3
WORK PAPER 28

	Initials	Date
Prepared By	C F	2-14-77
Approved By	R W	2-16-77

MULTI-PRODUCTS, INCORPORATED
Notes Payable, Bank, December 31, 1976

Balance, per client and audit, December 31, 1976   40 000 ✓∧

Demand note, $40,000
Note dated November 2, 1976
Interest rate 4½ percent

Accrued interest: $40,000 x 0.045 x $\frac{60}{360}$ = $300

✓ Confirmed.
∧ Examined authorization of board of directors.

Authorizations for the issuance of notes must be examined and reconciled with the notes issued for the period under examination. All notes issued during the period must be accounted for in order to detect the possibility of an unrecorded liability. Only serially prenumbered notes should be used. If notes are issued to client personnel, the auditor should ascertain the payment arrangements. Entries for notes issued for borrowing money must be traced to the cash receipts records. Credit entries for all other notes payable should be traced to the general journal, invoice register, note register, or other medium. Debits to Notes Payable are vouched by tracing the entries to the cash disbursements records and paid checks, or to other media—such as the general journal if a note is renewed. Paid notes should be voided to prevent reuse. The auditor should compare signatures on paid notes with the signatures of client personnel authorized to issue notes.

An auditor must inquire into and confirm collateral given as note security. The notes payable and accompanying collateral should be confirmed directly to the auditor. See Illustration 13–5. Notes payable to depository banks will be confirmed when bank balances are confirmed. See also Illustration 5–3. Confirmation replies should be watched for subordination of indebtedness.

Records must be examined for note renewals because, if notes are continuously renewed, (1) evidence of no intention to pay may exist, or (2) there may be an indication of forgiveness or indebtedness. The auditor should trace the history of renewed notes and, if necessary, render full disclosure of material situations in the audit report.

Notes paid during the period are examined for authenticity of signatures, proper voidance, and the correlation of issuance dates on the paid notes and in the financial records. If paid notes are not properly voided, the auditor must be certain that these notes are not a part of the ending balance of notes payable, even though entries have been made charging Notes Payable and crediting Cash.

Interest—expense, prepaid, and accrued—must be verified and tied up with the corresponding general-ledger accounts. When examining interest accounts, determination should be made (1) that the liability upon which the interest was paid was properly recorded and (2) that the interest was promptly paid.

After the end of the balance-sheet date and prior to closing the engagement, the auditor should compare note and interest payments with notes open at the end of the period in order to assist in detecting unrecorded liabilities.

It is also the responsibility of the auditor to accurately determine the client's intent as it relates to the renewal of notes classified as current liabilities. *Statement of Financial Accounting Standards No. 6,* issued by the FASB, states that if a client intends to refinance the obligation on a long-term basis and there is evidence that the client has the ability to consummate the refinancing, the amount so determined shall be shown as a long-term debt.

Accrued Expenses

Because all liabilities should be reflected in the financial statements, the audit of accrued expenses is important. However, unwarranted time should not be devoted to minutely small items of this type of liability which have no appreciable effect upon the financial statements. Good judgment must be exercised in all instances.

The audit procedures for each accrued expense are in some manner dependent upon the nature of each item. One effective method of determining expense accruals is to analyze the related expense accounts for the period of examination. Also, various original documents are examined for information concerning accruals. These original documents include minutes of directors and/or committees, patent licenses, salary and profit-sharing agreements, contracts, notes payable data, mortgages, trust indentures, and others. Client records of the subsequent period should be examined to determine if any items paid in that subsequent period were subject to accrual—but not accrued—at the end of the period under examination.

Accrued Salaries, Wages, and Commissions. If the fiscal closing date does not coincide with the end of a payroll period, there will be accruals of employees' earnings. These accruals are made from the payroll records. Accruals of commissions are made from source data, such as period-end

Illustration 13–4

THE BLANK COMPANY
Notes Payable Schedule, December 31, 1976

Note No.	Name of Payee	Date of Note	Maturity Date	Amount of Note	Unpaid 12-31-76	Rate
10	A Company	9-1-76	9-1-77	24000 //	12000 √	5%
11	B Finance	10-1-76	3-28-77	20000 zo	20000 √	6%
12	C Company	11-1-76	4-29-77	10000 //	10000 √	6%
13	D Company	11-1-76	2-28-77	8000 //	8000 √	6%
14	First National Bank	12-1-76	Demand	24000 ⊙	24000 √	4%
15	E Company	12-31-76	1-30-77	6000 //	6000 √	5%
				92000	80000 ∧	

√ Confirmed.
∧ Agrees with control.
⊙ Traced to cash receipts.
∅ Traced to cash disbursements.
// Traced to inventory purchased.
z $20,000 - $1,200 interest deducted.
 All notes paid during 1976 were inspected and traced to cash disbursements.
 All are mutilated.
 All notes are authorized by board of directors.

reports submitted by salesmen and sales records. If debit balances exist in commission liability accounts, investigation must be made of the commission agreement in order to determine the propriety of the commission accruals. In accordance with the agreement, debit balances may or may not have to be earned in the following period. Also, a debit balance may exist for a terminated employee—and the amount may or may not be collectible.

If vacation pay is accrued by charges spread throughout the year (a good practice), charges for vacation pay made to the liability account must be reviewed in order to determine the accuracy of the period-end balance. The auditor also should examine the provisions of union contracts for vacation pay provisions. Such contracts may specify that employees will earn one day's vacation pay for a stated number of days worked and are entitled to this pay in any case involving termination of employment.

Accrued Interest. Interest accrues on a time basis. Interest accruals usually are verified at the time of examining the related interest-bearing liability. Provisions also must include accruals on past-due liabilities.

Accrued Royalties. Royalties are based either on sales or on production. In accordance with the terms of the royalty agreement, sales records

	Initials	Date
Prepared By	CF	2-12-77
Approved By	RW	2-15-77

Total Days' Interest	1976 Expense	Interest 12-31-76 Prepaid	12-31-76 Accrued	Collateral Description	Market Price 12-31-76	Remarks
360	400				Ø	$6,000 and interest
180	300	900				paid on 12-30-76
				Merchandise		
				inventory	30000	
180	100		100			
120	96		96	Bonds, U.S.		
				Treasury	10000	
0	80	0				Interest paid
30	0	0				each 30 days
	976	900	196			

or production records are examined, and all accruals to the last day of the period must be brought into the records.

Accrued Taxes. Taxes commonly subject to accrual include federal, state, and city income taxes; federal and state unemployment taxes; the employer's portion of the Federal Insurance Contributions Act tax; real estate and personal property taxes; and franchise taxes. Normally, an auditor prepares many of the year-end tax returns. If the client has prepared the year-end returns, the auditor verifies them, examines related financial records, and traces payments to cash disbursements.

Federal, state, and city income taxes are computed on the taxable net income provided for in the income tax acts of each taxing authority. The auditor must determine the taxable net income base for each type of income tax. Accruals of each tax for the end of the period must be brought into the records. A portion of each tax, or all of each tax, or an amount in excess of the actual tax liability may have been paid prior to the close of the period. Refundable amounts which have *been approved* by the taxing authority should be shown as current assets.

Additional federal, state, and city tax assessments for *prior* years and refunds from prior years may be charged or credited to Retained Earnings, in accordance with the appropriate opinions of the APB.

Illustration 13–5
NOTES PAYABLE CONFIRMATION

THE RIPPIE COMPANY

Cincinnati, Ohio

January 10, 1977

Name of Bank: Southern Ohio Bank
or
Name of Broker or Other Creditor

Gentlemen:

Prince and Penz, Certified Public Accountants, are now conducting their annual audit of our records.

Please confirm directly to them our indebtedness for notes due you (or sold to you, if a broker) as of December 31, 1976. Our liability to you as of that date stands on our records at $10,000. Please list in the space provided any collateral held as security for the loan. An envelope is enclosed for your convenience. Thank you.

Very truly yours,
THE RIPPIE COMPANY
James Copeland, Treasurer

DETACH HERE

— —

January 12, 1977

Prince and Penz, Certified Public Accountants
5 East Fourth Street
Cincinnati, Ohio 45202

Gentlemen:

Amount of loan to the Rippie Company $10,000
Date of loan . . . .   November 10, 1976
Date Due . . . .   February 10, 1977
Collateral held . . . .   None
Differences:
                        None

(Signed) A. J. Pringle
SOUTHERN OHIO BANK

Federal and state unemployment taxes levied on employers are based on wages *paid*. The federal unemployment tax is payable annually. The majority of states require quarterly returns and payments. Unemployment tax accruals are verified by reference to payroll records. The auditor must ascertain that payments were not made on wages in excess of the amounts stipulated in the various tax acts. See Illustrations 13–6, 13–7, and 13–8.

The Federal Insurance Contributions Act is paid partially by the employee and partially by the employer. The employee's portion is withheld

Illustration 13–6
WORK PAPER 29

	Initials	Date
MULTI-PRODUCTS, INCORPORATED	Prepared By *CF*	*2-23-77*
Analysis of Liabilities for: F.I.C.A. Tax, State Unemployment Tax, Approved By	*RW*	*2-25-77*
Income Tax Withheld, and Workmen's Compensation Insurance, December 31, 1976		

Explanation	Adminis-trative Salaries	Sales Salaries	Direct Factory Payroll	Indirect Factory Payroll	Total	
Expense, 1976	359578	173800	674102	204600	1412080	
Add: Accrual, 1-1-76 ≠	0	0	0	0	0	
	359578	173800	674102	204600	1412080	
Deduct: Accrual, 12-31-76 ≠	0	0	0	0	0	
Paid: 1976	359578	173800	674102	204600	1412080	
Less amounts over maximum	263638	107134	322588	109448	802808	
F.I.C.A. taxable, per audit	95940	66666	351514	95152	609272	
F.I.C.A. tax	7750	5500	29000	7850	50100	
Amounts over maximum	256968	103478	247006	96214	703666	
Federal unemployment taxable	102580	70322	427096	108386	708384	
Federal unemployment tax	318	218	1324	336	2196 ⊙	
State unemployment tax at	2866	1958	11924	3028	19776	
state rates						
Income tax withheld-December, 1976				19248	∧	
Quarter ended (1976):						
March 31				48484	✓	
June 30				44336	✓	
September 30				40082	✓	
December 31				28608	✓	
Total general ledger credits				161510	✗	
Workmen's compensation insurance accrued						
Payroll, first six months				675246		
Rate: $0.21 per $100				1418		
Payroll, second six months				736834		
Rate: $0.21 per $100 (AJE 13)				1548		

≠On each December 31, the company pays all personnel for all amounts due
    through that date. Therefore, there are no accruals.
⊙ Balance per general ledger.
∧ Examined paid check No. 14267, issued on January 20, 1977, to Internal Revenue
    Service.
✓ Compared with general ledger and with return copies.
✗ Compared 10 percent of W-2's with earnings records.
    Exemption certificates were tested for the accuracy of income taxes
    withheld for the first pay period in March and November. In four
    instances the amounts withheld were incorrect and were called
    to the attention of the payroll department.

Illustration 13–7
WORK PAPER 30

	Initials	Date
MULTI-PRODUCTS, INCORPORATED	Prepared By	C F	2-13-77
F.I.C.A. Tax Liability, December 31, 1976	Approved By	R W	2-15-77

Balance, December 31, 1976			1 250	
December payroll	148140			
Less: Amounts in excess of maximum	132988			
F.I.C.A. Taxable	15152			
Tax	1250			
Total F.I.C.A. taxable wages paid in fourth quarter, 1976.				
Total wages	407778			
Less: Nontaxable	262354			
Taxable	145424			
Tax			11 750	
Less: Depository receipts:				
November	6352	∧		
December	4148	∧	10 500	
Balance, paid January 20, 1977			1 250	✗

∧ Examined prior to filing Form 941.
✗ Examined paid check.

Illustration 13–8
WORK PAPER 31

	Initials	Date
	Prepared By	L R	2-13-77
MULTI-PRODUCTS, INCORPORATED	Approved By	R W	2-15-77
State Unemployment Tax Liability, December 31, 1976			

Balance, per company, December 31, 1976			3 188	
Payments to state treasurer:				
First quarter	6 170	∧		
Second quarter	5 582	∧		
Third quarter	4 836	∧		
Fourth quarter--accrued	3 188			
Per audit, December 31, 1976	19 776	✓		

∧ Paid checks examined.
✓ Compared with general ledger.

from his salary on the base wage paid during each calendar year. The employer's portion must be accrued—preferably each pay period or each month. Payroll records are used by the auditor to determine the propriety of the amount withheld and the employer's matching amount paid or to be accrued. The auditor must watch for proper cutoff at the base level; this may be accomplished by scrutinizing Forms W–2. Adequate payroll records are necessary for the proper audit of all social security taxes.

Real estate and personal property taxes are levied as of a certain date. However, a business organization should accrue such taxes over the intervals between assessment dates. For real estate taxes—which frequently are levied and paid months after the applicable tax period—the auditor should refer to current tax bills for assessed values and, using the current tax rate plus or minus contemplated changes in valuations and rates, arrive at the accrued real estate taxes for the current period.

Personal property taxes normally are levied as of each year-end. After computing the tax in accordance with the personal property tax laws of the community, unpaid balances will appear as current liabilities.

Franchise taxes, levied for the privilege of conducting business for the following year, usually are levied as of the first day of the current period. The Franchise Tax account frequently changes—during the year—from a prepaid item to an accrued item. In accordance with the franchise tax law of each state, the auditor must compute the tax and determine that it is properly recorded; or if the governing authority computes the tax and renders an invoice, the auditor must verify the accuracy of the computations.

Amounts Withheld

When amounts are withheld from employees, the employer—by law or by agreement—is charged with the responsibility of remitting to the proper organization or government authority. The auditor must reasonably test the accuracy of the amounts withheld under the terms of the applicable agreement or law. He then must correlate paid checks with the records of the amounts withheld and with tax returns and reports filed with organizations—such as unions, community chests, and others.

Declared Dividends

Cash and other asset dividends declared but not paid at the balance-sheet date are liabilities. Declared but unpaid stock dividends are not liabilities but they should be indicated in the capital section of the balance sheet. The auditor must examine dividend actions of the board of directors in order to determine the existence of a liability for asset dividends declared and not paid.

If a paid dividend is unclaimed by its recipient, a liability remains. At the same time, a cash balance will remain if a dividend fund bank account has been established. This bank account should be examined for unauthorized withdrawals. In determining the period for which unclaimed dividends are allowed to stand before being returned to capital, and before a special Cash account balance is returned to general cash, good judgment must be used, and applicable laws of the state of incorporation must be followed.

If a dividend-disbursing agent is employed, the paying corporation has fulfilled its obligations when it remits to the agent the funds required to pay the dividend. In these instances the auditor should confirm unclaimed dividend amounts remaining with the disbursing agent. The auditor also should determine that the disbursing agent periodically remits unclaimed amounts to the paying corporation in accordance with the statute of limitations of the state.

Unclaimed Wages

Unclaimed wages should be deposited in the bank, and an Unclaimed Wages account should be credited. Amounts withdrawn from this account should be verified to be certain that they were paid to employees or to ex-employees entitled to the amounts. If after a reasonable time it is evident that certain wages will not be claimed, the liability may be transferred to income, provided that state laws do not require that unclaimed wages revert to the state.

Deposits

Deposits received from customers and from employees are liabilities—usually current. Compulsory deposits may be received or withheld from employees for tools, lockers, and so on. Voluntary deposits may be received or withheld from employees for savings, stock and/or bond purchases, or personal asset purchases. Compulsory deposits may be received from customers for such items as returnable containers, service deposits, and so forth.

The auditor should confirm deposits from employees. If receipts or passbooks are held by employees and if they reasonably are obtainable, they should be compared with company records for agreement of amounts. Company receipt copies of amounts received or withheld should be compared with general-ledger account balances for gross periodic credits. Debits to the liability accounts should be tested by comparing paid checks therewith.

In many cases, deposits are never claimed. Balances that evidently never will be claimed should be transferred to income, unless state laws prohibit such procedure.

The IRS has ruled (1975) that if a landlord is required to deposit all security deposits from residential tenants in a single interest-bearing account, the deposit plus interest belongs to the tenant with the landlord entitled to a 1 percent administrative fee. Therefore, the landlord must file a fiduciary income tax return, Form 1041 and the related schedules.

Revenues Received in Advance

Revenues received in advance (sometimes improperly termed deferred credits to income) are classed as current liabilities if they are short-term items. The auditor has a twofold interest in the examination of short-term revenues received in advance, as follows: (1) to ascertain that proper periodic allocation has been made, and (2) to determine that the deferred portion of the revenues received in advance is properly stated in the balance sheet.

Rent Received in Advance. Rent received in advance originally may be credited to a revenue account or to a liability account. Rental agreements and leases are examined to determine rental periods, rental cost, and payment arrangements, and are compared with the cash records in order to prorate the amounts received between revenue and the remaining liability at the balance-sheet date. Rental Revenue accounts and related liability accounts must be analyzed. Material advance payments should be confirmed directly to the auditor.

Interest Received in Advance. The period of the loan upon which interest was received in advance must be determined, and proper proration must be made between the amount of periodic interest earned and the amount applicable to future periods.

Subscriptions Received in Advance. Advance payments received from subscriptions must be totaled, and the total prorated between the current period and future periods on the basis of the time limits involved in the subscriptions. The total cash received—in accordance with available subscriptions records—must be reconciled with the total debits to the Cash account arising from subscriptions received in advance.

Tickets Sold in Advance. Proper accounting demands rigid internal control of tickets. Amounts received from tickets sold in advance but not used at the balance-sheet date should be set up in proper liability accounts. Verification of the accuracy of the liability should proceed as follows: determine the beginning inventory of the tickets; determine the number of tickets printed during the period; account for tickets redeemed during the period; verify the inventory of unsold tickets; the result will be the tickets sold and not used. Many sold tickets are never used, due to loss or negligence on the part of the customer. If tickets are serially numbered—and they should be—extremely old unredeemed numbers may be transferred to revenue.

Collections in Advance on Contracts and on Sales. Amounts received in advance on contracts and on sales for future delivery are verified by reference to the contracts and to sales orders. If no work has been performed on the contracts or if no deliveries have been made from sales orders, the entire amount received is revenue received in advance. If partial work has been done or if partial deliveries have been made, the amount received in advance must be separated for its revenue and liability elements.

CONTINGENCIES

A liability is a debt resulting from a past act. A contingency (sometimes called a contingent liability) is a *possible* future direct obligation. It is the result of a past act or of a possible future act. As of a balance-sheet date, there is no actual liability of determinable amount. However, the future financial condition of a company may be seriously affected by contingencies. Therefore, the auditor should investigate all contingencies and, for material items, set forth the contingency as a financial statement footnote, or provide reserves for specific contingencies. Full disclosure should be given contingencies in the audit report.

Contingencies are of two general classes:

1. Possible direct financial obligations, such as:
    a) Additional federal income (or other) tax assessments.
    b) Lawsuits.
    c) Breaches of contract, including leased equipment.
    d) Product guarantees.
    e) Sale of mortgaged properties.
2. Secondary obligations in which no liability will exist unless a primary obligor fails to act; a few examples include:
    a) Notes receivable discounted.
    b) Notes endorsed for others.
    c) Guarantees of obligations of others.
    d) Unused balances of outstanding letters of credit.

Contingencies may be difficult to determine because evidence of their existence may not appear in the accounting or other records.

AUDIT OF CONTINGENCIES

Minutes of meetings of the board of directors, partners, and special committees should be examined for information concerning contingencies. Correspondence with the client's attorney also should be examined.

If current assessments are in dispute, a contingency may be provided for by a charge to Income. If adverse judgment finally is rendered, the contingency becomes a liability.

The client's legal division should be requested to supply information concerning possible losses from lawsuits—in process and pending.

Examination should be made of purchase contracts, sales contracts, lease agreements, correspondence, and invoices for professional services. Special attention should be directed to these items, as they frequently divulge contingencies. If extraordinarily large purchase orders are protected by firm sales contracts, the probabilities of a liability from this source are reduced.

Product quality, performance, and service guarantees usually result in real liabilities. It is customary procedure to segregate a portion of the sales price as a liability for parts and services to be rendered. The auditor should examine debits to the liability account and determine the reasonableness of the total periodic debits and credits. The liability account should not become excessively large, nor too small to provide for parts and service in accordance with the terms of the guarantees. Work papers of the auditor should contain analyses of the conditions under which sales are made, together with an indication of the extent of the existence of these real liabilities or contingencies.

If real estate subject to a mortgage has been sold and if the purchaser did not assume the mortgage, the seller may become liable for a deficiency judgment if the mortgagee forecloses and if the amount realized is not sufficient to cover the loan.

If notes and/or acceptances receivable are discounted and if the primary obligor fails to liquidate, the party who discounted the paper becomes directly liable. If properly accounted for by the client, discounted items are readily revealed to the auditor. Also, bank confirmation replies disclose contingencies of this nature.

Endorsements of notes of other parties may be difficult to detect, because normally there is no record of such endorsement. Therefore, the auditor should request a liability certificate setting forth the amount and nature of all contingencies not recorded. If an accommodation endorser has taken up the instrument, a charge to a receivable and a credit to Cash should appear in his records. The allowance for doubtful items should contain adequate provisions for the noncollectibility of such items.

LIABILITY CERTIFICATE

To protect creditors, stockholders, and himself, the auditor should obtain from the client a certification of liabilities. This constitutes evidence that the auditor directed important questions to management and that management answered the questions. See Illustration 13–9. The certification is to the effect that all known direct liabilities and contingencies

Illustration 13–9

LIABILITY CERTIFICATE

Arch and Company   Date _____
Certified Public Accountants

In connection with the audit of our records for the year ended December 31, 1976,
we certify that to the best of our knowledge:

1. All direct liabilities have been recorded in the accounts, including all items in
   transit for which we had been billed and/or to which we had title.
2. As of December 31, 1976, contingencies are as noted below:
   a) Discounted notes, drafts, and acceptances ....$ _____
   b) Accounts or notes assigned .... _____
   c) Accommodation endorsements of the paper of others.......... _____
   d) Lawsuits and judgments .... _____
   e) Financial commitments not in the regular course of ordinary
      business .... _____
   f) Open balances on letters of credit .... _____
   g) Additional taxes for prior years .... _____
   h) Purchase commitments for materials at prices in excess of cur-
      rent market quotations or for quantities in excess of normal re-
      quirements .... _____
   i) Guarantees of debts of affiliated companies .... _____
   j) Renegotiation of government contracts...................... _____
3. There is no subordination of liabilities.
4. Company assets were pledged or hypothecated as liability
   security, other than as noted in 2, above, in the amount of......$ _____
5. The contracts for construction and/or purchase of fixed assets
   amount to ....$ _____
6. Advance receipts on construction contracts in process.......... $ _____

Signed _____ Title _____
Signed _____ Title _____

are properly disclosed in the financial statements. The certificate does not relieve the auditor of any responsibility for determining the proper inclusion of all liabilities. The certification may or may not be referred to in the audit report.

FINANCIAL STATEMENT CONSIDERATIONS

In the financial statements, current liabilities should be properly subdivided into trade accounts payable, nontrade accounts payable, amounts due affiliated companies, declared dividends payable, trade notes payable, nontrade notes payable, bank loans payable, deposit liabilities, accrued items, amounts withheld from employees, and short-term deferred credits to revenue. Amounts due officers, stockholders, directors, and other company personnel, other than for wages, should be separately set forth in the balance sheet. To reduce the detail in a formal balance sheet, the preceding related items may be grouped.

If notes or accounts payable are secured by pledged assets, that fact should be stated parenthetically in the balance sheet, or should appear as a footnote. Material amounts of notes or accounts payable due to parent or subsidiary companies should be separately set forth.

Debit balances in Accounts Payable, if material in amount, should be set forth as current assets.

Currently maturing portions of long-term indebtedness should be shown among the current liabilities, or they may remain in the long-term liability section of the balance sheet if accompanied by a statement of maturity date. However, the latter treatment affects a proper current ratio.

Revenues received in advance of being earned should be shown as current liabilities. Long-term deferred credits are shown separately classified, or placed in the long-term liability section of the balance sheet.

If material in amount or nature, contingencies must be properly disclosed by footnote or by creating contingency reserves. If contingency reserves are set up by action of the board of directors, they should appear in the proprietorship section of the balance sheet.

Unfilled purchase commitments of extraordinary amount should be disclosed by balance-sheet footnote, unless the extraordinary commitments are offset by firm sales orders. Purchase commitments of normal amount need not be mentioned.

Equipment lease agreements that are of an extraordinary amount should be disclosed by balance-sheet footnotes.

RELATED COSTS AND EXPENSES

Expense examination, in addition to that performed in the audit of original records, depends upon the adequacy of the system of internal control. Also, expense accounts of material amounts, those that may serve as hiding places for items that should be capitalized, and those that may be of a questionable nature, are analyzed in greater detail than other expense accounts. Many expense accounts are scanned and are not proved by the examination of underlying evidence in the form of authorizations, invoices, and paid checks. Material variations in the same expense items from the prior year should be investigated for cause and effect.

The audit objectives of expense account examination are:

1. To determine the adequacy of the system of internal control of expenses.
2. To determine the purpose of the expense.
3. To determine the correctness of the expense, based upon authorization, invoices, and paid checks.
4. To determine that the expenses are properly recorded.
5. To ascertain that each expense is properly classified.

INTERNAL CONTROL OF EXPENSES

The principal points of internal control of expenses involve approval for the initial authorization of the expenses, centralized control points for approval for payment, proper recording, and proper payment. An internal control questionnaire for expenses other than payroll is presented in Illustration 13–10. An internal control questionnaire for payroll appears in Illustration 13–14.

AUDIT OF EXPENSES

The audit procedures for expenses in general are:

1. Review the internal control and internal audit over expenses.
2. Verify the authority for incurrence of the expenses.
3. Compare major expenses with the similar items of the prior period.
4. Prove the mathematical accuracy of selected major invoices.
5. Test trace invoices and related documents to records of original entry and to the accounts.
6. Ascertain the propriety of the contra credit for the expense debits.
7. Analyze selected expense accounts.
8. Ascertain that all expenses have been recorded.
9. Determine the propriety of expense account classifications.
10. Examine expense accounts for items which should be charged to assets.
11. Examine major expense accounts to establish the recorded accuracy of related asset or liability accounts.
12. Verify expense account distributions.

Illustration 13–10

INTERNAL CONTROL QUESTIONNAIRE
Expenses

Company _____ Period Covered _____	Yes	No	Not Appli- cable	Remarks
1. Is there centralization of approval for expenses?	___	___	___	___
2. Are all but petty cash fund expenses routed through the central point of approval for expenses?	___	___	___	___
3. Are expense authorizations executed in writing?	___	___	___	___
4. Are expense orders sequentially numbered?	___	___	___	___
5. Are expense orders properly approved for price, quantity, and supplier?	___	___	___	___
6. Are invoices properly approved for payment?	___	___	___	___
7. Are invoices verified for prices, extensions, and footings?	___	___	___	___
8. Do expense orders originate in one place?	___	___	___	___
9. Is a postage meter used for outgoing mail?	___	___	___	___
10. Prior to authorization for payment, are invoices and all related documents signed by a properly authorized person?	___	___	___	___
11. Does the accounting department receive directly a copy of the expense authorization?	___	___	___	___
12. Does the accounting department match invoices and authorizations?	___	___	___	___
13. Are invoices received from creditors compared—by the accounting department—with open accounts?	___	___	___	___
14. Are invoices entered by a person who does not have access to cash?	___	___	___	___
15. Are invoices entered by a person who cannot authorize expenses?	___	___	___	___

Prepared by _____   Reviewed by _____
Date _____   Date _____

Taxes

When verifying tax liabilities in connection with the audit of current liabilities, the auditor has examined related tax expenses as presented earlier in this chapter.

Tax accounts require analysis for proper distribution of a total to selling, administrative, and manufacturing—unless separate accounts are carried and properly handled.

Repairs and Maintenance

In order to determine that capital expenditures have not been charged to expense, repair and maintenance accounts should be carefully examined. In many audits, repair and maintenance accounts are analyzed and the entries examined at the time of examining fixed assets. Invoices, shop orders, and payroll records are examined to determine the propriety

Illustration 13–11
WORK PAPER 32

	Initials	Date
MULTI-PRODUCTS, INCORPORATED — Prepared By	PM	2-4-77
Machinery Maintenance, December 31, 1976 — Approved By	RW	2-7-77

Month--1976	Material	Labor	Total
January	1238 ✓⊙	1706 ⊙	2944
February	422	700	1122
March	552	592	1144
April	1072	1870	2942
May	666 ✓⊙	1124 ∧⊙	1790
June	362	504	866
July	1052	1226	2278
August	1618	388	2006
September	318	1020	1338
October	1150	260	1410
November	1166	728	1894
December (see AJE 1)	386 ✓⊙	800 ∧⊙	1186
Total	10002	10918	20920
Add: AJE 1	50		50
Audit Total	10052	10918	20970

✓ Examined requisitions and invoices.
∧ Examined payroll distributions.
⊙ Reviewed repair orders.

	AJE 1	
Cost of Sales (Machinery Maintenance)	50	
Petty Cash		50
In December petty cash vouchers.		

of the debits to repair and maintenance accounts. These accounts also are analyzed on a comparative basis for the determination of upkeep between periods and between different types of equipment. Illustration 13–11 presents a work paper for the analysis of machinery repairs for Multi-Products, Incorporated. Illustration 13–12 presents a work paper for the analysis of nonpayroll factory costs.

Depreciation and Amortization

Charges for depreciation and amortization ordinarily are verified when fixed assets and intangible assets and their related accumulated depreciation or amortization accounts are examined. See Chapters 11 and 12. Credits to depreciation expense accounts represent errors of judgment or overcharges in all months of a year except the final month. Debits to accu-

Illustration 13-12

THE BLANK COMPANY

Nonpayroll Factory Costs, December 31, 1976

Month--1976	Repairs	Depreciation	Utilities	Supplies	Insurance	Property Taxes	Payroll Taxes	Total
January	1201	1536	1002	806	240	288	906	5979
February	1488	1536	1090	739	240	288	814	6195
March	825	1536	1001	702	240	288	827	5419
April	624	1536	933	718	240	288	798	5137
May	1072	1536	787	900	240	288	769	5592
June	1175 ✓	1536	718 ✓	816 ✓	240	288 ✓	760	5533
July	791	1536	675	460	240	288	710	4700
August	1065	1536	610	744	240	288	750	5233
September	1128	1536	902	566	240	288	672	5332
October	1202	1536	979	704	240	288	568	5517
November	1378	1536	1092	796	240	288	326	5656
December	614 ✓	1420	1173 ✓	993 ✓	318	230 ✓	182	4930
Totals	12563	18316 ✓	10962	8944	2958 ✓	3398	8082 ✓	65223

✓ Analyzed on related item work papers.

✓ Examined in detail. Ok.

mulated depreciation accounts represent fixed asset dispositions, or corrections of prior depreciation provisions.

Pension Plans

When a qualified pension plan is in effect and the fund is under the control of a trustee, the auditor for the company establishing the plan must ascertain the costs based on past services (services rendered prior to the adoption of the plan) and the expenses attributable to the present and future services of covered employees. All pension plan expenses—those for past, present, and future services—should be charged to current and future periods expenses.

The auditor must ascertain that retained earnings has not been charged for the services of past periods. When the plan is established, the cost of the services for past periods should be debited to a deferred charge account and a liability account should be credited because a definite liability exists. Periodically, as portions of the liability are currently paid, the deferred charge should be reduced and the expense recognized, together with the expense of the current period. The portion of the established liability currently payable, together with the liability for the expense of the current period is a current liability, and the remainder of the liability set up when the plan was established is a long-term liability. Current federal income tax regulations permit pension expenses for past services to be amortized over not less than ten years.

The auditor should also determine that the client has followed the requirements of the Employee Retirement Income Security Act of 1974 (Pension Reform Act of 1974).

Supplies Expense

In view of the materiality of the items and the effectiveness of internal control over physical quantities, supplies expenses are to be verified to the extent necessary. Remaining supplies inventories should be set up as assets in order properly to state periodic net income. Invoices should be vouched to the original records and traced to the accounts, and paid checks examined—all on a reasonable test basis.

Spoiled Work

Preferably, spoiled work costs should be charged to a Spoiled Work account; the offsetting credit is to Work in Process or to Finished Goods. Regardless of how spoiled work costs are handled, the auditor must ascertain that the accounting treatment is proper. Unreasonably high spoiled work costs should receive special comment in a management letter, and the effect of the lost costs should be pointed out.

Delivery Expenses

Delivery expenses should be examined in sufficient detail to determine that all expense charges are proper. Truck operating expense compiled on a comparative basis, by such factors as depreciation, gasoline, oil, and repairs, often reveals the efficiency of both equipment and drivers. Comparative analyses of hired delivery services may reveal expense variances.

If the client is the vendor, shipments may be made f.o.b. destination, with the understanding that the vendee will pay transportation and then deduct the amount from the remittance made to the vendor. By test, the auditor should verify the correctness of such deductions and should point out deductions in excess of allowable amounts.

Travel Expenses

Expenses for traveling should be investigated to determine their reasonableness and to determine that the expenses are properly supported by evidences of the expenditures. Obviously padded expense reports should be directed to the attention of the client. Travel expense reports should be reviewed, footed, and traced to the accounting records. Travel expenses may or may not appear to be reasonable, but the auditor cannot sit in judgment on the manner in which a client's staff travels.

Sales Discounts

Normally, sales discounts are verified in the course of examining original cash receipts records. Discounts should be tested for correctness of amount and traced to cash receipts records. Recorded discounts should not exceed the amount of the computations, unless the excess discount bears official approval. See Chapter 6.

Interest Expense

Interest rates and amounts must be verified. The entries for interest expense are traced through original records to the ledger accounts. Normally, interest expenses are verified when interest-bearing obligations are examined. The amortization of interest paid in advance must be verified, and interest accruals must be computed.

Illustration 13–13 sets forth a work paper for the analysis of the office operating expenses of Multi-Products, Incorporated.

INTERNAL CONTROL OF PAYROLL

Proper internal control over payroll demands that payments of proper amounts be made to eligible employees. Also, the following payroll duties

Illustration 13–13
WORK PAPER 33

MULTI-PRODUCTS, INCORPORATED

Analysis of Office Operating Expense, December 31, 1976

	Initials	Date
Prepared By	Pm	2-12
Approved By	QW	2-14

Month--1976	Telephone	Postage	Contributions	Maintenance of Office Equipment	Entertainment	Total
January	496	90	1000 ✓	334 ✓	54	1974
February	624	104		48	30	796
March	530	134			20	694
April	386	162		70	24	642
May	370	152	1000 ✓		36	1558
June	544 ✓✓	190		720 ✓✓	44	1498
July	408	76		22	34	540
August	376	88		84	22	570
September	348	138		796 ∧✓	38	1320
October	492	144	2000 ✓	24	66	2726
November	584 ✓✓	170			152	906
December	562	192	1000 ✓	142	184 ✓✓	2080
Total, general ledger	5720	1640	5000	2240	704 ✓✓	15304
Add: AJE 1, petty cash					162 ✓	162
	5720	1640	5000	2240	866	15466
Deduct: AJE 10.						
adding machine				720		720
Audit Balance	5720	1640	5000	1520	866	14746

✓ Invoices examined.
∧ Annual maintenance policies.
✓ Paid checks examined.

	AJE 10		
Office Equipment		720	
Office Operating Expense			720
Adding machine charged to expense.			

Contributions:		
Polio Fund		1000
American Cancer Society		1000
United Appeal		2000
American Heart Association		1000
		5000

must be separated: computing the payroll, preparing the checks or cash, and paying the employees. An internal control questionnaire for payroll appears in Illustration 13–14.

AUDIT OF PAYROLL

Internal payroll procedure differs widely between companies. However, minimum requirements for adequate payroll procedure and control include authorization to place employees on the payroll, an original source (clock cards, for example) for payroll computation, an earnings record for each employee, and a periodic payroll summary or journal. The auditor must understand the payroll procedure of each client.

A list of all persons employed during the period under examination should be obtained, together with individual rates of pay and pay-rate changes made during the period. The auditor must be certain that ex-employees do not remain on the payroll—to the benefit of some active employee. Therefore, termination methods must be investigated. Names appearing on authorized employment records must be compared with names appearing on periodic payroll records.

Illustration 13–14

INTERNAL CONTROL QUESTIONNAIRE
Payroll

Company_____ Period Covered_____	Yes	No	Not Appli-cable	Remarks
1. Is employment properly authorized?	___	___	___	_____
2. Is separation immediately reported to the payroll department?	___	___	___	_____
3. Are pay increases and decreases properly authorized?	___	___	___	_____
4. Are original time records properly prepared and controlled to avoid alteration?	___	___	___	_____
5. Are time clocks used?	___	___	___	_____
6. Are piecework records compared with actual production?	___	___	___	_____
7. Is the preparation of the payroll divided over the maximum number of employees appropriate in the circumstances?	___	___	___	_____
8. Are the payroll records regularly compared with the records of the personnel department?	___	___	___	_____
9. Are calculations rechecked prior to payment?	___	___	___	_____
10. Is the total time for each employee approved by a departmental foreman or by a timekeeper?	___	___	___	_____
11. Are all employees paid by check?	___	___	___	_____
12. If employees are paid by check:				
a) Are the checks sequentially prenumbered?	___	___	___	_____
b) Are spoiled checks properly voided?	___	___	___	_____
c) Are voided checks retained?	___	___	___	_____
d) Are unused payroll checks rigidly controlled?	___	___	___	_____
e) Does the client use a check protector?	___	___	___	_____
13. If a facsimile signature is used through a mechanical or electronic check signer, is access to the machine properly controlled?	___	___	___	_____
14. Does the person who signs the payroll checks participate in the preparation of the payroll?	___	___	___	_____
15. Does the person who signs the payroll checks have access to the accounting records?	___	___	___	_____
16. If the payroll is paid in currency and coin:				
a) Are receipts obtained from employees?	___	___	___	_____
b) Are the receipts compared with the payroll by a person not connected with preparing the payroll?	___	___	___	_____
c) Is each distribution of the payroll witnessed by a person independent of the preparation of the payroll?	___	___	___	_____
d) Does the paymaster have access to the cash records?	___	___	___	_____
e) Is the paymaster independent of the payroll preparation?	___	___	___	_____
f) Is the paymaster function rotated?	___	___	___	_____
17. Is the payroll paid through a separate bank account?	___	___	___	_____

Illustration 13–14—Continued

	Yes	No	Not Appli-cable	Remarks
18. Is the payroll bank account reconciled each month?				
19. Is the reconciliation made by a person independent of the entire payroll preparation and payment?				
20. Are returned checks and bank statements restricted to the person preparing the reconciliation?				
21. When the reconciliation is made, are individual checks ticked off on the payroll records?				
22. Is proper control exercised over unclaimed wages?				
23. Are unclaimed cash wages deposited in a bank account and a liability set up?				
24. Is proper disposition made of long-outstanding payroll checks?				
25. Did we:				
a) Witness a distribution of payroll?				
b) Perform a distribution of payroll?				
c) Immediately control unclaimed wages?				
26. Are payroll tax reporting requirements met?				
27. Are union fringe benefit reporting requirements followed?				
28. Are minority employee reporting requirements met?				
29. Are pension reporting requirements followed?				

Prepared by _____   Reviewed by_____

Date_____   Date_____

From individual clock cards, time tickets, and other original data, tests are made of hours worked which, when multiplied by approved pay rates, result in total pay accumulation. The pay accumulations tested then are traced to the individual earnings records and to the payroll journals or other control records. Deductions for taxes withheld, union dues, hospitalization insurance, employee purchases, and other items should be tested at the same time and for the same employees whose total pay accumulations were tested.

If payroll records are electronically prepared, an auditor may examine printouts, or he may operate the computer for a test period.

The total of the net cash periodic (week, month) payroll according to the payroll record should be accumulated and compared with the total credit to Cash. Tests should be made of the payroll control records for footings, crossfootings, and postings to proper wage accounts, if those records are prepared manually or mechanically.

Paid checks should be compared with cash disbursement entries and with individual earnings records for net pay. Endorsements should be scanned, although multiple endorsements are not uncommon on payroll checks. Checks bearing endorsements of more than one company employee should be investigated and satisfactory explanations obtained. All check numbers should be accounted for, and the procedure for reconciling special payroll bank accounts is the same as for reconciling any bank account. Unclaimed wages—cash or check—must be properly controlled. Unclaimed pay immediately should be transferred to someone who does not have access to payroll records. If not claimed in a reasonable time, the unclaimed wages should be deposited in the bank and an Unclaimed Wage account should be credited. Amounts never claimed should be disposed of in accordance with the laws of the state.

If possible, the auditor should mail federal Form W–2 to all employed personnel as of the end of the year. Differences should be reported directly to the auditor. Under any circumstances, the auditor should test-compare Form W–2 information with individual earnings records—both in detail and in terms of total gross wages, amounts withheld, and net payments. The total of the payroll should be reconciled with the total of the returns filed under the FICA, the sum of the W–2's, the federal and state unemployment tax returns, and all related accounts. A test of the accuracy of the total payroll may be made by analyzing the payroll into its component parts, as shown in Illustration 13–15.

The accuracy of accrued wages must be determined by reference to timecards and payday in relation to the end of the period. For accruals of salaries and commissions, it may be necessary to refer to minutes of certain committees, bonus agreements, employment contracts, commission agreements, and pension plans.

The auditor either should prepare or attend a distribution of the payroll to the employees. In this way the auditor will become familiar with the payroll operation and the system of internal control. Payroll distribution or attendance should be made without prior notice; while witnessing or paying, the auditor must be alert to the possibility of an employee's receiving duplicate payment. He should control unclaimed wages and follow their disposition.

FINANCIAL STATEMENT CONSIDERATIONS

As a minimum, for only modest disclosure of all material operating data, an income statement should include sales revenues, cost of sales, selling expense, administrative expense, nonoperating revenues and expenses, federal income tax, and net income. Preferably, income statements should be prepared in comparative form with the preceding year. Many corporations present stockholders with income statement data for ten consecutive years.

Sales revenue may be shown net, unless sales returns and allowances are material in amount. Sales revenue (whether gross or net) should not be shown net of cost of sales. In the event that a company has several categories of revenues, preferable treatment is to the effect that each sales

Illustration 13–15
WORK PAPER 34

		Initials	Date
MULTI-PRODUCTS, INCORPORATED	Prepared By	*pm*	2-12-7
Payroll Analysis, December 31, 1976	Approved By	*R w*	2-14-7

Month--1976	Administrative Salaries	Sales Salaries	Direct Factory Payroll	Indirect Factory Payroll	Total	
January	24000	13640	56174	17246	111060	∧
February	24000	13420	58528	17930	113878	
March	27000	13900	58036	17082	116018	
April	27000	14500	54484	17752	113736	
May	28000	14080	53112	15842	110034	
June	29000	13840	50956 ✓	15724 ◀	109520	∧
July	29200	11400	52232	15682	108514	
August	29320	11300	51638	15794	108052	
September	30258	14480	53224	14528	112490	
October	36400 ⊙	16160 ⊙	57596 ⊙	16178	126334	
November	36400	17660 ⊖	60912	18332	133304	
December	39000 ✗	19420	67210 ✓	22510 ✓	148140	∧
Total	359578	173800	674102	204600	1412080	◀
Less: Amount over F.I.C.A. limit	265638	107134	322588	109448	802808	
F.I.C.A. taxable	93940	66666	351514	95152	607272	
Less: Amount over F.U.T. limit	256998	103478	247006	96214	703696	
Federal unemployment taxable	102580	70322	427096	108386	708384	

✓ Traced direct and indirect labor to clock cards.
∧ Footed payroll journals.
◀ Compared Form W-2 totals with payroll summaries.
∅ Compared 10 percent of individual earnings records with W-2's.
⊙ Examined authorizations for increases.
✗ Examined salary and bonus agreements for officers for December.

Workmen's Compensation insurance:*		
Payroll, first 6 months		675246
At $0.21 per $100 (charged to insurance expense)		1418
Payroll, second 6 months		736834
At $0.21 per $100 (Accrual) (AJE 13)		1548

*State laws vary widely for workmen's compensation.

category be shown separately—and totaled—in order to offer full disclosure of all material facts.

Expenses of material amount should be separately set forth and not combined with other items. Such expenses normally include cost of sales, depreciation, major selling and administrative expenses, interest charges, and federal income tax.

Nonrecurring revenues and gains of material amount, and expenses and losses of material amount, should be clearly set forth as such (together with applicable income tax adjustments) in the income statement in a manner which will not distort normal net income.

Earnings per share of common stock should be shown, both undiluted and fully diluted.

SUGGESTED ADDITIONAL READING:

FASB Statements of Financial Accounting Standards Nos. 5 and *6.*
APB Opinions Nos. 21 and *26.*
Employee Retirement Income Security Act of 1974.

QUESTIONS

1. How can a list of open accounts payable assist the auditor in starting his audit?

2. Why should an auditor review cash discounts?

3. What are the audit objectives in examining current liabilities?

4. Summarize the principal points of internal control over current liabilities.

5. *a)* Why should long-standing credit balances in accounts payable be investigated by the auditor?

   b) Why should debit balances in accounts payable be investigated by the auditor?

   c) Name all possible sources of debit balances in accounts payable, and indicate the adjustment necessary for each.

6. *a)* Outline a program for the verification of notes payable.

   b) Of what value is the Interest Expense account in the audit of notes payable?

7. How can the auditor accomplish the objective of proper inclusion of all current liabilities in his report?

8. During the examination of the records of the Spring Company for the year ended December 31, 1976, you find that the client's internal control over payrolls is not perfect, because the size of the organization does not permit proper separation of duties; otherwise, there are no outstanding weaknesses in the system. Two hundred hourly employees are paid by check every two weeks. Wage rates are set forth in a union contract, which you have examined.

   a) Prepare an audit program for the examination of hourly payrolls to be performed during preliminary work period in November 1976.

   b) What additional audit procedures, if any, would be necessary in connection with the hourly payrolls as of December 31, 1976?

9. If the notes payable schedule prepared from documents submitted to the auditor does not agree with the general-ledger account, what errors should the auditor look for as an explanation for this difference?

10. What are the objectives of auditing accrued expenses?

11. What is involved in determining the liability for dividends payable?

12. What are the audit objectives for the examination of revenues received in advance?

13. What are the audit objectives to determine the existence and nature of contingencies?

14. Why should management receive monthly reports on the status of current liabilities? Of what benefit could this be to the auditor?

15. For each of the following indicate the preferred title and balance sheet classification:

a) Amount due trade creditors.

b) Deposits received from customers to assure delivery of merchandise.

c) Interest received on notes receivable due in 60 days.

d) Employees' wages earned but not paid.

e) Endorsed subsidiary's bank loan.

f) Signed contract for anticipated plant rearrangement costs.

g) Cash received from a customer, along with order, covering material cost of items to be produced to specification.

h) Sales tax collected, to be remitted to state in 90 days.

i) Mortgage bonds payable, 8 percent due 2001.

j) Advanced rent received—five years in advance.

k) One for one common stock dividend declared.

l) Discounted customer notes receivable.

m) Premium received on 8 percent mortgage bonds payable.

n) Accrued estimated state income tax payable.

o) Sinking fund cash accumulating for use to retire mortgage bonds.

p) Appropriation of retained earnings for bond sinking fund.

q) Portion of 80 percent mortgage bonds to be retired next year.

r) Secured a 90-day loan from the bank on a discounted note payable.

s) Estimated amount of redeemable coupons.

t) Advance receipts on a contract that will be completed next year.

u) Cash dividends in arrears, but not declared.

v) Interest due on mortgage bonds, but not paid.

w) Estimated three-year warranty cost on products sold this year.

x) Cash received for concert series, half of which will be given in this year and the balance next year.

y) Deposits on containers held by customers.

PROBLEMS

1. From the following information, prepare the current liabilities section of the balance sheet for Karen, Inc., as of December 31, 1976.

(1) Notes payable arising from the purchase of raw materials, $116,600.

(2) Notes payable—bank, due in 90 days, $60,000. (Collateral consists of $80,000 of marketable securities.)

(3) Notes payable to officers, due on demand, $40,000.

(4) Accounts payable from the purchase of materials, $88,000.

(5) Cash balance in First Bank, $28,000; cash overdraft in College Bank, $35,000.

(6) Dividends in arrears on cumulative preferred stock, $48,000.

(7) Advance receipts on special jobs being manufactured to specification for customers, $6,000.

(8) Installment notes on equipment purchased, $40,000 of which $20,000 is due in 1977 and the balance in 1978.

(9) Accounts receivable, credit balances, $3,600.

(10) Estimated costs of meeting service requirement guarantees on products produced and sold, $14,400.

(11) One of the company's products exploded causing injury to a customer's employee. The estimated claim is $4,800. The company has no insurance to cover a loss of this nature.

(12) Karen borrowed $20,000 on the cash surrender value of an officer's life insurance. Cash value amounts to $80,000. Interest on this loan has been paid to the balance sheet date.

2. *a)* On April 1, 1976, a client, Electro, Inc., was licensed to manufacture a patented power unit. The license called for a royalty of $0.20 for each unit manufactured. What procedures would you follow in the first annual audit as of December 31, 1976, to determine that the liability for royalties is correctly stated?

b) After your audit was completed, you were asked to prepare a certified report for the owner of the patent on the power unit, covering therein your findings as to royalty payable. Prepare the report you would submit. Pertinent data are: 613,500 units were placed in production, of which 62,720 were rejected or spoiled; on July 26, 1976, a royalty of $6,300 was incurred; and on October 30, 1976, a royalty of $49,520 was incurred.

(AICPA, adapted)

3. As of January 1, 1970, Katey leased a building for ten years; the building was to be used as a retail store. The agreement with the owner was as follows: The annual rent was to be based on sales. On sales up to $300,000 per year the rate was to be 3 percent. On sales in excess of $300,000 per year, the rate was to be 2 percent. However, during the first five years of the term of the lease, the annual rental was to be a minimum of $8,000 per year, after which the minimum was to be increased by 12½ percent.

The lease provided that if in any one year the rent based on sales did not equal the minimum annual rental, the minimum would be payable, but the amount paid solely as a result of such minimum could be applied in reduction of the next year's rent to the extent that the next year's rent exceeded the minimum for that year. Sales by years were as follows:

1970	$192,000	1975	$282,000
1971	258,000	1976	330,000
1972	296,000	1977	284,000
1973	322,000	1978	340,000
1974	248,000	1979	394,000

a) Compute the amount of rent payable each year under the lease.

b) Discuss the financial statement treatment of any amounts payable under the provision for payment of a minimum amount of rent.

(AICPA, adapted)

4. The following data are submitted for a magazine publishing company. All subscriptions were received on July 1, 1976, to start in that month. There is no prior revenue or revenue received in advance.

Subscription for Period of—	Number of Subscriptions	Subscription Price for Period Indicated	Total Cash Received
1 year	40,000	$12.00	$ 480,000
2 years	40,000	21.00	840,000
3 years	40,000	30.00	1,200,000
5 years	40,000	36.00	1,440,000

a) Prepare an audit program for verification of the revenue received in advance from subscriptions as of the year ended December 31, 1976.

b) Prepare work papers setting forth the revenue earned in 1976 and the amount deferred by years as of December 31, 1976.

5. Based upon an audit (for year ended December 31, 1976) certain adjustments must be made. For the client to realize the importance of these adjustments it is necessary to discuss with him the effect on (*a*) net income (before income tax), (*b*) current liabilities, (*c*) net working capital, (*d*) provision for federal income tax, and (*e*) retained earnings.

Prepare an analysis which will indicate whether each of the above is increased (I), decreased (D), or no effect (N).

The adjusting entries follow:

(1) Interest Expense	1,000	
Accrued Interest Payable		1,000
Error in not accruing interest on note.		
(2) Retained Earnings	2,000	
Stock Dividend Payable		2,000
Error in recording stock dividend calculation on 6/30/76.		
(3) Accrued Interest Payable	200	
Interest Expense		200
Interest due 1/1/77 recorded twice.		
(4) Notes Payable—Trade	4,000	
Accounts Payable—Trade		4,000
Payment on note recorded as payment on account payable.		
(5) Profit Sharing Plan Expense	6,000	
Profit Sharing Plan Payable		6,000
Record provision of plan approved by the directors.		
(6) FICA Tax Expense	4,000	
Accrued FICA Tax Payable		4,000
Record employer's FICA tax for week ended 12/31/76.		
(7) Accrued Payroll Insurance Payable	3,000	
Payroll Insurance Expense		3,000
Cancel the accrual of federal unemployment insurance.		

(8)	Notes Payable—Bank	10,000	
	First Mortgage Loan Payable		10,000
	Correct payment to bank made on short-term		
	notes and not on the first mortgage.		
(9)	Federal Income Tax	6,000	
	Provision for Federal Income Tax		6,000
	Record additional federal income tax		
	due for 1976.		
(10)	Retained Earnings	2,000	
	Dividend Payable		2,000
	Record cash dividend declaration as of		
	12/28/76 record date.		

6. Prepare any necessary adjustments for the following audit findings of unrecorded transactions for the year ended December 31, 1976:

   a) An invoice for an insurance premium of $18,000 dated December 31, 1976. Effective date of policy 12/1/76–11/30/79. Invoice unpaid at December 31, 1976, due to the invoice being misplaced. Premium was paid January 10, 1977 and the check cleared the bank on January 12, 1977.

   b) An invoice for 10,000 computer payroll checks in the amount of $1,000 dated December 15, 1976. Checks had been received, but inspection confirms that none had been used by December 31, 1976. Invoice paid on January 22, 1976.

   c) An invoice for a three-year service contract on the client's typewriters in the amount of $1,800, dated December 1, 1976. Effective date of service contract, 11/1/76–10/31/79. The office manager overlooked approving this invoice until the date of payment—January 10, 1977.

   d) The audit of the client's Form 941—Employer's Report of Federal Income Tax and FICA tax liability for the fourth quarter of 1976, revealed that the employer's share of the FICA tax, $1,000, had not been recorded at December 31, 1976.

   e) The return of your account payable verification letter from Research, Inc., indicated a balance due of $1,200. The client's subsidiary ledger showed a balance of $1,800. The difference was due to a client error in crediting Dryer, Inc., for the $600 received from Research.

   f) A review of the client's profit sharing plan revealed:
      (1) No contribution if profits are $25,000 or less.
      (2) When profits are in excess of $25,000, contribution is to be 10 percent of such excess, but not to exceed 20 percent of participants' annual salary.
      (3) Profits are $90,000 and participants' salaries are $120,000. No entry has been made to date.

   g) A noninterest-bearing note to the president, in the amount of $24,000, has been included in Accounts Payable—Nontrade. After discussing this situation with the board of directors on January 10, 1977, it was recorded in the minutes of that meeting as an approval of the loan, at an interest rate of 9 percent. The note was dated November 1, 1976, and due on demand.

h)   The review of the sales bonus plan revealed that no entry had been made for bonuses due December 31, 1976. The provision of the plan stipulated the following:

No bonus on first $250,000 sales

10 percent on next $500,000 sales

5 percent on next $1,000,000 sales

2 percent on any sales in excess of $1,750,000 sales

Total audited net sales—$2,500,000 (disregarded payroll taxes).

14

Long-Term Liabilities

Corporate long-term debt obligations, many with varying features, have entered corporate financing fund raising methods over the past several years. In an audit of long-term liabilities, it is the duty of the auditor to obtain satisfactory evidence of the authority to issue such obligations and to ascertain that all provisions of the agreements of each item are being followed. Related funds must be accounted for in accordance with necessary requirements under the debt obligation agreement.

AUDIT OBJECTIVES

For long-term liabilities the audit objectives are: (1) to determine the adequacy of the system of internal control; (2) to obtain satisfactory evidence of the authority to incur long-term obligations; (3) to ascertain that all long-term liabilities are properly recorded and are properly classified; (4) to determine that interest (including amortization of premiums and discounts) is proper; (5) to determine that the debtor has conformed to all requirements in accordance with contracts regarding sinking funds, restrictions, and the like; and (6) to ascertain that assets pledged (if any) as security to loans are properly disclosed.

INTERNAL CONTROL OF LONG-TERM LIABILITIES

Internal control features applicable to long-term liabilities primarily involve (1) control over the issued and unissued obligations and (2) control over the receipt of cash from an issue and the payment of interest of the proper amount.

Long-term liabilities normally are authorized by the board of directors, or by a stipulated majority of the holders of other long-term obligations, or by a required majority of stockholders.

Proper internal control dictates that long-term debt obligations authorized but unissued be independently prenumbered. Authorized but unissued obligations should be in the controlled possession of the properly authorized corporate officer, or in the possession of an independent trustee. When authorized items are sold, the trustee or the proper corporation official should receive and retain—from the board of directors—a written order to release the items (bonds, debentures, etc.).

Internal control of long-term obligations may be effected by the employment of a trust company as trustee for the obligations. Also, if there are many holders of long-term obligations in the form of (assume) bonds, a registrar, a transfer agent, and an interest-disbursing agent may be independently employed in order to add to the effectiveness of the control.

Redeemed obligations should be canceled and properly mutilated in order to prevent their unauthorized reissuance, and they should be retained for audit.

For registered bonds, a ledger or other record should be used, in which should be shown details of the bonds issued, canceled, and outstanding. A subsidiary ledger normally is and should be maintained by the issuing corporation or by the trustee, for bonds registered as to principal or interest. When summarized, the details of the subsidiary ledger should serve as control data for the auditor. Similar internal control features are applicable to other long-term liabilities.

Proper internal control must be exercised over the payment of interest on long-term liabilities so that amounts in excess of the correct amount will not be paid. Interest on long-term liabilities will be paid directly, either by the debtor or by an interest-paying agent. The use of an interest-paying agent facilitates internal control because there would be no point in issuing excess cash for interest to the agent.

Returned uncashed interest payment checks should be set forth as a liability. If a corporation pays its own interest, proper control should be exercised over authorizing, preparing, and signing the interest checks exactly as in the issuance of checks for the payment of any liability.

An internal control questionnaire for long-term liabilities is set forth in Illustration 14–1.

AUDIT OF LONG-TERM LIABILITIES

In an audit of long-term liabilities, it is normal procedure to examine accounts and entries related to those items, such as interest expense, and premium or discount and its amortization; also, when auditing long-term liabilities and the records pertaining to them, entries for assets received in exchange for the issuance of the liabilities are examined. At any time

Illustration 14–1

| INTERNAL CONTROL QUESTIONNAIRE | | | | |
| Long-Term Liabilities | | | | |

Company_____ Period Covered_____	Yes	No	Not Appli-cable	Remarks
1. Are all long-term liabilities properly authorized by:				
a) The board of directors, and/or	____	____	____	____
b) A required majority of the stockholders, and/or	____	____	____	____
c) A required majority of the holders of other bonds?	____	____	____	____
2. Does the client employ an independent transfer agent for registered bonds?	____	____	____	____
3. Does the client employ an independent registrar for registered bonds?	____	____	____	____
4. If the client does not employ an independent transfer agent or registrar:				
a) Are unsigned bonds properly controlled?	____	____	____	____
b) Are bonds and other obligations signed prior to issuance?	____	____	____	____
c) Are canceled obligations properly mutilated?	____	____	____	____
5. Are at least two signatures necessary to validate an instrument for long-term borrowing?	____	____	____	____
6. Does the client employ an interest-paying agent?	____	____	____	____
7. If the client does not employ an independent interest-paying agent, is the control over coupons or interest checks proper?	____	____	____	____
8. Are unclaimed interest amounts properly handled?	____	____	____	____
9. Have any gains or loss been incurred as the result of extinguishment of debt?	____	____	____	____
10. Is convertible debt and/or debt issued with stock purchase warrants?	____	____	____	____

| Prepared by_____ Date_____ | Reviewed by_____ Date _____ |

prior to closing the records, interim transactions may be examined, thereby affording relief from work at the fiscal period-end.

Bonds Payable

The audit procedures for bonds payable of any type depends on whether a bond trustee is employed or whether the issuing corporation attends to the details of issuance, registration, and transfer.

On an initial engagement, or upon the issuance of new bonds, the auditor should examine a signed copy of the trust indenture in order to become familiar with its provisions and requirements and to determine the authority to issue the bonds. Neglect or violation of the provisions of the trust indenture should be brought to the attention of the client for correction. Notes concerning the trust indenture and the financial provisions contained therein should be prepared and retained for review in future examinations; or a copy of the trust indenture and the financial provisions may be obtained. Pertinent data in a trust indenture include the amounts authorized; dates of issuance and retirement (serial retirements may be provided); interest rates and dates; sinking fund provisions and the disposition of sinking fund balances; property pledged (if any) under the mortgage; redemption features; working capital maintenance requirements; dividend restrictions; provisions for the issuance of additional obligations, the sale of mortgaged property, insurance coverage of mortgaged property, and all other provisions.

If a bond trustee is *not* employed, work papers similar to those in Illustration 14–2 should be prepared, setting forth the data contained therein.

If a bond trustee *is* employed, a confirmation similar to that shown in Illustration 14–3 should be obtained from the trustee, setting forth the original issue, retirements, balance outstanding at the audit date, and other pertinent data. Periodic trustee reports serve as the data for verification of bond transactions. Work papers should be prepared for interest

Illustration 14–2
WORK PAPER 35

		Initials	Date
MULTI-PRODUCTS, INCORPORATED	Prepared By	EF	2-15-77
Bonds Payable, December 31, 1976	Approved By	RW	2-16-77

Date of Issue: January 1, 1970
Type of Bond: Debenture
Maturity Dates: $100,000 each July 1, starting July 1, 1971
Interest Rate: 4 percent January 1 and July 1

Total original issue: 1,000 at $1,000 each, issued at par — 1 000000
Retired and canceled to December 31, 1976 — 600000 W⊙
Balance of bonds outstanding, December 31, 1976, per audit — 400000

Accrued interest on bonds:
Interest paid, July 1, 1976: $500,000 at 4 percent for half year — 10000 ∧∅
Interest accrued, December 31, 1976: $200,000 at 4 percent for one-half year — 8000
Total interest, 1976 — 18000

W In company files, Mutilated.
⊙ Inspected canceled bonds Nos. 1-300 inclusive.
∧ Vouched to cash disbursements.
∅ Agrees with general ledger.

expense, accrued interest, and the verification of the amortization of premium or discount. The details of the bond issue and its activity would be the same as those appearing in a bond schedule when there is no trustee.

If the bond-issuing corporation has not received the latest report of the trustee, the bonds-outstanding balance according to the trustee and the corporation will not agree. All differences must be reconciled, and audit adjustments must be prepared for the Bond liability account and for the Sinking Fund or Bond Retirement account.

Illustration 14–3
THE GOODMAN COMPANY
Report from Bond Trustee, December 31, 1976

```
                         SEVENTH BANK

                      10 East 7th Street

                    Cincinnati, Ohio 45202



                                        January 15, 1977


    Way and Hall
    Certified Public Accountants
    Federal Reserve Bank Building
    Cincinnati, Ohio 45202

    Gentlemen:

    At your request, we are submitting the following data
    pertaining to the first-mortgage bonds of the Goldman
    Company, for which bond issue we serve as trustee.

    We certify to the following data as of December 31, 1976:

         Original issue: 20-year, 5 percent
           first-mortgage bonds; authorized
           and issued.........................$500,000
         Retirements, at par: 150 bonds
           at $1,000...........................150,000
         Bonds outstanding, December 31, 1976:
           350 at $1,000.......................$350,000
         Treasury bonds..........................      0
         Uncashed bond interest coupons.........    250
         Sinking fund balance................. 120,000


                             Very truly yours,

                             SEVENTH BANK

                             George Forrest

                             Trust Officer
```

If there is no trustee, a reconciliation of the bond liability may be effected by starting with the bonds outstanding at the beginning of the year under examination, adding bonds issued during the year, and deducting bonds retired, thus arriving at the bonds outstanding at the end of the year. Bonds sold should be traced to the cash records. Confirmation of bonds outstanding normally is considered necessary only in the event of suspected fraud, or if internal control over bond transactions is weak.

By corresponding with the client's attorney, an auditor should confirm the recording of any mortgage underlying the bond issue. Ownership of property pledged under the trust indenture should be verified by the examination of contracts, deeds, bills of sale, and cash disbursed. Insurance coverage should be reviewed in order to determine that indenture requirements are being fulfilled and in order to determine the adequacy of insurance from the point of view of present market values of the property pledged.

When bonds are issued for cash, the price must be determined and the receipts traced to the cash records. Offsetting entries in the liability account and in the Bond Premium or Discount also must be examined. If bonds were sold for cash to an underwriting syndicate, remittance advices from the syndicate should be examined and compared with entries for cash received, premium or discount, and syndicate charges. In a repeat examination, if a trustee exists, the auditor should request a statement setting forth the following data:

1. Bonds outstanding at the beginning of the period.
2. Bonds issued during the period and premium or discount.
3. Bonds retired during the period; the prices at which they were retired; the disposition of any unamortized premium or discount; and the treatment of loss or gain upon retirement.
4. Bond balance outstanding at the end of the year.
5. The composition of the sinking fund and an analysis of sinking fund transactions for the period of examination.
6. A statement of interest accrued on sinking fund assets as of the date of examination.

When bonds are issued in exchange for assets other than cash, the auditor should examine the entries for the exchange. He also should investigate the reasonableness of the recorded values of the properties acquired in the exchange.

If bonds are issued in exchange for other outstanding liabilities (usually other bonds), the terms of the exchange agreement should be examined. Accounting entries also must be examined.

If a corporation holds treasury bonds, their numbers should be listed on the audit work papers. If a bond trustee holds treasury bonds, he should be requested to confirm them directly to the auditor. Minutes of the board of directors should indicate treasury bond purchases and sales.

The Treasury Bond account at the beginning of the period, plus purchased treasury bonds, less treasury bond credits, equals the end-of-the-period treasury bond balance. The auditor must vouch treasury bond transactions occurring during the period under audit. At a balance sheet date, the Treasury Bond account should be adjusted to par in order to prevent understating or overstating the bond liability. If treasury bonds have been charged—at purchase—to the Treasury Bond account at other than par, adjustments must be prepared charging a loss or a gain if purchased above or below par. Adjustments also must be made for unamortized premium or discount on the treasury bonds as of the date of their acquisition.

A cremation certificate or mutilated bonds should be present for bonds retired during the period. If retired bonds are not canceled or destroyed (and supported by a cremation certificate), a possibility exists that they may have been reissued and the cash proceeds fraudulently used, or the trust indenture violated.

Entries for bond retirements will appear in the cash disbursements records; the auditor should examine the entries. Debits to the Bonds Payable account should represent retirement entries. Bond coupons maturing after the date of bond retirement should be attached to the retired bonds. Profit or loss on retirement must be verified. If all bonds of an issue have been retired, the auditor must verify the cancellation of the deed of trust.

Examination must be made to ascertain that unamortized premium or discount applicable to retired bonds has been eliminated and that any remaining unamortized premium or discount applies only to the remaining bonds outstanding. At this point, it may be well to note that original bond premiums or discounts should be prorated over the shorter of the life of the bonds or an earlier retirement date.

If bonds of the issuing corporation are purchased by the trustee as an investment, which bonds the trustee may sell later, the bonds are kept alive. Usually, the issuing corporation pays interest to the trustee on these bonds.

When a sinking fund trustee is employed, the auditor must obtain confirmation of the fund balance at the audit date and the charges and credits to the fund during the period under examination.

If a sinking fund exists and is administered by the issuing company, a schedule must be prepared setting forth the detail of the periodic charges and credits to the fund and its audit date balance. If the fund is administered by the issuing company, the auditor must verify the sinking fund transactions. In addition, the auditor must examine the sinking fund assets, normally composed of stocks, bonds, cash, and accrued interest. The bonds in the fund may include bonds of the issuing company. Deficiencies in the sinking fund must be covered by additional contributions by the bond-issuing company.

If a sinking fund trustee is not employed, bonds of the issuing company, in the sinking fund, should be valued at par and deducted from bonds outstanding in the balance sheet, exactly as treasury bonds are shown. Discounts and premiums on company bonds purchased and in the fund should be credited or charged to a profit and loss account, just as if the bonds are retired. If the issuing company bonds are held by a sinking fund trustee, they should be priced at cost in a manner similar to any investment; the issuing company has no control over them.

In the exceptional event that a sinking fund reserve is used, the auditor must ascertain that the amount of the reserve is correct and must verify the disposition of the reserve when the bonds are retired.

Bond interest expense for each interest period included in the period of audit must be verified. This verification may be set forth on the work papers for bonds payable. In computing interest expense, additional bonds issued during the period of examination and bonds retired during the period must be taken into consideration.

If a company issues its own checks in payment of interest, the paid checks should be test-compared with a list of the registered bondholders at each interest date for bondholder name, amount, and endorsements. Unclaimed interest checks should be controlled and listed by the auditor. If unclaimed interest checks at an interest date are cashed before the next audit, the auditor should examine bondholder records for transfers; endorsements should be examined.

Mortgages Payable

Mortgages payable may be scheduled in a manner similar to Illustration 14–4. The data for mortgages are obtained from the general ledger, subsidiary ledgers, correspondence, and the client's copy of the mortgage. The authority to mortgage property is determined from an examination of charters, bylaws, and minutes of the meetings of stockholders and directors. Existing agreements or the provisions contained in each mortgage must be examined and noted in the work papers for such items as the purpose of mortgaging the property, interest rate, interest and principal payments, insurance, taxes, and the maintenance of the mortgaged property. The auditor must determine that all provisions are adhered to by the mortgagor.

The authenticity of credits to the Mortgages Payable account must be verified by tracing the offsetting debit to other accounts, supported by entries in the records of original entry, authorization data, and by copies of the mortgage. Each credit must be fully supported and understood.

Debits to the Mortgages Payable account when principal payments are made should be verified by examining the original cash disbursements records, paid checks, and confirmations from the mortgagee.

Confirmations of mortgages should be obtained from the mortgagees

Illustration 14–4

THE BLANK COMPANY
Schedule of Mortgages Payable, December 31, 1976

Mortgagee	Property Mortgaged	Amount	Installments			Maturity Date	Interest			
			Prior to 1976	1976	Balance 12-31-76		Rate	Dates	Paid in 1976	Accrued 12-31-76
Northside Bank	Plant No. 1	200,000 √	120,000	20,000 (10-1-76)	60,000	10-1-78	6%	4-1 10-1	4,800 Ø	900 Ø 3 mo. on $60,000
Central Trust Co.	Plant No. 2	120,000 √	None	None	120,000	1-1-80	6%	1-1 7-1	7,200 Ø	3,600 Ø
First Federal Bank	Plant No. 3 ⊙ ∧ √	300,000 √Z	None	15,000 (12-31-76)	285,000 W	7-2-86	5%	1-2 7-2	None	7,500 Ø
		620,000	120,000	35,000	465,000 W				12,000	12,000

Appraised values:
Plant No. 1 .... $440,000
Plant No. 2 200,000
Plant No. 3 800,000

√ Confirmed.
⊙ Mortgage on Plant No. 3 negotiated on July 2, 1975.
∧ Twenty (20) notes of $15,000 each; payable one each on January 2 and July 2.
Z Proceeds traced to records and to bank.
√ Proceeds used to build plant.
Ø Interest paid and accrued agrees with company's records.
W Agrees with control account.

on a test basis. The confirmation requests should include the balance of the mortgage at the beginning of the year, dates and amounts of principal payments made during the year, the balance of the mortgage at the end of the year, interest dates, interest rates, total interest paid during the year, and necessary data concerning payment arrangements. Confirmation replies are compared with the auditor's work paper data.

Mortgage interest should be further verified by a test sufficient to assure its accuracy and to convince the auditor that unrecorded liabilities do not exist. Paid checks issued for interest payments should be traced through the original records to the interest accounts on a test basis. Interest must be accrued from the last interest payment date to the balance-sheet date.

When mortgages are canceled, the auditor should examine the canceled mortgage, notes, and correspondence from the client's attorney. Evidence of cancellation on county records is obtained by attorney confirmation or by examination of county records.

Long-Term Notes Payable

Notes payable due after one year commonly are classed as long-term liabilities. Audit procedures are the same for long-term notes payable and short-term notes payable.

PENSION PLANS

Pension plans assume a variety of forms. If an employer has a liability to make current deposits into a pension plan fund at a balance sheet date, that liability should be set forth. The funds provided by the employer may be periodically deposited with a trustee (insurance company, bank, or trust company) under the approved plan.

The periodic premiums are expense charges in the period of incurrence, and all accrued premiums should be set forth as such in the balance sheet. *Accounting Research Bulletin No. 43,* chapter 13, treats of pension plan costs which are known as annuity costs—the costs necessary to cover an employee for services performed *prior* to the adoption of the plan, and *Opinion No. 8* of the Accounting Principles Board now supersedes chapter 13, and also supersedes *Accounting Research Bulletin No. 47. Opinion No. 8* of the Accounting Principles Board comprehensively covers pension plan costs and related problems and should be followed.

Pension costs based on past services should *not* be charged to Retained Earnings simply because those past services already have been rendered. The costs based on past services should be charged to expense systematically over the present period and a reasonable period following the adoption of the pension plan—because obviously any plan is adopted with the sole thought of the future. Again, see *Opinion No. 8* of the APB.

In order to qualify under the Internal Revenue Code, annuity costs based on past services must be spread over the present and future periods. If payments into the pension fund for past services were made in a lump sum and if a deferred charge to future operations is charged at that time, the allocation to future expense periods in the past has been a matter of management's decision; for federal income tax purposes the prepaid costs are allocable over a minimum of ten years if the initial past-period service cost is immediately paid in full.

Generally, in order to qualify under the Internal Revenue Code, pension funds must be deposited with an approved fund trustee. In this case, the company establishing the fund is not in possession of the fund assets and does not show fund assets or liabilities, other than currently due payments. Also, if the pension funds are trusteed, any future financial difficulty of the employer will not threaten the balance in the accumulated funds.

As stated earlier in this section, an accrual to make current deposits into a pension fund should be clearly set forth. How should *total* pension plan obligations be shown? In practice, there is no uniformity of answer to the question. Some companies show the total of the obligation as a liability, a very few still show it as a retained earnings segregation, and a few show the item separately between liabilities and capital. The authors are of the opinion that prior service cost of a pension plan which is not funded is not a liability but should be systematically charged to expense in the future—based on an accounting method that uses an acceptable actuarial cost method; if the vested rights of participants are liabilities of an employer, the present value of the amount not funded should be shown as an accrual.

In the examination of the obligation of a client for the maintenance of pension agreements, the auditor's investigation should be made so that certainty exists that pension agreement terms are being fulfilled by the client and that liabilities under the agreement are properly stated. The auditor should include in his permanent file a copy of the pension plan agreement. Also, the auditor is urged to follow *Opinion No. 8* of the APB in order to narrow the areas of differences in financial reporting.

FINANCIAL STATEMENT CONSIDERATIONS

In a balance sheet it is essential that each long-term liability be fully disclosed and adequately described. Bonds payable (including today's "funny money" obligations) may be carried in the balance sheet at par, together with maturity dates and interest rates, or they may be carried at par plus unamortized premium (or minus unamortized discount). It is important to show interest rates if those rates are higher than the current price of borrowing, and particularly if the bonds are not callable. If a trustee is not employed, sinking fund bonds of the issuing company, retired bonds, unissued bonds, and treasury bonds (whether or not they are kept alive) should be deducted at par from the total authorized issue and the net par liability extended. Treasury bonds kept alive for resale very often are shown as assets; but they should be shown as deductions from the gross liability because the liability to be liquidated has been reduced by the acquisition of the bonds, in spite of intentions which at the balance sheet date are not fulfilled. A balance sheet should show existing conditions and not expectations.

If a bond issue—or one series of a total serial issue—is payable within one year and if a special fund is not available for the payment, the amount currently due should be moved to the current liability classification. If a special fund is available for the repayment of amounts currently due, the fund becomes a current asset at the time the transfer is made from long-term to current liabilities. However, where special payment funds are available, it must be remembered that the removal of the special fund and the currently due portion of the liability to the current sections may disturb the current ratio. In addition, if gains or losses from extinguishment of debt are incurred, they should be classified as extraordinary items and should be sufficiently described to enable users of financial statements to objectively evaluate their importance.

Mortgages should be shown in the balance sheet as first mortgages, second mortgages, chattel mortgages, and so on. Each mortgage should be shown at its net payable amount. Where assets are pledged as security for a mortgage, this fact should be so indicated on the asset side of the balance sheet.

Long-term notes issued to banks and insurance companies are a prominent method of financing employed by industrial concerns. All long-term notes should be classified with long-term liabilities.

Pension fund liabilities do not enjoy a uniform placement in the balance sheet. However, it is the opinion of the authors that amounts currently due should be shown as current liabilities, and that the total of the liability under the fund should be shown as a long-term liability if the vested rights of participants are liabilities of an employer. Also, *Opinion No. 8* of the APB should be followed, and an acceptable actuarial cost method should be used.

SUGGESTED ADDITIONAL READING

Statement of Financial Accounting Standards No. 4.
APB Opinions Nos. 8, 14, 26, and *30.*

QUESTIONS

1. What are the audit objectives in the examination of long-term liabilities?
2. What factors should be present for a company to have good internal control over its long-term liabilities?

3. *a)* Describe several types of bonds.
   b) What are treasury bonds?
   c) What steps are involved in the audit of a client's treasury bonds?

4. What procedures must the auditor follow where a bond sinking fund is in operation?

5. One principle of internal control over long-term liabilities is that instruments of indebtedness be physically controlled prior to authorized issuance. Why might a company be interested in increasing its indebtedness by issuing long-term obligations if it did not need the funds provided by such issuance?

6. How should bonds payable be carried in the balance sheet?

7. How should a series of serial bonds be shown on the balance sheet when they are due in the next year and how should a special fund which is available for repayment be shown?

8. *a)* How should mortgages be shown in the financial statements?
   b) How should mortgaged property be shown in a balance sheet?

9. How should costs of pension plan annuities be handled that are in consideration of past services?

10. How can a company limit its legal obligation of a pension plan?

11. What must an auditor do in the financial statements to insure full disclosure of leases?

PROBLEMS

1. As of December 31, 1976, the Bonds Payable account of a client contains the following entries:

   October 1, 1975, cash . . . . 448,000 Cr.
   April 1, 1976, cash . . . . 37,600 Dr.
   October 1, 1976, cash . . . . 42,400 Dr.

   The bond maturity date is October 1, 1995.
   As auditor, state the examination procedures you would follow for:
   a) Confirmations, assuming a trustee.
   b) Assurance of the accuracy of the account balance of $368,000.
   c) Acceptable financial statement presentation.

2. In reviewing the accounts of Boon, Inc., at the beginning of 1976, you find that on January 1, 1977, it had acquired a new building in exchange for its own 6 percent First Subordinated Bonds with a par value of $400,000 that mature January 1, 1982. You determine that the bonds had a market value on the date of exchange of $368,000; however, the building was recorded at par value of the bonds and depreciation was recognized for 1972 through 1975 at the rate of 4 percent annually. What compound entry would you make to correct the accounts?

3. A client is advised by a pension consultant at the beginning of 1976 that the cost of establishing a certain pension plan with full recognition of past services of all present employees is $1,800,000. The payment needed

to recognize services for 1976 is calculated at the end of 1976 to be $160,000; this amount is payable in January 1977.

Prepare the journal entries that will appear on the records of the client in 1976 assuming that:

a) The cost of recognizing past service is paid in 1976, and such cost is to be assigned to revenue in equal installments over a ten-year period.

b) The cost of recognizing past services is to be paid in ten equal annual installments, and the client wishes to report the full amount payable on the plan as a liability.

4. On July 1, 1972, Welch, Inc., issued $300,000, 5 percent, 20-year mortgage bonds. The bond indenture provided that the company deposit with the trustee on June 30, 1973, and annually thereafter, the sum necessary for the accumulation at 3 percent, compounded annually, for a sinking fund to retire the bonds at maturity. The fiscal year ends June 30.

On June 30, 1977, the balance sheet contains only the following accounts relative to the bond issued.

Bond Sinking Fund . . . . $ 25,000
Bonds Payable 300,000

Your initial audit shows that the $25,000 was deposited on June 30, 1975, that $11,164.71 should have been set aside annually at 3 percent if the fund is to be accumulated in 16 deposits. Bond interest dates are January 1 and July 1, and the interest has been paid when due.

Prepare the entries to correct the records as of June 30, 1977, and show account balances relative to the bond issue as they should appear on the June 30, 1977, balance sheet.

5. Your corporate client was considering the issuance of bonds as of January 1, 1976, under either of the two following plans:

Plan 1: $500,000 par value, 8 percent, first-mortgage, 20-year bonds, due on December 31, 1995, to be issued at 94 percent of par.

Plan 2: $500,000 par value, 8 percent, first-mortgage, 20-year bonds, due on December 31, 1995, to be issued at par, with provision for payment of a 6 percent premium upon maturity.

The client requests that you prepare separate sets of journal entries for each plan, with explanations:

a) At the date of issue.
b) Monthly thereafter.
c) Upon payment at the date of maturity.
d) Which plan is the more advantageous to the client?

Discounts and premiums are to be allocated to accounting periods on a straight-line basis. Issuance costs are to be ignored.

6. On July 1, 1966, Jaws, Inc., issued $500,000 of 40-year, 5 percent, first-mortgage bonds at 95. During the past ten years, the company annually charged to expense 2½ percent of the unamortized discount. On July 1, 1976, the company purchased $100,000 of the bonds at 90 and retired

and canceled them. During the course of your audit for the year 1976, you noted that the $10,000 discount at the acquisition date had been credited to a nonrecurring income account. Is the transaction correctly recorded? If not, what should be the correct entry?

7. From the following data, show how the information might be set forth in an acceptable balance sheet.

1976

July 20 Bonds authorized, first-mortgage, 20-year, 5 percent, $5,000,-000.

Aug. 1 Of the bonds authorized, $4,000,000 were sold to an under-writer, at par.

1977

Mar. 10 Bonds of a par of $200,000 were purchased at par and were to be held alive in the treasury.

July 18 The bonds acquired on March 10, 1977, plus $300,000 of the unissued bonds were pledged as collateral for a loan of $375,-000.

8. One of your clients has the following bond issues outstanding at December 31, 1975.

Series I: $15,000,000, 6 percent, due on January 1, 1998, callable at 105 until January 1, 1993, and thereafter at 103.

Series II: $30,000,000, 5 percent, due January 1, 2008, callable at 104 until January, 1988, and thereafter at 102.

The company plans to refund both issues by issuing $50,000,000 of 4 percent bonds, due January 1, 2008. The bonds are to be issued at 96. The original issue of Series I was $20,000,000; and $5,000,000 had been purchased and retired by the sinking fund trustee in accordance with the provisions of the trust indenture. On January 1, 1976, there was no cash in the sinking fund, due to purchases of the Series I bonds. Assuming that the refunding operation is to be effective on January 1, 1976, what is the total saving effected by the operation? Assume that no additional bonds will be called.

9. A client corporation has just entered into an employee pension plan. The plan became effective January 1, 1976. During the course of your audit for the year ended December 31, 1976 you find that two entries, in connection with the pension plan, have been made as follows:

Retained Earnings 5,000
    Cash 5,000
    To record the first of a series of five equal annual
    payments required to be made to an insurance company
    to cover the cost of pensions based on past services.

Factory Wages 3,000
    Cash 3,000
    To record the 1976 contribution to the insurance company
    for pension costs based on the 1976 factory wages.

Did the two entries reflect properly the facts regarding the pension plan? Present your reasons and describe any changes considered necessary.

15

Owners' Equities

CAPITAL

The synonymous terms "owners' equities," "capital," "proprietorship," or "net worth" represent the difference between total assets and total liabilities. These equivalent terms have no relationship to any asset, working capital, or "how much the business is worth."

Corporate capital is composed of the dollar amounts allocated to issued and outstanding shares of capital stock, capital contributed in excess of the par or stated value of capital stock, donated capital, appreciation of assets (if recorded), retained earnings appropriations, and unappropriated retained earnings.

Partnership capital is composed of the sum of the algebraic balances of the partners' capital accounts and personal accounts.

Single proprietorship capital is the algebraic balance of the owner's capital account and personal account—if one is used.

Normally, the audit of equity capital items is not extensively time-consuming, because ordinarily the number of transactions to be examined is not large; however, the majority of transactions in this area are material in amount, and consequently are important.

AUDIT OBJECTIVES FOR CORPORATE CAPITAL

The objectives of auditing corporate capital are (1) to evaluate the internal control over stock transactions and stock certificates; (2) to determine that transactions affecting equity accounts have been properly authorized, approved, and recorded; (3) to determine the propriety of ledger accounts and financial statement presentation of authorized capital stocks, issued and outstanding capital stocks, other permanent capital items not represented by capital stock, treasury stocks, retained earnings, and retained earnings reservations; (4) to determine that the privileges of each class of stockholder have been observed by the corporation; and (5) to determine that statutory requirements have not been violated.

INTERNAL CONTROL OF CORPORATE CAPITAL

For capital stock, the principal points of internal control are the prevention of the issuance of unauthorized stock certificates and the proper accounting for transfers of shares.

Corporations having a large number of stockholders and actively traded stocks employ independent transfer agents (banks or trust companies), who prepare stock certificates, maintain a ledger of the stockholders, approve transfers of share ownership, issue new certificates and prepare and mail dividend checks. The corporation also employs an independent registrar who signs the certificates and determines that the stock is not overissued.

When a corporation acts as its own registrar and transfer agent, proper internal control demands that stock certificates be serially prenumbered, and that authority for the signing and issuance of certificates be delegated by the board of directors. As one certificate is issued, corresponding records (certificate stub blanks or a record of the certificates) should be prepared containing the name and address of the stockholder and the number of shares—spelled out and in numbers. Canceled certificates should be mutilated. Entries for stock issuances and transfers should be made by a person who does not have the authority to sign and issue certificates.

An internal control questionnaire for corporate capital is presented in Illustration 15–1.

AUDIT OF CAPITAL STOCK

In examining capital stock issues, state requirements relative to incorporation procedures, the qualification of securities, treasury stock regulations, par value and no-par-value shares, the requirements of the Securities and Exchange Commission, and other pertinent requirements must be fully understood.

In starting an audit of capital stock, the auditor must examine the articles of incorporation and any amendments thereto which may affect the accounting for capital stock and the audit, including (a) the names of the various classes of stock; (b) the number of authorized shares of each class; (c) the par value, stated value, or no-par-value features of each class; (d) any special rights of each class; and (e) normal and liquidating dividend features.

In an initial audit, each class of capital stock should be scheduled from

Illustration 15–1

INTERNAL CONTROL QUESTIONNAIRE
Corporate Capital

Company_____ Period Covered _____	Yes	No	Not Appli- cable	Remarks
1. Is an independent transfer agent employed for capital stock?	___	___	___	_____
2. Is an independent registrar employed for capital stock?	___	___	___	_____
3. If the client does not employ an independent transfer agent or registrar:				
a) Are unissued stock certificates under the control of an officer?	___	___	___	_____
b) Are stock certificates signed in advance of issuance?	___	___	___	_____
c) Are blank stock certificates and matching stubs prenumbered by the printer?	___	___	___	_____
d) Are canceled stock certificates properly voided?	___	___	___	_____
4. Does an independent agent pay the dividends?	___	___	___	_____
5. If an independent dividend-paying agent is not employed, is proper control exercised over dividend checks?	___	___	___	_____
6. Are unclaimed dividend checks redeposited and set up as liabilities?	___	___	___	_____
7. Is the dividend bank account regularly reconciled:				
a) By a person who does not maintain the dividend records?	___	___	___	_____
b) By a person who does not mail the dividend checks?	___	___	___	_____
8. If there is no registrar, does the client regularly reconcile the number of shares outstanding—according to the stockholders' records—with the control account balance in terms of shares?	___	___	___	_____
9. If capital stock is exchanged for noncash assets, is proper valuation applied to the assets received?	___	___	___	_____
10. Has the Securities and Exchange Commission ever rejected asset valuations referred to in Question 9?	___	___	___	_____
11. If retained earnings reserves exist, were they properly authorized, established, and canceled?	___	___	___	_____
12. Have stock dividends or splits been:				
(a) properly authorized?	___	___	___	_____
(b) properly entered?	___	___	___	_____

Prepared by_____   Reviewed by_____
Date_____   Date _____

the beginning of the business or for a number of years to insure accuracy of recording and the accuracy of the balance at the beginning of the year under audit. In a repeat engagement the schedule may follow the pattern shown in Illustration 15–2, in which the number of shares of each class at the beginning of the period represents the starting point. If company purchases and original issuances are involved, entries must be vouched to cash or other original asset records, to other capital stock accounts, and to

Illustration 15–2
WORK PAPER 36

		Initials	Date
MULTI-PRODUCTS, INCORPORATED	Prepared By	PM	2-25-77
Common Stock Certificate Data, December 31, 1976	Approved By	RW	2-26-77

Certificate Number	Stockholder Name	Balance Dec. 31, 1976	Issued or Canceled 1976	Balance Dec. 31, 1976
101		10,000 ✓		10,000 T
102		5,000 ✓		5,000 T
103 C		10,000 ✓	10,000 C	
104		4,000 ✓		4,000 T
105 C		6,000 ✓	6,000 C	
106		5,000 ✓		5,000 T
107			3,000 I ✓	3,500 T
108			6,000 I ✓	6,500 T
109			3,000 I ✓	3,000 T
110			3,000 I ✓	3,000 T
		40,000		40,000 B

C Canceled, Examined for mutilation.
✓ Certificate record examined.
I Issued
T Traced to stockholders' ledger
B Balance per audit

paid-in capital accounts if original issues are sold at amounts in excess of par or stated values. The schedule concludes with the share balance at the end of the year. Support for debits and credits to capital stock accounts for original and subsequent issuance, for treasury stock transactions, for cancellations, for stock dividends, and for stock splits originate not only in the original financial records but also in the minutes of the meetings of stockholders and directors.

All shares outstanding must be accounted for by the auditor. If a corporation retains a capital stock registrar or a transfer agent, the auditor should obtain confirmations of the shares outstanding at the end of the period. If a corporation maintains its own capital stock records, the auditor must total the stockholders' open share records (certificate stubs for small companies) in order to prove the share balance of the controlling account for the number of shares outstanding; all certificate numbers should be accounted for, including those canceled during the year under audit. The beginning balance of the number of shares, plus the number of shares issued during the year, minus the number of shares canceled during the year, equals the number of shares outstanding at the end of the year. Canceled certificates should be defaced to prevent their reuse. Each accompanying transfer record should indicate the number of shares canceled, the name of the persons to whom new certificates were issued, and the number of shares issued. This is necessary in order to ascertain to whom dividends should be paid.

Treasury stock transactions should be verified and proper disposition given to the differences between cost and resale price of the treasury shares. The auditor must determine that dividends are not paid on treasury stock. Treasury stock is "issued," but it is not outstanding; therefore, it is not a permanent reduction of capital stock or a retirement of shares. Local statutory requirements for the acquisition and disposition of treasury stock must be followed. Normally, treasury stock is recorded at cost of acquisition; and as treasury shares are resold, the Treasury Stock account should be credited at cost. Any difference between cost price and disposition price should be charged or credited to a special permanent noncap:tal stock equity account. It may be necessary to charge Retained Earnings if there is no appropriate special permanent noncapital stock equity account.

AUDIT OF PARTNERSHIP AND SINGLE PROPRIETORSHIP CAPITAL

A copy of the partnership agreement should be in the auditor's permanent file. The current agreement should be examined and the following minimum data excerpted:

1. Name, address, and fiscal year of the partnership.
2. Name of each partner.
3. Classification of each partner, i.e., general, limited, or silent.
4. Capital contributed by each partner.
5. Duties of each partner.
6. Drawing arrangements for each partner.
7. Interest arrangements on capital account balances.
8. Interest charges on excess drawings.
9. Profit- and loss-sharing ratios.
10. Provisions for withdrawal of a partner.
11. Partnership dissolution and liquidation provisions.
12. Reciprocal life insurance arrangements.
13. Retirement pension plan arrangements.

Violation of any portion of a partnership agreement should be directed to the attention of the partners.

In an initial audit of the financial statements of a partnership, opening entries should be verified for assets contributed, liabilities assumed, and the capital credit for each partner. In a first examination, if the original partnership personnel has changed or if the original partnership has been dissolved, followed by the formation of a succeeding partnership, the accuracy of the accounting for withdrawals, dissolutions, and new formations should be verified in order to avoid future complications. Also, in a first audit, it *may* be necessary to vouch entries in both capital and personal accounts from the beginning of the partnership. If this is not necessary, entries should be vouched for a period of time sufficient to assure the auditor of the accuracy of the accounts as of the beginning of the year under examination.

For the period under examination, each capital account and each personal account should be analyzed, and each transaction in each account should be vouched to the original records. In verifying account entries, the auditor must ascertain that drawing arrangements have not been violated and that capital account contributions have been maintained in accordance with the partnership agreement. The auditor must ascertain that current-period net income or loss has been properly distributed to the partners.

In the first audit of a single proprietorship, it usually is not necessary to analyze the capital account (and drawing account, if used) from the inception of the business. A review of tax returns of prior periods and the accounting records for assets and liabilities normally will establish the validity of the owner's equity. For the period under audit, the auditor must analyze the capital and drawing accounts of the owner and must vouch the entries in these accounts.

AUDIT OF STOCKHOLDERS' EQUITIES OTHER THAN CAPITAL STOCK

This section of the chapter will set forth the audit procedures for equity capital amounts not credited to capital stock accounts. The excess of net assets over capital stock is divided into various accounts—each account being created on a functional basis. Retained earnings, or earnings retained for use in the business, represent accumulated periodic net income, after dividends and other appropriate charges, transferred to the account at closing time each year. The accumulation is from the date of incorporation, or from the date when a deficit was eliminated in a quasi-reorganization. Retained earnings reservations represent retained earnings amounts transferred to specifically named appropriations, such as a reserve for a specific contingency, a reserve for treasury stock acquisitions, and others.

Paid-in capital in excess of the par or stated value of capital stock arises when par value stock is sold at a premium, when stock of a stated value is sold above that price, when voluntary amounts are paid in by shareholders, when shareholders are assessed for fund-raising purposes (this is unusual), when treasury stock is sold at a price in excess of acquisition cost, and in any other instances resulting from transactions between the corporate entity and its stockholders; these transactions should not be entered in the capital stock accounts.

Appreciation of assets (excess of appreciation over cost) arises when assets are written upward on the accounting records.

For each class of noncapital stock equity and for each account involved, the auditor must determine its composition, source, and dispositions. Restrictions—legal or by company action—placed on each class must be determined, as must the propriety of all charges and credits. Reservations or appropriations of retained earnings must be analyzed to determine the adequacy and propriety of each appropriation and to determine that the appropriations are disposed of in accordance with the purpose of the creation and in accordance with accepted principles of accounting.

Each noncapital stock equity account should be scheduled, all entries in each account should be vouched, the restrictions on retained earnings should be verified, and deductions from each noncapital stock equity account must be properly authorized.

A noncapital stock equity account should not be distributed without proper action of the board of directors and/or the stockholders—except debits to Retained Earnings for current-period losses. Distributions of (debits to) any class of noncapital stock equity must not violate either the legal or contractual debits when that item is segregated for special purposes.

Retained Earnings

In a first audit, retained earnings should be analyzed for a number of prior periods adequate to establish the balance of the account at the beginning of the period under audit. The audit objectives of such an analysis are:

1. To determine the propriety of the debits and the credits from the point of view of ascertaining that the entries properly belong in this capital account.
2. To obtain a condensed picture of the net income productivity of the business.
3. To obtain a picture of dividend policies in the past.
4. To determine whether the theory of clean retained earnings has or has not been consistently followed, in accordance with modern and approved practice.

In a repeat engagement the Retained Earnings account is analyzed for the period under examination. All entries should be verified by reference to the records of original entry. Charges to the account should be properly supported by action of the board of directors for such items as dividend declarations and appropriations of retained earnings. The mathematical correctness of the entries should be proved.

Restrictions on retained earnings should be fully understood, verified,

Illustration 15–3
WORK PAPER 37

	Initials	Date
MULTI-PRODUCTS, INCORPORATED	Prepared By *pm*	2·25·77
Retained Earnings, December 31, 1976	Approved By *RW*	2·26·77

Balance, per audit, December 31, 1975			575274	
Add: Net income, 1976			271010	
			846284	
Deduct: Dividends, 1976			100000 ✓∅	
Balance, per audit, December 31, 1976			746284	

✓Traced to cash disbursements.
∅No checks outstanding.

and fully disclosed in the audit report. Appropriations of retained earnings, when disposed of, should be returned to the Retained Earnings account.

In the absence of fraud and discrimination, the board of directors has the power to distribute retained earnings as it wishes, after providing for proper debits to the account for appropriations. See Illustration 15–3.

Paid-in Capital

The following comments apply to amounts paid in which are in excess of the par or stated value of capital stock, donated amounts, capital arising from treasury stock transactions, and any other noncapital stock equity, except retained earnings and appreciation of assets.

In a first audit, each account should be analyzed from its inception (if necessary) in order to ascertain the propriety of the entries. In a repeat engagement, current-period entries should be vouched. Capital contributed in excess of the par or stated value of the capital stock issued should appear only upon authorization of the board of directors.

Debits to a paid-in capital (and other similar nonstock) equity account should be investigated critically to determine not only their propriety but also their legality. Cash dividends may or may not be permissibly declared from these sources. See Illustration 15–4.

Appreciation of Assets

In a first audit it may be necessary to analyze this account from its inception to determine the propriety of all entries. Source entries must be

Illustration 15–4
WORK PAPER 38

	Initials	Date
Prepared By	PM	2-23-77
Approved By	RW	2-26-77

MULTI-PRODUCTS, INCORPORATED
Paid-In-Capital--Excess of Issuance Price over Par, December 31, 1976

Balance, per audit, December 31, 1975		200000		
Changes in 1976		0		
Balance, December 31, 1976		200000		
When the common stock originally was issued on October 2, 1967, in the amount of 40,000 shares of a par value of $20 each, it was sold for $15 per share; and $5 per share was credited to paid-in capital.				

vouched to the related asset accounts. In a repeat engagement, all current-period entries should be examined and traced to original authorizations and records.

The auditor must ascertain if depreciation on appreciated assets is computed on original cost or on the increased valuations; the latter treatment is preferable.

If a discovery capital account is in existence, geological reports should be examined to determine the validity and reasonableness of the account. Debits to the account may represent capital distributions to stockholders or reductions caused by revaluations.

Retained Earnings Appropriations or Reserves

A true "reserve" is a segregation—or appropriation—of retained earnings for a specific purpose. Retained earnings appropriations are established voluntarily by the board of directors or by required legal or contractual obligation.

In examining retained earnings appropriations, the auditor must ascertain the authority for the segregation, the purpose for which it was created, and whether it is optional or contractual. If contractual, the auditor must examine the underlying agreements and determine whether the terms of the agreement are being followed.

Each retained earnings appropriation should be analyzed, and all entries should be vouched. Examples of retained earnings appropriations include those for specific contingencies, such as fire losses, conservation of business capital, and for capital stock redemptions. Upon the fulfillment of the purpose for which a retained earnings appropriation was created, it should be returned to unappropriated retained earnings; or it may be permanently capitalized by a transfer to capital stock—with or without the payment of a stock dividend.

A retained earnings appropriation should *not* be treated as a liability— because a liability does not exist.

DIVIDENDS

In the examination of dividends declared and/or paid, the auditor should refer to the minutes of the board of directors to determine the dates of declaration, record, and payment; he should determine the amount per share and the kind of dividend. These data are compared with the accounting records, and with stockholders' subsidiary records. Verification of the total dollar amount of the dividends for any one dividend payment is made by multiplying the dividend per share by the number of shares outstanding at the record-closing date.

A stock dividend is not considered taxable income to the recipient. However, its realistic effect is to transfer a part of the retained earnings to permanent capital, and to distribute that transferred portion to the stockholders. Consequently, the stockholders have received tangible wealth, just as though cash had been received.

In a stock split, only the number of shares is changed. There is no transfer of retained earnings to permanent capital. Stock splits usually are used when it is desired to reduce the market price per share of stock outstanding.

To be legal, a dividend should be authorized by the board of directors and the action recorded. If a cash dividend has been declared but not paid at the end of the accounting period, it should appear as a liability. When dividends are paid in capital stock, the auditor must determine that such action did not result in the issuance of shares in excess of those authorized by the charter. In order to ascertain the propriety of a dividend declaration and the correctness of the accounting entries, the source of the dividend must be ascertained. When a dividend is declared from retained earnings, a deficit should not thereby be created. Also, if there are restrictions on retained earnings, a dividend declaration should not reduce the Retained Earnings account below the appropriated amounts required by those other actions.

If dividend payments represent a partial or full return of capital—exemplified in some extractive industries and public utilities cases—a notice of such action should accompany the dividend check or be imprinted on the check.

Paid dividend checks should be test-compared with the stockholders' subsidiary ledger records for name, amount, and endorsement. In order to complete a bank reconciliation, all dividend checks must be accounted for. Computers are useful for this operation. Unclaimed dividend checks should be deposited in the bank and a liability account credited.

If dividends on cumulative preferred stock are in arrears, the balance sheet should contain a footnote to that effect.

FINANCIAL STATEMENT CONSIDERATIONS

In the balance sheet, capital stock should be separately set forth for each class in terms of authorized shares, par or stated values per share, shares outstanding, shares unissued, treasury shares, and dividend rates on preferred stock. Cumulative dividends in arrears on preferred stock should be shown by balance-sheet footnote.

Short-term equalization allowances should not appear in the capital section of a balance sheet—because they are not a part of owners' equities.

Uncollected capital stock subscriptions normally are current assets, unless (1) there is no immediate intention of collecting the subscriptions, or (2) there is a contingency with respect to their collection. In the two latter cases the uncollected subscriptions are shown as deductions from the capital stock.

Treasury stock is not an asset but may be shown either as a deduction from the shares authorized or as in Illustrations 15–5 or 15–6. Today,

Illustration 15–5
CAPITAL SECTION OF A BALANCE SHEET

Stockholders' Equities:

Preferred stock: authorized 10,000 shares of $100 par value, of which 8,000 shares are issued and outstanding, and 1,500 shares are unissued, and 500 shares are in the treasury	$ 800,000	
Common stock "A," authorized and issued, 100,000 shares of a par value of $10 per share	1,000,000	
Common stock "B," no par value, 1,000,000 shares authorized and issued at a stated value of $8 per share	8,000,000	
Total Capital Stock		$ 9,800,000
Paid-in capital from premium on preferred stock .	$ 100,000	
Paid-in capital from the sale of "B" common stock in excess of stated value	3,000,000	3,100,000
Total Paid-In Capital		$12,900,000
Discovery value capital—excess over cost	1,000,000	1,400,000
Retained earnings appropriated for:		
Reserve for self-insured risks	1,200,000	
Reserve for plant expansion	5,000,000	6,200,000
Unappropriated earnings retained for use in the business		24,500,000
Total Paid-In Capital and Retained Earnings		$45,000,000
Less: Reacquired common shares (36,400), at cost		1,108,000
Total Stockholders' Equities		$43,892,000

Illustration 15–6
CONSOLIDATED STATEMENT OF SHAREHOLDER'S EQUITY
(in thousands)

	Par Value of Capital Stock	Capital in Excess of Par Value	Earnings Retained and Invested in the Business	Treasury Shares at Cost	Total
Balance, Dec. 31, 1972 . . .	$ 923,786	$115,378	$2,878,223	$(118,466)	$3,798,921
Net income			511,249		511,249
Cash dividends at $1.29 a share			(180,304)		(180,304)
Acquisitions and issuance of treasury shares (net)				(4,598)	(4,598)
Balance, Dec. 31, 1973 . . .	923,786	115,378	3,209,168	(123,064)	4,125,268
Net income			970,266		970,266
Cash dividends at $1.65 a share			(233,876)		(233,876)
100 percent stock distribution	908,625	(238,403)	(670,222)		
Capital stock issued upon conversion of debentures	43,127	155,574		47,082	245,783
Acquisitions and issuances of treasury shares (net) excluding shares issued upon conversion of debentures		6,010		11,656	17,666
Balance, Dec. 31, 1974 . . .	$1,875,538	$ 38,559	$3,275,336	$ (64,326)	$5,125,107

many companies show treasury stock as an asset when it is acquired for future sale under stock option plans. This is not proper. Capital paid in from each source should be clearly, definitely, and separately set forth and explained. Retained earnings is shown divided into its appropriated and unappropriated portions. Illustration 15–5 includes more items than normally found in the stockholders' equity section of any one balance sheet.

SUGGESTED ADDITIONAL READING:

Statement on Auditing Standards No. 1, Section 420, Paragraphs 11, 13, 14; Section 545, Paragraph 1.
Annual reports to stockholders of various major corporations.

QUESTIONS

1. In the early stage of an audit of the financial statements of a corporation, an auditor would obtain information that would become a part of the permanent file. What are the types, sources, and nature of this information?

2. What are the audit objectives in examining corporate owners' equities?

3. What are the principal points of internal control for corporate capital stock?

4. During the current year the authorized capital stock of a corporation has been increased and the additional shares were sold. Outline the procedures to be followed in the verification of the capital stock if the corporation (a) employs a capital stock transfer agent and (b) if the corporation does not employ a transfer agent.

5. During the course of the audit of the records of a company, you compared the balance of the shares in the Common Stock controlling account with the sum of the duplicate stock certificates and with the share balances in the subsidiary stockholders' ledger. Three months after completion of the audit, it was discovered that all the common stock outstanding at the balance sheet date had not been accounted for in a proper manner. What possibilities might have caused this situation?

6. When examining a Development Expense account for a new corporation, you noted that one charge was for discount granted the corporate president for par value common stock issued to him. As auditor, what position would you take?

7. In the audit of the financial statements of a partnership, what steps would you follow in examining the Personal accounts of the partners?

8. In the course of an audit of the financial statements of the partnership of A, B, and C, what would be your guide in the following circumstances? What action would you take in each instance?
   a) In determining the division of profits.
   b) The drawings of partner A are above the permitted amount.
   c) The drawings of partner B are above the permitted amount.

9. Under what conditions would an auditor find appropriations limiting the use of retained earnings?

10. Plants, Inc., has appropriated retained earnings of $4 million over a ten-year period for the purpose of plant expansion. The company completed the expansion program at a cost of $6 million in year 11. The expansion was financed through company funds of $3.5 million and borrowed funds of $2.5 million. What disposition of the appropriation for plant expansion should the auditor recommend?

11. All of the common capital stock of 200,000 shares, par value $10 each, of End, Inc., has been subscribed for. On December 31, 1975, $5 per share had been received on *all* of the subscriptions. The business was successful, and the Retained Earnings account showed a balance of $4,000,000 on December 31, 1976. At the first board meeting of January 1977 a motion was passed to make the stock—of which $5 per share

was still uncollected—fully paid. You, as auditor, were called in to offer your advice as to how the motion should be brought into the records.

12. Outline the procedure for an audit of dividends paid.

13. Audits of five clients showed that each has cumulative preferred stock dividends in arrears at a certain date. Each company had adequate free retained earnings to cover the dividend.

Client 1 did not show the accumulation in the balance sheet but appended a footnote stating the amount of the accumulation.

Client 2 showed the dividend in arrears as a current liability; Retained Earnings had been debited.

Client 3 completely ignored the dividend.

Client 4 set up a reserve for unpaid dividends, from retained earnings.

Client 5 showed the Dividend account as a current liability; it debited Dividends, which it showed as a deduction from retained earnings in the balance sheet.

Which client or clients followed correct procedure? Explain.

14. *a)* What are three methods of creating a so-called secret reserve?

b) As auditor, how would you proceed to detect secret reserves?

c) Explain how the interests of minority stockholders might be affected by the existence of secret reserves.

d) Should secret reserves be mentioned in an audit report?

PROBLEMS

1. As auditor, you are to prepare the contributed capital section of the balance sheet of Globe, Inc., at the end of the fiscal year, June 30, 1977. Globe was organized under a charter authorizing 10,000 shares of 6 percent preferred stock; the stock is cumulative, and preferred as to dividends and in liquidation. The par is $100 per share and the liquidation value is $105. In addition, 20,000 shares of common stock having no par or stated value were authorized. During the first year, the following transactions occurred.

a) Subscriptions were received for 8,000 shares of 6 percent preferred stock at $115 per share; a down payment of $368,000 was received, and the balance is due in two equal installments.

b) Of the common stock, 12,000 shares were sold for cash at $10 per share.

c) Of the common, 2,000 shares and 60 shares of the preferred were issued for reimbursement for legal fees incurred in organizing the corporation.

d) The first and second installments on the preferred stock subscriptions were collected, except on 500 shares. Stock certificates were issued fully paid shares.

e) 3,000 shares of common stock and 1,000 shares of the preferred stock, plus $50,000 cash were given in payment for a building the company needed to store its finished product. The former owners had purchased the building for $80,000 and it was depreciated to a book value of $24,000 at the date of disposition.

f)   100 shares of preferred were sold for cash of $120,000.

g)   The annual dividend was declared on the preferred stock and a $1 per share dividend was declared on the common stock. No dividends were declared on the subscribed stock.

2.   The Pecan Company was incorporated in 1976, with an authorized capital consisting of two classes of common stock: Class A, 10,000 shares, par value $50 per share; and Class B, 50,000 shares, par value $10. Voting privileges were the same for both classes. Dividend stipulations differed for the two in a respect that has no significance in this problem. During 1976, 5000 shares of Class A, and 25,000 shares of Class B were sold at par. The Capital Stock account shows credits for $500,000 for the stock sold. The sum of the certificate records disclosed that 50,000 shares of both classes were issued. From the stockholders' ledger, the auditor ran an adding machine tape of the number of shares issued, and his total agreed with the 50,000 shown in the stock certificate record. He therefore assumed that everything was in proper order and proceeded to prepare a balance sheet. Did the auditor perform his proper duties? How should the stock be shown in the balance sheet? What probably was wrong with the stock certificate record?

3.   The following account balances are on your audit work sheet and your audit supervisor assigned you the responsibility of preparing the Stockholders' Equity section of the balance sheet. From the following information, prepare that section.

Reacquired common shares (18,200) at cost	$ 554,000
Preferred stock: authorized 5,000 shares, $100 par value of which 4,000 shares are issued and outstanding	400,000
Additional capital paid in in excess of par value on preferred stock	50,000
Appreciation of fixed assets—excess over cost	200,000
Reserve for self-insured risks	600,000
Common stock "B," no par value, 1,000,000 shares authorized and issued at a stated value of $4 per share	4,000,000
Additional paid in capital in excess of stated value on "B" common stock	1,500,000
Unappropriated earnings retained for use in the business	12,250,000
Common stock "A," authorized and issued 50,000 shares of $10 par value	500,000
Discovery value capital—excess over cost	500,000
Reserve for plant expansion	2,500,000

4.   The stockholders' equities accounts for the Janis Barger Company on October 31, 1976, are as follows:

Capital stock, $100 par, 25,000 shares	$2,500,000
Premium on capital stock	1,000,000
Retained earnings	5,000,000

Shares of the Company's stock are selling at this time at $150. The client requests you to prepare the entries for each case below:

a)   A stock dividend of 10 percent is declared and issued.

b)   A 100 percent stock dividend is declared and issued.

5.   Capital accounts for the Data Company on December 31 are as follows:

Preferred stock, $100 par, 5,000 shares issued
and outstanding .... $ 500,000
Premium on preferred stock 50,000
Common stock, $10 par, 100,000 shares issued
and outstanding 1,000,000
Premium on common stock 125,000
Retained earnings 1,500,000

Preferred stock is convertible into common stock. Prepare the entry to be made on the corporation's records assuming that all of the preferred stock is converted under each of the following assumptions:

a)   Preferred shares are convertible into common on a share-for-share basis.

b)   Each share of preferred is convertible into five shares of common.

6.   The capital section of the balance sheet of the Major Company, December 31, 1975, appears as follows:

Preferred stock, 6 percent, $50 par, 5,000 shares ... $ 250,000
Equity of common stock, 50,000 shares, no par 1,750,000
Total Capital $2,000,000

At December 31, 1976 the capital section appears as follows:

Preferred stock, 6 percent, $50 par, 4,500 shares ... $ 225,000
Equity of common stock, 60,000 shares, no par 2,275,000
Total Capital $2,500,000

Certain 1976 transactions follow. From the available information, and as a result of your audit, redraft the capital section of the balance sheet as of December 31, 1976.

a)   The additional 10,000 shares of no-par common stock were sold at $30 per share. The stated value of all no-par common stock is $20 per share. The first 50,000 shares were issued at $25.

b)   Net income for 1976 was $332,500.

c)   Preferred stock (500 shares) was purchased for the treasury at $55 each.

d)   Cash dividends paid: preferred, $15,000; common, $90,000.

7.   The income statement for the Upgrade Company for the year ended December 31, 1976, shows:

Net income before provision for federal income tax ... $200,000
Less: Provision for federal income tax 90,000
Net income $110,000
Add extraordinary gain (net of taxes) from sale
of subsidiary 100,000
Net income and Extraordinary Gain $210,000

Calculate per-share earnings for 1976 under *(a)* and *(b)* below:

a)   The Company has only common stock, the number of shares outstanding totaling 200,000.

b) The Company has 200,000 shares of common stock plus 100,000 shares of convertible preferred stock outstanding. The preferred stock is convertible into common stock at the rate of one preferred share for each two shares of common held.

8. The records of Spark, Inc., have not been audited for the three-year period ended December 31, 1976. As a result of your audit for the year ended December 31, 1976, and your review of the records of the two prior years, it is necessary to revise the net income and the retained earnings. Based upon the audited data which follow:

a) Prepare work papers for the correction of the retained earnings for the year ended December 31, 1974, and for the correction of the net incomes for the years ended December 31, 1975 and 1976.

b) From the results of (a), prepare work papers setting forth the adjusted balance of the retained earnings at the end of each of the three years and the adjusted net incomes for 1975 and 1976. The company's retained earnings at December 31, 1976, follow:

Balance, December 31, 1974	$180,000
Net income, 1975	200,000
Net income, 1976	220,000
Balance, December 31, 1976	$600,000

No dividends were declared or paid during the three-year period.

From your examination, you obtained the following information which must be taken into consideration at the close of the years involved:

December 31, 1974:

(1) Goods consigned out to consignees are included in the inventory at $120,000, which is 20 percent in excess of cost.

(2) The following liabilities are omitted from the records:

New construction	$25,000
Material included in inventory	7,100

December 31, 1975:

(3) Uncollectible accounts receivable of $9,000 are to be written off.

(4) Goods consigned out to consignees are included in the inventory at $180,000, which is 20 percent in excess of cost.

(5) Accrued taxes of $2,100 were omitted from the records.

(6) Plant additions of $9,000 have been charged to expense.

(7) The inventory is overstated by $14,300.

(8) Depreciation was omitted; $5,000 should be provided.

December 31, 1976:

(9) Uncollectible accounts receivable of $11,000 are to be written off.

(10) The following liabilities are omitted from the records:

For purchase of new machinery	$12,000
Accrued taxes	5,900

16

Completing an Audit;
Post-Statement Disclosures

CLOSING AN AUDIT

Upon the conclusion of an audit and the completion of all work papers, the auditor is in possession of all data necessary for the adjustment of a client's records, and the preparation of the audit report which will include the rendition of an opinion—unqualified, qualified, disclaimed, or adverse.

Before departing from a client's office, the auditor should assemble all work papers and compare them with the internal control questionnaire and the audit program in order to be certain that all necessary data have been accumulated and that all audit work is completed. All material belonging to a client should be returned to him as it was presented to the author.

Financial statements preferably should be drafted prior to departure from the client's office. Depending upon the accounting firm's office review, copies of audit adjustments may be submitted to the client prior to departure; or they may be submitted after the work papers and the financial statements have been reviewed by high-level accounting firm personnel. Audit adjustments are reviewed for accounting accuracy, mathematical accuracy, adequacy of explanations, and propriety of the entries.

The papers accumulated by an auditor prior to drafting an audit report may be summarized as follows:

1. A completed internal control questionnaire.
2. An audit program.
3. Balance sheets.
4. Income statements and statements of retained earnings.

5. Statements of changes in financial position.
6. All schedules supporting the financial statements.
7. All work papers prepared during the course of the examination.
8. Audit adjusting journal entries.
9. Copies of the proceedings of meetings of the stockholders, the board of directors, and important committees.
10. Copies of up-to-date pension and bonus plans.
11. Copies of necessary contracts (or notes pertaining to them).
12. Copies of new bond indentures.
13. Copies of tax returns—federal, state, local.
14. Copies of all filings with the SEC.
15. Copies of all other necessary and desirable papers.
16. An index of the work papers.

If the auditor has followed the plans set forth in this book, all audit adjustments will be recorded in three places: (1) on the work papers for the particular accounts being adjusted, (2) on the working trial balance papers, and (3) on the audit adjustment work papers. The adjustments should be reviewed critically before leaving the engagement.

FINANCIAL STATEMENT PREPARATION

Financial statements must be prepared in accordance with consistently applied recognized accounting principles and in accordance with recognized standards of preparation, and they must be prepared so that they will enhance the communication of financial data. Financial statements must be adequate, and they must offer full disclosure of all material data. In addition to a client's interest in its financial statements, present and prospective stockholders, creditors, governmental agencies, the press, financial analysts, and labor organizations also are interested. The physical form of financial statements may vary in accordance with (1) preference, (2) the purpose of preparation, and (3) regulatory requirements.

Standards of financial statement preparation may be summarized as follows:

1. Assets should be classified in a manner that will—
   a) Facilitate the accounting for their utilization.
   b) Facilitate the interpretation of the statements.
2. If assets are expressed on a basis other than cost of acquisition, that different basis should be indicated.
3. Accumulated provisions for doubtful accounts, depreciation, and depletion should be deducted from the related asset in the balance sheet.
4. Assets and related liabilities should not be offset unless such offset is required by law or by contract.

5. The balance sheet should not contain a special section for reserves, allowances, or depreciation accumulations. Each reserve, allowance, or accumulation should be identified as a subdivision of retained earnings, or as an asset reduction account, or as a liability, and the position of each in the balance sheet should be established accordingly.
6. Significant characteristics of long-term liabilities should be disclosed in the balance sheet. This is *especially* important today.
7. Changes in paid-in capital and retained earnings should be disclosed in the balance sheet in the period in which the changes occur.
8. Statements of retained earnings should disclose the detail of charges and credits.
9. The income statement should be arranged to report in a consistent manner the proper detail of revenues, expenses, periodic net income or net loss, and earnings per share of common stock—primary and fully diluted.
10. The net income or net loss in the income statement must be clearly set forth.
11. The statement of changes in financial position should follow the pattern of presenting the sources of funds and the uses of funds, and close with the components which constitute working capital.

BALANCE SHEETS

Modern balance sheets emphasize the working capital position and the source of the net assets, as shown in Chapter 1. At all times a balance sheet must be so prepared and presented that it is understandable, that it fulfills the requirements of the business organization for which it is prepared, and that full disclosure is given to all material items.

In a balance sheet, asset and liability classifications should be indicated; the classifications may be as follows:

ASSETS:
1. Current assets (including short-term prepayments).
2. Investment assets (other than current assets).
3. Fixed tangible assets.
4. Intangible assets.
5. Long-term deferred charges.

LIABILITIES:
1. Current liabilities (including short-term deferred credits).
2. Long-term deferred credits.
3. Long-term liabilities.

Any interchange of the preceding order may be followed, but it is good practice to arrange the assets and liabilities so that classifications coincide—that is, if current assets are listed first among the assets, current liabilities should be listed first in the liability section.

Each of the preceding classifications is mutually exclusive. Unrelated items within a classification should not be combined. A few examples follow:

1. Cash available for general commercial purposes must be shown separately from restricted funds.
2. Accounts receivable should be properly subdivided.
3. Inventories should be divided between raw materials, work in process, finished goods, and supplies, either in the balance sheet or a footnote thereto.
4. Long-term investments should be divided between investments in stocks, bonds, cash or cash values of life insurance, and other items.
5. Fixed tangible assets should be separated by items or by groups, with each depreciation and amortization provision properly shown.

In the balance sheet, each class of capital stock must be separately presented. Capital items other than capital stock are divided between permanent paid-in-capital, capital credits arising from asset appreciation, retained earnings, and retained earnings reserves (if applicable). With regard to treasury stock, the Securities and Exchange Commission has established the following rule for corporations filing under its jurisdiction: "Reacquired shares, if significant in amount, shall be shown separately as a deduction from capital shares, or from the total of the capital shares and surplus, or from surplus, at either par or stated value or cost, as circumstances require." It is the opinion of the authors that treasury stock (not acquired for resale) should be deducted (at cost) from the total of the appropriate capital stock and retained earnings—and not from capital stock alone. The restriction on retained earnings should be explained parenthetically or in a footnote.

Balance sheets should be prepared in comparative form. Important comparative data are included in the audit report, accompanied by appropriate comment. (See Chapter 1, and annual reports of major corporations.) Comparative financial statements for several years increase the significance of a statement for any one year. Changes in the application of accounting principles should be pointed out. Explanations, qualifications, and footnotes of any preceding year should be referred to or restated in the comparative financial statements currently prepared.

INCOME STATEMENTS

In the preparation of an income statement, there must be no attempt to shift profits or losses from one period to another in an attempt to equalize periodic net income for two or more periods.

The income statement details the periodic operations that have brought about the majority of the changes in the retained earnings. It is based on the concept of a going concern; consequently, the income statement is an interim report, since profits and losses are not fundamentally the result of short-time operations. The net income for the year must be clearly and unequivocally set forth. Net income should be appraised not only in terms of its total amount but also in terms of earnings per share of capital stock. One of the primary functions of a published income statement is to enable outsiders to predict the *future* course of earning capacity.

For only modest disclosure of all material operating data, an income statement should show—as a minimum—sales, cost of goods sold, selling expense, administrative expense, nonoperating revenues and expenses, nonrecurring items of gain or loss (except for adjustments of *prior* years income taxes), federal income tax, and net income. Nonrecurring items of gain or loss should not be buried in sales or expense figures; if this were practiced, comparative sales and other analyses would be meaningless. Either the multistep form of income statement or the single-step form may be used; the majority of companies use the multistep form because major items of expense are then shown by functions.

In order to afford full disclosure of all material data, the minimum requirements for the preparation of income statements, set forth in the preceding paragraph, should be expanded, and normally are expanded. The expansion may be within the income statement proper, or it may appear in supplementary data, as exemplified by separately stating total depreciation expense, the total of all types of taxes, taxes per share of stock, net income per share of stock, etc. Most companies prefer not to show total detail in income statements because they do not wish to divulge total information to competitors. For registered companies, the requirements of the Securities and Exchange Commission must be followed in all financial reporting.

The only acceptable income statement is the "all-inclusive" type. The all-inclusive type, if properly prepared, adheres to the theory of maintaining a clean retained earnings and follows the concept that the net income of a business is not accurately measurable for short periods of time. See Illustration 16–1.

The reader should examine annual published reports of corporations for variations in the presentation of financial statements.

Miscellaneous Income Statement Considerations

The importance of proper income statements cannot be overemphasized; in their preparation, the principle of consistency must not be violated, and there must be proper matching of periodic revenues and related expenses. Income statements prepared in comparative form are

Illustration 16–1

THE GENERAL COMPANY
Statement of Income and Retained Earnings
For Years Ended December 31

	1975	1974
Net Sales	$3,570,426	$3,096,369
Cost of sales	2,788,307	2,400,253
Gross profit	$ 782,119	$ 696,116
Advertising, selling and administrative expenses	424,031	366,146
Operating income	$ 358,088	$ 329,970
Other income	15,491	6,457
	$ 373,579	$ 336,427
Interest and related charges	71,901	46,938
Other deductions	11,467	8,534
	$ 83,368	$ 55,472
Income before provision for taxes on income and minority interest	$ 290,211	$ 280,955
Provision for taxes on income:		
Currently payable:		
Federal	91,109	87,277
Foreign	37,736	30,845
Other	12,669	11,314
Deferred.		
Federal and other	(2,326)	1,229
Foreign	4,496	7,240
	$ 143,684	$ 137,905
Income before minority interest	146,527	143,050
Minority interest in earnings of subsidiaries	9,864	11,752
Net income	$ 136,663	$ 131,298
Retained earnings at beginning of year	818,043	752,843
	$ 954,706	$ 884,141
Cash dividends:		
Common stock: 1975, $2.50 per share; 1974, $2.38 per share	65,586	61,598
Preferred stock: 1975 and 1974, $6.00 per share	4,497	4,500
Retained earnings at end of year	$ 884,623	$ 818,043
Net income per common share:		
Undiluted	$5.16	$4.90
Fully diluted	4.94	4.72

valuable for purposes of trend studies; percentage figures can be used easily and afford the basis for valuable analyses for management purposes. In general, the percentages should be in terms of net sales as the base and/or in terms of the percentage increase or decrease in each item; comparisons must be for the same time intervals. Income statements may be prepared in long form or in short form, the latter being supported by schedules for cost of sales, selling expenses, administrative expenses, and other expenses and other revenues.

Federal income taxes may be shown in the income statements as follows:

Income before federal income taxes $200,000
Deduct: Federal income taxes   95,000
Net income transferred to retained earnings $105,000

THE STATEMENT OF CHANGES IN FINANCIAL POSITION

This statement (Illustration 16–2) now is recognized as one of the three major financial statements, and it is mentioned in both the scope section and the opinion section of the audit certificate. It is the modern evolvement of the old "statement of sources and application of funds,"

Illustration 16–2

THE GENERAL COMPANY
Statement of Changes in Financial Position
For the Years Ended December 31

	1975	1974
Source of funds:		
Net income	$136,663	$131,298
Charges to income not requiring use of working capital:		
Depreciation and amortization	48,286	44,870
Minority interest in earnings of subsidiaries	9,864	11,752
Net provision for noncurrent deferred income taxes . . .	5,780	8,725
Working capital provided from operations	200,593	196,645
Issuance of additional long-term debt	152,631	70,911
Deferral of liability for foreign income taxes	22,287	–
Conversion of debentures and proceeds from stock options		
exercised	1,456	922
Disposition of property, plant, and equipment	6,220	15,735
	383,187	284,213
Application of funds:		
Additions to property, plant, and equipment	68,151	67,868
Investments in subsidiaries which were not consolidated		
in year of acquisition		
1974	(52,316)	52,316
1975	16,100	–
Net noncurrent assets of businesses acquired	13,573	–
Cost in excess of net assets of businesses acquired	35,896	–
Decrease in long-term debt (including transfer to current) . .	164,221	97,341
Dividends to stockholders	70,083	66,098
Dividends to minority stockholders of a subsidiary	3,252	4,708
Purchases of Common stock for treasury	3,174	20,087
Other, net	(1,087)	(6,692)
	321,047	301,726
Increase (decrease) in working capital	$ 62,140	$(17,513)
Components increasing (decreasing) working capital:		
Cash	$ (9,724)	$ (239)
Receivables, customers	62,519	16,844
Inventories	196,299	85,414
Other current assets	6,330	9,879
Notes payable to banks	14,123	(13,204)
Commercial paper	(23,243)	(1,560)
Short-term borrowings by a foreign subsidiary	(57,360)	(9,895)
Accounts payable and accrued expenses	(27,491)	(92,099)
Current portion of a long-term debt	(99,313)	(12,653)
Increase (decrease) in working capital	$ 62,140	$(17,513)

and it emphasizes changes in net working capital. One illustration appears in Chapter 1, and a more comprehensive example is shown on page 433.

POST-STATEMENT DISCLOSURES

Events which occurred after the date of the financial statements—which were revealed prior to closing an audit, and are material and would have an effect on the financial statements, or which were significant and unusual—should be disclosed.

The importance of disclosing events occurring subsequent to the date of the financial statements has increased because the income statement is now emphasized, and because the Securities Act requires that registration statements filed with the SEC be representative as of the date of registration.

Prior to drafting an audit report, the auditor should—and normally does—review the events occurring subsequent to the date of the financial statements. These reviews are made primarily to determine whether any of the events are of sufficient magnitude materially to affect the reported financial condition or operations of the client. The time required to complete an audit varies, and it is entirely possible that events have taken place after the end of the fiscal year which may affect the client's financial position or operations *subsequent thereto,* and *prior to* or *subsequent to* the issuance of the audit report. However, it does not follow that a report should be delayed on the premise that an event might occur. Also, an audit report should be completed and delivered as rapidly as possible after concluding the field work.

It must be remembered that an audit report and its accompanying financial statements primarily are historical—they are not future projections. Also, if there is no necessity for disclosure of events subsequent to the date of financial statements, the disclosure serves no purpose. Perhaps the point should be reemphasized that the work of concluding an examination and rendering the report takes place after the date of the financial statements. The auditor ordinarily determines the cutoff of cash receipts and disbursements, and expense and payable recognition; reviews the collection of receivables; follows confirmation requests; and discusses the affairs of the client with management. While these procedures vary with the circumstances of each audit, the auditor nevertheless is placed in a position whereby he is able to determine the necessity for reporting events occurring subsequent to the date of the financial statements.

Post-statement events of financial importance constitute:

1. Those that directly affect the financial statements and should be given recognition in the year-end statements by adjustment of those statements.

2. Those that do not require adjustment of the financial statements but may warrant comment, as footnotes to the statements or comments in the report.
3. Those that may fall into a questionable category between (1) and (2), in which case the decision is difficult for disclosure or nondisclosure, and about which there may be disagreement among accountants.

In general, audit reports should include comments on post-statement events that:

1. May affect the financial statements being audited.
2. May affect future operations and subsequent financial statements.
3. Do not fall under the requirements of the SEC.
4. Do involve the Securities and Exchange Commission.

Prior to preparing the audit report but after having completed all routine post-period work, the auditor should:

1. Read the new-period minutes of the meetings of stockholders, the board of directors, and major committees, in order to determine if major financial events have occurred which would have an effect on the fairness of the presentation of the financial statements of the year under examination.
2. Review the client's financial statements prepared in the interim between the financial statement date and the date of submitting the audit report.
3. If applicable, study the prospectus.
4. Review registration statements.
5. Discuss, with the client's officers, events that may be material.
6. Obtain a letter from the client's attorney concerning pending litigation.

In the opinion of the authors, post-statement disclosure should be granted (1) if the amount is material, (2) if the event is significant and is extraordinary, and (3) if the event occurs after the financial statement date but prior to closing the audit. The only exceptions are in those cases where *only* the interests of owners are involved *and* where the events are of a normally routine nature. The requirements for disclosure depend upon the circumstances of each case; consequently, reasoned opinion is required to judge between extraordinary and ordinary occurrences and their effect on financial position, financial operations, creditors, and investors. Both adverse and advantageous incidents should be given equal prominence in the audit report.

The following are illustrative of the accounts affected and the events that may take place subsequent to the date of the financial statements but prior to the preparation of the report:

Items Affected	*Post-Statement Event*
Cash:	Bank failure.
	Court action impounding funds.
	Robbery, burglary, or theft of money in an amount materially in excess of insurance.
Receivables.	Bank moratorium.
	Failure of major customer.
	Large unforeseen note or account losses.
Investments:	Drastic declines in market price.
	Financial difficulties of issuing companies.
	Default in interest or principal payments.
	Sale of investments at prices materially above or below cost.
Inventories:	Uninsured fire losses and other casualty losses.
	Drastic increases or decreases in market price.
	Changes in methods of pricing inventories.
	Unusual use of inventory as loan collateral.
Fixed Assets:	Uninsured fire and other casualty losses.
	Proposed expansion or contraction plans.
	Asset appraisals upward or downward.
	Obsolescence caused by sudden changes in products or demand.
Current Liabilities:	Unusual purchase commitments, accompanied by decreased selling prices.
	Purchase contract cancellations.
	Default in note payments.
Long-Term Liabilities:	Large increases in funded debt.
	Default in interest or principal payments.
	Refunding operations.
Capital Stock:	Increases or decreases in number of shares.
	Unusual treasury stock transactions.
	Reorganization of capital stock structure.
	Changes in the form of organization, that is, from a partnership to a corporation, or vice versa.
Paid-In Capital:	Transfers to or from capital stock caused by changes in par or stated value.
	Unusual changes in paid-in capital.
Retained Earnings:	Unusual dividends that impair working capital.
	Unusual appropriations.
	Material losses or profits directly charged or credited.
Other Items:	Changes in key executive personnel.
	Changes in management policies.
	Changes in laws.
	Unusual additional tax assessments or refunds.
	Securities and Exchange Commission requirements.
	Court judgments rendered.

The events occurring subsequent to the date of the financial statements should be of sufficient importance to warrant one or more of the following actions:

1. Amending the year-end financial statements.
2. Footnoting the financial statements.
3. Placing parenthetical notations in the financial statements.
4. Commenting in the text of the audit report. If an item is commented upon in the text of the report, the auditor should connect the financial

statements and the report in a manner similar to the following: "These financial statements are an integral part of and are subject to the text comments of the accompanying report. The report text must be read in conjunction with these statements."

CERTAIN SEC REQUIREMENTS

The SEC is tightening its requirements in the area of financial reporting, and the presentation of financial statements; consequently, an auditor must remain familiar with all changing and new requirements of the Commission. Certain requirements of the SEC regarding reporting and financial statements are briefed at this point; *there are many more.*

Financial statements must be submitted in comparative form for two consecutive years. This can result in a drastic work-increase for the certifying accountant if the client is a new one that has been in business for more than one year.

Only unqualified opinions will be accepted in connection with a public offering of securities.

Normally, financial statements are representative *only* as of a given date—and not as of their later date of issuance; this is not the case for financial statements incorporated in registration statements filed with the SEC under the Securities Act of 1933. Under that act, the statements assumedly represent conditions and operations as of the statement registration date. Consequently, an auditor *must* investigate nonroutine events which occurred between the date of the financial statements and the effective date of the registration statement.

With the exception of public utility holding companies and registered investment companies, the SEC has not set forth a statement of accounting principles, but it is moving rapidly in that direction in all areas of financial reporting—and the Commission has the power of law behind it. Accounting requirements and regulations of the SEC are published in Regulations S–X, relating to the forms and content of financial statements and to auditing regulations, in the Commission's *Accounting Series Releases,* and in its formal findings and opinions.

Under Article 5 of Regulation S–X, the balance sheet is presented in the order of "current to fixed"; the income statement shows sales, cost of sales, selling expense, general expense, administrative expense, other deductions, special items, and net income before and after federal income tax provisions. An analysis of retained earnings is required, and it may be combined with the income statement.

Full and adequate disclosure in financial statements reduces the necessity for reporting accounting methods in detail. In some cases the Commission has held that the financial statements did not result in full disclosure when the accompanying report offered explanations.

Rule 3–11 of Regulation S–X requires a statement of the policy followed for the fiscal period for which income statements are filed with respect to the following: (1) depreciation, depletion, and obsolescence of physical assets, including the methods and rates used; (2) provisions for the amortization of intangibles, including the methods and rates used; (3) the accounting treatment for maintenance, repairs, renewals, and betterments; and (4) the adjustment of the accumulated provisions for each item in (1) and (2) above, at the time the properties are retired or otherwise disposed of.

Upon review by the Commission, if the statements are considered to have been prepared contrary to generally accepted accounting principles, or if they otherwise fail to meet the requirements of the Commission, a deficiency letter is sent to the company allegedly at fault. The deficiency letter, followed by correspondence (or conference) with the registrant and its accountants (normally independent CPAs) frequently constitute methods of resolving accounting questions which otherwise might have to be settled through formal hearings with the Commission.

Rules 14a–3 and 14c–3 require that a summary of operations and management's analysis of the summary must now be included in annual published reports. This summary must be filed annually as Item 2 of Form 10–K. It must show revenues, expenses, other gains and losses for the past five years; additional years summaries are required if the past five-year period is misleading. The analysis of management must explain material changes in revenues and expenses, and in the application of accounting principles.

Form 10–Q and Regulation S–X have been amended to require additional quarterly reporting by registrants and footnote disclosure of selected quarterly data in the annual financial statements. The footnote may be set forth as "unaudited," but a limited review (not defined as of December 31, 1975) is mandatory. In *ASR No. 33–5612*, the SEC has stated it prefers that the accounting profession establishes the standards for the limited review, and the auditing standards division of the AICPA has this opportunity.

SUGGESTED ADDITIONAL READING

Statement on Auditing Standards No. 1, Sections 560 and 561.
Accounting Series Releases of the Securities and Exchange Commission.
Rules and Regulations of the Securities and Exchange Commission.

QUESTIONS

1. The following events occurred prior to drafting the audit reports for five clients, but after the effective date of the financial statements.

a) Explain how each item might have come to the attention of the auditor.

b) What is the responsibility of the auditor to recognize each item in the preparation of the audit report?

Client:

1. The granting of a retroactive wage increase.
2. Additional federal income tax for a prior year, which was not disputed.
3. An antitrust suit filed by the federal government.
4. The declaration of a 200 percent stock dividend.
5. The sale of fixed assets at a material loss.

2. The auditor in charge requests that the work papers indicated below be arranged in proper order. Prepare a proper sequential listing.

a) Certificate from the register of the outstanding common stock.

b) Analysis of the Preferred Capital Stock account and the listing of the preferred stock shareholders.

c) Schedule of prepaid casualty insurance.

d) Analysis of the Factory Machinery account.

e) Analysis of taxes accrued.

f) Inventory price-test sheets.

g) Reconciliation of the First Bank checking account.

h) Certification from the trustee of a bond redemption sinking fund.

i) Analysis of marketable securities and accrued interest thereon.

j) Petty cash count.

k) Analysis of notes payable.

l) Notations regarding subsequent audits.

m) Minutes of meetings of the stockholders and the board of directors.

n) Sales analysis.

o) Confirmation certificate from the First Bank.

p) Analysis of retired earnings.

q) Working trial balances as of the end of the fiscal year.

r) Analysis of the accumulated depreciation of factory machinery.

s) Audit adjusting entries.

t) Notes regarding work performed in connection with the cash receipts records.

u) Notes regarding work performed in connection with the record of assets purchased and expenses incurred (voucher register).

v) Analysis of accounts receivable.

w) Analysis of maintenance of factory machinery.

x) Summary of fixed assets.

y) Payroll analysis.

3. When an audit report is drafted there are ethical considerations that the auditor should bear in mind. Discuss.

4. a) What is a footnote, as used in an audit report?

b) What is the similarity between footnotes to financial statements and report qualifications?

c) What are the differences?

5. Near the completion of a periodic examination, the auditor asked his client for certain contracts and tax returns. The auditor started to prepare

copies of the contracts and tax returns when the client suggested that the auditor take them to his office. What course should the auditor follow?

6. *a)* At the conclusion of an audit, but prior to drafting the audit report, what papers normally will be accumulated by the auditor?

   b) In closing an audit, it is customary for the auditor to submit to his client a copy of his audit adjustments, to be journalized and posted by the client. Upon the auditor's return to a client for a subsequent audit, it was discovered that the client had not taken up the auditor's adjustments of the preceding period and that he had no intention of doing so.

   How should the auditor proceed with the second examination? (1) In the subsequent audit, should the auditor start with the client's post-closing trial balance of the preceding year, or (2) should he start with the figures of the preceding year according to his work papers? Present reasons for your answer.

7. You were examining the financial statements of Wilt, Inc., for the year ended December 31, 1976, when you were consulted by the corporation's president, who believes there is no point in examining the 1977 voucher register and testing data in support of 1976 entries. He stated that (1) bills for 1976 which were received too late to be included in the December voucher register were recorded as of the year-end by journal entry, (2) the internal auditor made tests after the year-end, and (3) he would furnish you with a letter certifying that there were no unrecorded liabilities.

   a) Should the auditor's test for unrecorded liabilities be affected by the fact that the client prepared entries to record 1976 bills which were received late? Explain.

   b) Should the auditor's test for unrecorded liabilities be affected by the fact that a letter is obtained in which a responsible official certifies that all liabilities have been recorded? Explain.

   c) Should the auditor's test for unrecorded liabilities be eliminated or reduced because of the internal audit tests? Explain.

   d) Assume that the corporation, which handled some government contracts, had no internal auditor but that an auditor for a federal agency spent three weeks auditing the records and was just completing his work at this time. How would the auditor's unrecorded liability test be effected by the work of the auditor for a federal agency?

   e) What sources in addition to the 1977 voucher register should the auditor consider to locate possible unrecorded liabilities?

8. You are conducting an annual examination of the financial statements of a corporation for the purpose of rendering an opinion regarding financial statements for use in an annual report to the stockholders.

   Answer the following questions concerning events occurring subsequent to the date of the financial statements:

   a) What audit procedures should normally be followed in order to obtain knowledge of post-financial statement events?

b) What is the period with which the auditor is normally concerned with regard to post-financial statement events?

c) List five different examples of events or transactions which might occur in the subsequent period.

d) What is the auditor's general responsibility, if any, for reporting such events or transactions?

e) In your audit report, how would you deal with each of the examples you listed in (c)?

(AICPA)

9. Prepare a list of events occurring after the effective date of the financial statements, but prior to rendering the audit report, that might be mentioned in the audit report or have an effect on it.

10. The following events, each of material amount, occurred in the course of the audit of the financial statements of each company indicated below. Each event occurred after the end of the year under examination (December 31, 1976, in each case) but prior to the completion of the field work early in 1977.

In your reports of examination and/or as a footnote to the integral financial statements, what comments would you make, if any?

Client No. 1 has oil properties of $500 million in a foreign country. On January 10, 1977, the foreign government expropriated the assets of all American companies having properties in the foreign country.

Client No. 2 incurred a loss of $35,000,000 when on January 19, 1977, fire destroyed the largest of four of the company's buildings. The gross loss was $95,000,000, and the insurance recovery was $40,000,000. Income insurance was not carried.

Client No. 3 has a material portfolio of U.S. Treasury securities. On February 1, 1977, the company sold all the securities and invested the total proceeds in various common stocks, all listed on major stock exchanges.

Client No. 4 has completed plans for a plant expansion program, and on March 1, 1977, an underwriting syndicate will offer for sale $60,000,000 of the company's bonds at 102 plus accrued interest.

11. As of December 1, 1976, negotiations were in process between your client, a corporation, and one of its stockholders for the purchase and retirement by the corporation of the shares owned by the stockholder at a price still to be determined. The company is a close corporation with 20,000 shares of only common stock outstanding, with a stated value of $3,000,000. The retained earnings are $5,000,000. The stockholder who desires to dispose of his stock owns 1,000 shares and wants a price of $800 per share. The corporation has offered to purchase and retire the shares at 80 percent of book value. The corporation has adequate cash to pay the stockholder. The entire transaction and its consummation or failure to be concluded lies in the price per share. Should this matter be mentioned in the audit report for the year ended December 31, 1976? Present reasons for your answer.

12. As of December 31, 1976, your firm is conducting its first audit of the financial statements of Henn, Inc. The accountant of the Company

already has prepared financial statements for the year, including the following analysis of retained earnings:

Balance, January 1, 1976	$190,028	
Net income for 1976	64,848	
Profit on sale of fixed assets	4,584	
Premium on sale of capital stock	8,800	
Total credits		$268,260
Provision for 1976 federal income taxes	$ 20,000	
Dividends paid	20,000	
Pension payments to retired officers	8,000	
Total debits		48,000
Balance, December 31, 1976		$220,260

a) Detail the procedure to be followed in the audit of each item above, except net income for 1976. Your engagement does not include the preparation of the federal income tax return.

b) What changes would you recommend in the presentation of these items in the financial statements? What are your reasons for any changes recommended? Present reasons for not changing the items which you believe are properly presented.

(AICPA, adapted)

PROBLEMS

1. Captain, Inc., manufactures electronic systems, which it sells to manufacturers of television sets and stereo systems. In connection with your examination of the financial statements for the year ended December 31, 1976, you completed all field work February 1, 1977, at which time you are attempting to evaluate the significance of the following items prior to drafting the audit report. Unless otherwise noted, none of the items have been disclosed in the financial statements.

Item 1

Captain stopped its policy of paying quarterly cash dividends. Dividends were paid regularly through 1975, discontinued for all of 1976 in order to finance equipment for a new plant, and resumed in the first quarter of 1977. In the annual report, dividend policy is to be discussed in the president's letter to stockholders.

Item 2

A ten-year loan agreement, entered into three years ago, provides that dividends may not exceed net income after taxes subsequent to the date of the agreement. The balance of retained earnings at the date of the loan was $298,000. From that date through December 31, 1976, net income after taxes totaled $360,000 and cash dividends totaled $130,000. Based upon these data it was concluded that there was no retained earnings restriction at December 31, 1976.

Item 3

Captain's new factory, which cost $600,000 and has an estimated life of 25 years, is leased from the National Bank at an annual rental of $100,000. The company is to pay property taxes, insurance and maintenance. At the conclusion of its ten-year noncancelable lease, the company has the option of purchasing the property for $1. In Captain's income statement the rental payment is reported on a separate line.

Item 4

A major electronics company has introduced a line of products that will compete directly with Captain's primary line, now being produced in a specially designed plant. Because of manufacturing innovations, the competitor's line will be of comparable quality but priced 50 percent below Captain's line. The competitor announced its new line during the week following completion of audit field work. You read the announcement in the newspaper and discussed the situation with Captain's executives. Captain will meet the lower prices, which are high enough to cover variable manufacturing and selling expenses but will permit recovery of only a portion of fixed costs.

For each of the preceding items, discuss:

a) Any additional disclosure in the financial statements and footnotes that you should recommend to your client.

b) The effect of the situation on the report upon Captain's financial statements. For this, assume that the client did not make the additional disclosure recommended in part (a).

Complete your discussion of each item—both parts (a) and (b)—before discussing the next item. The effects of each item on the financial statements and the audit report should be evaluated *independently* of the other items. The cumulative effects of the four items should not be considered.

(AICPA, adapted)

2. From the following data of a new client, The Hust Company, prepare a proper combined Statement of Income and Retained Earnings for the year ended December 31, 1976.

Retained earnings 1/1/76	$ 40,000
Current year dividends on common stocks	35,500
Net sales	600,000
Selling expenses	72,000
Interest expense	2,000
Provision for federal income tax, 1976	52,000
Uninsured flood loss in 1976	17,500
Federal income tax refund for 1974	5,000
Cancellation of a reserve for damages from a lawsuit successfully concluded	20,000
Profit on sale of long-term investments	8,000
Administrative expenses	74,000
Cost of goods manufactured and sold	330,000

The client has 10,000 shares of common stock outstanding and 10,000 shares of four-for-one convertible preferred outstanding.

3. From the financial statements presented below, prepare the following:
    a) A list of criticisms of the statements.
    b) An acceptable balance sheet.
    c) An acceptable combined statement of income and retained earnings.

GOLF, INC.
Balance Sheet
December 31, 1976

Assets

Buildings (Note 1)	$ 9,334,000
Short-term prepaid items	75,000
Treasury stock (25,000 shares, at par)	500,000
Assets allocated to insurance fund:	
Cash in banks (including $300,000 of time deposits)	650,000
U.S. Treasury bonds, at cost	500,000
Cash on hand and in banks	2,780,000
Accounts receivable	4,750,000
Inventories, at cost	3,411,000
	$22,000,000

Liabilities

Common stock; authorized and issued, 500,000 shares; par $20	$10,000,000
Accounts payable	3,566,000
Federal income taxes	440,000
Excess of revenue over disbursements on uncompleted contracts	690,000
Reserve for repairs of machinery (Note 2)	222,000
Reserve for self-insurance	650,000
Reserve for depreciation of buildings	2,805,000
Appreciation capital (Note 1)	285,000
Retained earnings	3,342,000
	$22,000,000

GOLF, INC.
Statement of Income, Retained Earnings, and Appreciation Capital
For the Year Ended December 31, 1976

Revenues	$17,500,000
Less: Operating expenses, except depreciation	14,170,000
	$ 3,330,000
Interest on investments	22,000
Excess of provision for self-insurance charged to operations in 1976 over net losses in 1976	360,000
Net profit before depreciation and federal income taxes	$ 3,712,000
Gain from sale of capital assets (Note 3)	1,410,000
	$ 5,122,000
Provision for depreciation	550,000
Total profit before federal taxes	$ 4,572,000
Less: Federal income taxes	1,760,000
Net Profit	$ 2,812,000

	Retained Earnings	Appreciation Capital
Balance, December 31, 1975	$ 795,000	$610,000
Net profit, above	2,812,000	
Transfer from appreciation capital to retained earnings of depreciation on appreciation charged to income in 1975 ($270,000) and of unamortized appreciation on buildings sold	+320,000	−320,000
Excess of cost of 25,000 shares of treasury stock purchased over par	−15,000	$ −5,000
	$3,912,000	
Deduct: Dividends paid in 1976	570,000	
Balance, December 31, 1976	$3,342,000	$285,000

Note 1: Buildings are stated at cost, except for three buildings recorded at appraised values when acquired in 1973. The excess of appraised values over original cost was credited to Appreciation Capital, and depreciation on appreciation has been accrued through charges to operations. On December 31, 1976, the unamortized balance of the appreciation was $290,000.

Note 2: This reserve is set up out of income in the amount of $40,000 per month; the system was started on January 1, 1976.

Note 3: Sale, in 1976, of five buildings in excess of book value; $50,000 of appreciation capital was applicable to two buildings acquired in 1973 and sold, above.

4. Below are presented some of the accounts appearing in the trial balance of The Fox Co., at December 31, 1976.

	Debit	Credit
No-par common stock, issued at $5		5,000
No-par common stock, issued at $4		152,000
Treasury stock, no-par common, acquired at $5 . . .	15,000	
Capital stock, $100 preferred A, 500 shares		55,000
Capital stock, $100 preferred B, 500 shares		47,000
No-par common stock, authorized, 50,000 shares	0	0
Class A preferred; authorized 1,000 shares, $100 par		100,000
Class A preferred; unissued, 500 shares	100,000	
Class B preferred; authorized, 500 shares		3,000
Class B preferred; unissued	3,000	
Reserve for 1976 federal income taxes (set up in 1976)		46,400
Reserve for loss on accounts (56,000 added in 1976)		7,200
Reserve for reduction of December 31, 1976, inventory to market (a 1976 revenue charge)		9,100
Reserve for possible 1977 inventory declines (set up in 1976)		10,000
Reserve for preferred dividends declared (a 1976 revenue charge)		2,750

Reserve for common stock dividends to be declared (a 1976 revenue charge)		7,300
Common stock dividend of 7,300 shares declared on common of record as of January 2, 1977 (a 1976 revenue charge)		7,300
Loss on sale of fixed assets (1976)	4,000	
Organization expense unamortized	2,500	
Bond discount unamortized	3,400	
Loss on inventory decline in 1976	9,100	
Retained earnings, January 1, 1976	22,070	
Profit, 1976		162,500
The remaining accounts comprised the following:		
Cash, receivables, inventories, and fixed assets	740,430	
Accounts, notes, and bonds payable		284,950
	899,500	899,500

From the information presented, prepare (1) the capital section of the December 31, 1976, balance sheet; (2) a schedule showing the changes you would make in the profit to arrive at the corrected net income for 1976 (ignore any revision of the 1976 income tax).

(AICPA, adapted)

5. You are completing an examination of the financial statements of Hill, Inc., for the year ended February 28, 1977. Hill's financial statements have not been examined previously. The controller of Hill has given you the following draft of proposed footnotes to the financial statements:

Note 1. With the approval of the Internal Revenue Service, the Company changed its method of accounting for inventories form Fifo to Lifo on March 1, 1976. In the opinion of the Company the effects of this change on the pricing of inventories and cost of goods sold were not material in the current year but are expected to be material in future years.

Note 2. The stock dividend described in our May 24, 1976, letter to stockholders has been recorded as a 105 for 100 stock split. Accordingly, there were no changes in the stockholders' equity account balances from this transaction.

Note 3. For many years the Company has maintained a pension plan for certain employees. Prior to the current year pension expense was recognized as payments were made to retired employees. There was no change in the plan in the current year, but upon the recommendation of its auditor, the Company provided $64,000, based upon an actuarial estimate, for pensions to be paid in the future to the current employees.

For each Note discuss:

a) The note's adequacy and needed revisions, if any, of the financial statements or the note.

b) The necessary disclosure in or opinion modification of the audit report. (For this requirement assume the revisions suggested in part (a), if any, have been made.)

Complete your discussion of each note (both parts (a) and (b)) before beginning discussion of the next one.

(AICPA, adapted)

6. You have completed your audit of Sands, Inc., for the year ended December 31, 1976, and were satisfied with the results of your examination. You have examined the financial statements of Sands for the past three years. The Corporation is now preparing its annual report to shareholders. The report will include the financial statements of Sands and your short-form audit report. During your audit the following matters came to your attention:

   (1) The Internal Revenue Service is currently examining the Corporation's 1974 federal income tax return and is questioning the amount of a deduction claimed by the Corporation's domestic subsidiary for a loss sustained in 1974. The examination is still in process and any additional tax liability is indeterminable at this time. The Corporation's tax counsel believes that there will be no substantial additional tax liability.

   (2) A vice president who is also a stockholder resigned on December 31, 1976, after an argument with the president. The vice president is soliciting proxies from stockholders and expects to obtain sufficient proxies to gain control of the board of directors so that a new president will be appointed. The president plans to have a footnote prepared which would include information of the pending proxy fight, management's accomplishments over the years, and an appeal by management for the support of stockholders.

   a) Prepare the footnotes you would suggest for the items listed above.

   b) State your reasons for not making disclosure by footnote for each of the listed items for which you did not prepare a footnote.

   (AICPA, adapted)

Index

449

This book has been set in 10 point and 9 point Caledonia, leaded 2 points. Chapter numbers are 30 point Helvetica and chapter titles are 18 point Helvetica. The size of the type page is 27 by 46½ picas.